THE BIBLE
THROUGH PICTURES

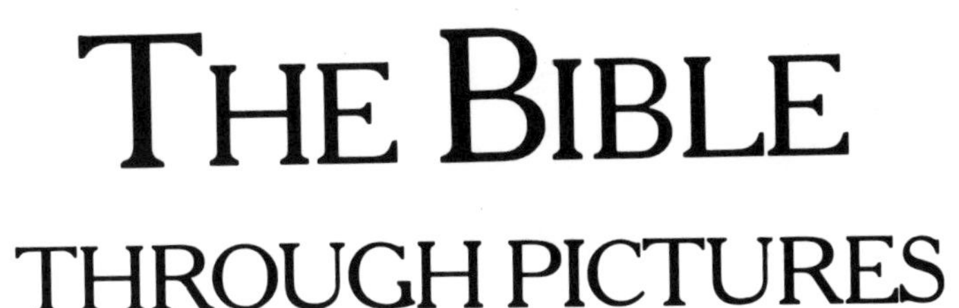

THE BIBLE
THROUGH PICTURES

The Choicest Passages of God's Word
put in the Fascinating Garb of Pictures by
FRANK BEARD
AND OTHERS

Designed and Arranged to Familiarize
Both Young and Old with the Great
Events of Bible History and to Stimu-
late Interest in the Holy Bible.

BONANZA BOOKS
New York

Originally published under the title *The New Bible Symbols*.

This 1989 edition is published by Bonanza Books,
distributed by Crown Publishers, Inc., 225 Park Avenue South, New York, New York 10003.

Printed and Bound in the United States of America

Library of Congress Cataloging-in-Publication Data

Beard, Frank, 1842-1905.
[Bible symbols]
The Bible through pictures / by Frank Beard.
Previously published as: Bible symbols. 1904.
ISBN 0-517-68238-9
1. Hieroglyphic Bibles. 2. Bible stories, English. I. Title.
BS560.B4 1989
220.9′505—dc20 89-1011
h g f e d c b a CIP

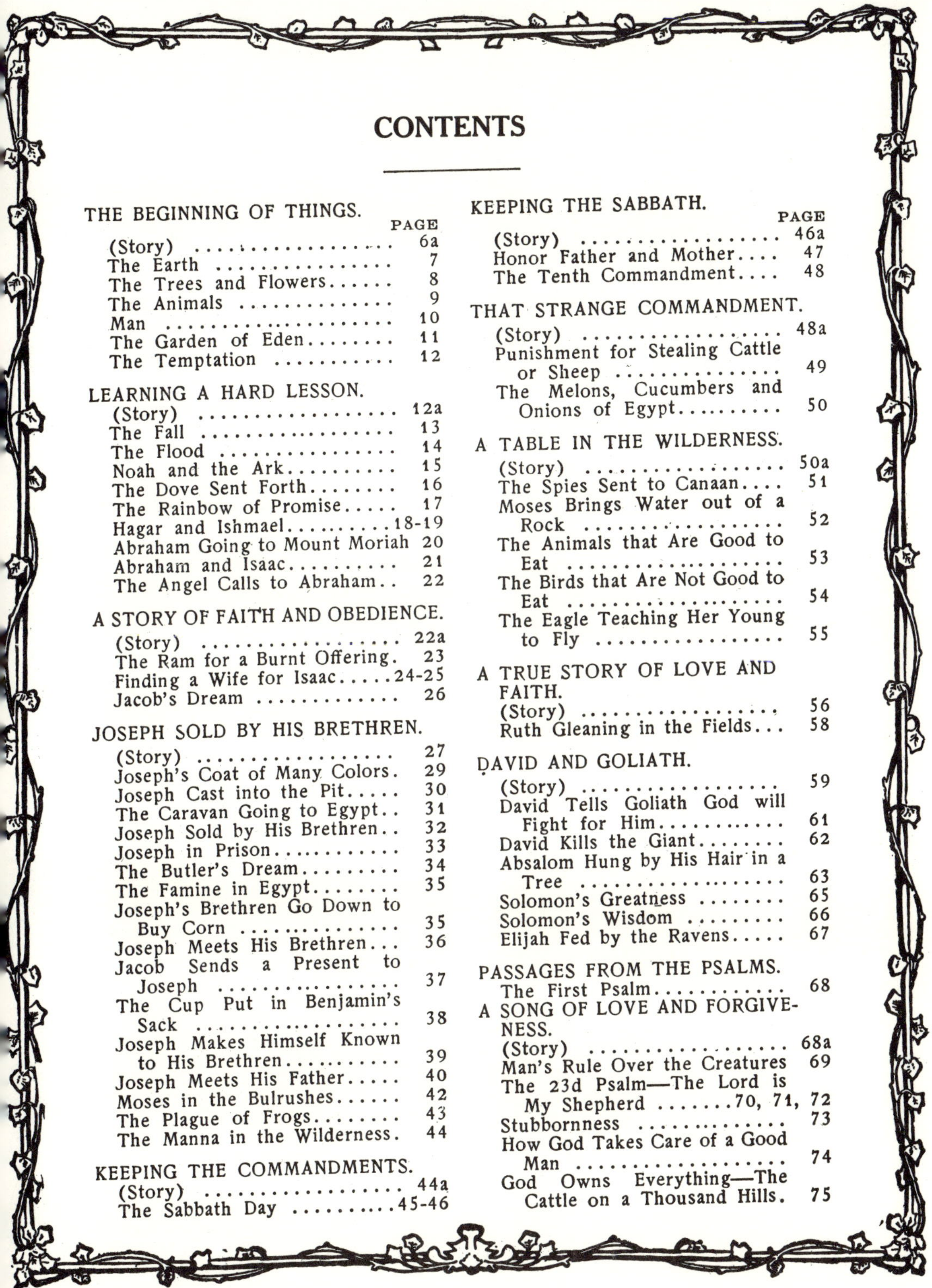

CONTENTS

HALF-TONES, ENGRAVINGS AND PLATES OF FAMOUS PICTURES.

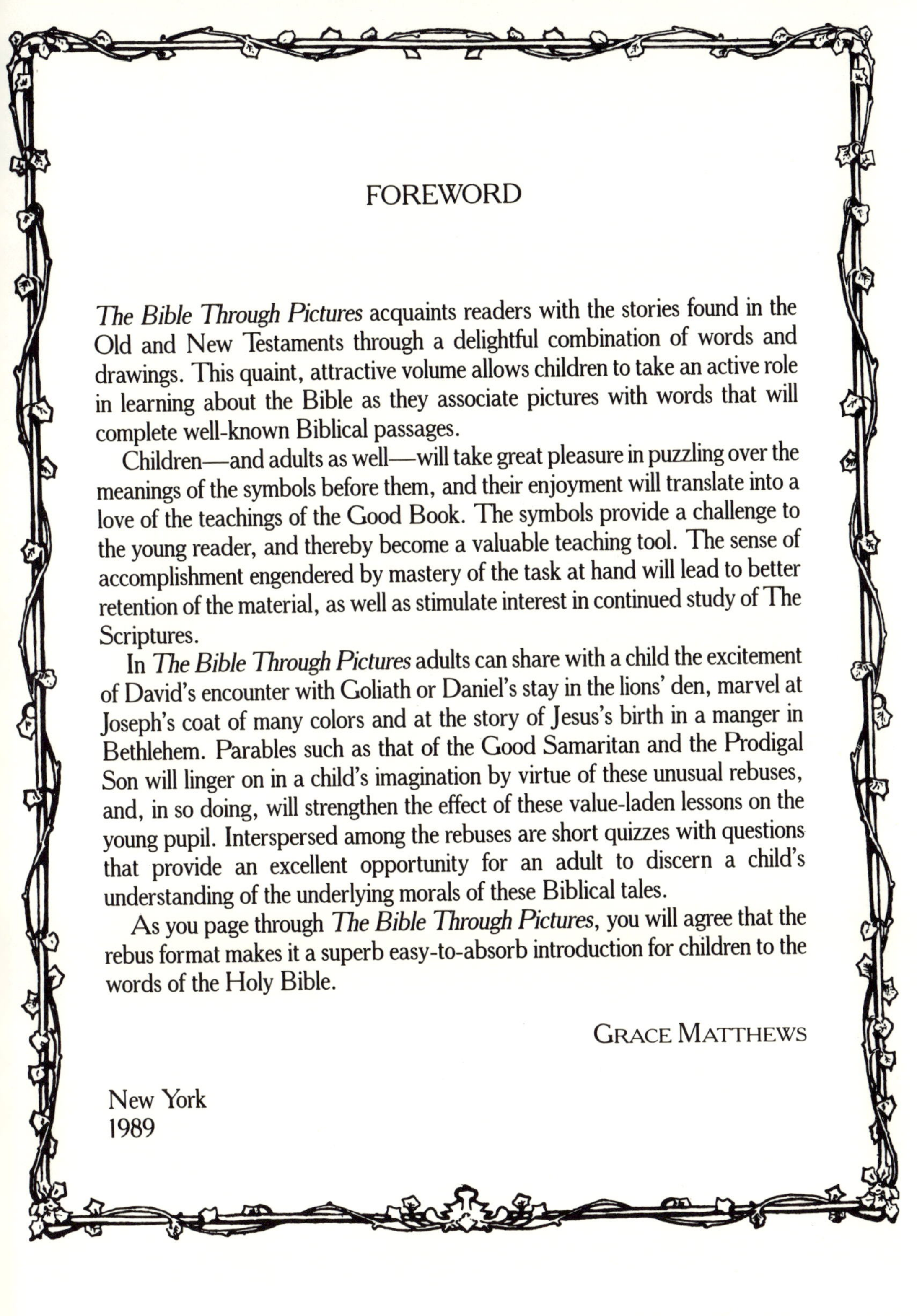

FOREWORD

The Bible Through Pictures acquaints readers with the stories found in the Old and New Testaments through a delightful combination of words and drawings. This quaint, attractive volume allows children to take an active role in learning about the Bible as they associate pictures with words that will complete well-known Biblical passages.

Children—and adults as well—will take great pleasure in puzzling over the meanings of the symbols before them, and their enjoyment will translate into a love of the teachings of the Good Book. The symbols provide a challenge to the young reader, and thereby become a valuable teaching tool. The sense of accomplishment engendered by mastery of the task at hand will lead to better retention of the material, as well as stimulate interest in continued study of The Scriptures.

In *The Bible Through Pictures* adults can share with a child the excitement of David's encounter with Goliath or Daniel's stay in the lions' den, marvel at Joseph's coat of many colors and at the story of Jesus's birth in a manger in Bethlehem. Parables such as that of the Good Samaritan and the Prodigal Son will linger on in a child's imagination by virtue of these unusual rebuses, and, in so doing, will strengthen the effect of these value-laden lessons on the young pupil. Interspersed among the rebuses are short quizzes with questions that provide an excellent opportunity for an adult to discern a child's understanding of the underlying morals of these Biblical tales.

As you page through *The Bible Through Pictures*, you will agree that the rebus format makes it a superb easy-to-absorb introduction for children to the words of the Holy Bible.

GRACE MATTHEWS

New York
1989

THE BIBLE
THROUGH PICTURES

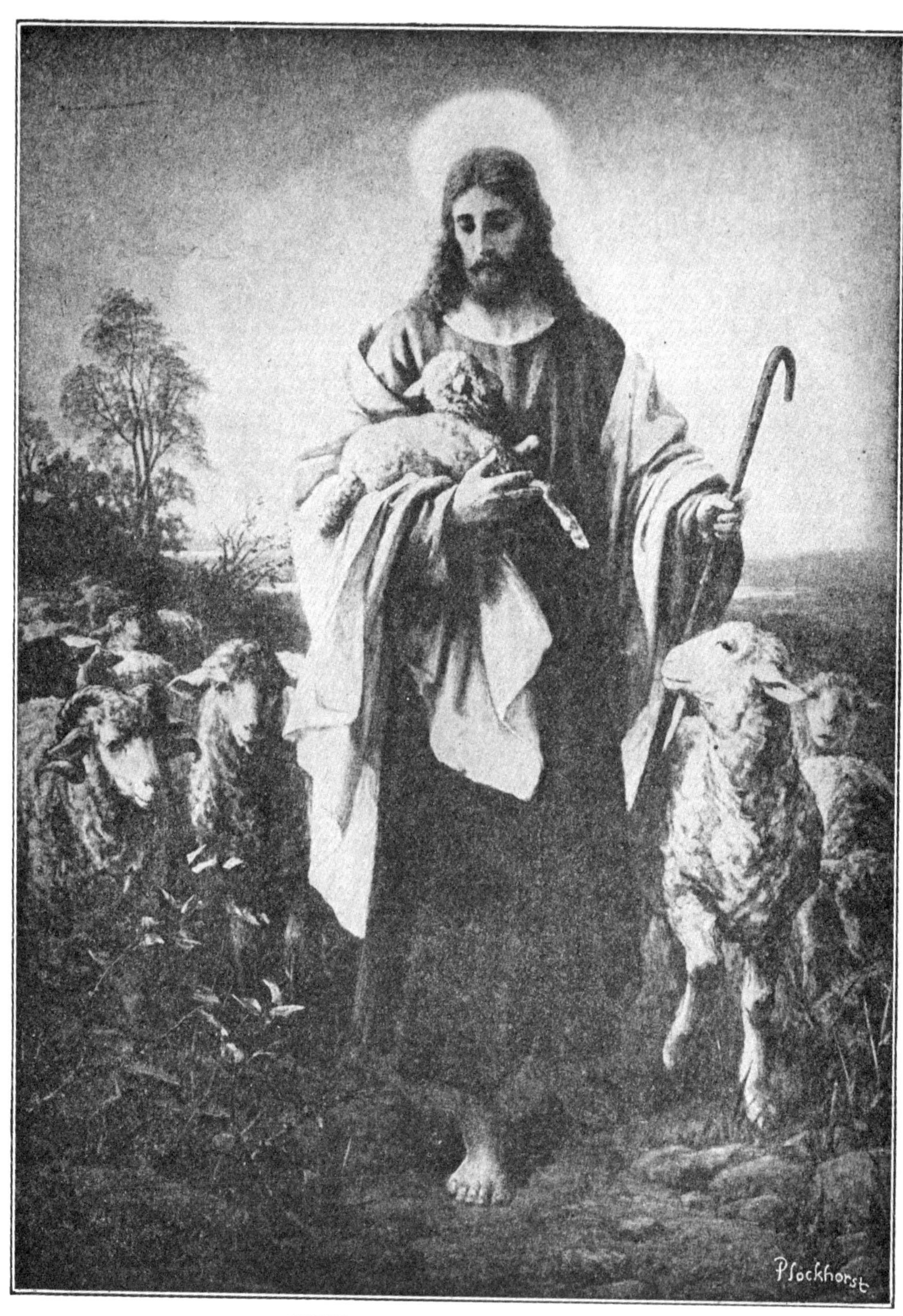

THE GOOD SHEPHERD.

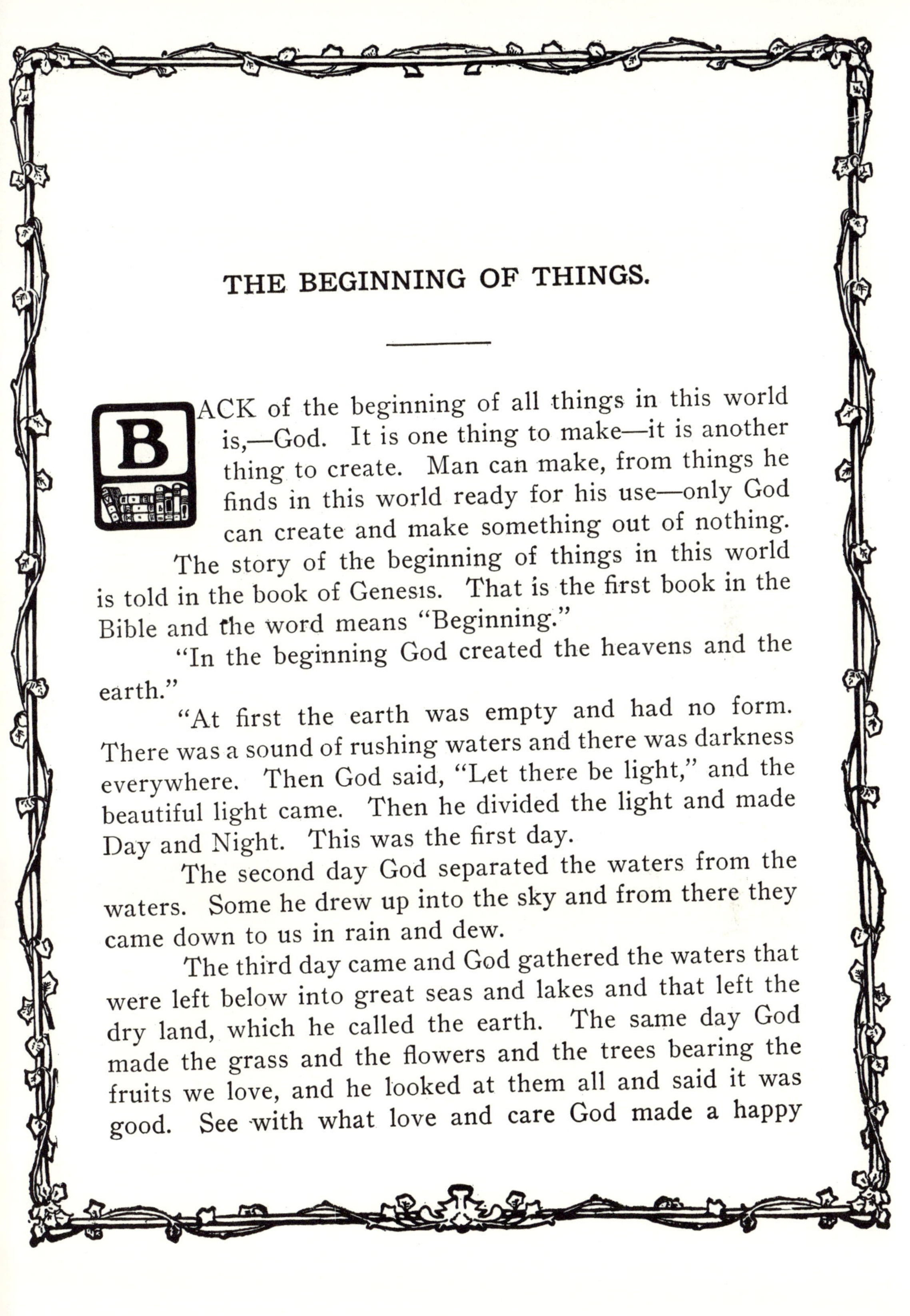

THE BEGINNING OF THINGS.

BACK of the beginning of all things in this world is,—God. It is one thing to make—it is another thing to create. Man can make, from things he finds in this world ready for his use—only God can create and make something out of nothing.

The story of the beginning of things in this world is told in the book of Genesis. That is the first book in the Bible and the word means "Beginning."

"In the beginning God created the heavens and the earth."

"At first the earth was empty and had no form. There was a sound of rushing waters and there was darkness everywhere. Then God said, "Let there be light," and the beautiful light came. Then he divided the light and made Day and Night. This was the first day.

The second day God separated the waters from the waters. Some he drew up into the sky and from there they came down to us in rain and dew.

The third day came and God gathered the waters that were left below into great seas and lakes and that left the dry land, which he called the earth. The same day God made the grass and the flowers and the trees bearing the fruits we love, and he looked at them all and said it was good. See with what love and care God made a happy place for you, his children, who were already living in his thoughts!

The work of the fourth day was as beautiful as it was wonderful, for then God made the sun, and the moon, and the stars. He gave to each one its place and its own work to do. Can you think of any work that is given these gems of the sky to do?

And then God began to make living creatures,—the fish that live in the great waters, and the fowl and birds that fly about the earth. Some were very small, but others were great like the whale in the sea and the noble eagle in the air. God blessed them, for he saw that his work was good, and this was the fifth day of the beginning.

On the sixth day God made the living creatures that dwell on the land—all kinds of cattle, and beasts of the field, the creeping things, he made. They are his creatures just as truly as we are, and God has put them here for some purpose, for he "saw that it was good."

And now God had made a place for man to live and had made many things to be a help and blessing to him, and he said, "Let us make man in our image." And so God created man. "Both male and female created he them," to rule over the fish of the sea, the fowl of the air, and the cattle of the earth. Then he blessed them and told them that all the good things he had made were for their use. He placed them in a beautiful garden to care for it and enjoy the good things that grew there.

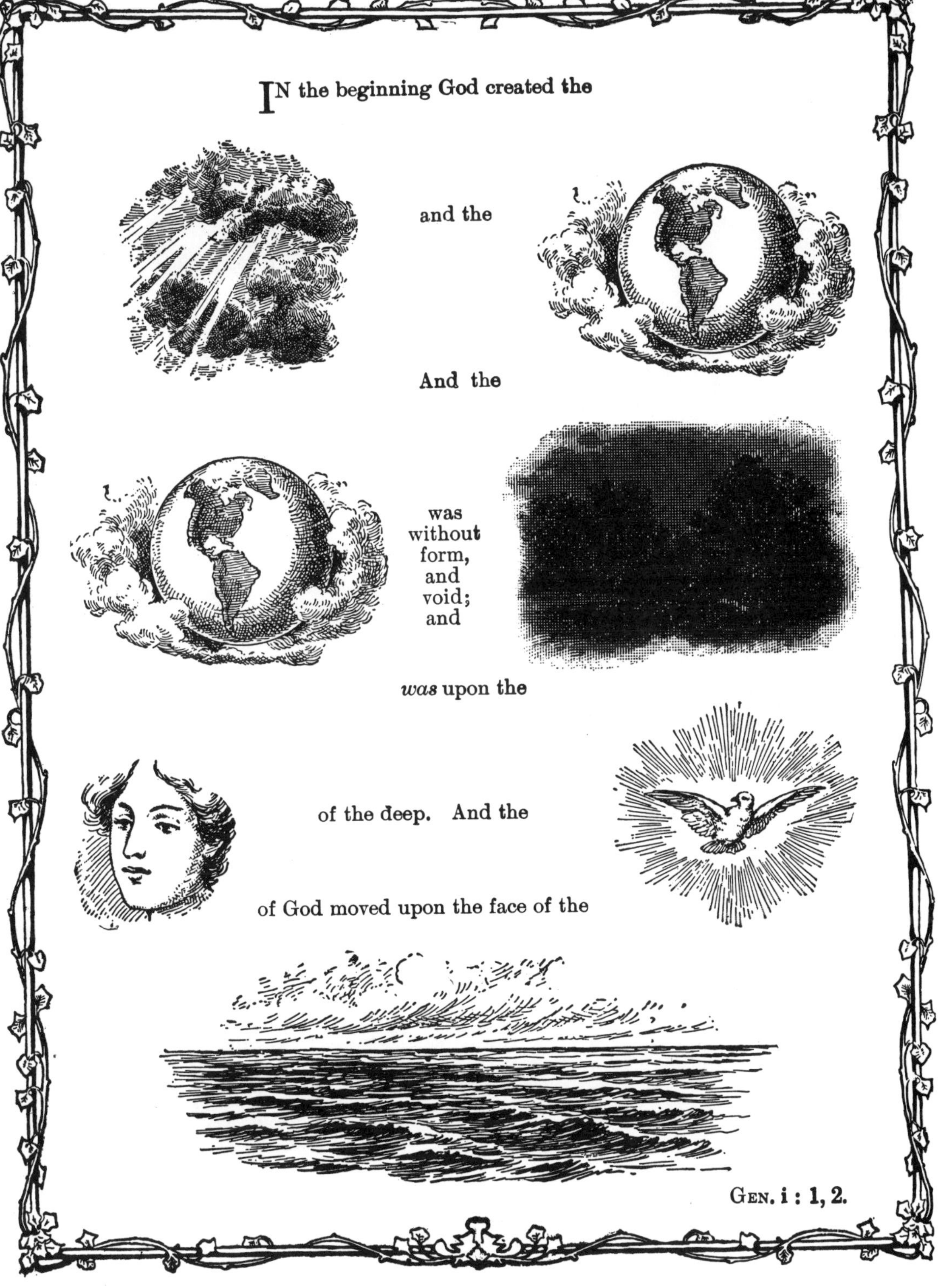

IN the beginning God created the

and the

And the

was without form, and void; and

was upon the

of the deep. And the

of God moved upon the face of the

GEN. i : 1, 2.

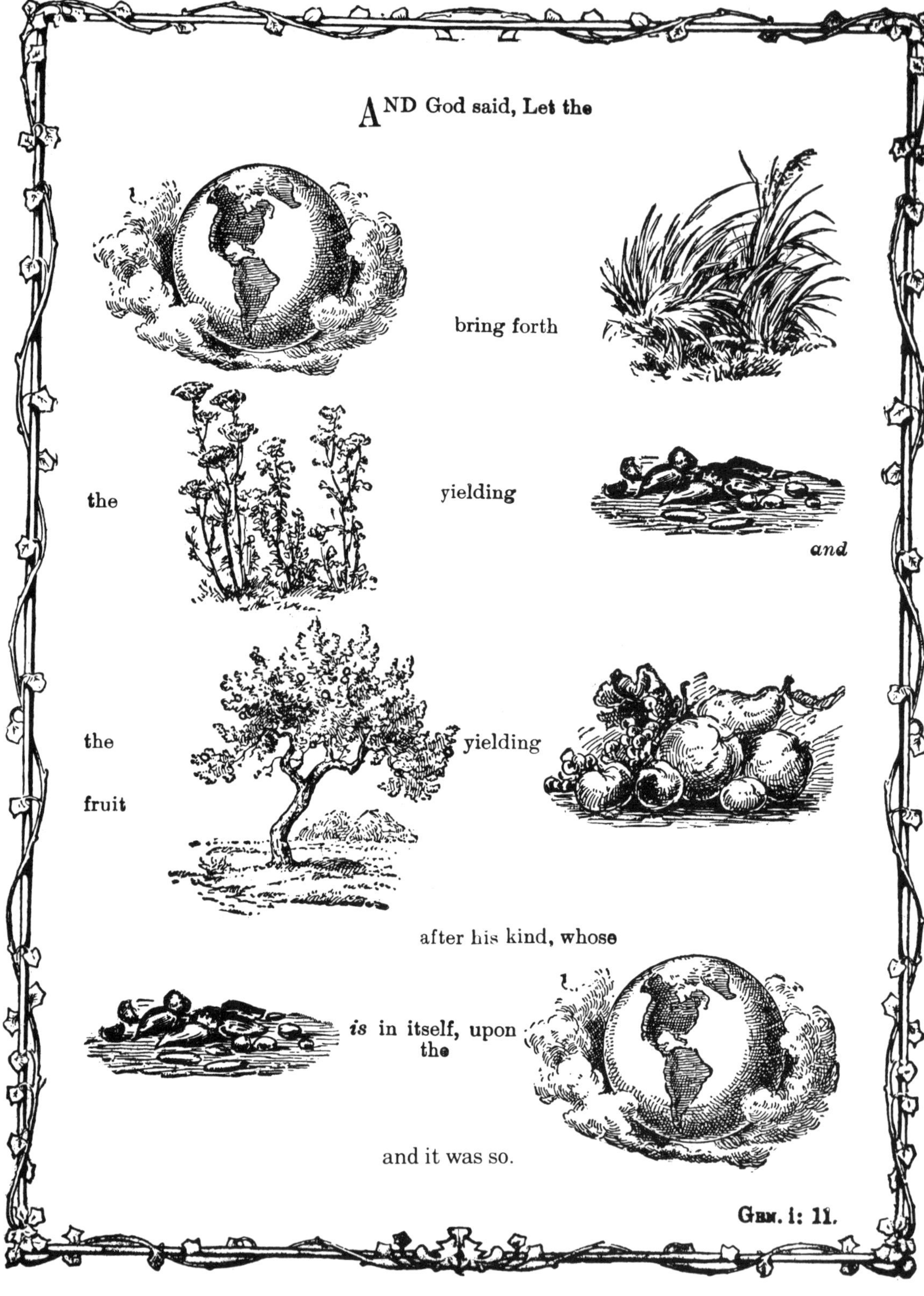
AND God said, Let the
bring forth
the
yielding
and
the
yielding
the fruit
after his kind, whose
is in itself, upon the
and it was so.
GEN. i: 11.

AND GOD made the

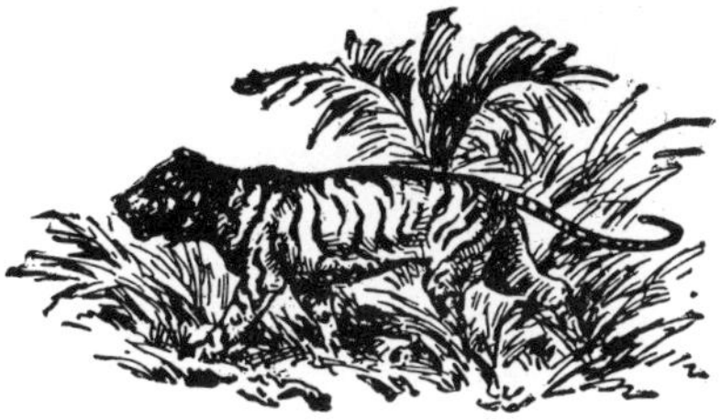

of the

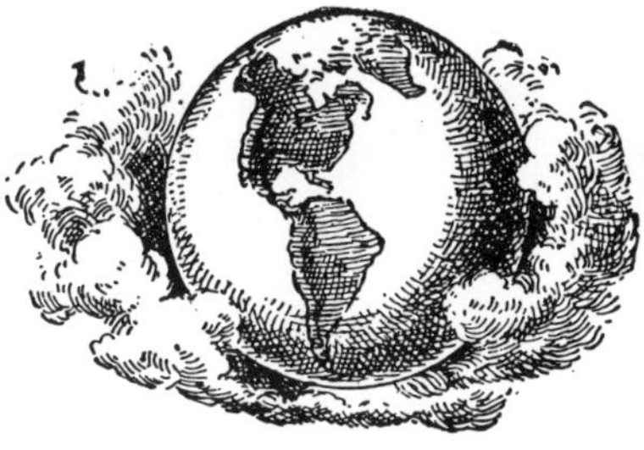

after his kind, and

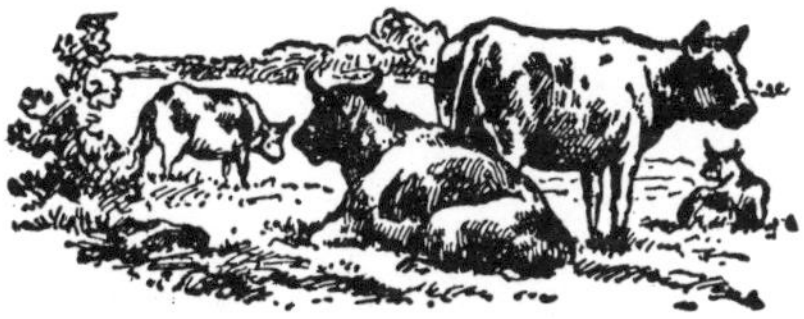

after their kind, and

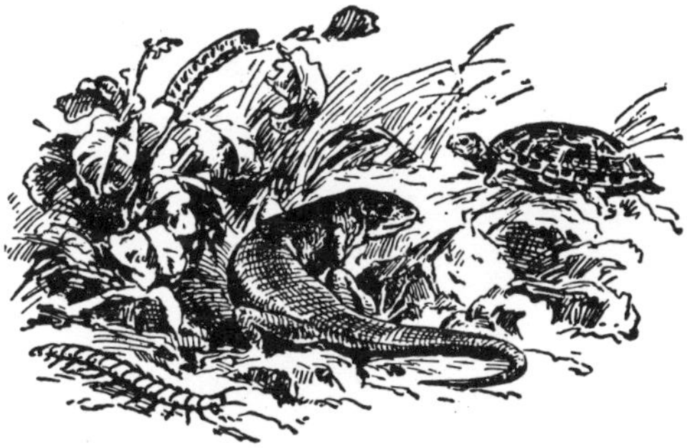

upon the

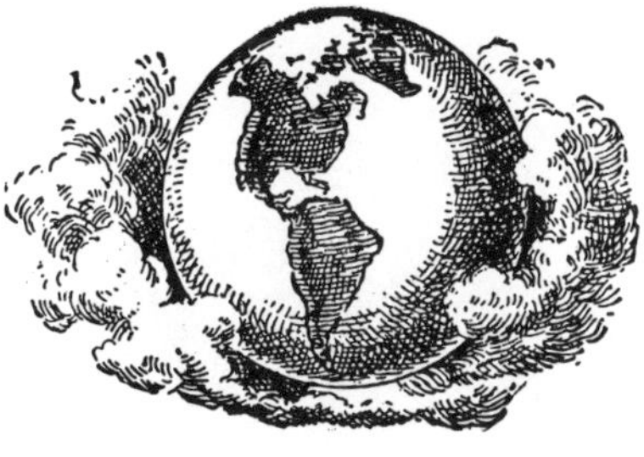

after his kind: and

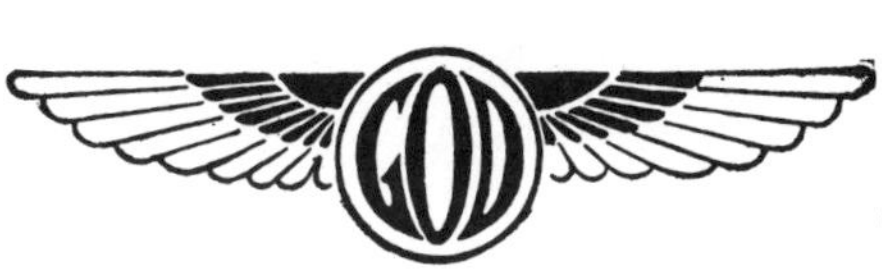

saw that *it was* good.

GEN. i : 25.

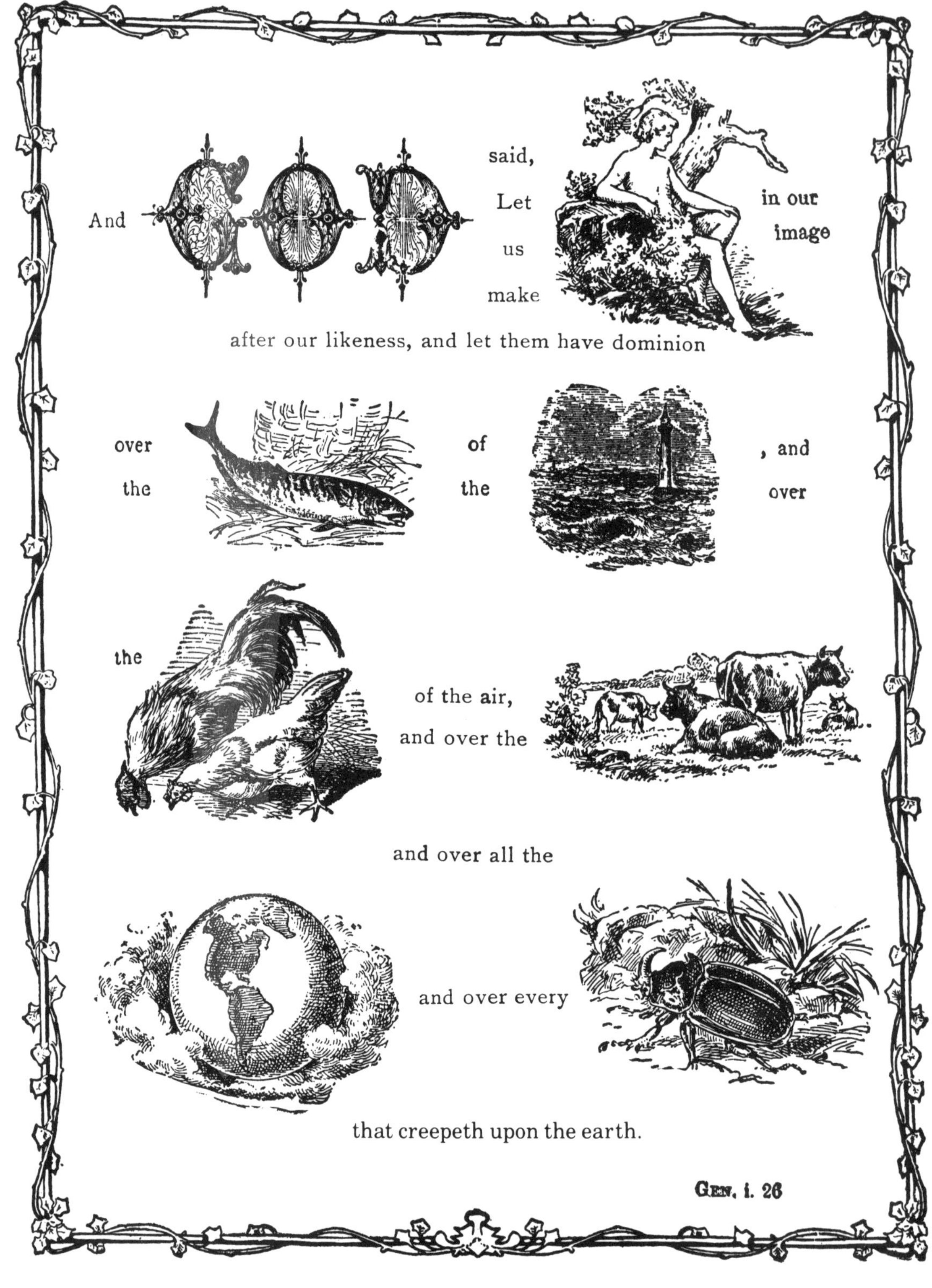

And GOD said, Let us make in our image

after our likeness, and let them have dominion

over the of the , and over

the of the air, and over the

and over all the

and over every

that creepeth upon the earth.

GEN. i. 26

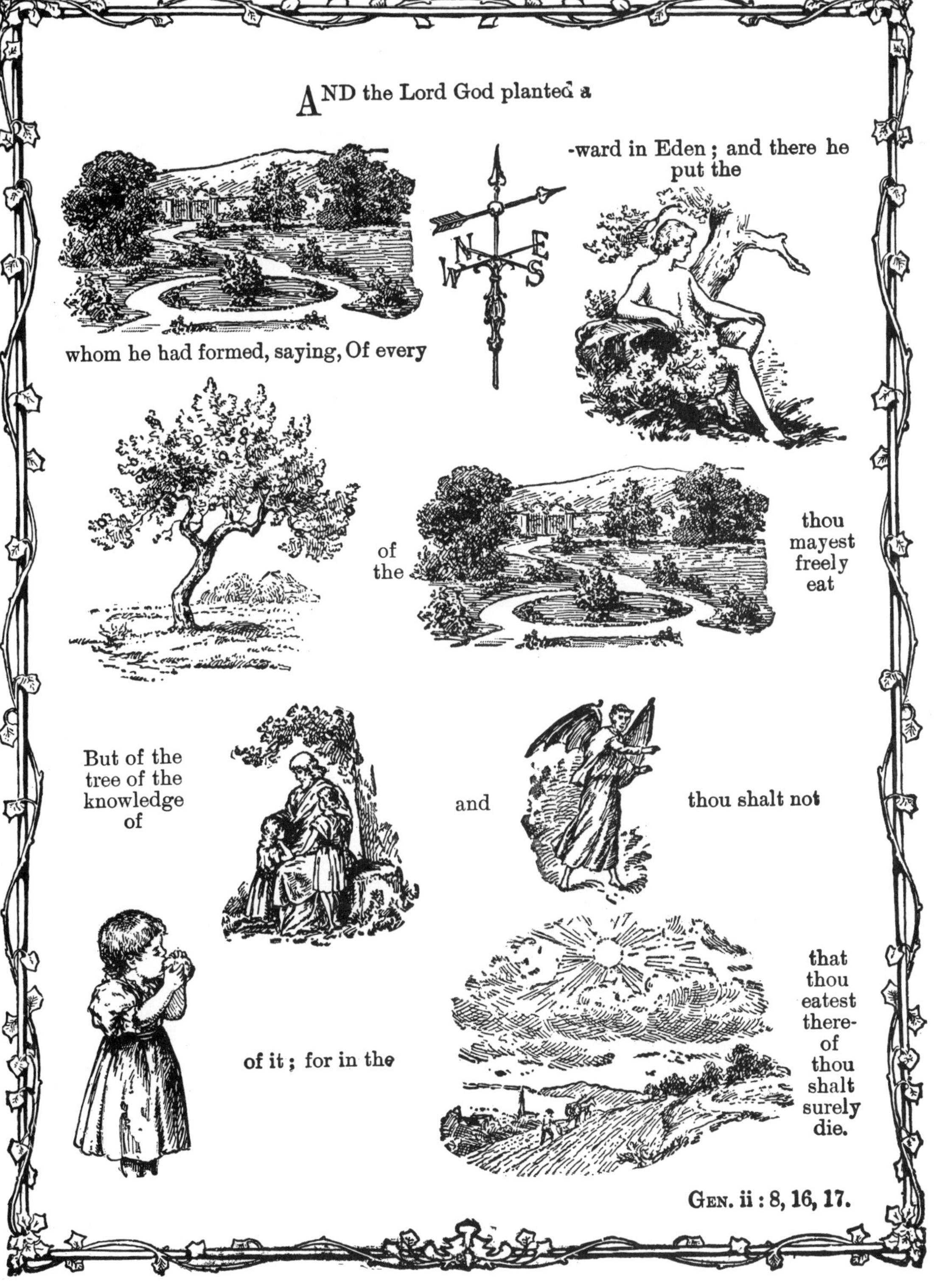
AND the Lord God planted a
-ward in Eden; and there he put the
whom he had formed, saying, Of every
of the
thou mayest freely eat
But of the tree of the knowledge of
and
thou shalt not
of it; for in the
that thou eatest thereof thou shalt surely die.
Gen. ii: 8, 16, 17.

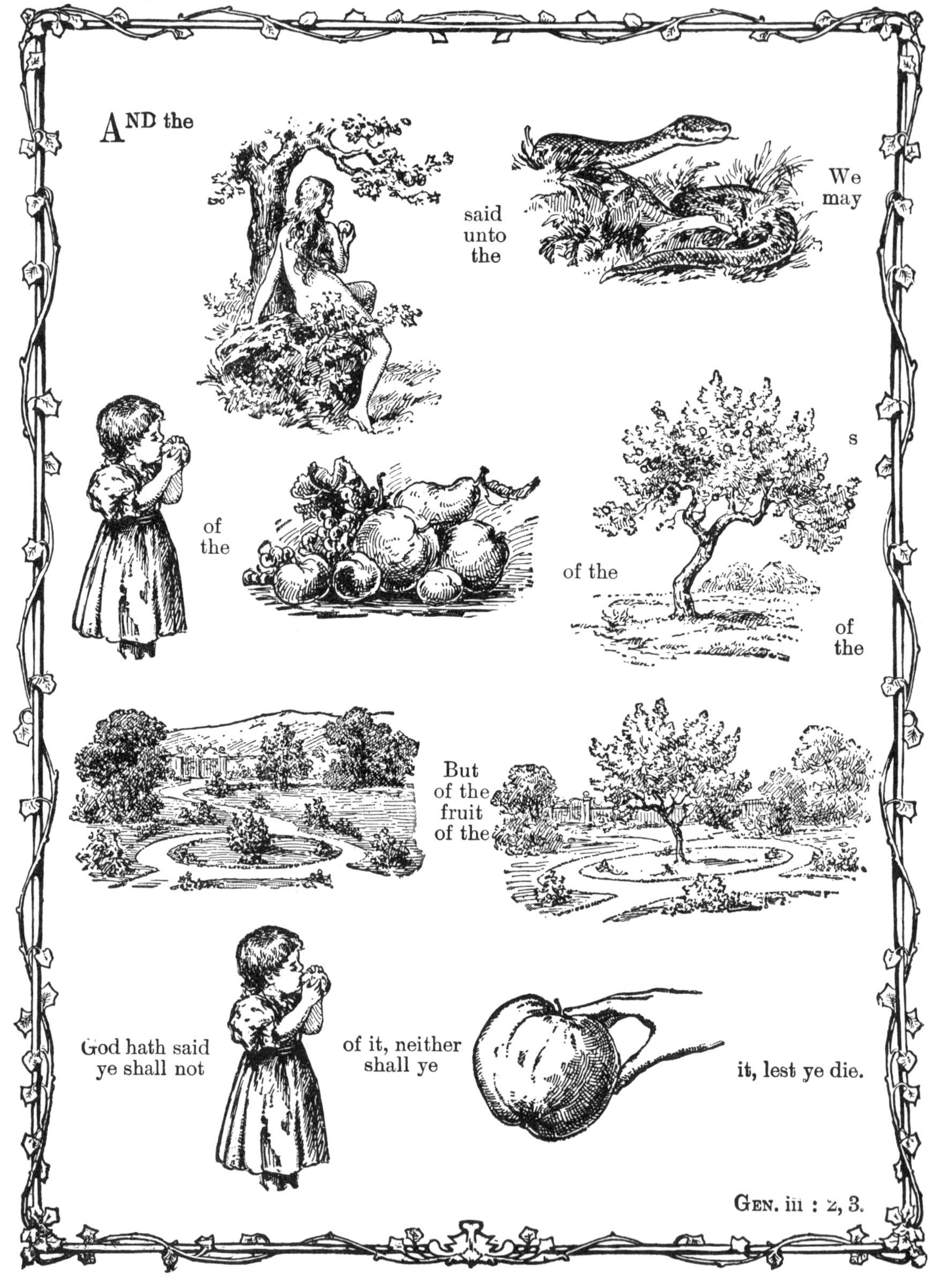
AND the
said
unto
the
We
may
s
of
the
of the
of
the
But
of the
fruit
of the
God hath said
ye shall not
of it, neither
shall ye
it, lest ye die.
GEN. iii : 2, 3.

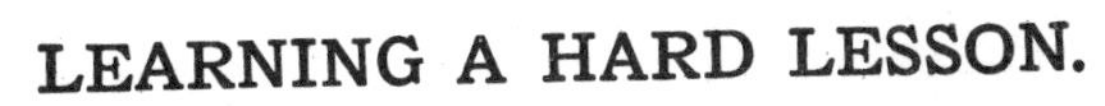

LEARNING A HARD LESSON.

THE first man God created was named "Adam" and the first woman "Eve." They were in a new, beautiful world and God gave them a home in the lovely garden of fruits and flowers. Sometimes he came and walked in the garden with these dear children of his and talked with them. What a happy life it was! No hard work, only to dress and keep the garden, no care, no pain, and no trouble, and God, their holy and loving creator, for their strong and constant Friend.

But a little cloud appeared in the clear sky of their happiness. When God gave this beautiful garden called the Garden of Eden for their home he told them that they might eat the fruit from every tree in it but one. If they should eat the fruit from that one he said they would surely die. Do you wonder why God should do this? He wanted them to learn to choose and obey. They were like children in a new world and with everything to learn. But they had God for their teacher and this lesson of obedience was one of the first he gave them to learn. Surely, you say, they will obey God!

Into this peaceful garden came the spirit of evil. He took the form of a serpent and whispered to Eve about the beauty of the fruit on the forbidden tree. He said that they would not die if they ate the fruit, but their eyes would be opened and they would then know all about good and evil. And Eve—poor, foolish Eve—believed the evil spirit and took some of the fruit and ate it. This was not all—she gave some to Adam and he ate it, and right away they knew they had done wrong. When they heard the voice of God in the garden they tried to hide themselves. As if anyone could ever hide from God!

And did they die? No, not then, but the spirit of innocence died in them and never again could they look into the face of God with clear, unafraid eyes. They lost their beautiful home, too, and went out to labor hard for their bread because they had chosen to please themselves rather than God.

But this was not all. They planted the seeds of disobedience and self-will, which grew great and strong in other hearts, and so the beautiful world God had made for his children to live in became a place in which there is sin, and sorrow, and pain, and death, and all this because Adam and Eve wanted to have their own way.

The child who chooses to obey finds his home a happy place. He is not afraid when he hears his father's or mother's voice, but is quick to answer and glad to hear all they say. But the child who loves his own way best and disobeys the commands that are given by those who love him, is not happy. He wants to hide away when he has done wrong, for his heart tells him that he has listened to the tempter and yielded as Adam and Eve did. Then, like Adam and Eve, he loses his sweet home joy and the gladness that comes from loving obedience.

"I'll see how Jesus lived
By reading in his Word,
And try to be his little child,
Just following my Lord."

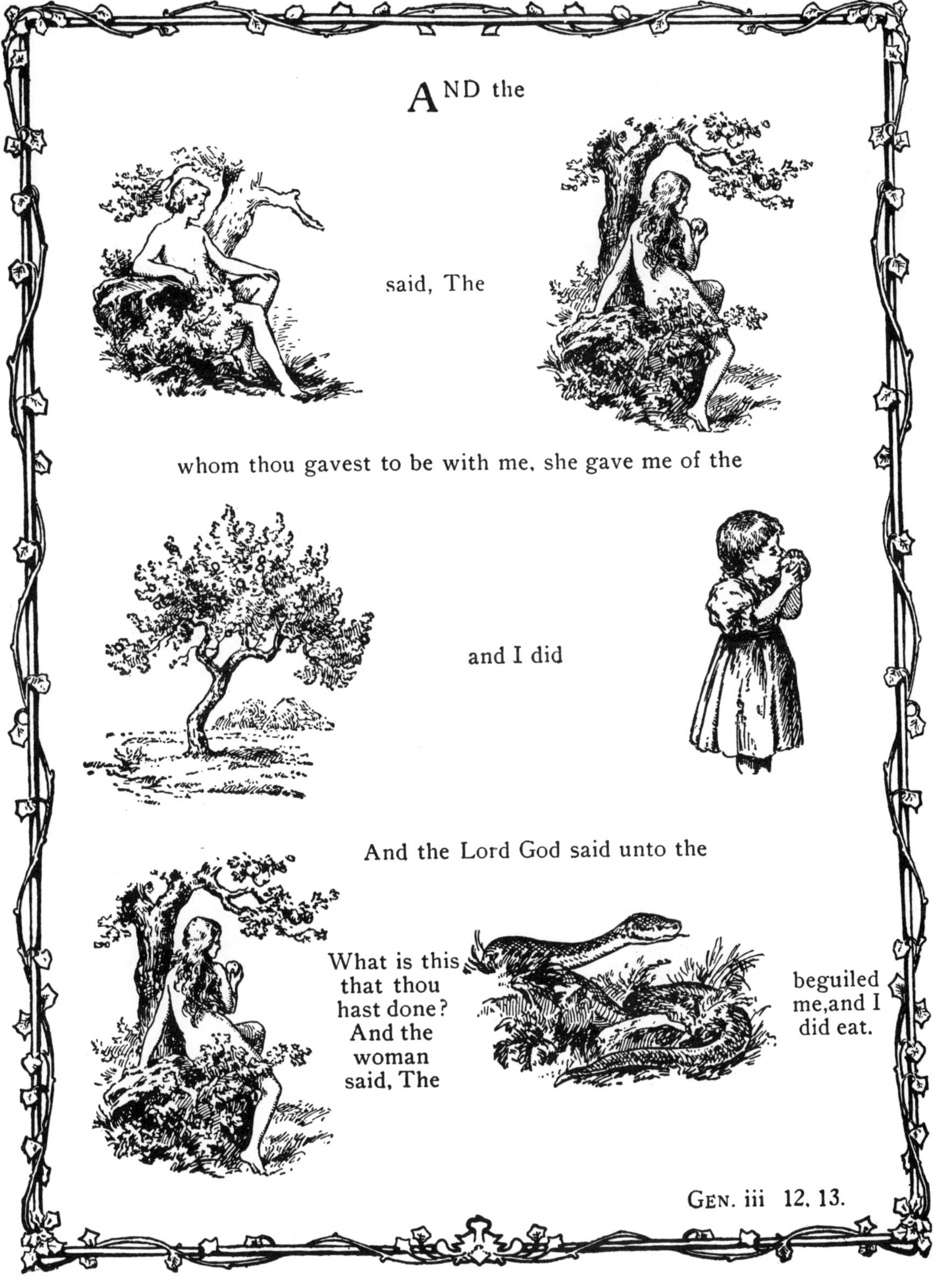

AND the

said, The

whom thou gavest to be with me, she gave me of the

and I did

And the Lord God said unto the

What is this that thou hast done? And the woman said, The

beguiled me, and I did eat.

GEN. iii 12, 13.

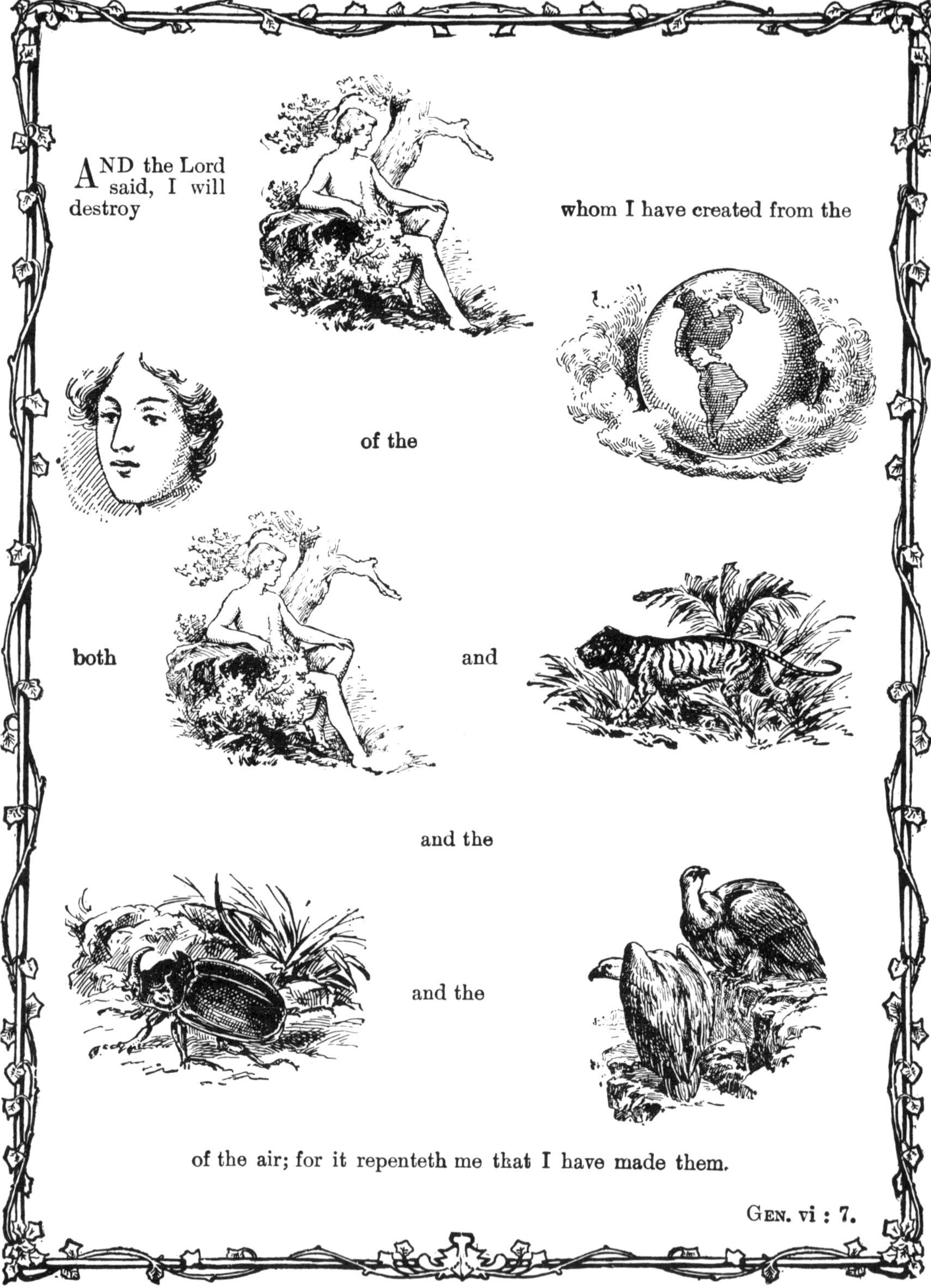

AND the Lord said, I will destroy

whom I have created from the

of the

both

and

and the

and the

of the air; for it repenteth me that I have made them.

GEN. vi : 7.

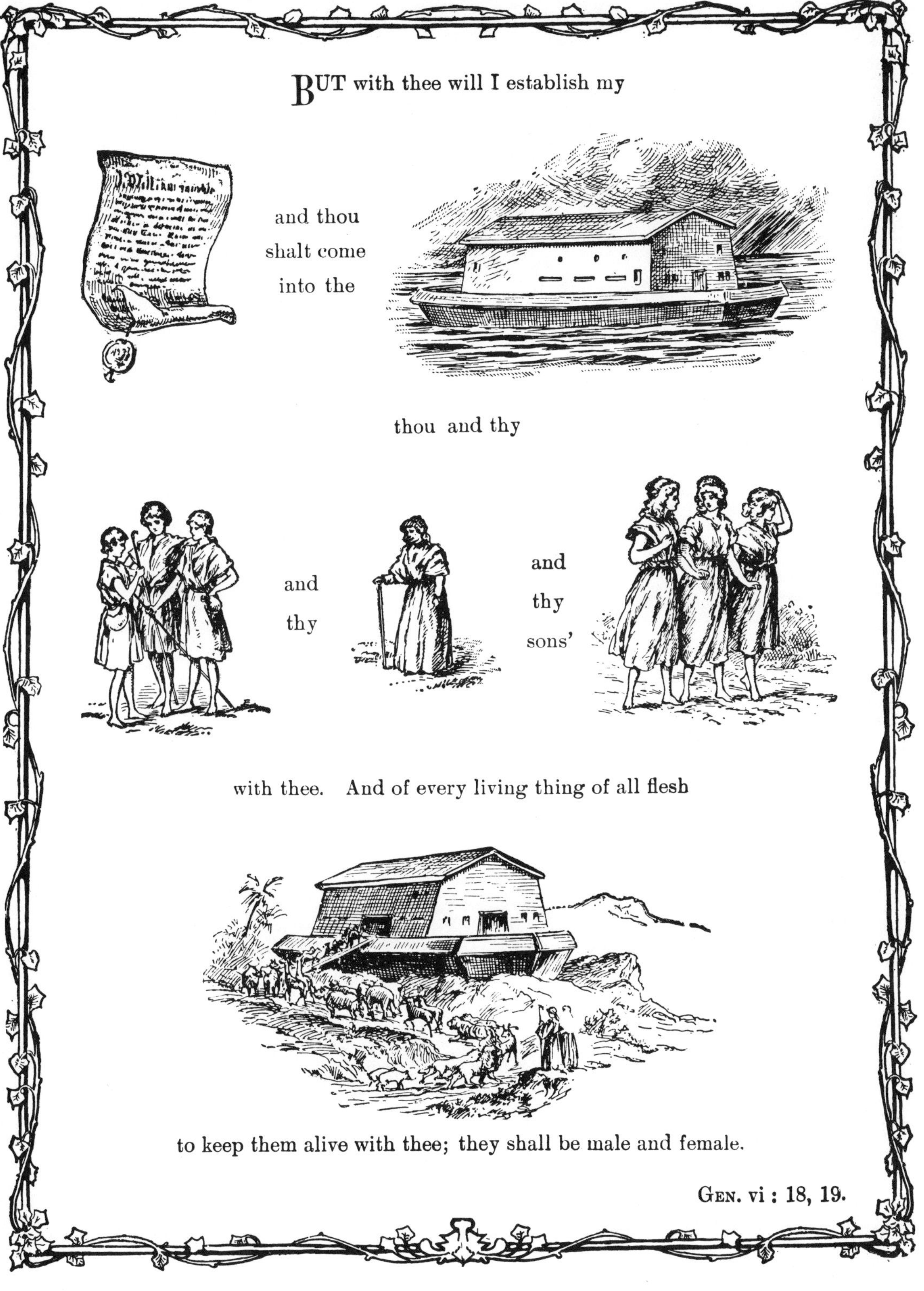

BUT with thee will I establish my

and thou shalt come into the

thou and thy

and thy

and thy sons'

with thee. And of every living thing of all flesh

to keep them alive with thee; they shall be male and female.

GEN. vi : 18, 19.

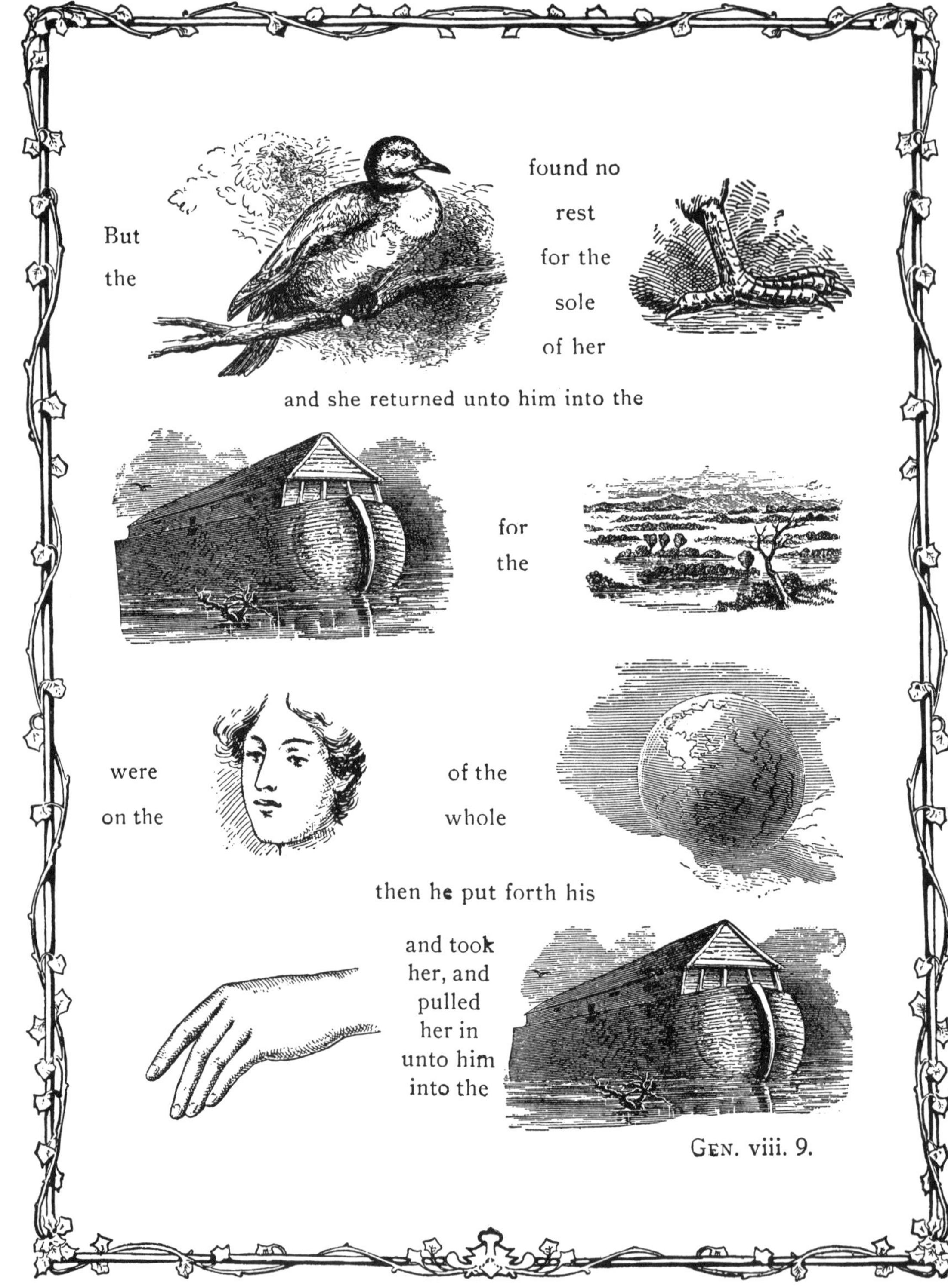

But the found no rest for the sole of her

and she returned unto him into the

for the

were on the of the whole

then he put forth his

and took her, and pulled her in unto him into the

GEN. viii. 9.

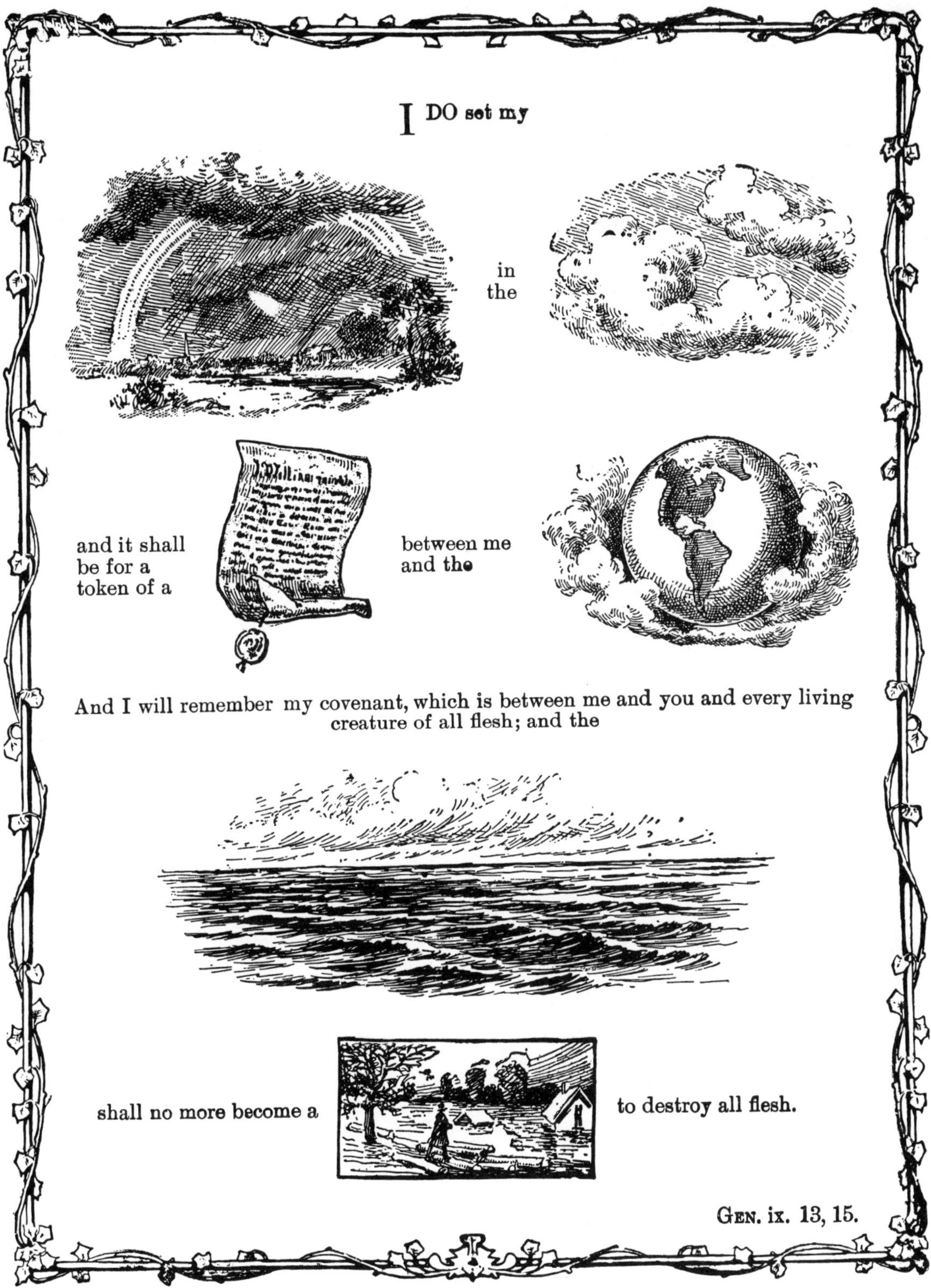

I DO set my [rainbow] in the [cloud]

and it shall be for a token of a [covenant] between me and the [earth].

And I will remember my covenant, which is between me and you and every living creature of all flesh; and the

[waters]

shall no more become a [flood] to destroy all flesh.

Gen. ix. 13, 15.

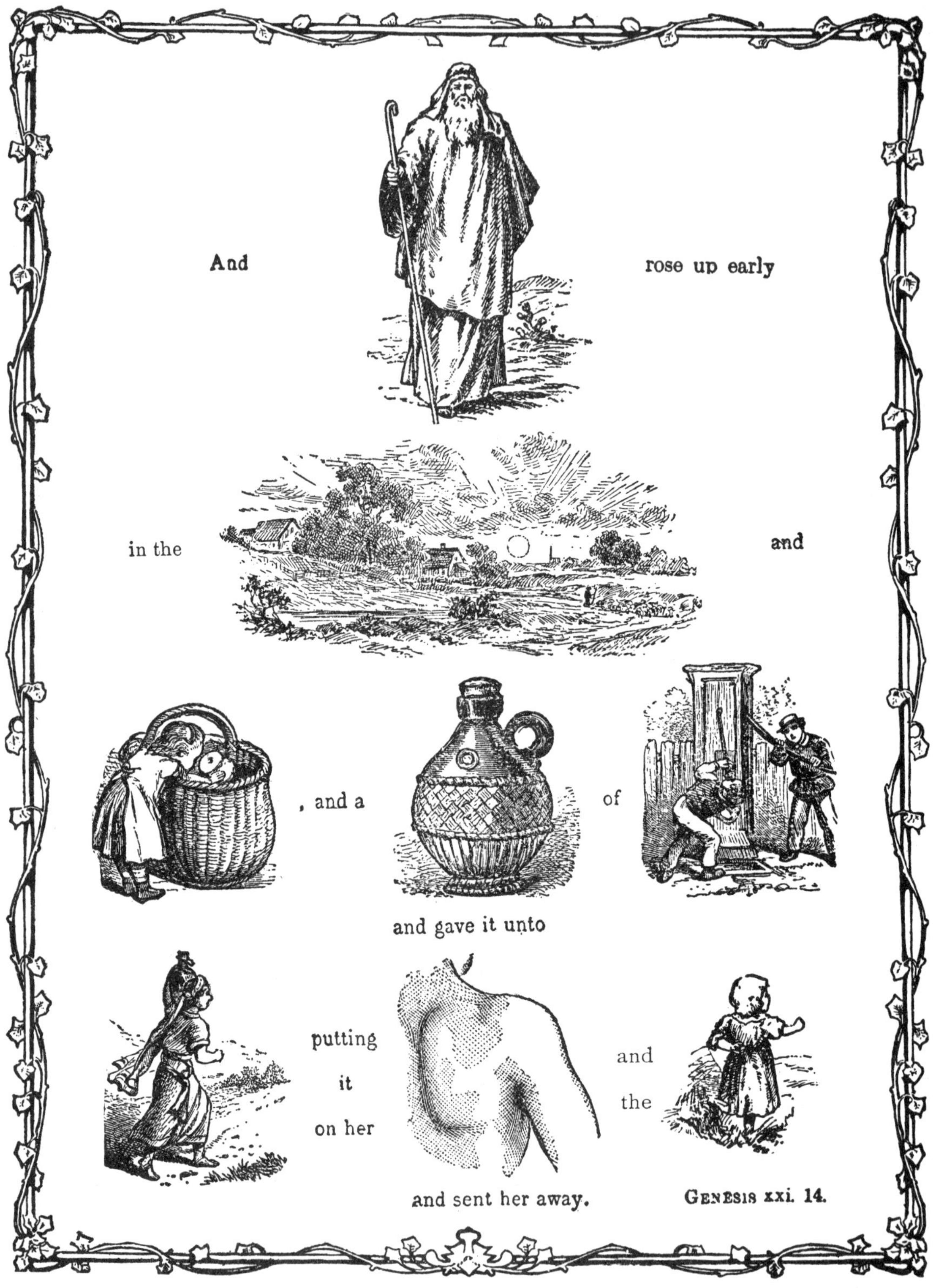
And
rose up early
in the
and
, and a
of
and gave it unto
putting
it
on her
and
the
and sent her away.
GENESIS xxi. 14.

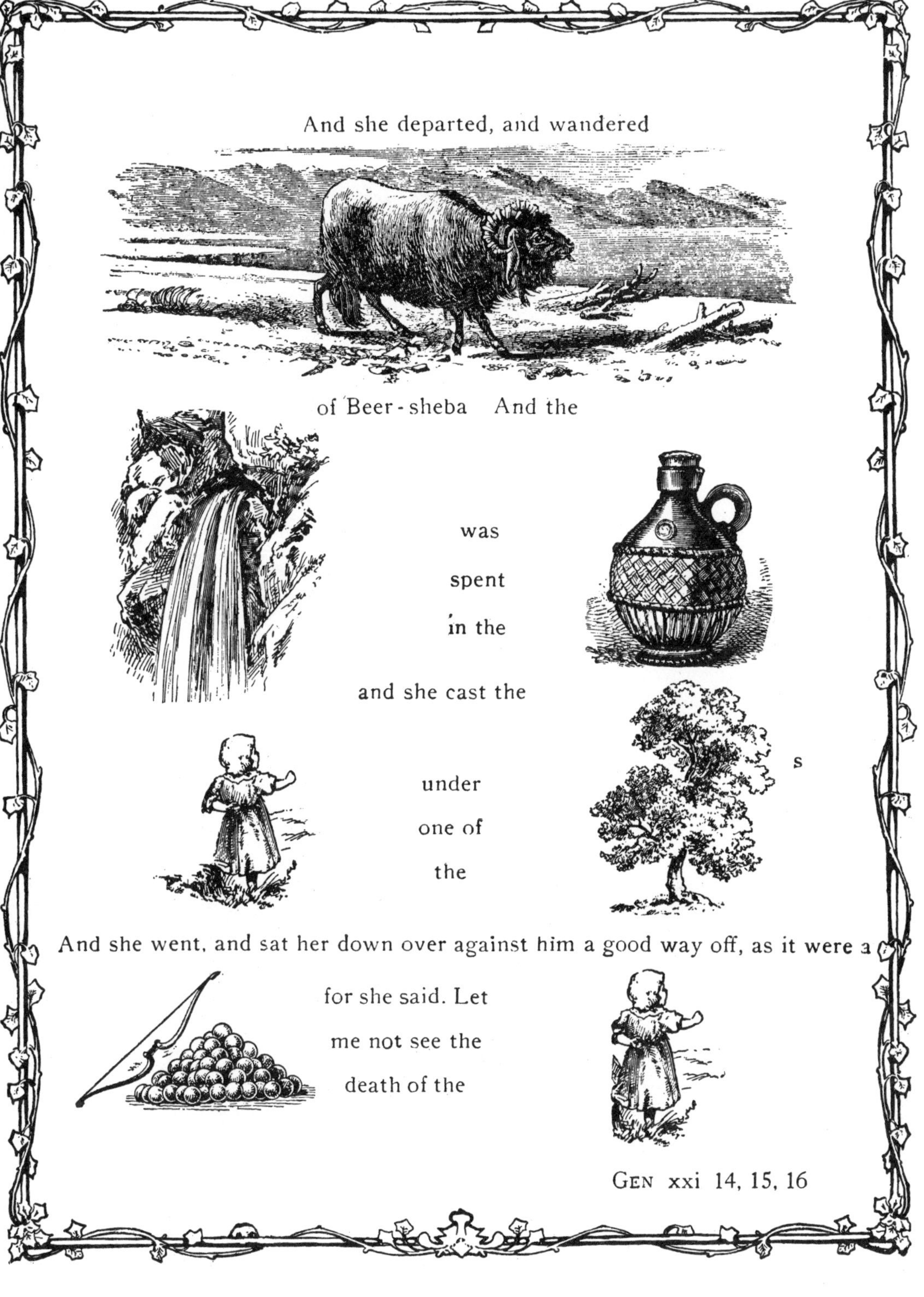

And she departed, and wandered

of Beer-sheba And the

was

spent

in the

and she cast the

s

under

one of

the

And she went, and sat her down over against him a good way off, as it were a

for she said. Let

me not see the

death of the

Gen xxi 14, 15, 16

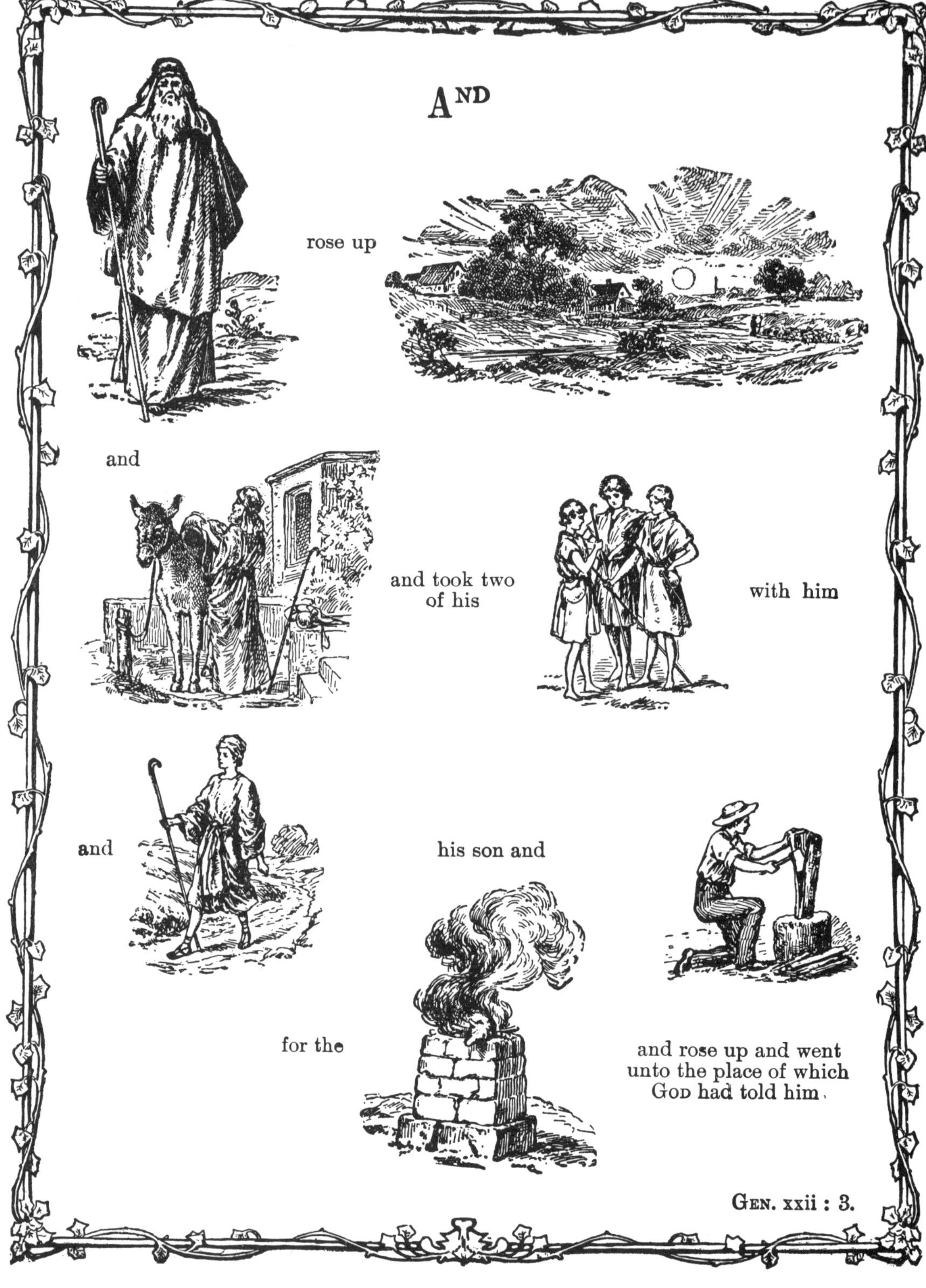
AND
rose up
and
and took two
of his
with him
and
his son and
for the
and rose up and went
unto the place of which
God had told him.
Gen. xxii : 3.

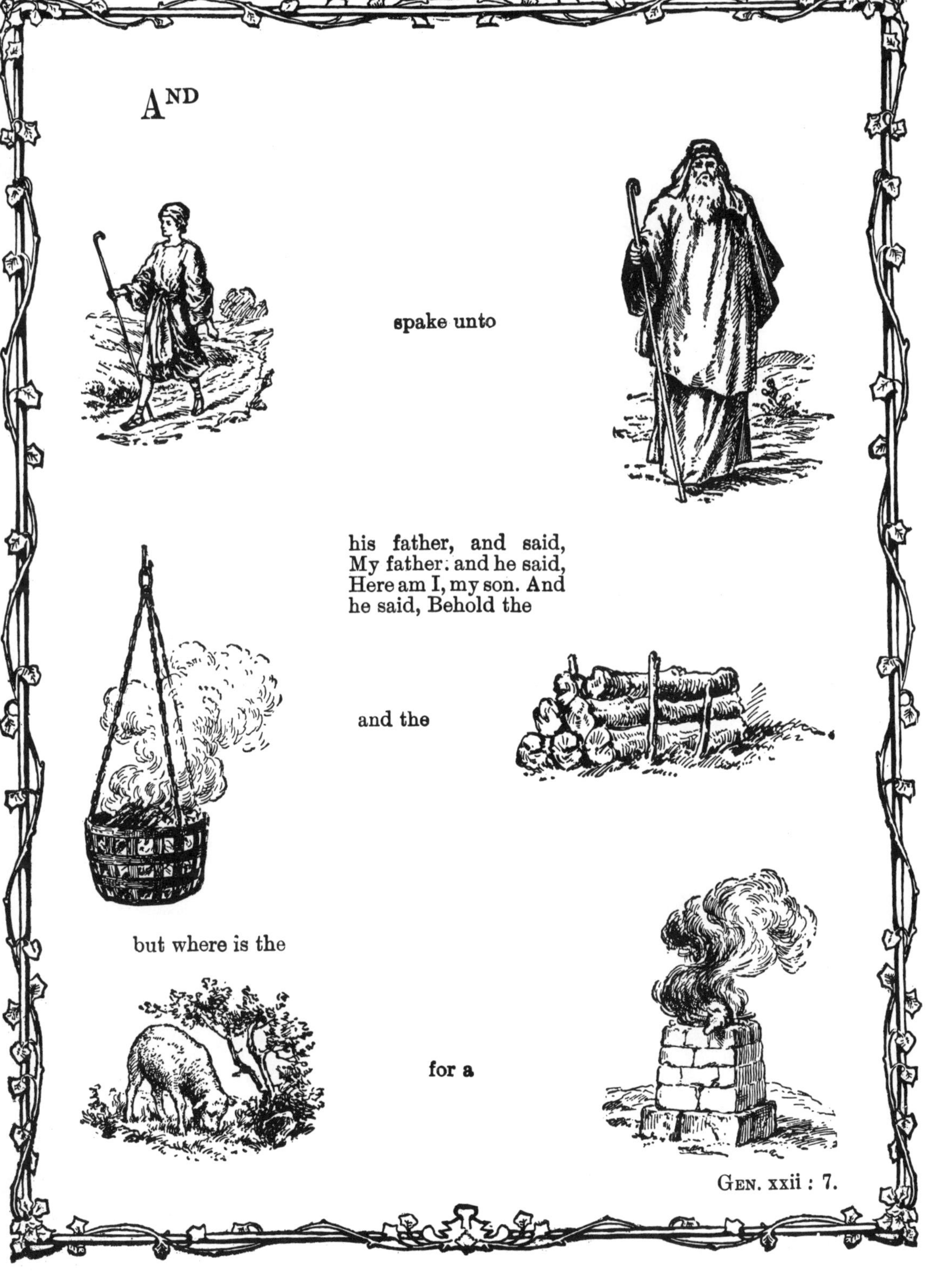

AND

spake unto

his father, and said, My father: and he said, Here am I, my son. And he said, Behold the

and the

but where is the

for a

GEN. xxii : 7.

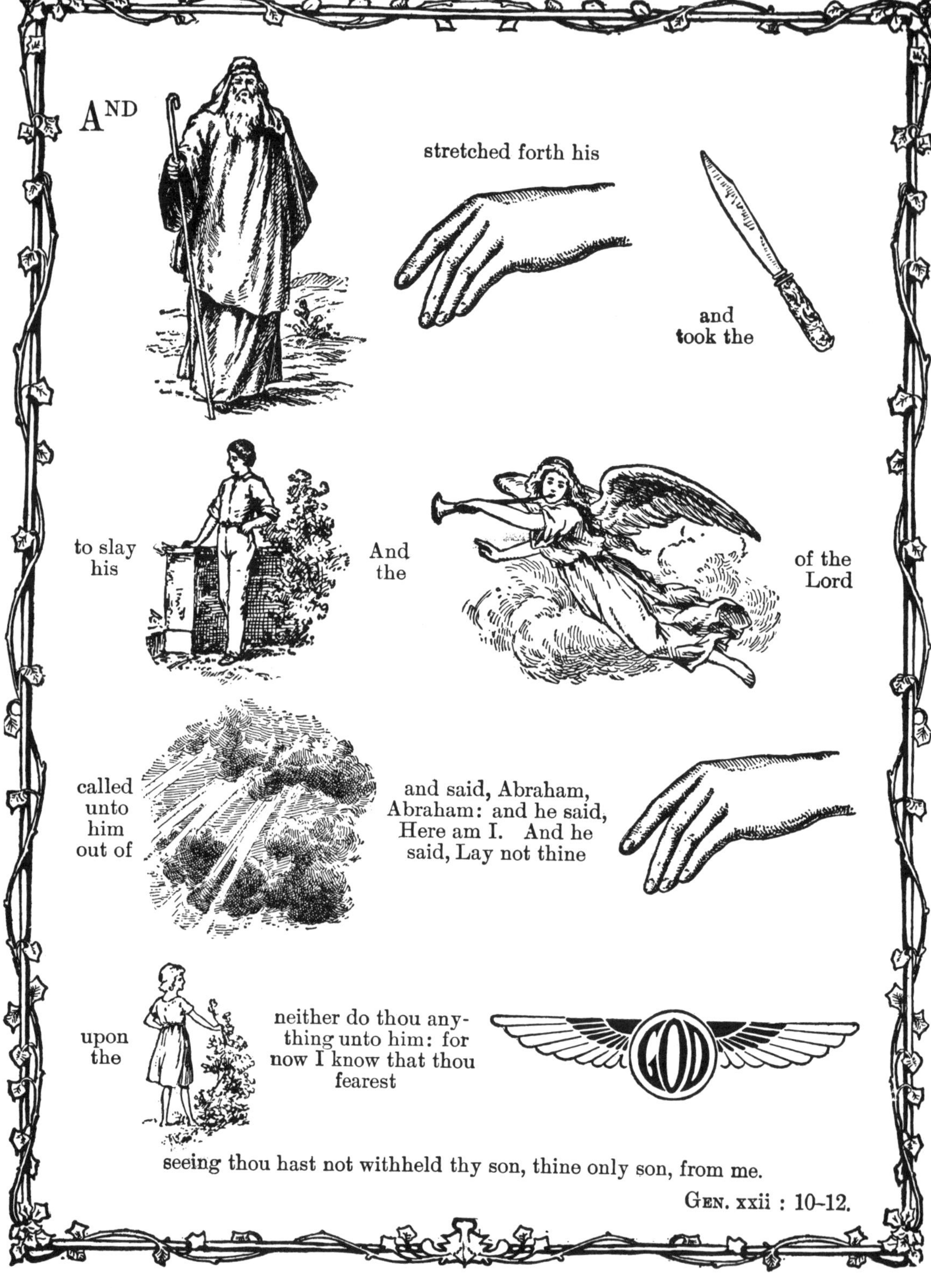

AND
stretched forth his
and
took the
to slay
his
And
the
of the
Lord
called
unto
him
out of
and said, Abraham,
Abraham: and he said,
Here am I. And he
said, Lay not thine
upon
the
neither do thou any-
thing unto him: for
now I know that thou
fearest
GOD
seeing thou hast not withheld thy son, thine only son, from me.
GEN. xxii : 10-12.

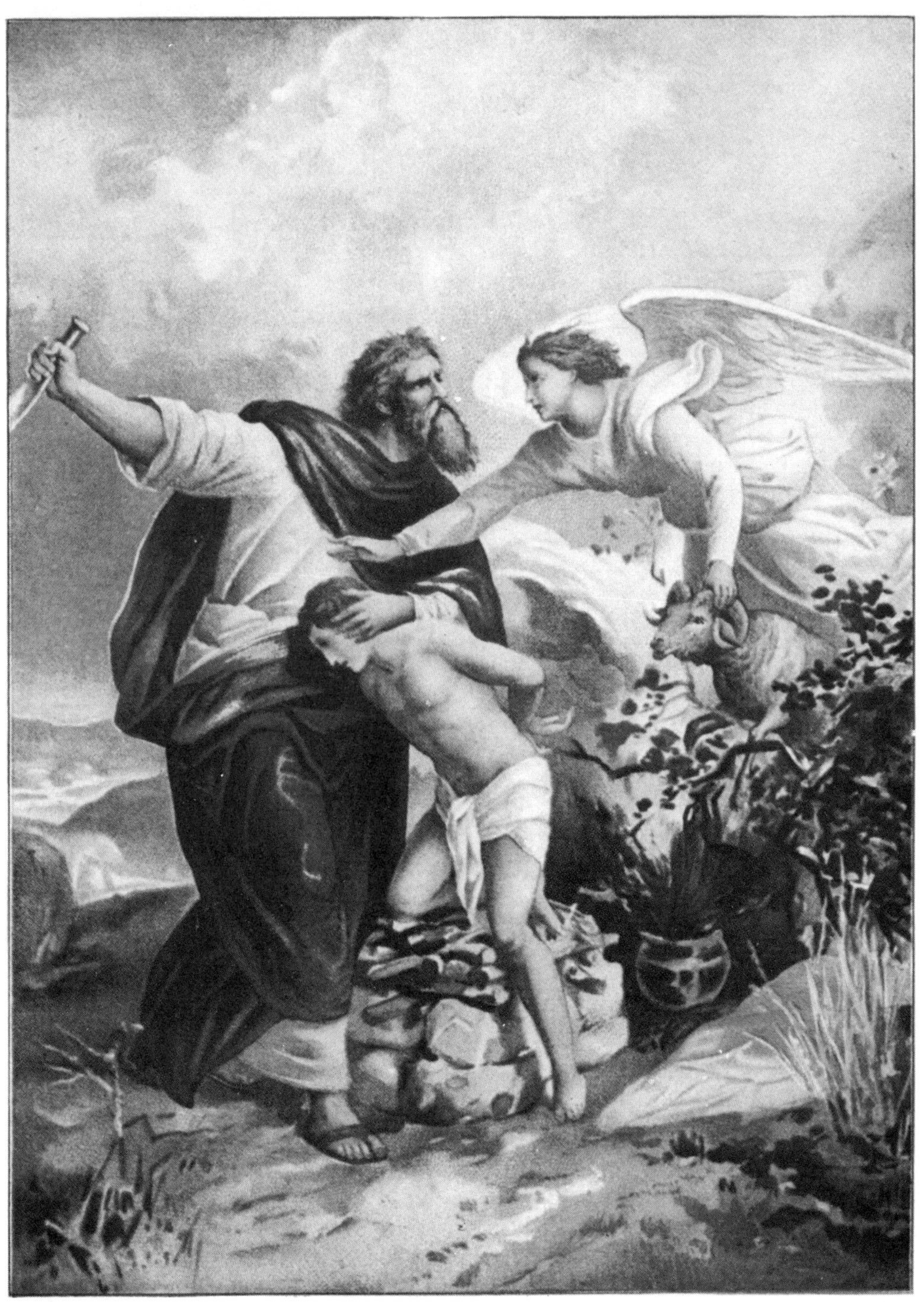

THE OFFERING OF ISAAC.

THE OFFERING OF ISAAC

In our story of the Patriarchs, page 24, we saw that Abraham and his wife Sarah had only one child, Isaac. God had promised him to them, but had kept them waiting till they were nearly a hundred years old. Yet they never gave up their faith in God's promise. "Abraham believed in God": he accepted what God told him as true, and he did what God told him to do without any questioning or doubting. This disposition made him very pleasing to God.

To give men an example at all times of the faith and obedience they should have toward God, Abraham was put to a great test. One day Abraham heard a voice calling him: "Abraham! Abraham!" He answered: "Here I am." It was an angel talking to him. "Get ready," continued the angel; "take your son Isaac and bring him over into the land where the Lord appeared to you, Moriah; and there I will show you which of the hills you will offer him on as a burnt-offering to the Lord."

Isaac was then a young man of some twenty-five years, and he was the only hope and love of his parents. But Abraham did not hesitate one moment: God wanted it, and that was enough. So the next morning before daybreak Abraham called Isaac and two of his servants. They put a few bundles of kindling wood on the back of an ass, Abraham got a big knife, and they all started out for the place the angel had said. They went on and on for three days. When they got near the hill, Abraham left the two servants down in the valley with the ass. He put the wood on Isaac's back and he carried the fire and the knife in his hand. "Father," said Isaac, "you are going to offer a sacrifice; but where is the victim?" "Oh! God will see to that, my boy," answered Abraham. Nothing more was said. Both went up onto the hill; both together gathered stones and heaped them into an altar; then they set the wood in place. Now Abraham tells his son that he is to be the victim. Isaac sets aside his clothes quietly while his father sets fire to the wood. Neither one hesitates. God wants it, that's enough. Now look at your picture: Abraham seizes his only dear boy; he raises his great knife to kill him. Down it's coming, when a hand out of the cloud grabs Abraham's, and a voice is heard: "Stop, Abraham, kill not your boy. Now I know that you fear God and are ready to do anything He wants you to do."

It was the angel who had spoken to him before and told him to come there. At the bidding of the angel Abraham offered to God, instead of his son, one of the sheep that were grazing there on the hill brow. After the sacrifice, God renewed all his promises to Abraham and praised him for his faithfulness.

Who was offered a long time after this on one of these hills of Moriah?

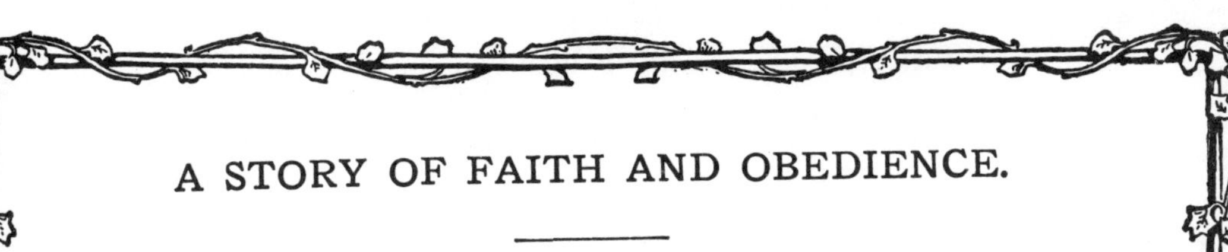

A STORY OF FAITH AND OBEDIENCE.

ABRAHAM, one of the Old Testament heroes, was a man of great faith and of perfect obedience. Perhaps he began to be obedient when he was a very little child and this helps us to believe that he had a good mother, though we do not know her name. His father's name was Terah and all his children were born in Ur of the Chaldees. But when God called them to go to Canaan they arose and went, but stopped at Haran on the way, and there Terah died. It was in Ur that Abraham found his beautiful wife Sarah, who had no child for many, many years until at last the Lord gave her a little son whom she named Isaac.

This story is about Abraham and Isaac. God knew that the faith and obedience of Abraham was almost perfect, but he wanted to try him once more and this is the story of the way he did it.

Among the heathen people who lived near Abraham in Canaan there was a dreadful kind of worship,—the offering up of children as sacrifices to the gods. This is done in some heathen lands to this very day. Abraham had been taught to offer lambs and bullocks. It was not because the Lord loved such worship, but because he knew that men were like children in these early days of the world, and that they must see a picture of prayer or of praise to help them to believe it. It seemed to these childish people that the smoke of the sacrifices and the incense carried their worship up to God, who was looking down from the Heavens and waiting for it.

The heathen people believed in this kind of worship, too, and sometimes offered their children to false gods. The true God never wanted such offerings. Yet, one day he spoke to Abraham to prove his faith and told him to take his only son Isaac, whom he loved, to Mount Moriah and there to offer him as a burnt sacrifice on the mountain top.

Do you think Abraham would say, "Why,"—or "How can I,"—or "Thou hast promised,"—? No, he arose up early in the morning, saddled his ass, cut the wood for the burnt offering, and taking his son and two men servants started toward the place that was afterward Jerusalem. For three days they walked, and when Abraham saw the high place before him he told the servants to wait with the ass while he and Isaac went up to worship. Abraham carried the fire and the knife, but Isaac carried the wood, and so they went up the rocky way together.

Isaac said:

"My father, behold the fire and the wood, but where is the lamb for a burnt offering?"

Abraham put aside his grief and said:

"God will provide himself the lamb for a burnt offering, my son."

When they came to the top of Moriah, where the great world altar has stood for ages, Abraham built the altar and laid on the wood,—and then,—could he do it? Yes, he did. He bound Isaac upon the wood, then he put forth his hand for the knife, but a voice from Heaven called him. It was the Lord, who had seen his perfect faith and his perfect obedience.

"Lay not thy hand upon the lad," he said. "Neither do thou anything to him: for now I know that thou fearest God, seeing thou hast not withheld thy son, thine only son, from me."

Then Abraham saw a ram caught in a thicket by his horns and he took it and offered it up as a burnt offering to the Lord. He also named the place "Jehovah-Jireh," or "The Lord Will Provide."

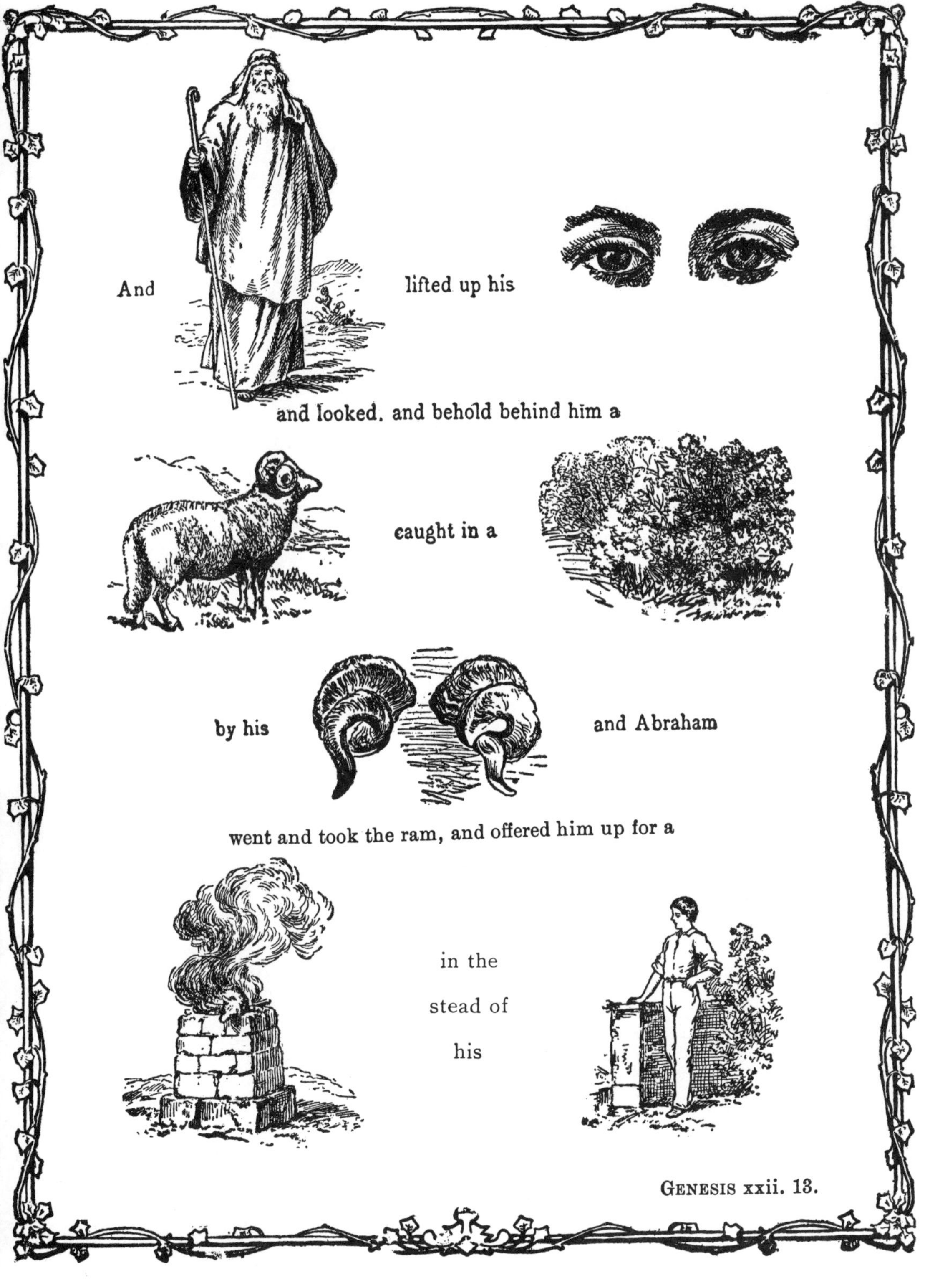

And lifted up his

and looked, and behold behind him a

caught in a

by his and Abraham

went and took the ram, and offered him up for a

in the

stead of

his

GENESIS xxii. 13.

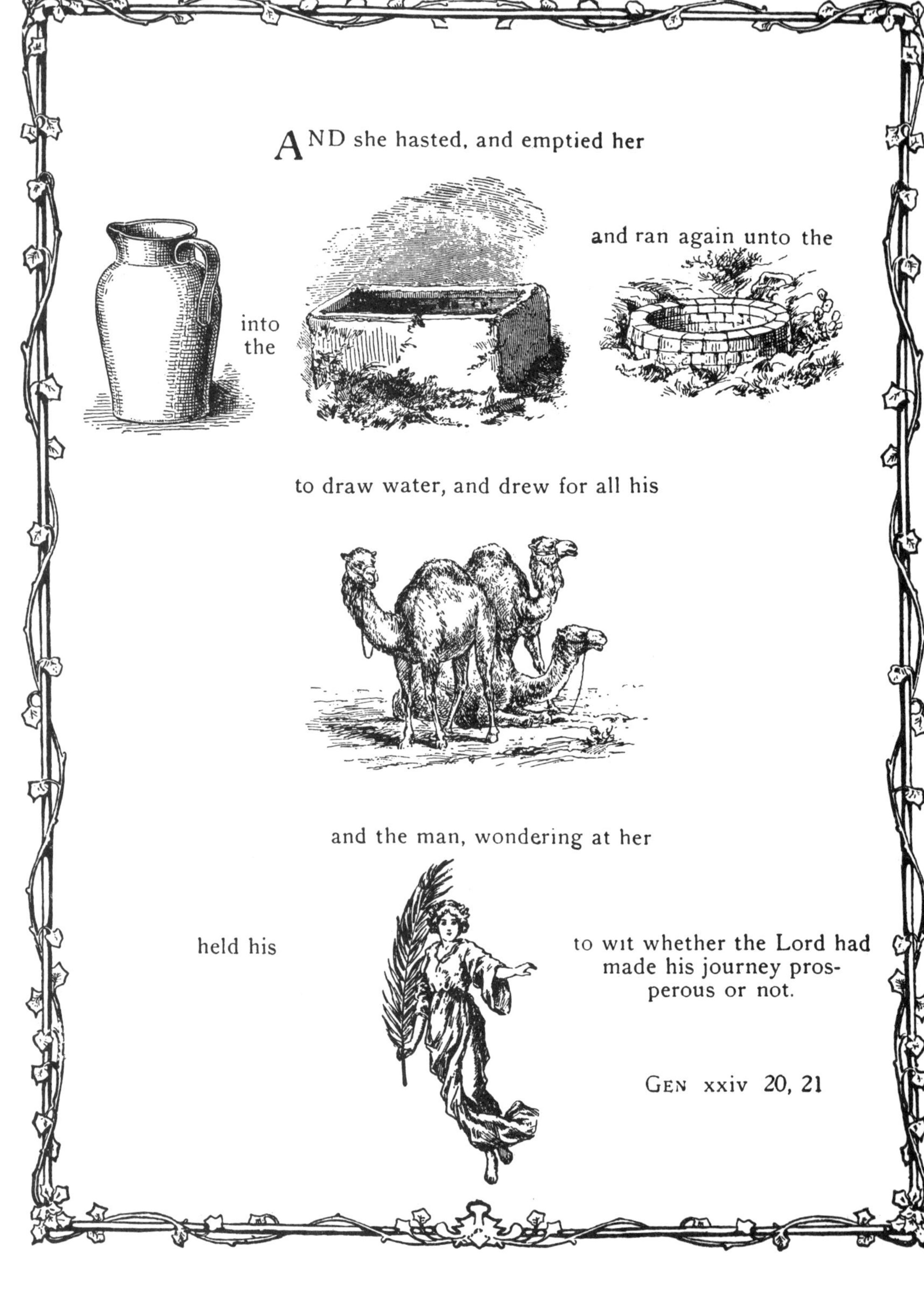
AND she hasted, and emptied her
into
the
and ran again unto the
to draw water, and drew for all his
and the man, wondering at her
held his
to wit whether the Lord had
made his journey pros-
perous or not.
GEN xxiv 20, 21

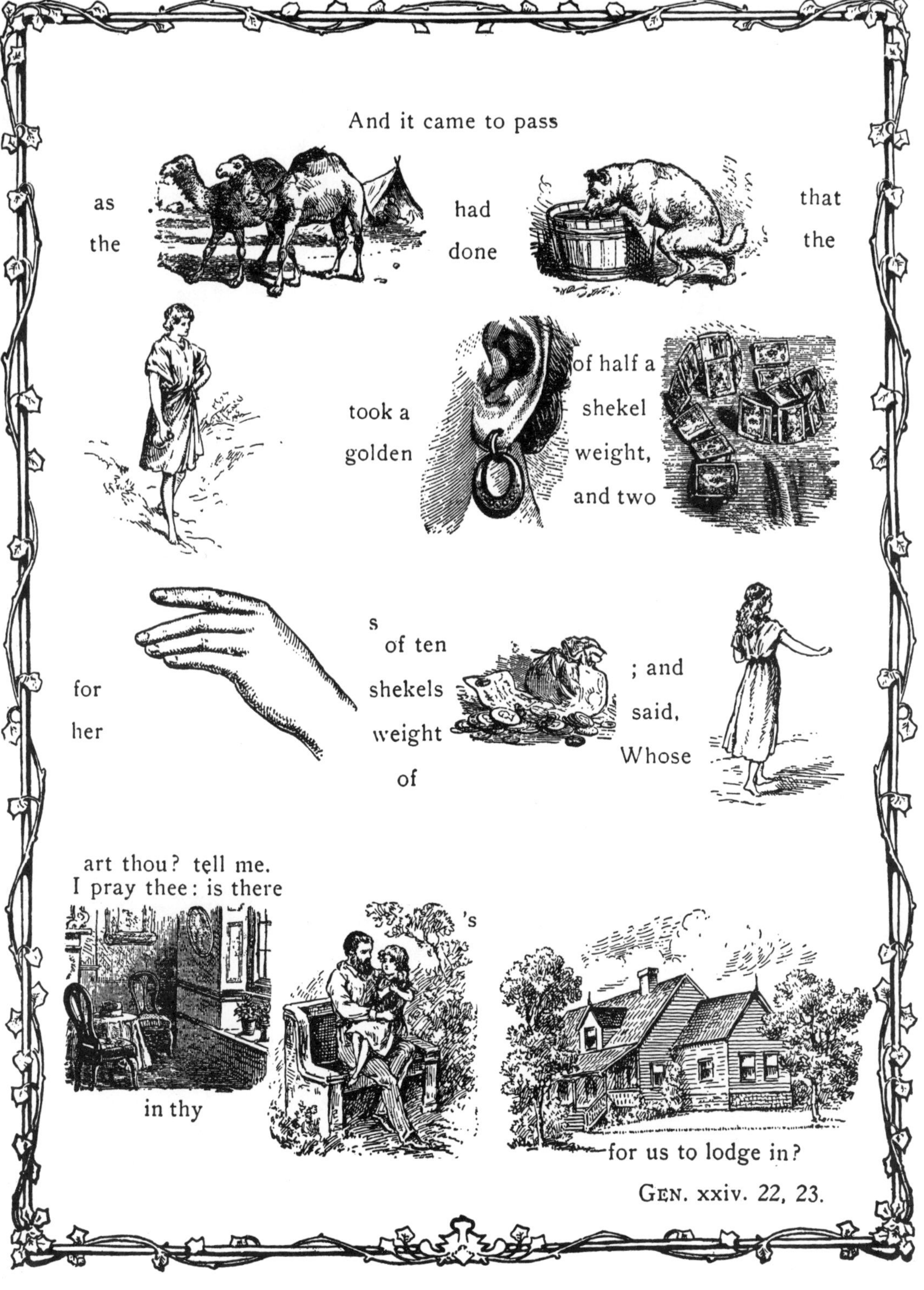
And it came to pass
as the
had done
that the
took a golden
of half a shekel weight, and two
for her
s
of ten shekels weight of
; and said, Whose
art thou? tell me.
I pray thee: is there
in thy
's
for us to lodge in?
GEN. xxiv. 22, 23.

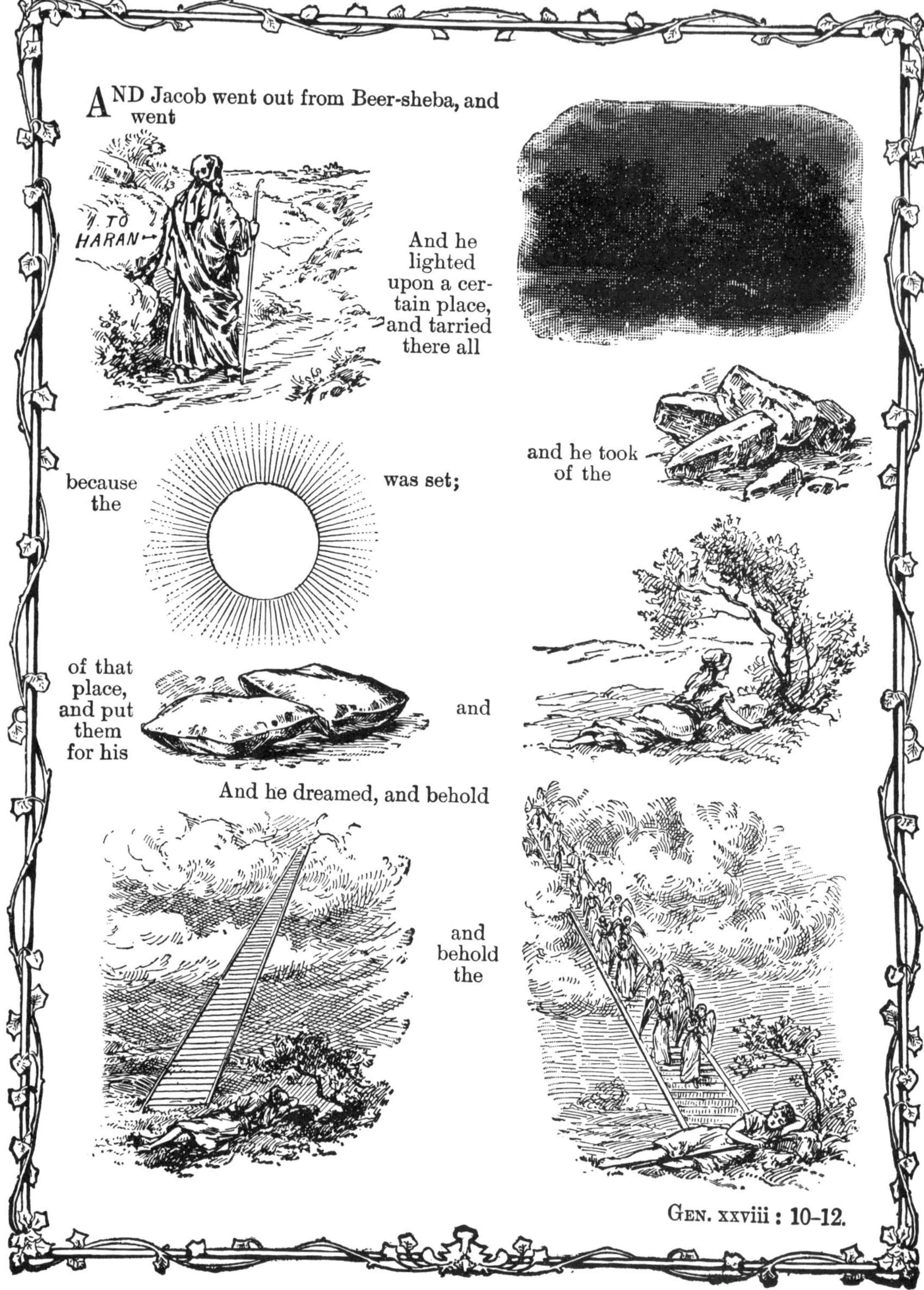

AND Jacob went out from Beer-sheba, and went

And he lighted upon a certain place, and tarried there all

because the

was set;

and he took of the

of that place, and put them for his

and

And he dreamed, and behold

and behold the

GEN. xxviii : 10–12.

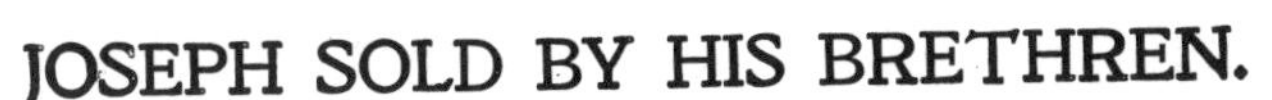

JOSEPH SOLD BY HIS BRETHREN.

"BEHOLD, this dreamer cometh." The words were spoken by one of a group of men in the fields of Dothan. They wore the loose, rough garb of the East, and their strong faces were browned by long exposure to an eastern sun.

"Come now, therefore," the harsh voices went on, "let us slay him, and cast him into some pit, and we will say, some evil beast hath devoured him; and we shall see what will become of his dreams."

But one of the brothers said, "Let us not kill him, but cast him into this pit that is in the wilderness." This was Reuben, one of the sons of Jacob, and he wanted the life of his young brother spared for his old father's sake. And so when young Joseph, the dreamer, and the darling of his father, came near, the hard-hearted brothers seized him and first stripping off the beautiful "coat of many colors," which had helped to cause their jealousy and ill feeling, they threw him into one of the pits so often found in that country.

Why had these men learned to hate their young brother, the son of Jacob's old age, and the firstborn of the beautiful Rachel? More than once Joseph had dreamed strange dreams, which he told in the innocence of his heart. Always the dreams seemed to mean that he would one day be in high honor, and his brothers would bow down to him and serve him. These dreams, and the fondness with which his father looked upon this beloved son, had stirred their hearts to hatred, and they allowed the spirit of envy and jealousy to drive them to thoughts of murder.

But now a new thought came to one of their number. A company of traveling merchants came in sight, and they agreed to sell their brother and let him be carried away into Egypt to be sold as a slave. This was done, and the "dreamer" was taken away from their sight, as they supposed, for all time.

And now, see how God cares for his children who are true to him, as Joseph was. Sold as a slave to Potiphar, a high officer of King Pharaoh's, he soon became a trusted servant, and his heathen master saw and believed that "the Lord was with him." He even found that he himself was blessed and prospered for Joseph's sake, and that this noble, handsome young man was of great value to him.

But trouble came through Potiphar's vain and foolish wife, and Joseph was thrown into prison, though he had done no wrong. Again we read, "But the Lord was with Joseph." Yes, even in prison and disgrace, the Lord stood by him, giving him wisdom and love, and sending him dreams, which in the end brought him out of prison, and placed him in still higher position than before!

The King of Egypt, the great Pharaoh, had a wonderful dream, which no wise man could interpret. He sent for Joseph, and the Lord showed Joseph the true meaning. When the King learned that a great famine was coming, he placed Joseph in charge, and during all the famine years, and the years of plenty that went before, it was Joseph's wisdom that planned, and carried out the plans which saved Egypt from great trouble and loss.

One day there came a company of men from Canaan, where the famine was sore, asking to buy bread from Joseph. He knew them at once for his brothers, but they knew him not. His loving heart went out to them, and when he at last made himself known to them, he wept aloud for joy and sorrow. The time had come, indeed, when the dreams of the dreamer had come true, and Joseph, the hated and despised brother, became, not only one to whom the brothers bowed down in love and reverence, but the one to whom they actually owed their lives.

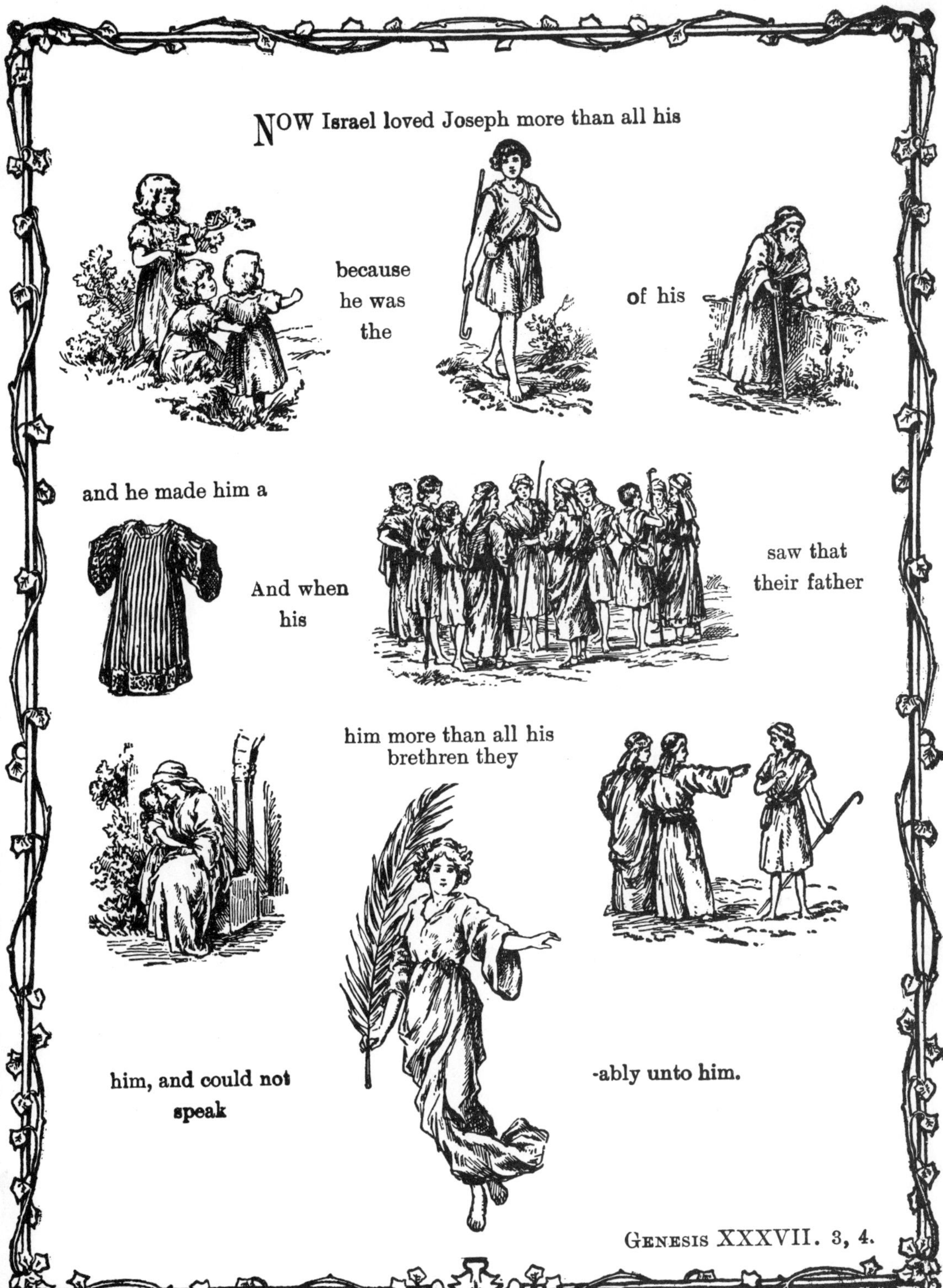
NOW Israel loved Joseph more than all his
because he was the
of his
and he made him a
And when his
saw that their father
him more than all his brethren they
him, and could not speak
-ably unto him.
GENESIS XXXVII. 3, 4.

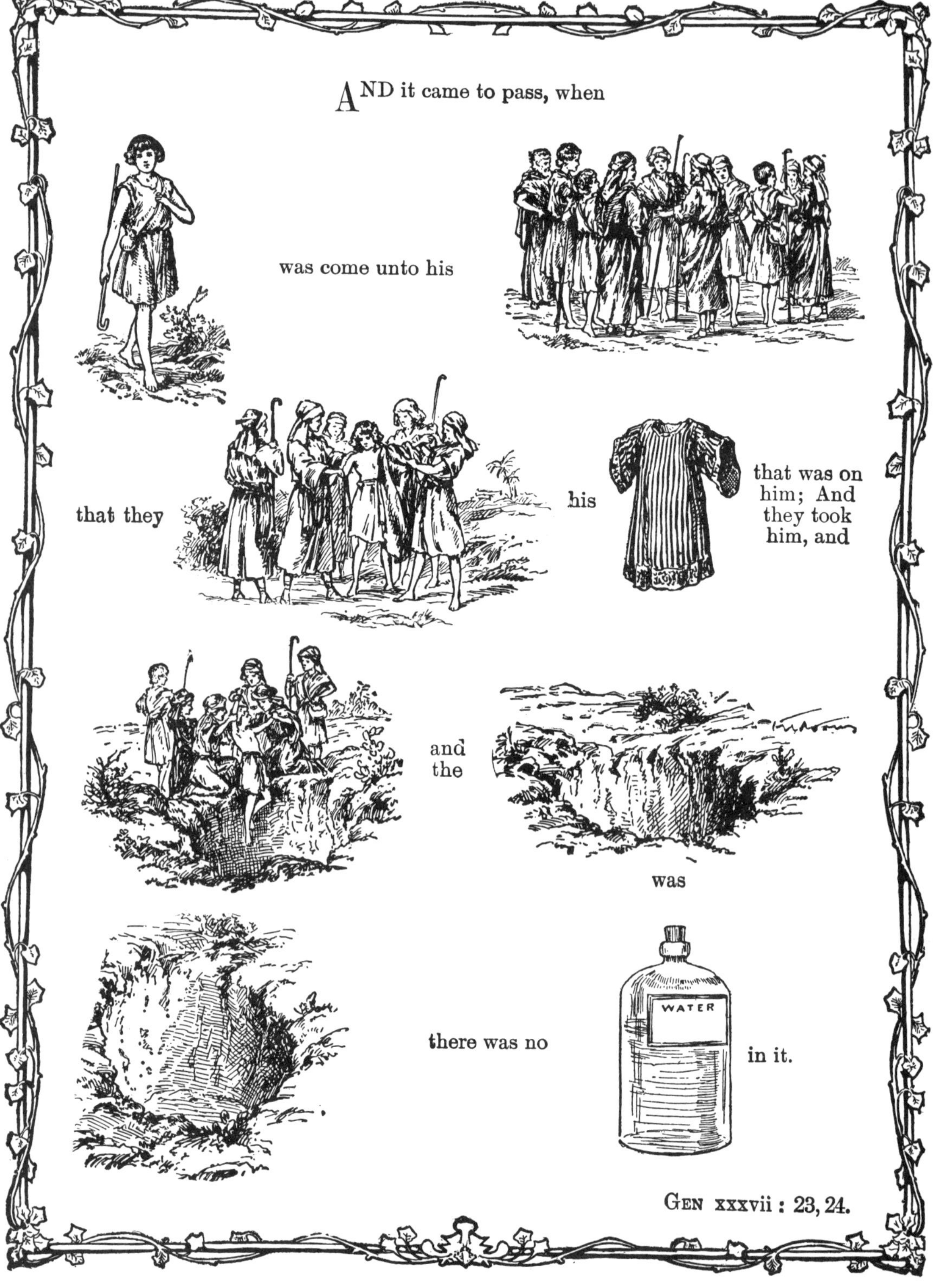
AND it came to pass, when
was come unto his
that they
his
that was on
him; And
they took
him, and
and
the
was
there was no
WATER
in it.
GEN xxxvii : 23, 24.

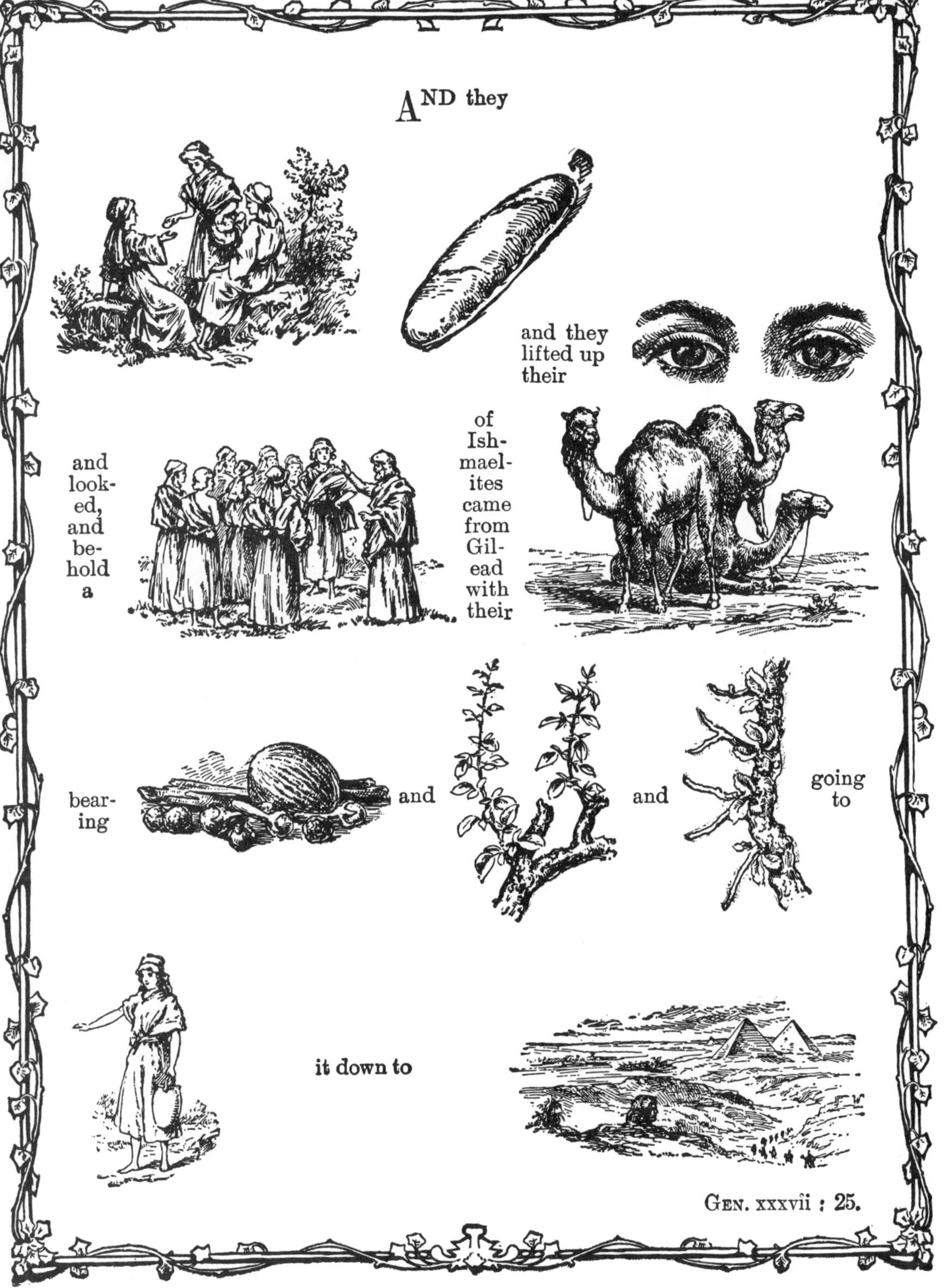
AND they
and they
lifted up
their
and
look-
ed,
and
be-
hold
a
of
Ish-
mael-
ites
came
from
Gil-
ead
with
their
bear-
ing
and
and
going
to
it down to
GEN. xxxvii : 25.

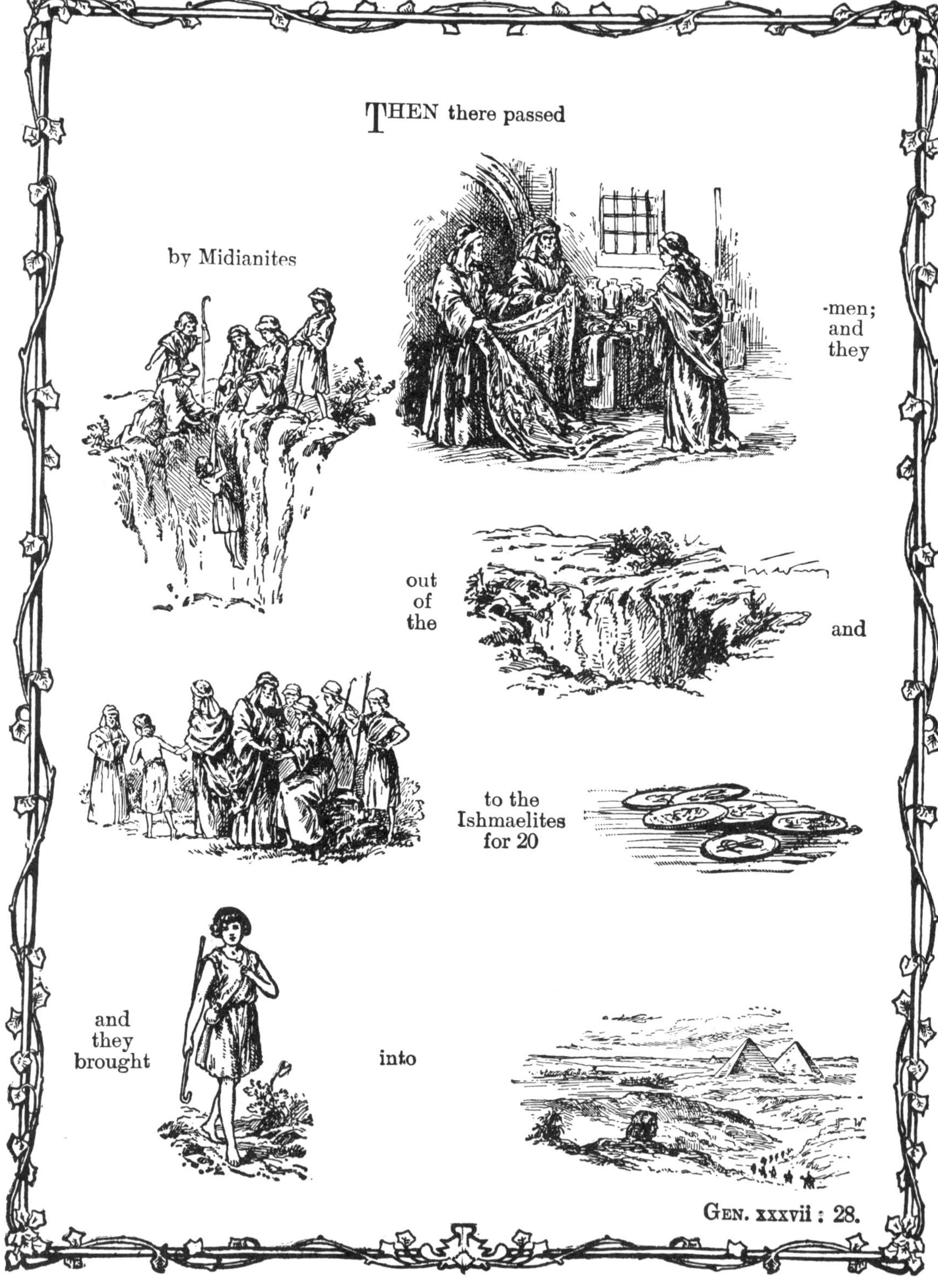
THEN there passed
by Midianites
-men; and they
out of the
and
to the Ishmaelites for 20
and they brought
into
GEN. xxxvii : 28.

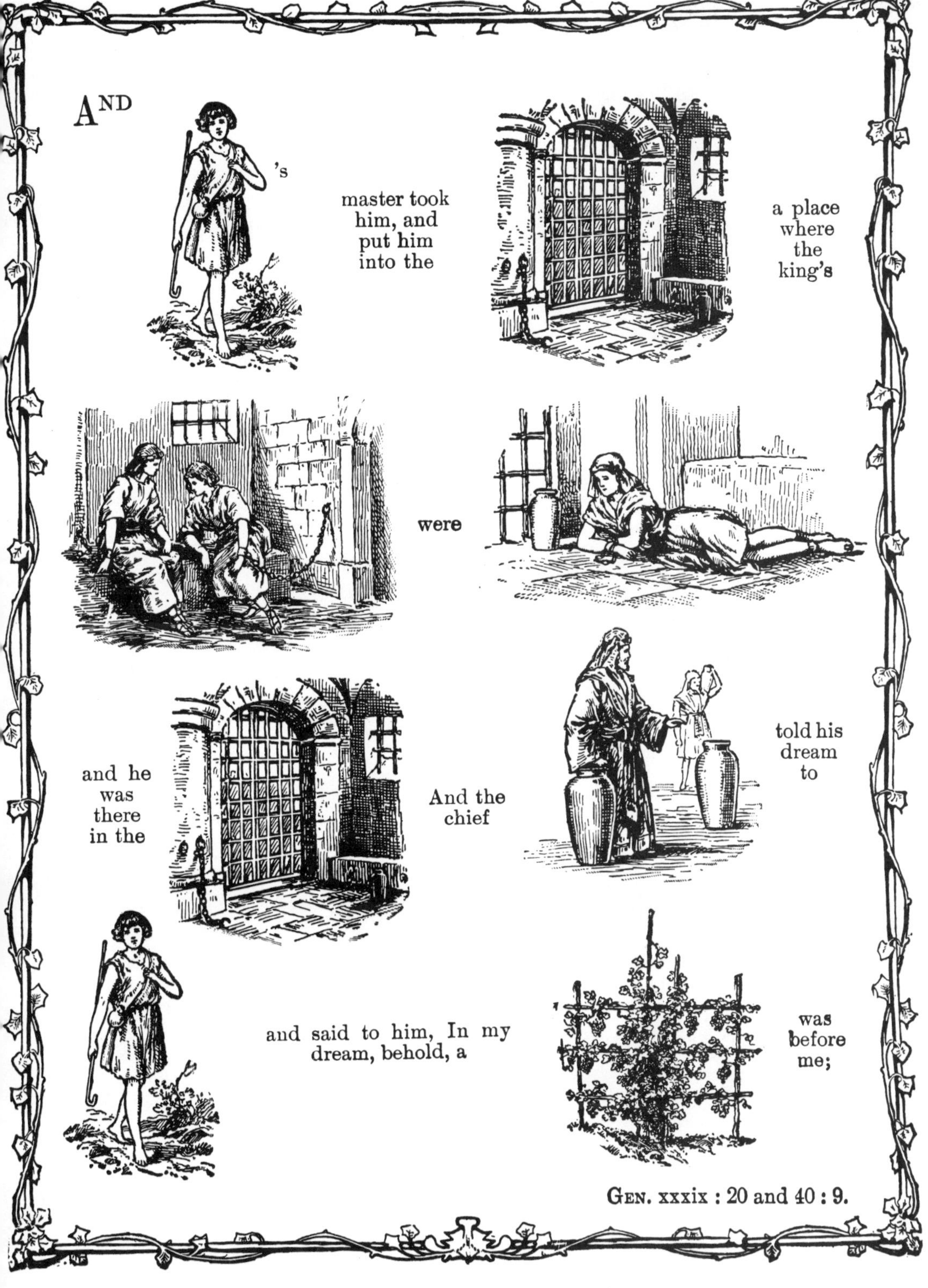

AND 's master took him, and put him into the a place where the king's were and he was there in the And the chief told his dream to and said to him, In my dream, behold, a was before me;

GEN. xxxix : 20 and 40 : 9.

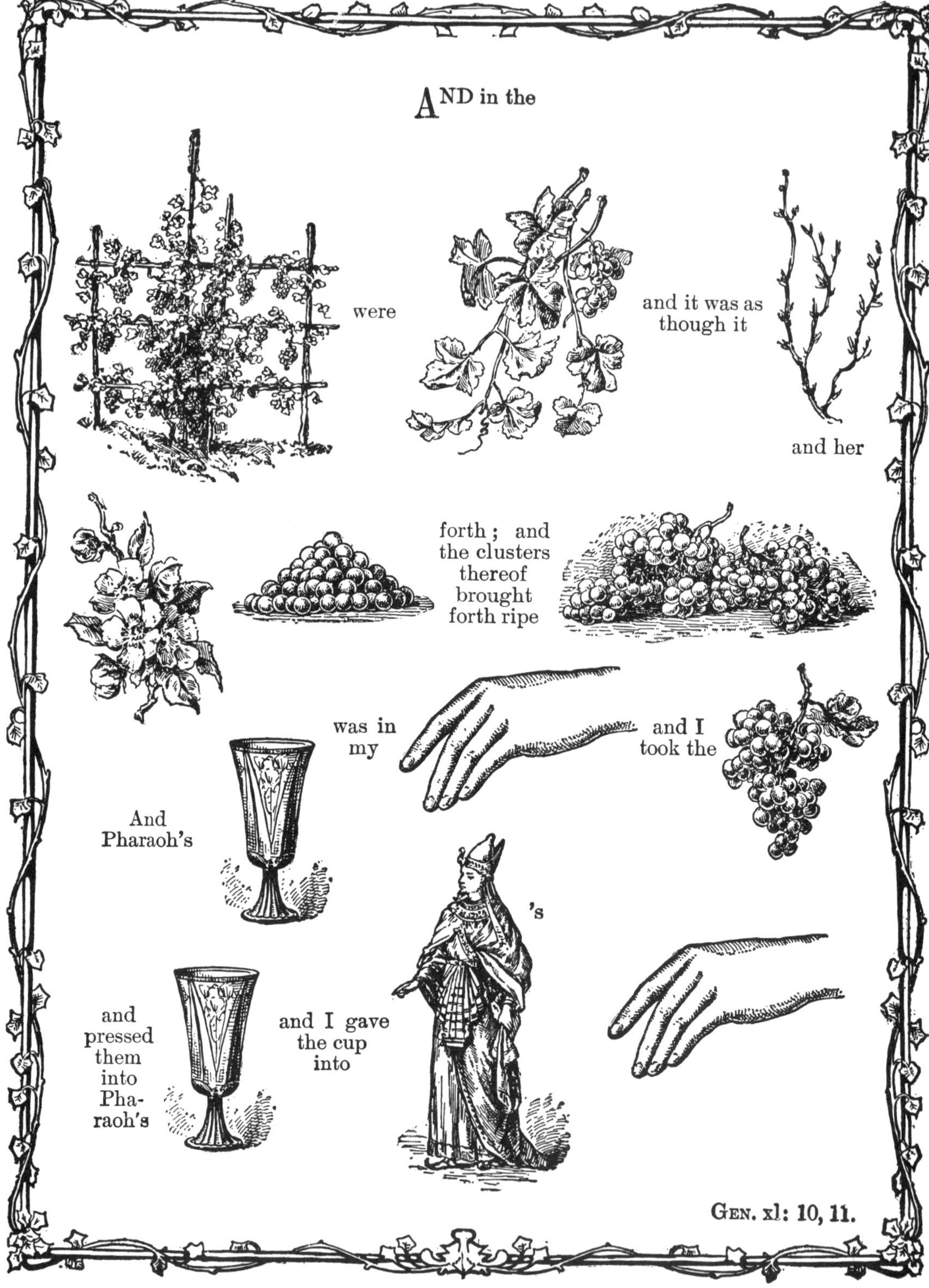
AND in the
were
and it was as
though it
and her
forth ; and
the clusters
thereof
brought
forth ripe
And
Pharaoh's
was in
my
and I
took the
's
and
pressed
them
into
Pha-
raoh's
and I gave
the cup
into
GEN. xl: 10, 11.

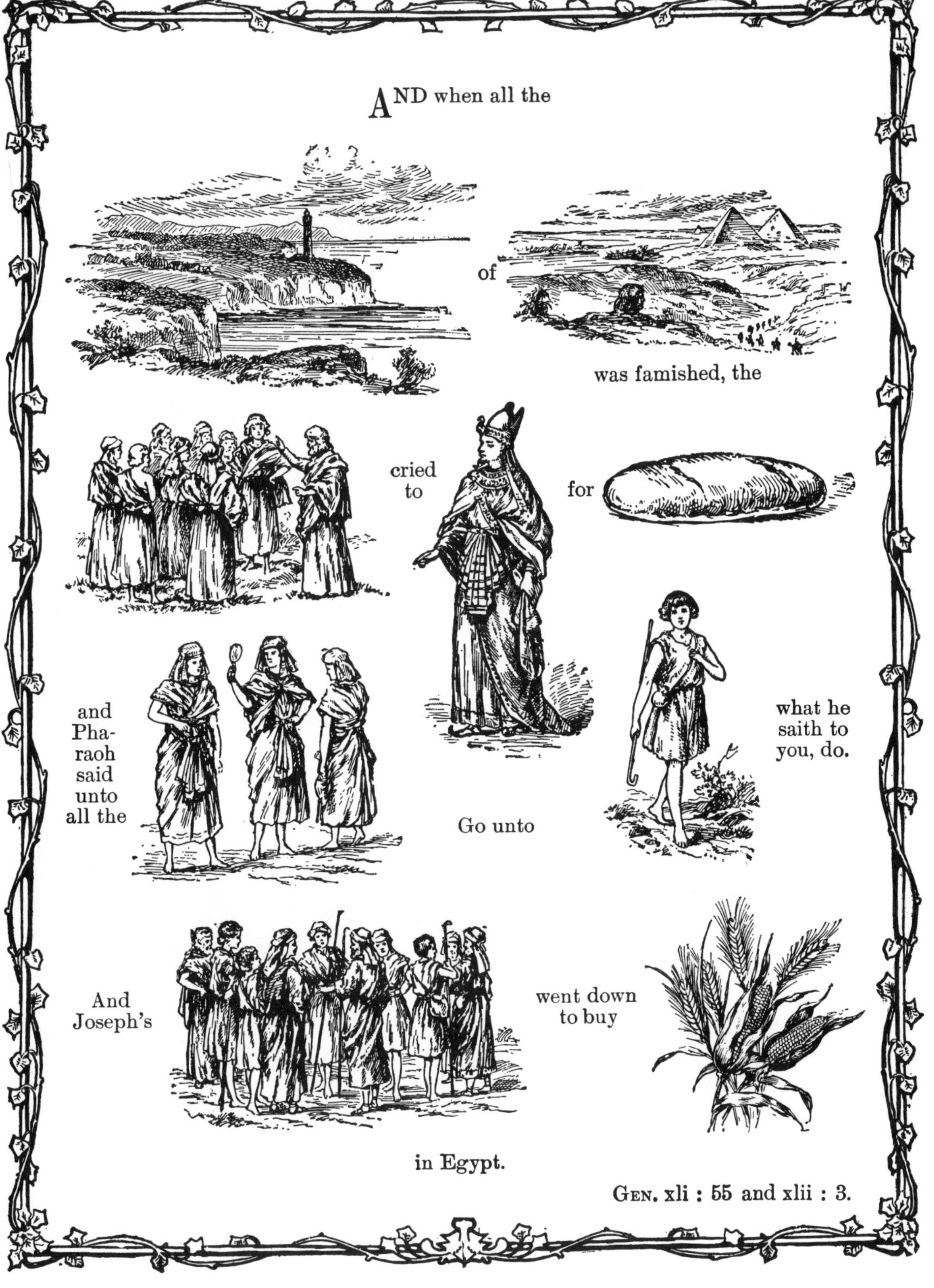

GEN. xli : 55 and xlii : 3.

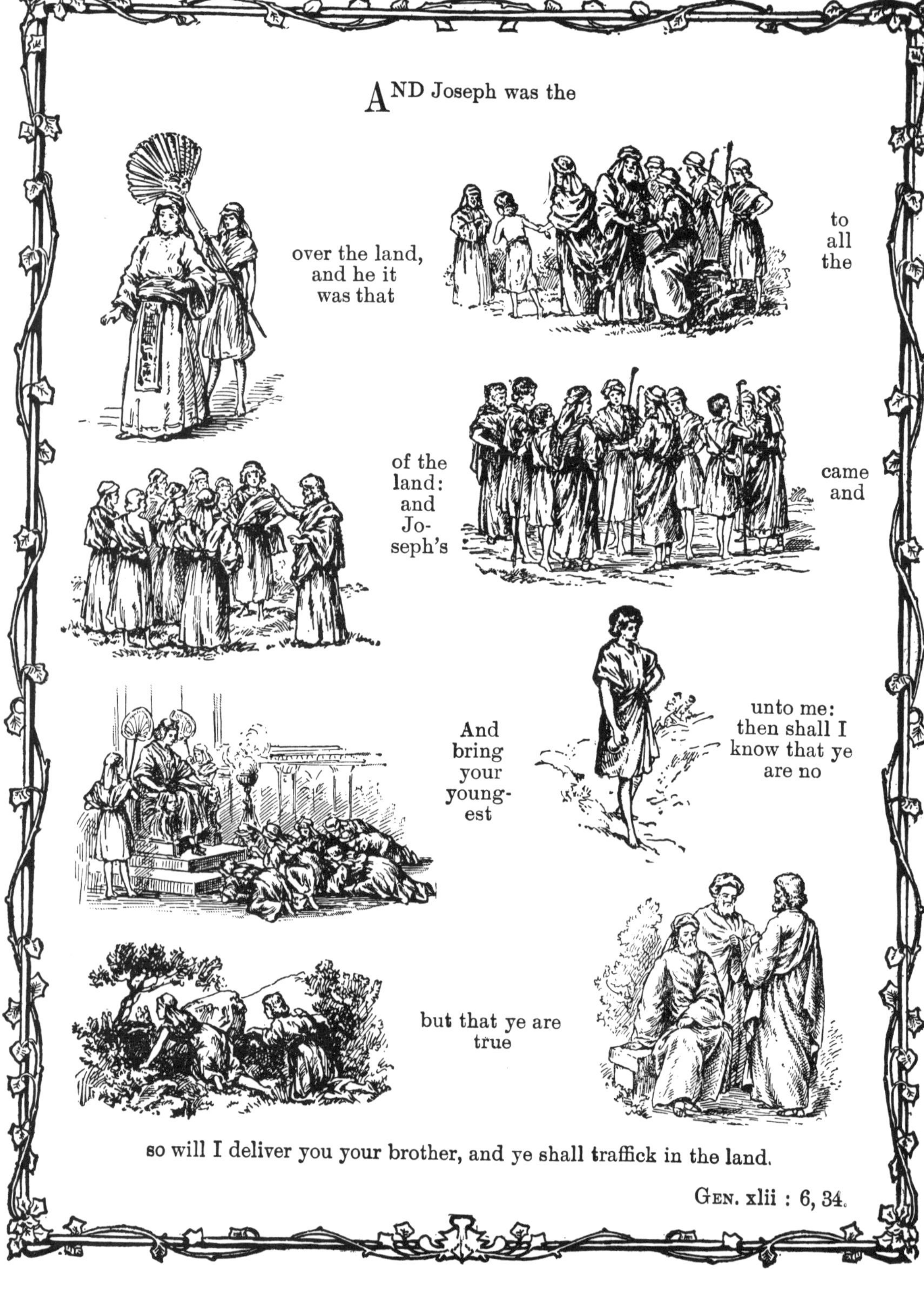

AND Joseph was the

over the land, and he it was that

to all the

of the land: and Jo-seph's

came and

And bring your young-est

unto me: then shall I know that ye are no

but that ye are true

so will I deliver you your brother, and ye shall traffick in the land.

GEN. xlii : 6, 34.

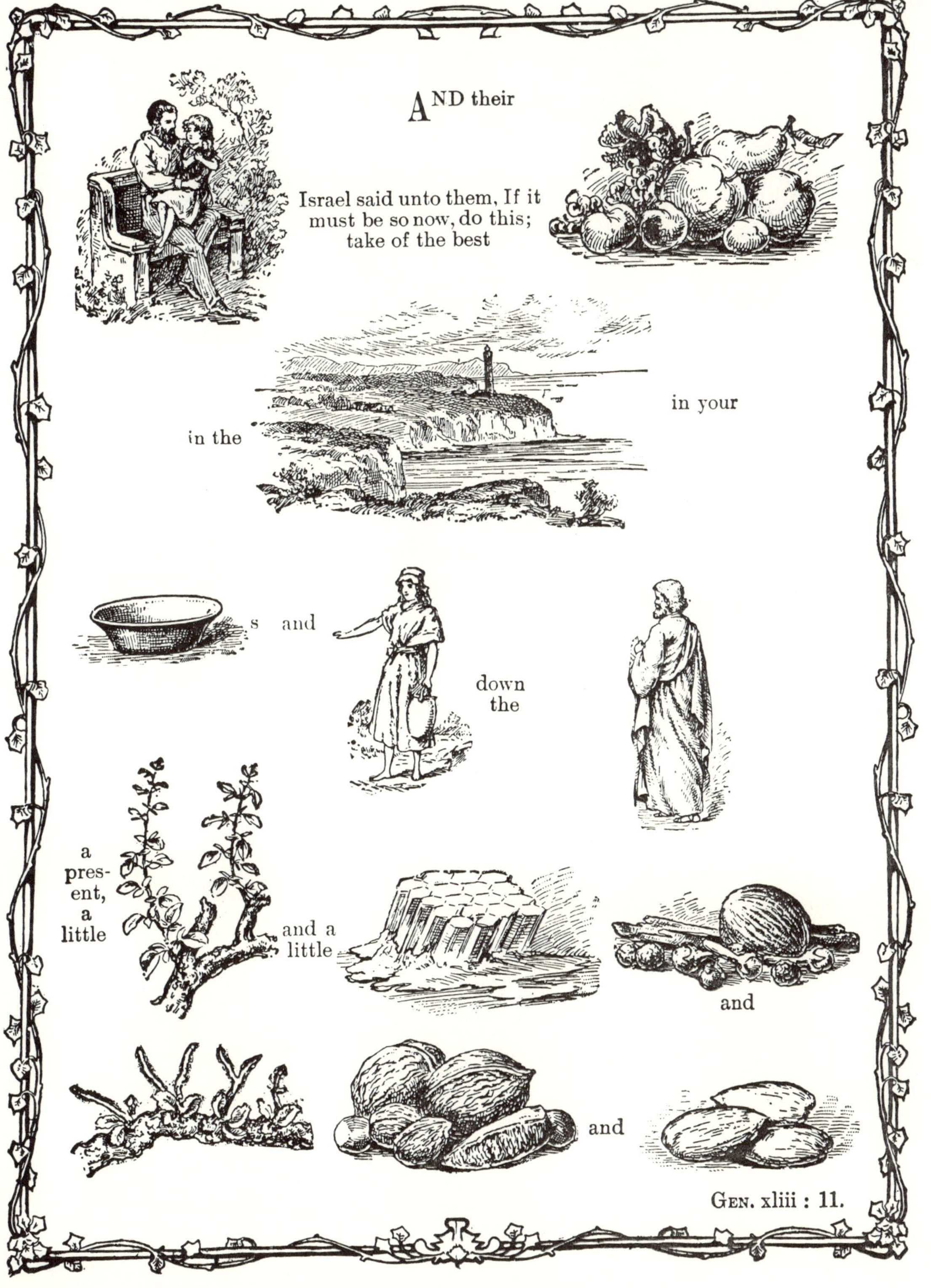

AND their

Israel said unto them, If it must be so now, do this; take of the best

in the

in your

s and

down the

a present, a little

and a little

and

and

Gen. xliii : 11.

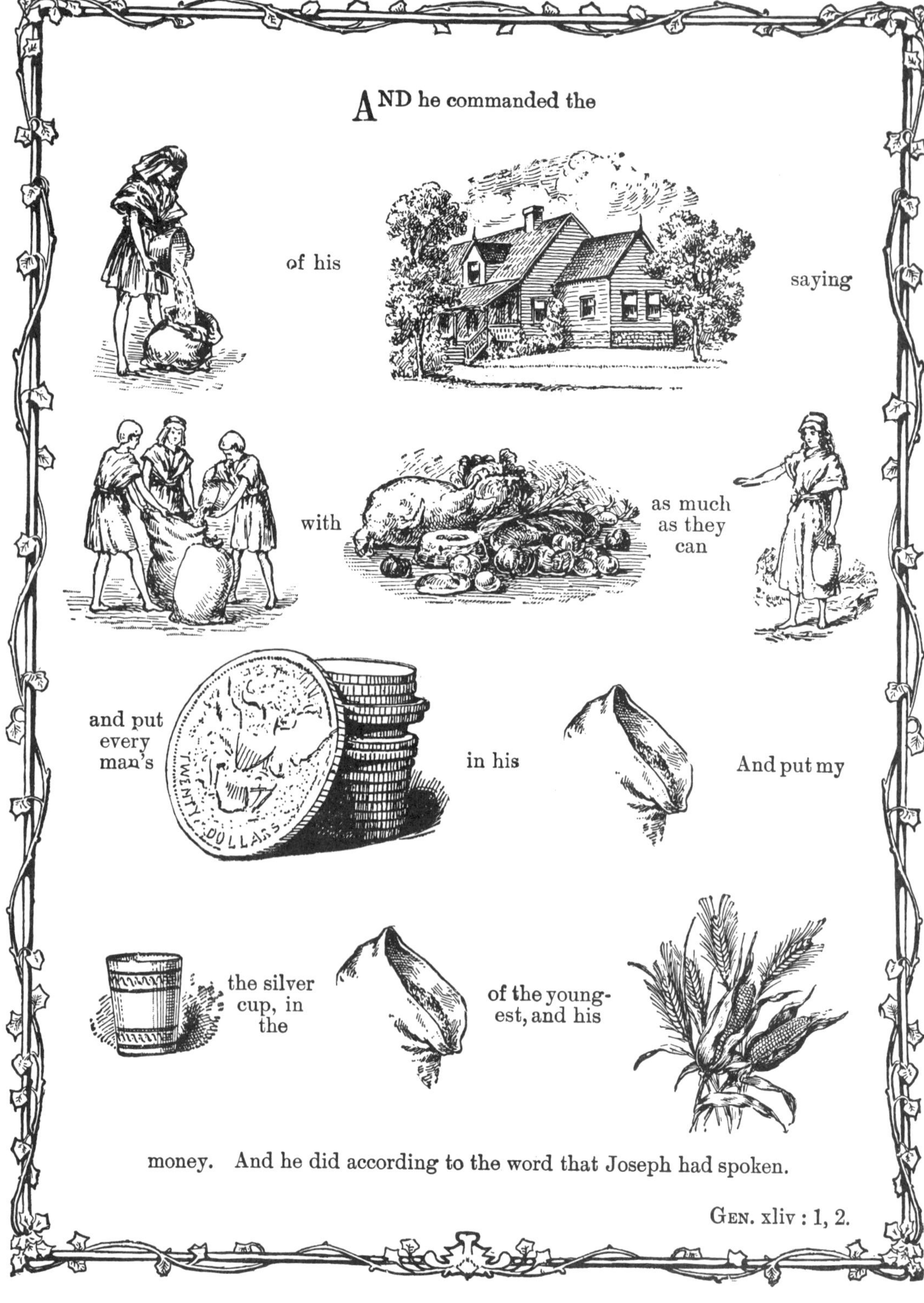
AND he commanded the
of his
saying
with
as much as they can
and put every man's
in his
And put my
the silver cup, in the
of the young-est, and his
money. And he did according to the word that Joseph had spoken.
GEN. xliv : 1, 2.

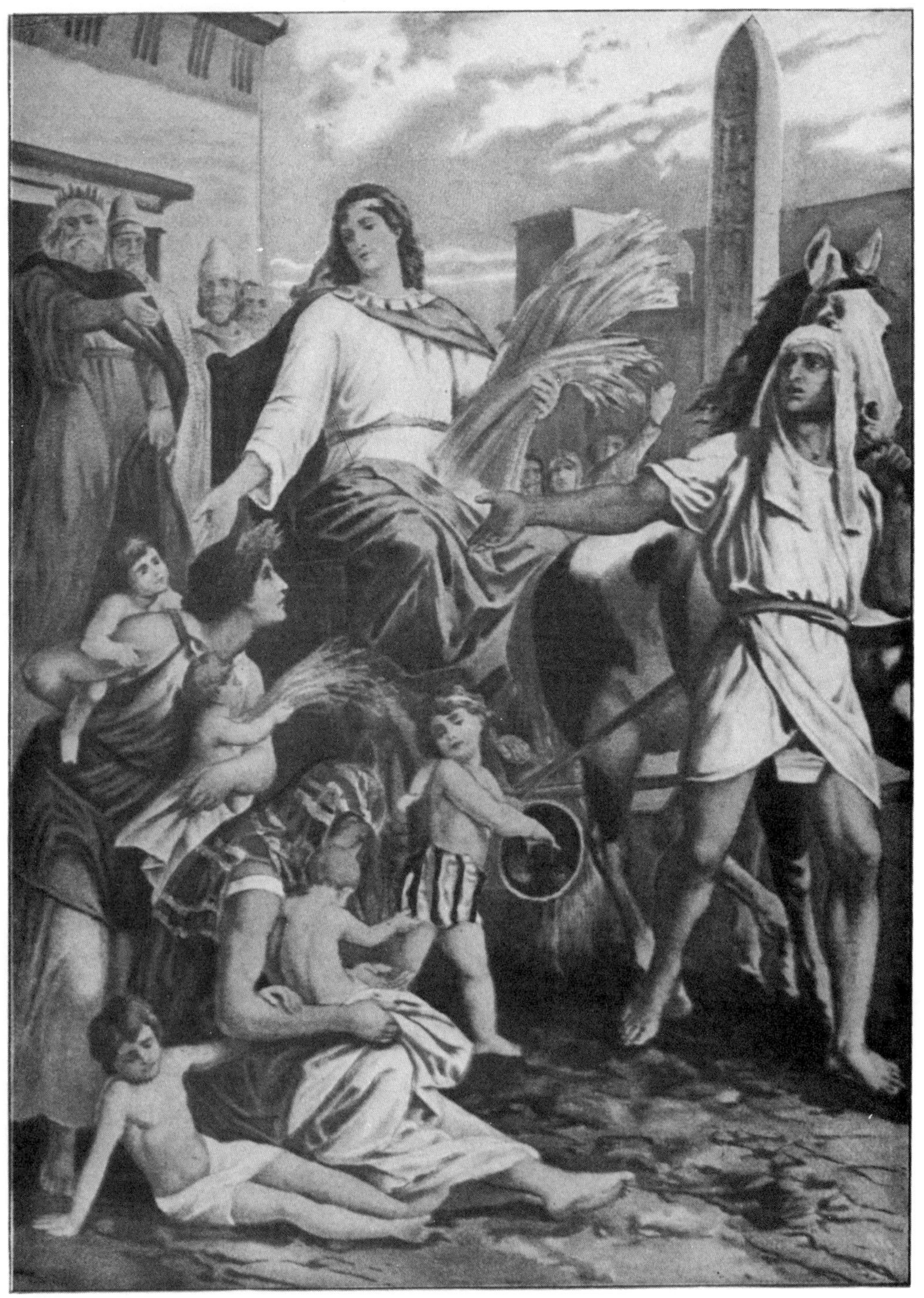

JOSEPH, THE RULER OF THE LAND.

JOSEPH, THE RULER OF THE LAND

On page 45, and again on page 52, you will find the story of Joseph. On the reverse of this page there is a picture of him when he was made prefect of all Egypt.

You remember how Joseph told the King of Egypt that there would be seven years of great plenty and then seven years of great scarcity of food. He told the king to pick out a wise man and send him all through the country, with authority to make the people save up one-fifth of their crops during the seven years of plenty. This man was to be the king's overseer or prefect. He was to build storehouses in which to keep the food supplies that the people brought to him. Later, during the years of famine, he was to sell these same supplies to those who needed them.

The Pharaoh said to Joseph: ''What man could I get who would do this better than you? I now place you over my entire kingdom: my people must do all that you tell them. I will keep only the throne above you.'' Then the king took a ring off his own finger and set it on Joseph's. He ordered that he be clad in the king's richest garments and that he be proclaimed the ruler of the land. Joseph was then about thirty years old. By the king's order he married a noble young woman by the name of Aseneth, whose father held one of the highest positions in the kingdom.

Joseph made the rounds of the whole land of Egypt and caused to be stored up large quantities of corn in every city. When the seven years of unwonted plenty were over, Joseph caused the stores to be opened, and the Egyptians were allowed to purchase what supplies they needed. Even the people from the neighboring countries came to buy corn in Egypt. When the buyers had no more money, Joseph gave them corn in exchange for their cattle; and when they had no more cattle, he took their lands for the corn that he gave them. By the end of the seven years' famine, he had bought up all the land of Egypt for the Pharaoh. Afterward he rented them back to their former owners for one-fifth of their annual produce. It was during this period that Jacob and his children came down into Egypt on the invitation of Joseph. To them Joseph gave a fertile district called Gessen, where they lived separated from the Egyptians and where Joseph supplied them with food free of charge.

At this stage of his career, Joseph is a type of our Lord Jesus Christ ruling and sustaining His Church.

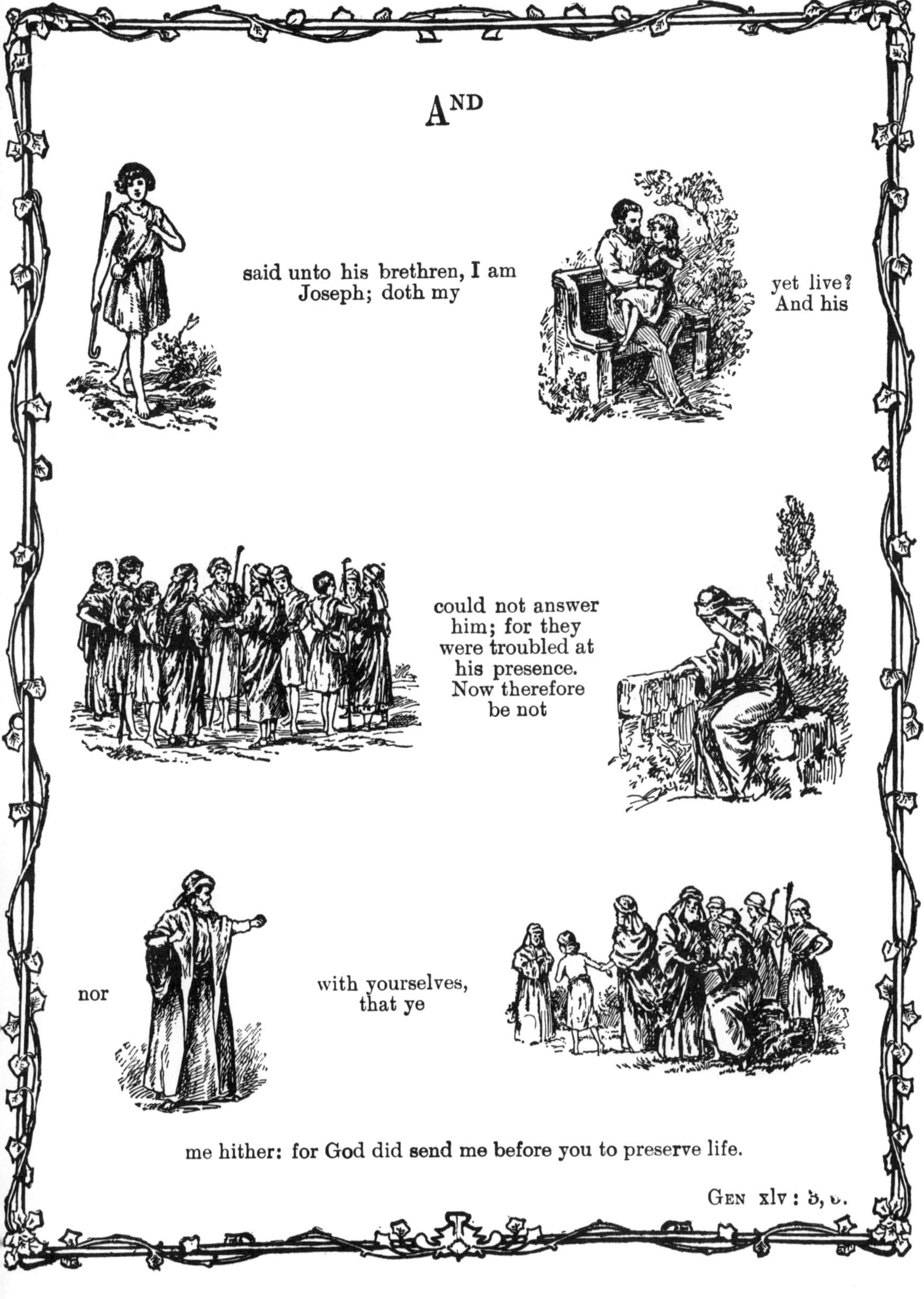

AND

said unto his brethren, I am Joseph; doth my

yet live? And his

could not answer him; for they were troubled at his presence. Now therefore be not

nor

with yourselves, that ye

me hither: for God did send me before you to preserve life.

GEN xlv: 3, 5.

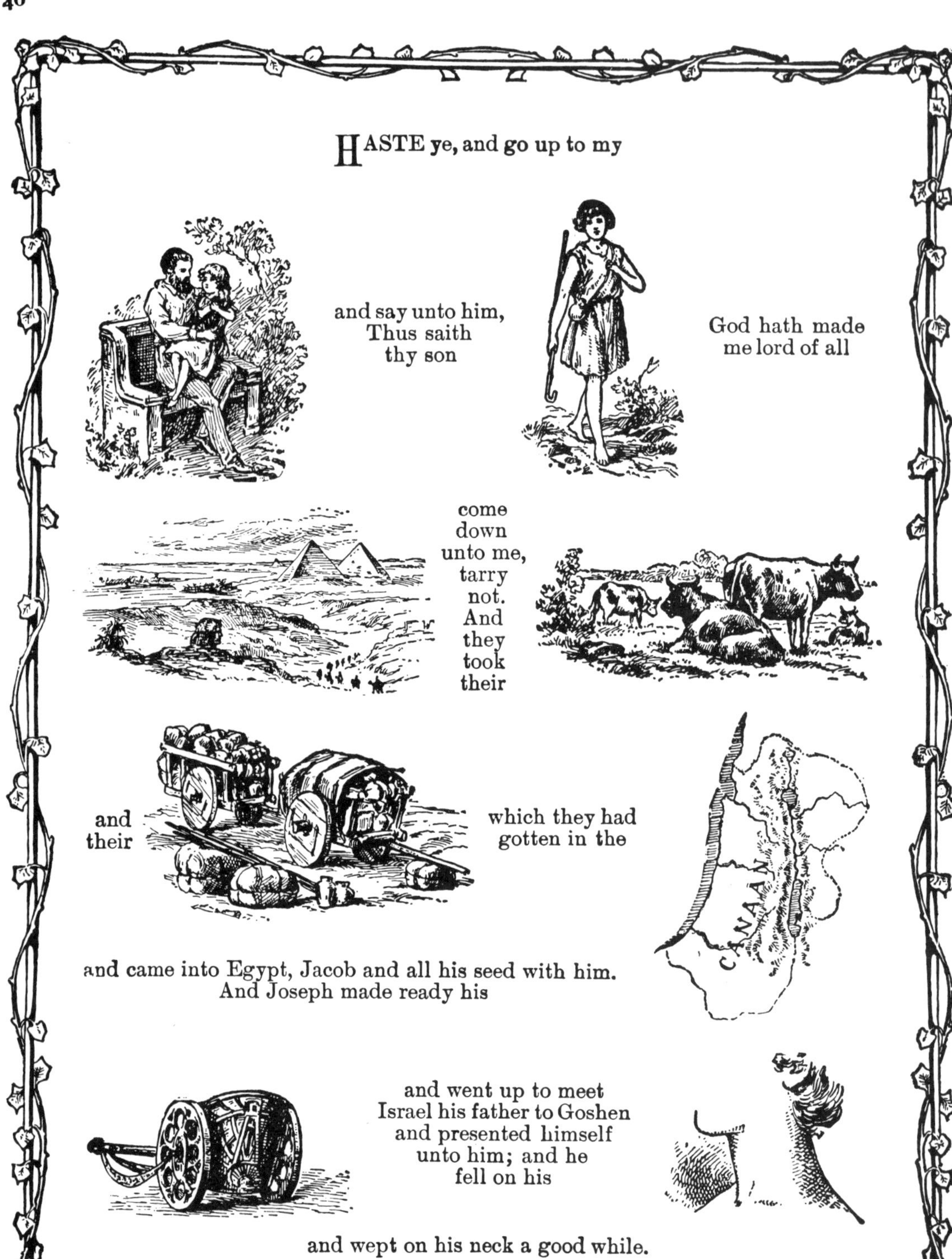

HASTE ye, and go up to my

and say unto him, Thus saith thy son

God hath made me lord of all

come down unto me, tarry not. And they took their

and their

which they had gotten in the

and came into Egypt, Jacob and all his seed with him. And Joseph made ready his

and went up to meet Israel his father to Goshen and presented himself unto him; and he fell on his

and wept on his neck a good while.

GEN. xlv : 9 and xlvi: 6, 29.

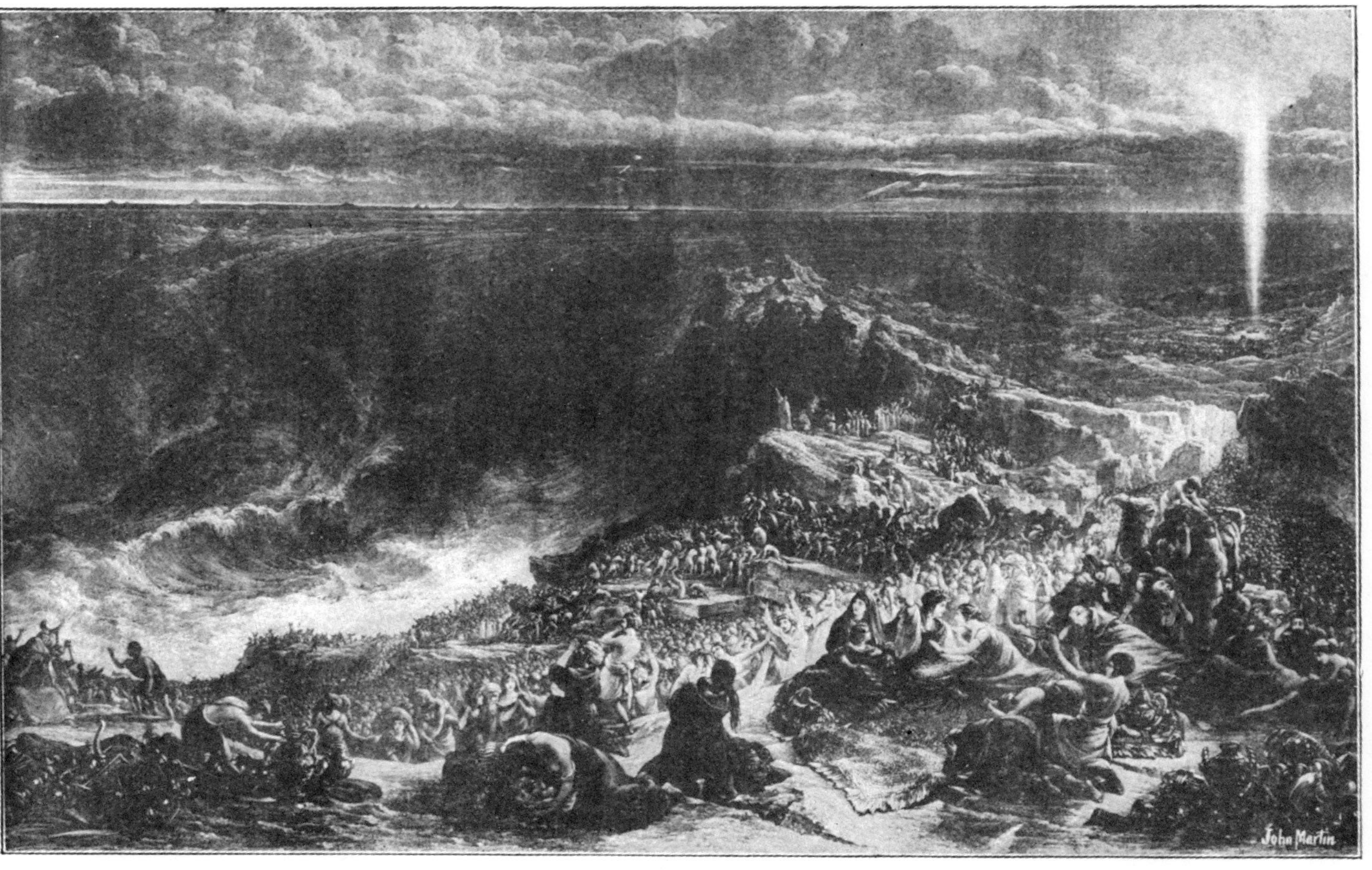

THE DESTRUCTION OF PHAROAH'S HOST.

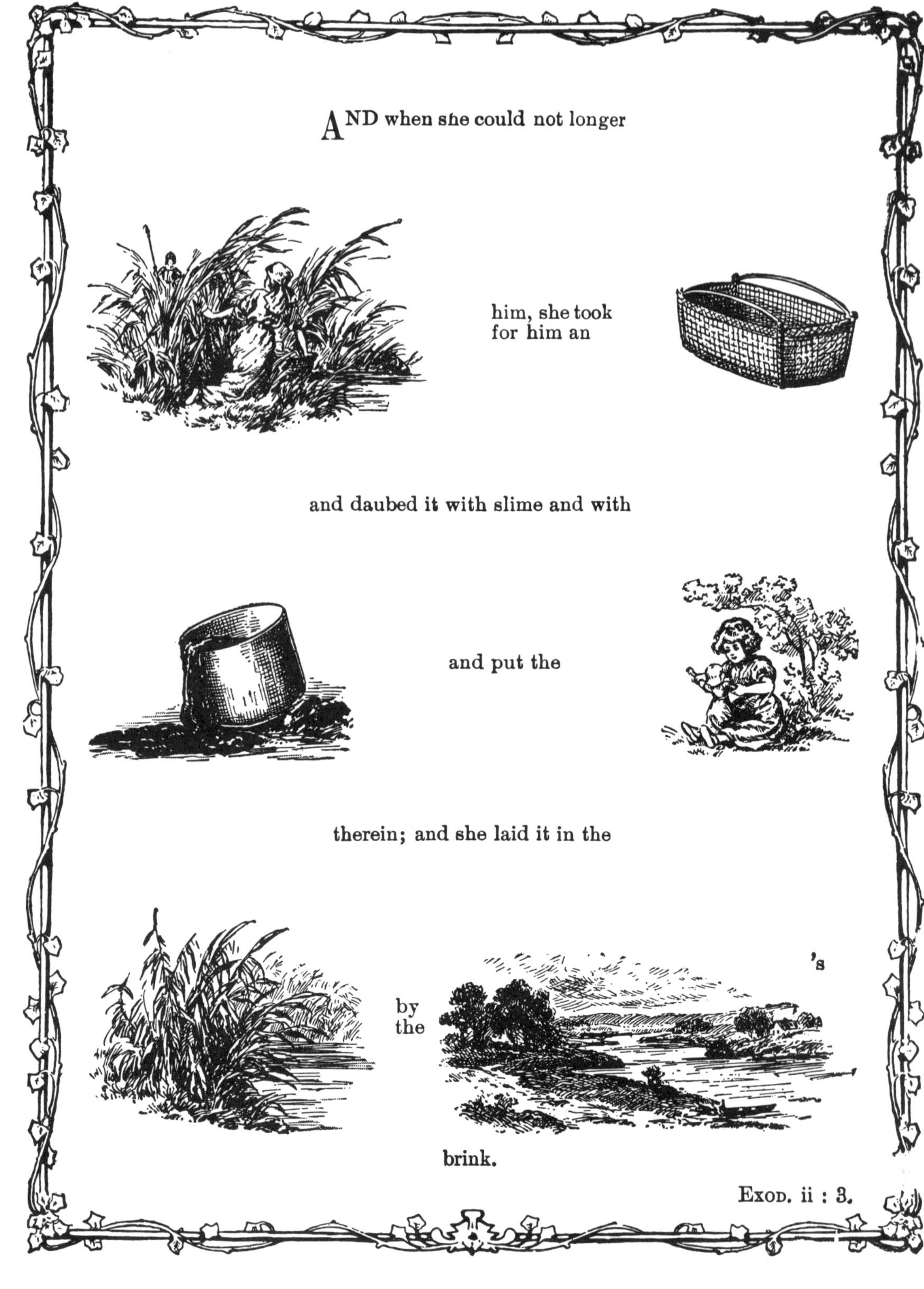

AND when she could not longer

him, she took
for him an

and daubed it with slime and with

and put the

therein; and she laid it in the

by
the

's

brink.

Exod. ii : 3.

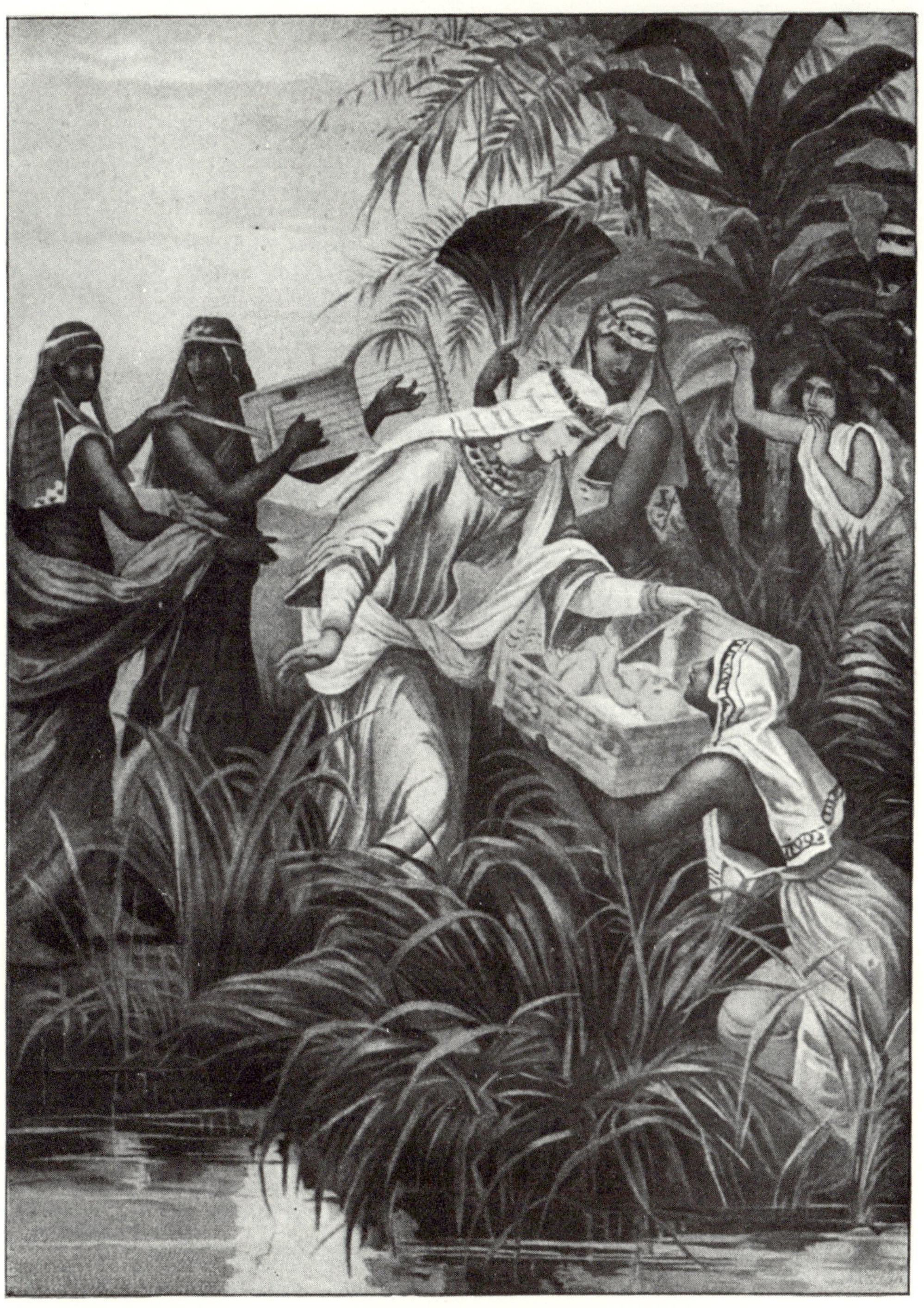

PHARAOH'S DAUGHTER FINDS MOSES.

PHARAOH'S DAUGHTER FINDS MOSES

On page 61 the story of this picture is told according to the Bible recital. But Jewish tradition has given us some curious details about the life of Moses.

One day, says Josephus, a famous soothsayer told the Pharaoh that, at the very moment they were talking, there was about to be born to a Hebrew couple a child who, should he reach to manhood, would humble the Egyptians and bring great glory upon his own people. So the king, to prevent anything of the kind happening, ordered that from that moment all the male children of the Israelites be thrown into the Nile soon after their birth. There was at that time a man called Amram, and his wife's name was Jocabed. God appeared to him in a dream and told him that a baby boy was about to come to them, and that the boy was to be the saviour and deliverer of his people.

In due course the child was born, and its parents kept it for three months hidden away from everybody. Then it was impossible to conceal it any longer, so they sent the child adrift on the waters of the Nile. That very day he was picked up by Termutis, the Pharaoh's daughter, while she and her maids were bathing in the river near the palace. The child was very beautiful, so she took him and adopted him as her own. She called him Moses because she had saved him from the waters, and later on she presented him to the king, her father.

As little Moses grew older he waxed more and more attractive, and both the princess and the king became very fond of him. They even talked of making him heir to the throne, as the Pharaoh had no sons. One day, when the boy was about three years old, the king playfully set his crown upon the lad's head; but little Moses snatched it off and threw it to the ground. Balaam, the magician, was present and counselled the king to put the boy to death. The Pharaoh ordered the execution. But as Moses was about to be slain, the angel Gabriel presented himself before Pharaoh and said: "O king, harm not the boy until we first see if he hath attained to reason and discretion." The king consented. Then Gabriel caused to be offered to the boy two platters, on the one were brilliant gems, on the other burning coals. Moses was told to take whichever he wanted. The boy was reaching his hand for the gems when the angel guided it toward the coals. The coals did not burn his fingers; but when he licked one with his tongue, he burned the tip off it. And that's why Moses stuttered ever after.

The daughter of Pharaoh then took Moses and had him educated in all the branches of knowledge known to the Egyptians, until he was considered the most learned of men.

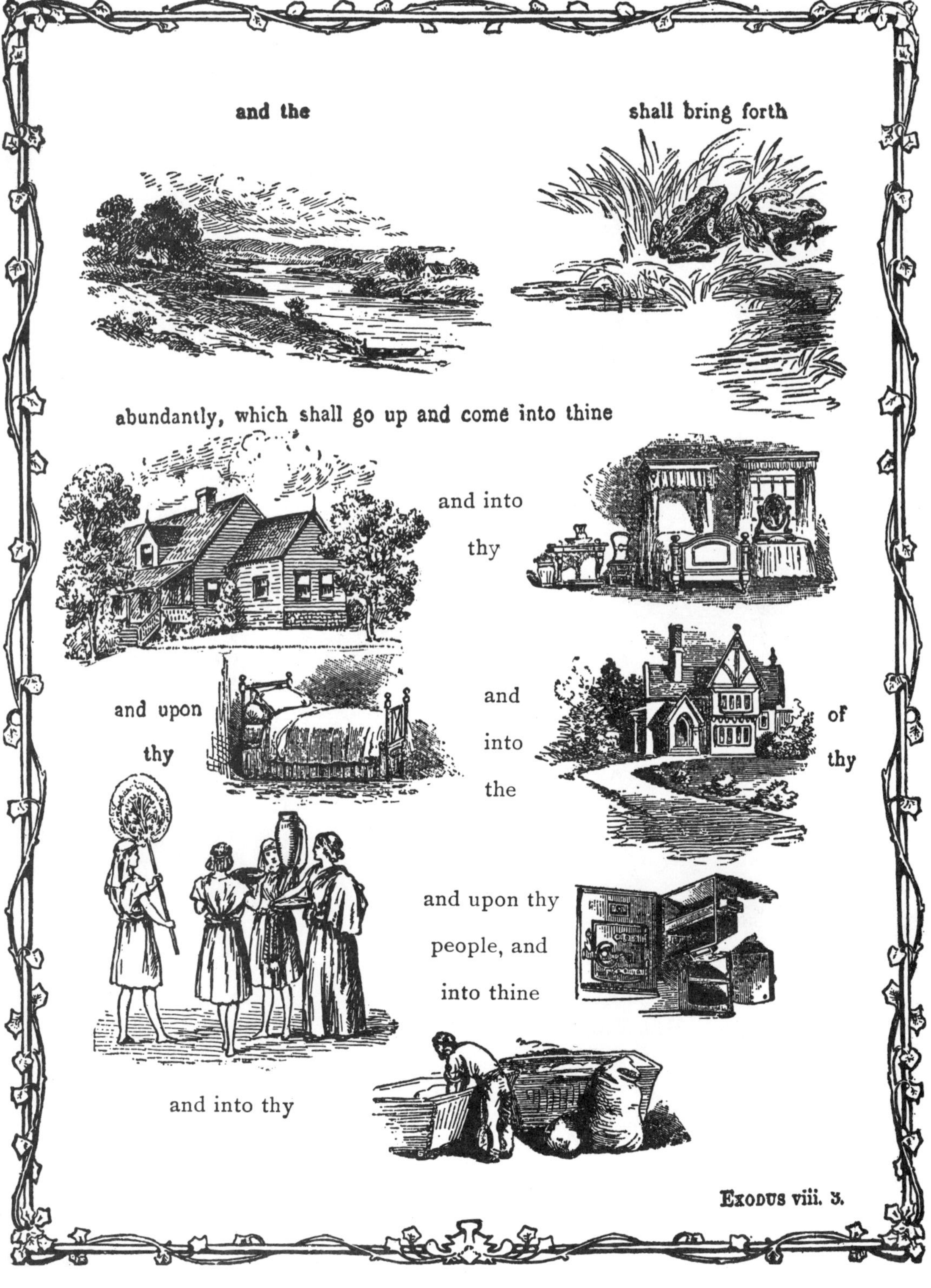
and the
shall bring forth
abundantly, which shall go up and come into thine
and into
thy
and upon
thy
and
into
the
of
thy
and upon thy
people, and
into thine
and into thy
Exodus viii. 3.

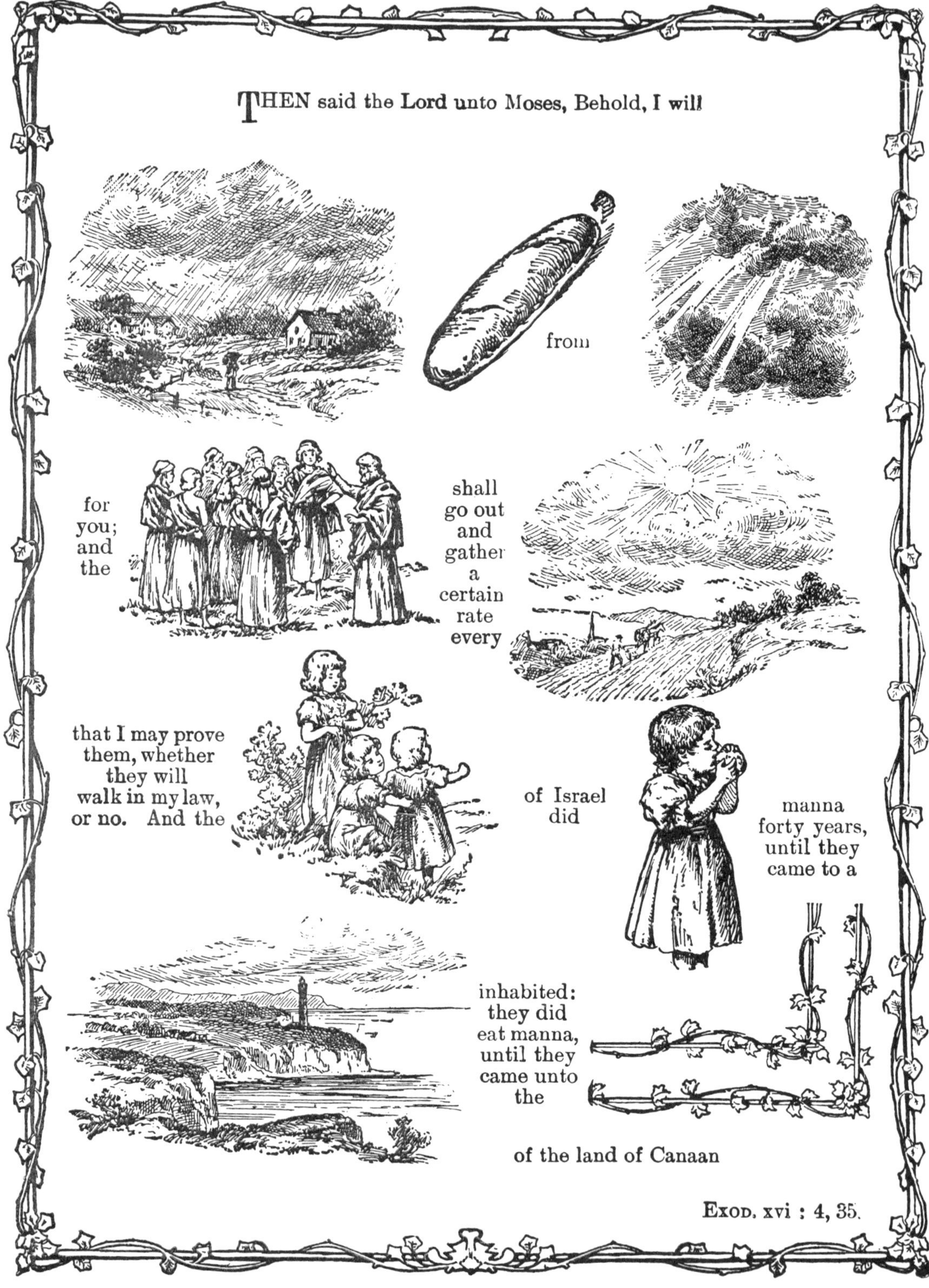
THEN said the Lord unto Moses, Behold, I will
from
for
you;
and
the
shall
go out
and
gather
a
certain
rate
every
that I may prove
them, whether
they will
walk in my law,
or no. And the
of Israel
did
manna
forty years,
until they
came to a
inhabited:
they did
eat manna,
until they
came unto
the
of the land of Canaan
Exod. xvi : 4, 35.

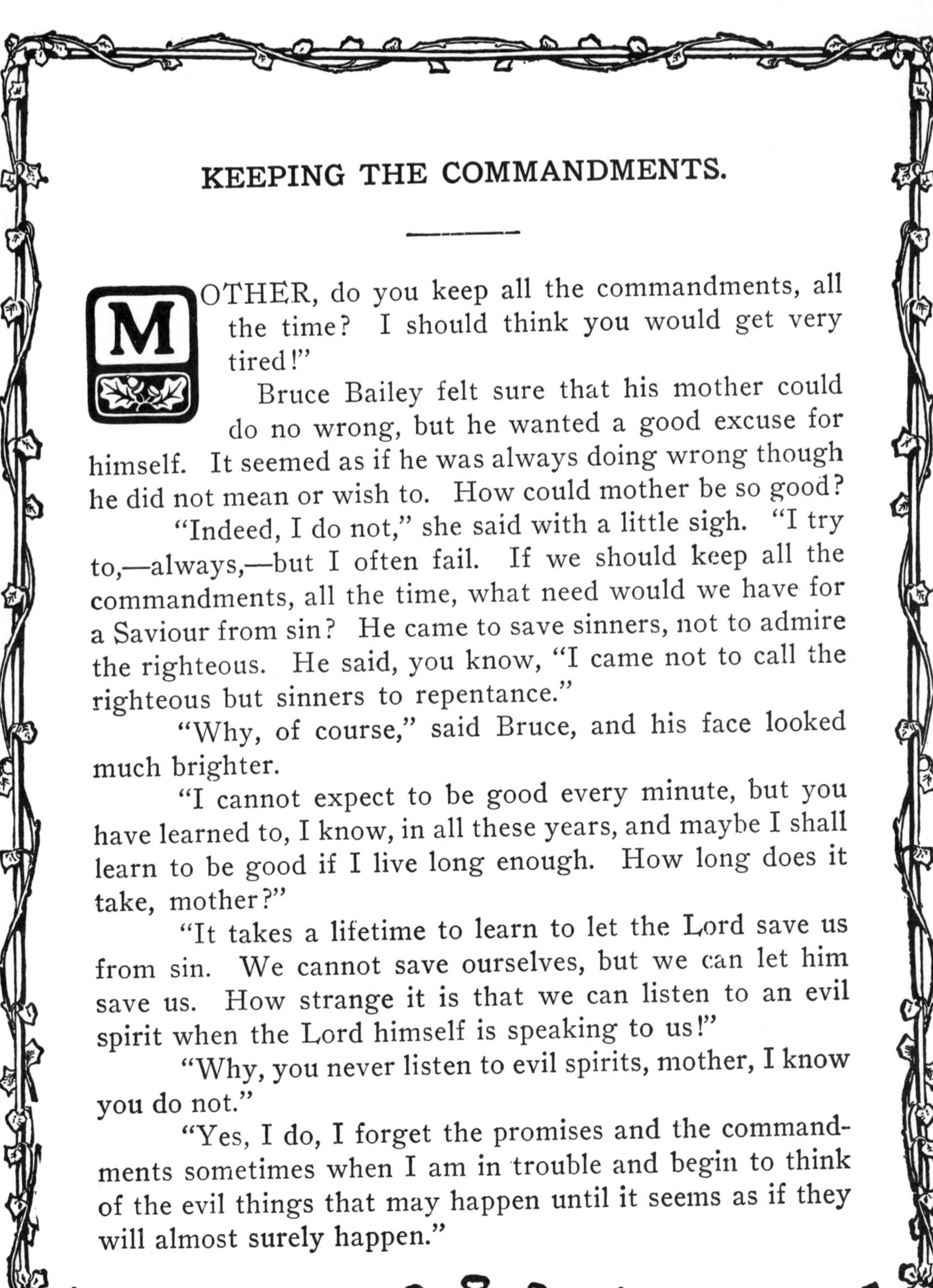

KEEPING THE COMMANDMENTS.

"MOTHER, do you keep all the commandments, all the time? I should think you would get very tired!"

Bruce Bailey felt sure that his mother could do no wrong, but he wanted a good excuse for himself. It seemed as if he was always doing wrong though he did not mean or wish to. How could mother be so good?

"Indeed, I do not," she said with a little sigh. "I try to,—always,—but I often fail. If we should keep all the commandments, all the time, what need would we have for a Saviour from sin? He came to save sinners, not to admire the righteous. He said, you know, "I came not to call the righteous but sinners to repentance."

"Why, of course," said Bruce, and his face looked much brighter.

"I cannot expect to be good every minute, but you have learned to, I know, in all these years, and maybe I shall learn to be good if I live long enough. How long does it take, mother?"

"It takes a lifetime to learn to let the Lord save us from sin. We cannot save ourselves, but we can let him save us. How strange it is that we can listen to an evil spirit when the Lord himself is speaking to us!"

"Why, you never listen to evil spirits, mother, I know you do not."

"Yes, I do, I forget the promises and the commandments sometimes when I am in trouble and begin to think of the evil things that may happen until it seems as if they will almost surely happen."

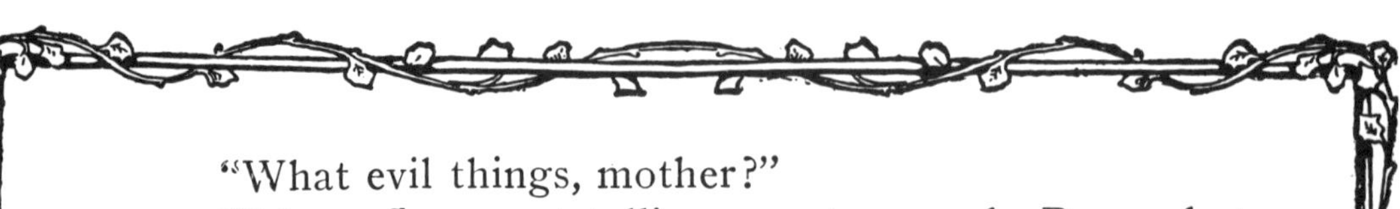

"What evil things, mother?"

"I hope I am not telling you too much, Bruce, but sometimes I fear you may grow up with that wilfulness that often troubles you and that will grow stronger and take you captive. Then what should we do? Just here I am always in much distress of mind until I remember my Father in Heaven who is your Father, too, and he gives me a little word that brings peace in like a flowing river. How good,—how good he is!"

"What does he say to you, mother?"

"Sometimes he has said, 'Fear not, Mary,' or 'Thy son liveth.' "

"Sometimes I have seen a drunken young man and have seemed to see you grow up to become like him. This would follow me all day; once it followed me three days and then suddenly a voice spoke to me in the night:

"Thou shall have joy and gladness; and many shall rejoice at his birth, for he shall be great in the sight of the Lord, and shall drink neither wine nor strong drink, and he shall be filled with the Holy Ghost."

"Then I thanked God with tears of gratitude and went to sleep in peace. You see, Bruce, that I do not keep all the commandments all the time, don't you?"

Bruce was full of tears himself, but he said: "You were only afraid mother, and afraid of me; you were not bad."

"Sometimes I feel fretful, Bruce, almost angry, but God forgives me."

"Well, mother," said Bruce, after a long silence, "you need never be sorry you told me these things. I am going to begin now to keep all the commandments as well as I can and to let God teach me just as you do. I just need to love him and trust him, I suppose."

"That is all, dear boy."

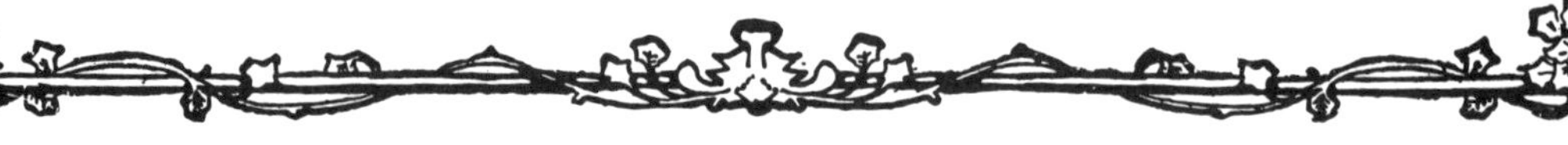

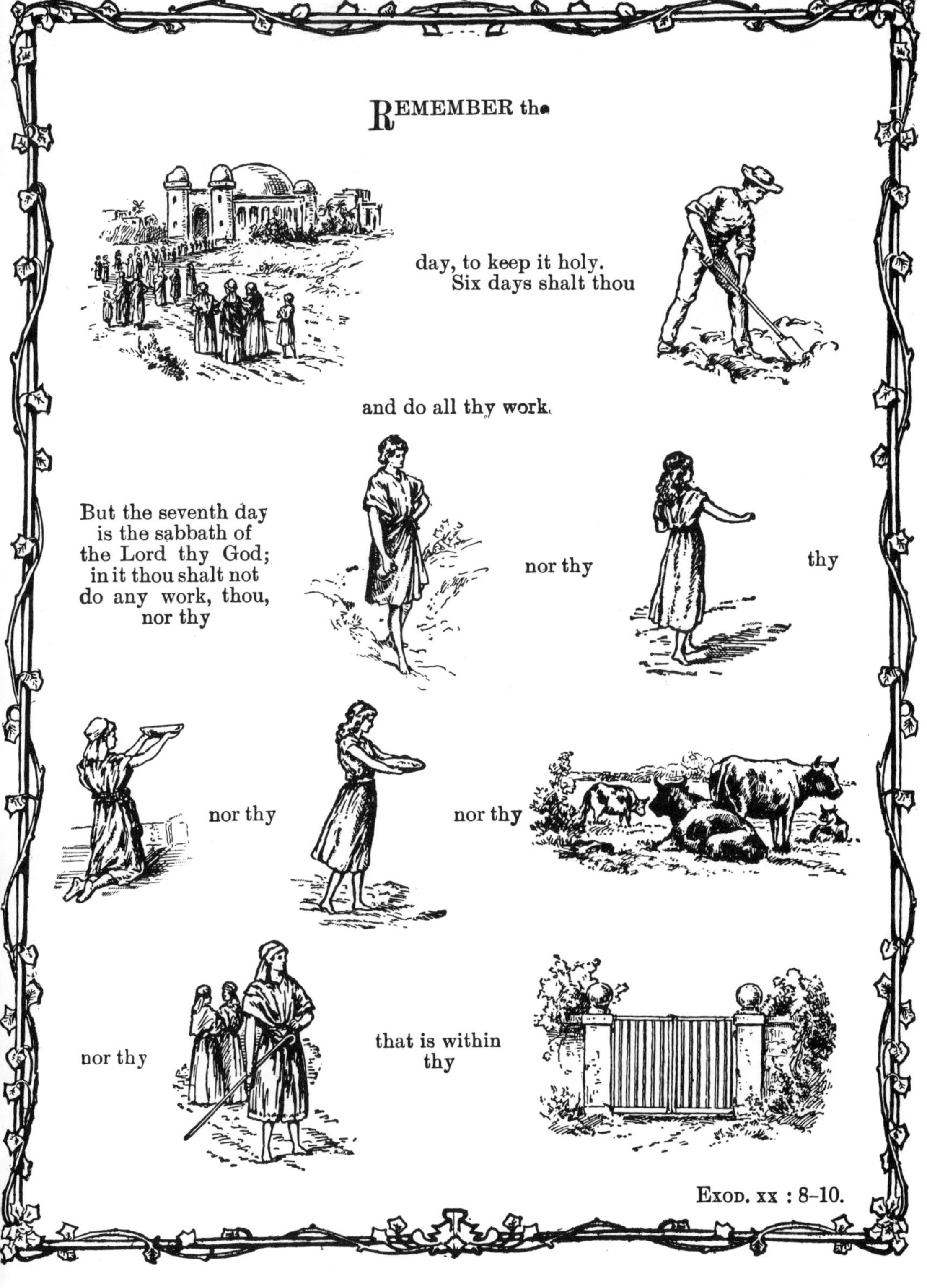
REMEMBER the
day, to keep it holy.
Six days shalt thou
and do all thy work.
But the seventh day
is the sabbath of
the Lord thy God;
in it thou shalt not
do any work, thou,
nor thy
nor thy
thy
nor thy
nor thy
nor thy
that is within
thy
Exod. xx : 8–10.

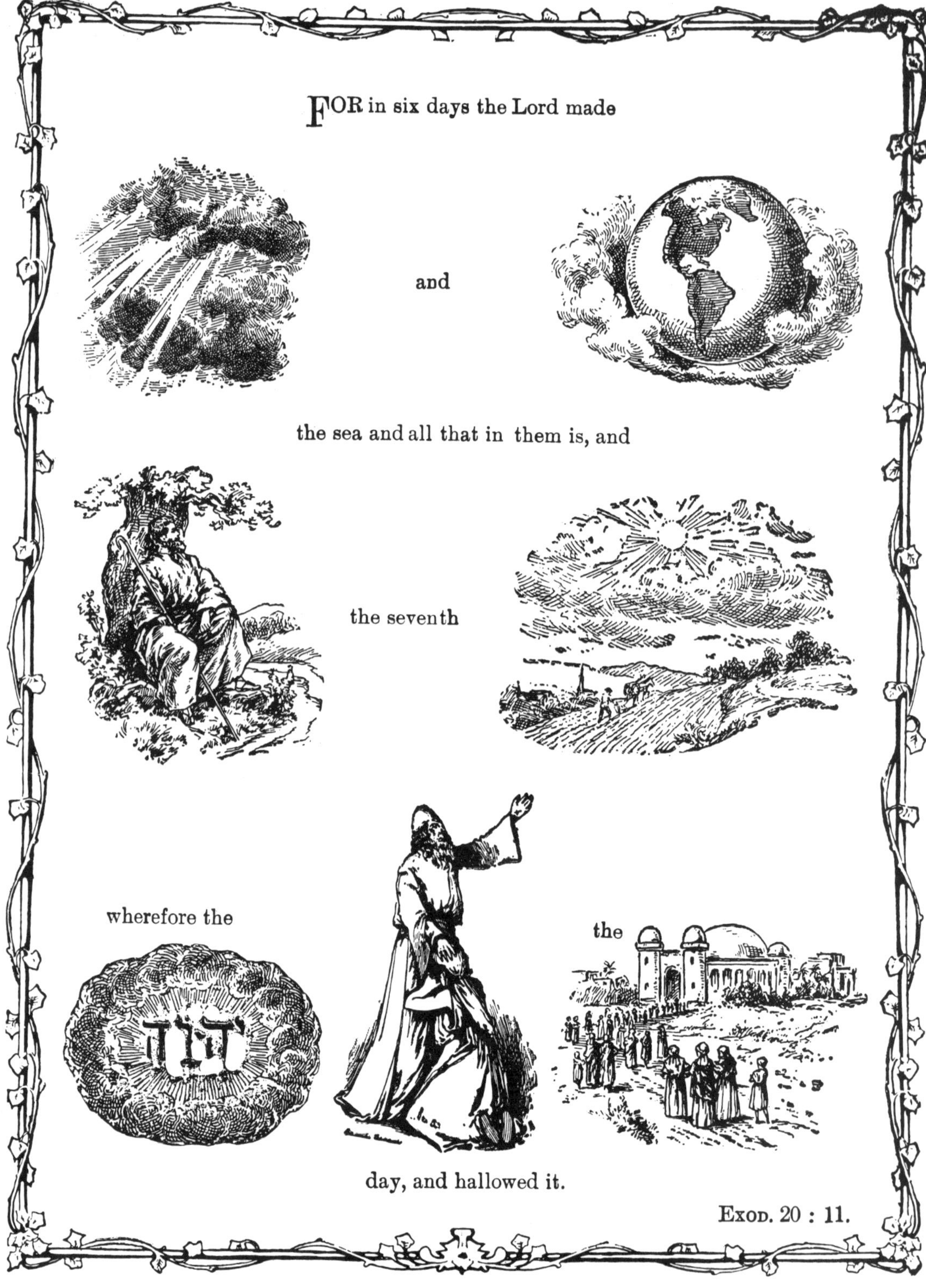

FOR in six days the Lord made

and

the sea and all that in them is, and

the seventh

wherefore the

the

day, and hallowed it.

Exod. 20 : 11.

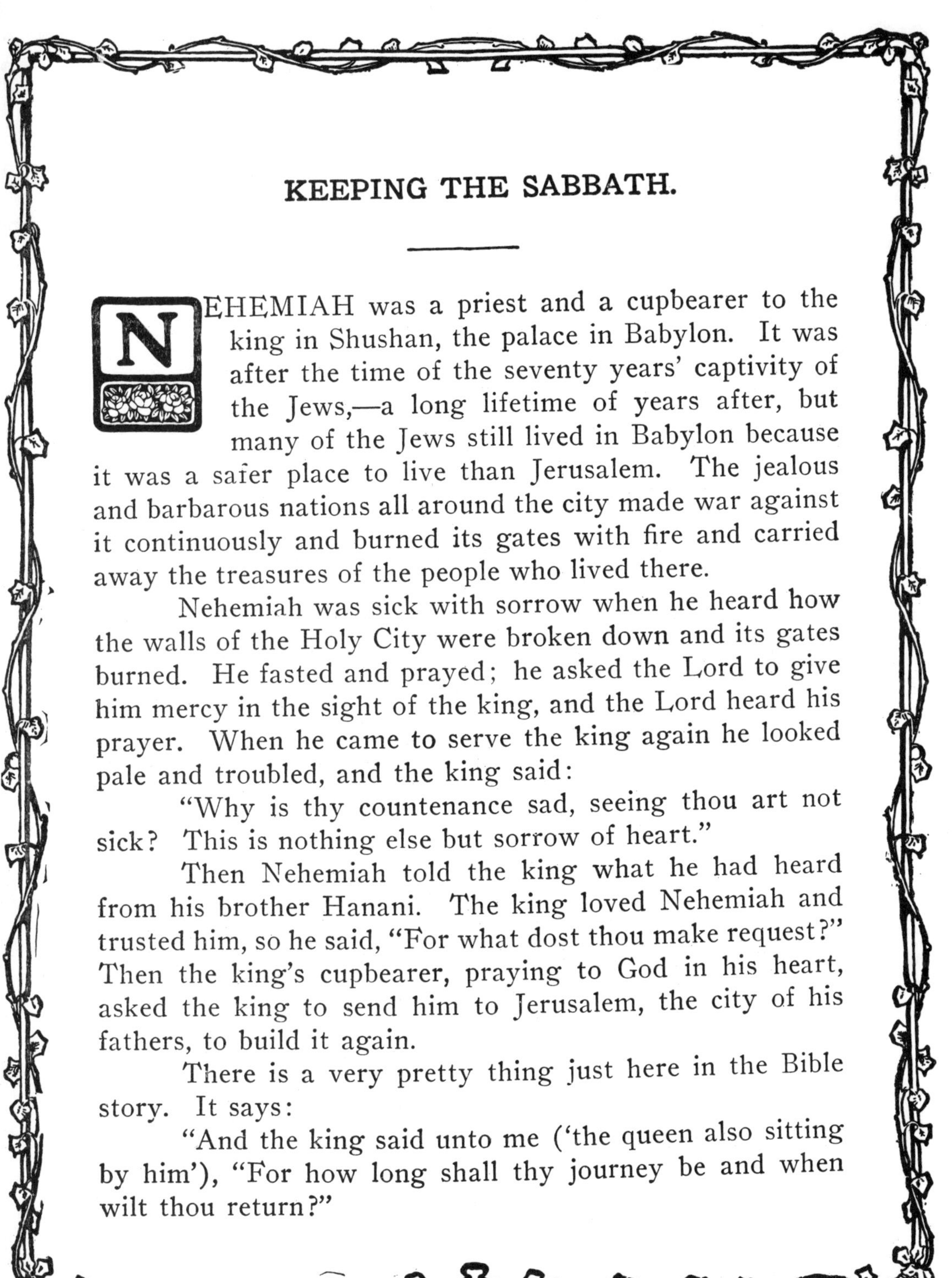

KEEPING THE SABBATH.

NEHEMIAH was a priest and a cupbearer to the king in Shushan, the palace in Babylon. It was after the time of the seventy years' captivity of the Jews,—a long lifetime of years after, but many of the Jews still lived in Babylon because it was a safer place to live than Jerusalem. The jealous and barbarous nations all around the city made war against it continuously and burned its gates with fire and carried away the treasures of the people who lived there.

Nehemiah was sick with sorrow when he heard how the walls of the Holy City were broken down and its gates burned. He fasted and prayed; he asked the Lord to give him mercy in the sight of the king, and the Lord heard his prayer. When he came to serve the king again he looked pale and troubled, and the king said:

"Why is thy countenance sad, seeing thou art not sick? This is nothing else but sorrow of heart."

Then Nehemiah told the king what he had heard from his brother Hanani. The king loved Nehemiah and trusted him, so he said, "For what dost thou make request?" Then the king's cupbearer, praying to God in his heart, asked the king to send him to Jerusalem, the city of his fathers, to build it again.

There is a very pretty thing just here in the Bible story. It says:

"And the king said unto me ('the queen also sitting by him'), "For how long shall thy journey be and when wilt thou return?"

Two things made the king very gentle: the spirit of God within him, and the spirit of a good wife beside him.

"So it pleased the king to send me," wrote Nehemiah, "and I set him a time."

Some time you will read the book of Nehemiah and find the wonderful story of the rebuilding of the walls of Jerusalem. Nehemiah had a great work to do and only a little time in which to do it. He worked with all the strength of his mind and body,—first to strengthen the hearts of a discouraged people, and then to teach them how to work. They built the walls with their weapons of war upon them.

"Every one," says the Bible story, "with one hand wrought on the work and with the other hand he held a weapon."

When all was builded and the gates barred they kept a joyful feast for seven days, and the streets and squares were full of little leafy houses made of the branches of olive and myrtle, and palm, and pine, which they had brought in from the Mount of Olives.

But almost the last great work that Nehemiah did for the Jews was to bring back their Sabbath. If you will look at the picture page you will see just what Nehemiah saw every Sunday. He knew that God saw it too and he could not go back to Babylon and remember that picture of a Sabbath in Jerusalem! What could he do?

He locked the city gates at sunset on the next Sabbath and set guards over them until the Sabbath was past. Then the merchants from Tyre, and the sellers of all kinds of wares, and grains, and wine, and fruits and foods camped outside the gates once or twice, until Nehemiah threatened to arrest them. Then they came no more on the Sabbath and the city had a peaceful, quiet day, as the Sabbath always should be.

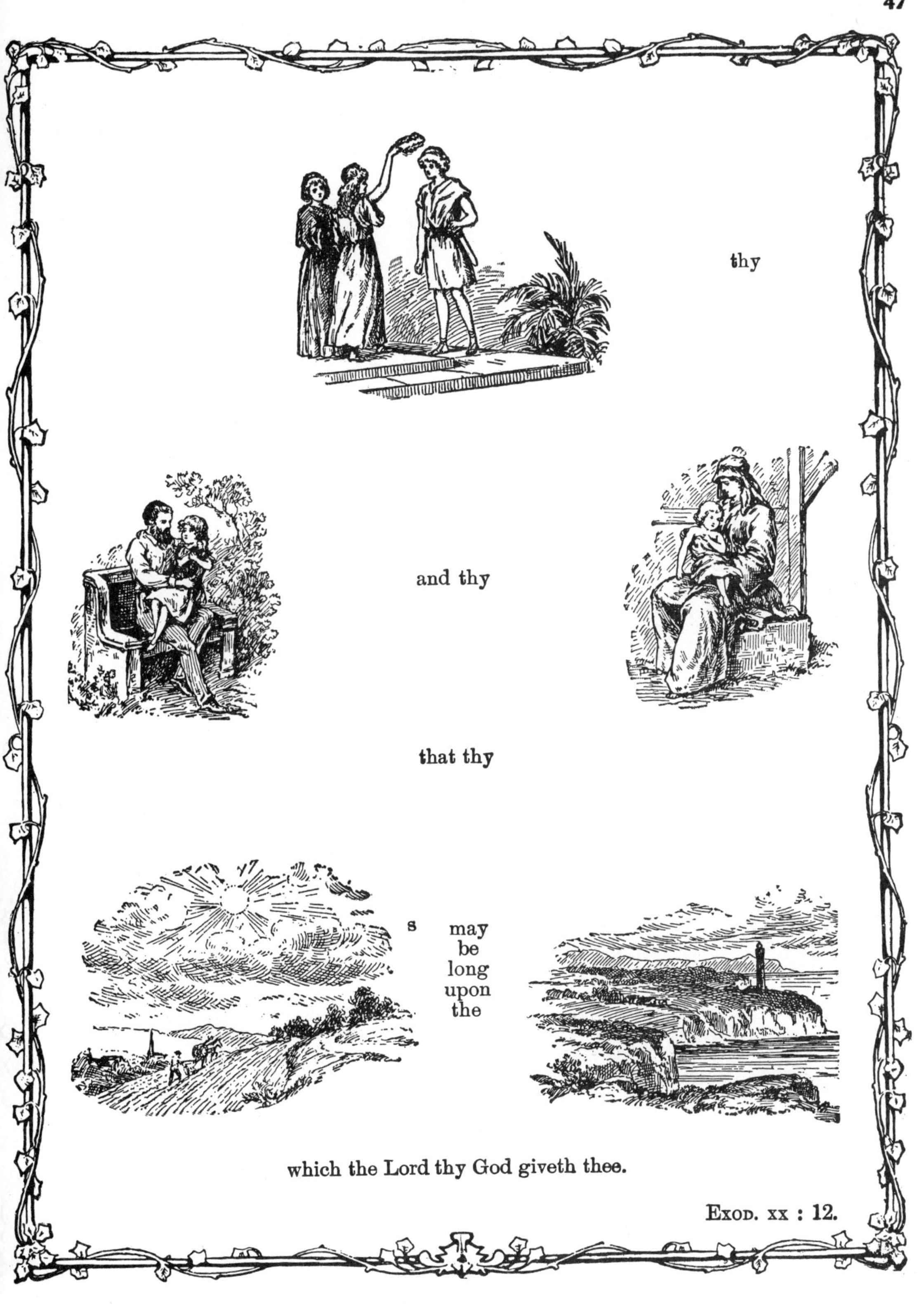

thy

and thy

that thy

s may be long upon the

which the Lord thy God giveth thee.

EXOD. XX : 12.

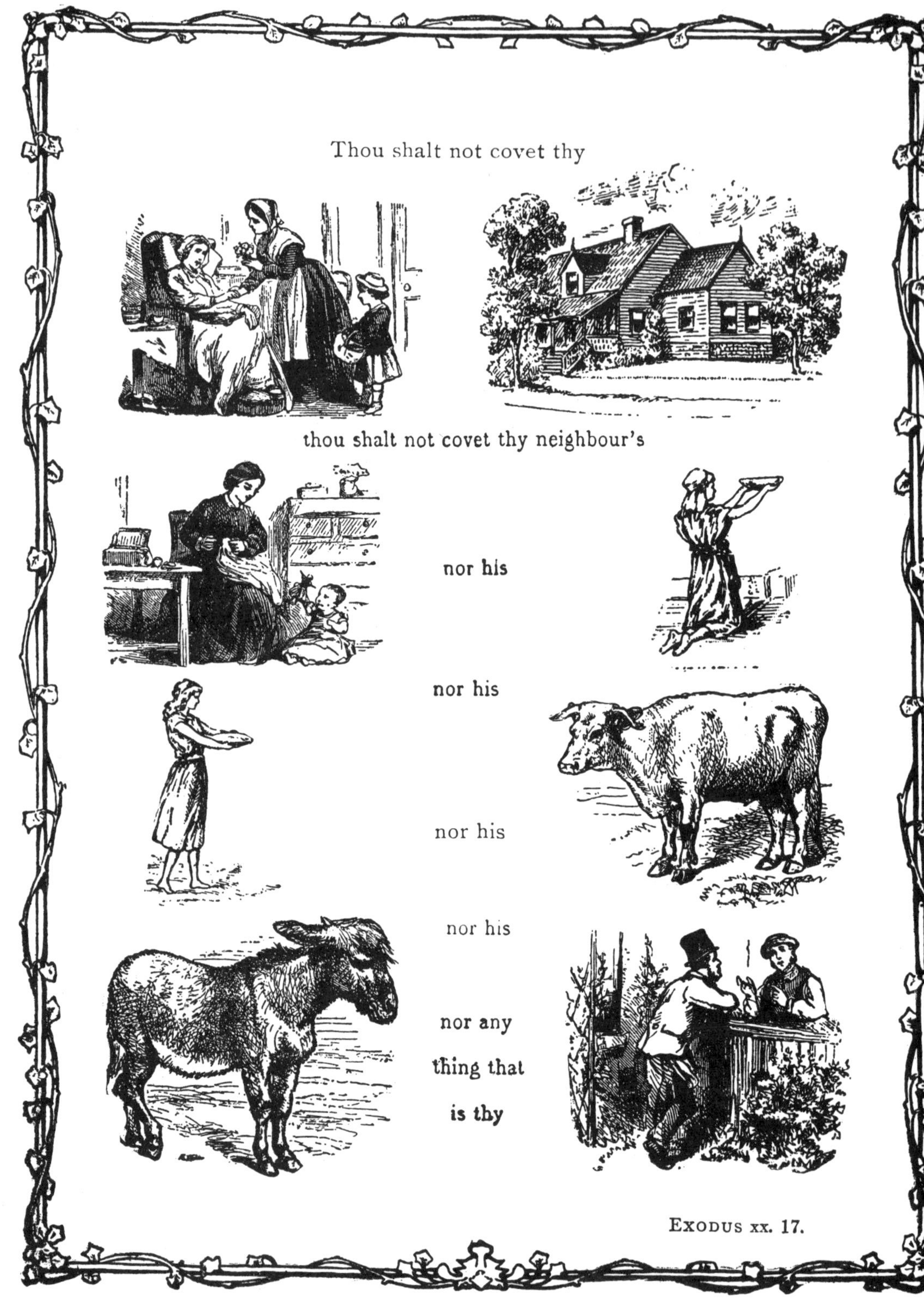

Thou shalt not covet thy

thou shalt not covet thy neighbour's

nor his

nor his

nor his

nor his

nor any thing that is thy

EXODUS xx. 17.

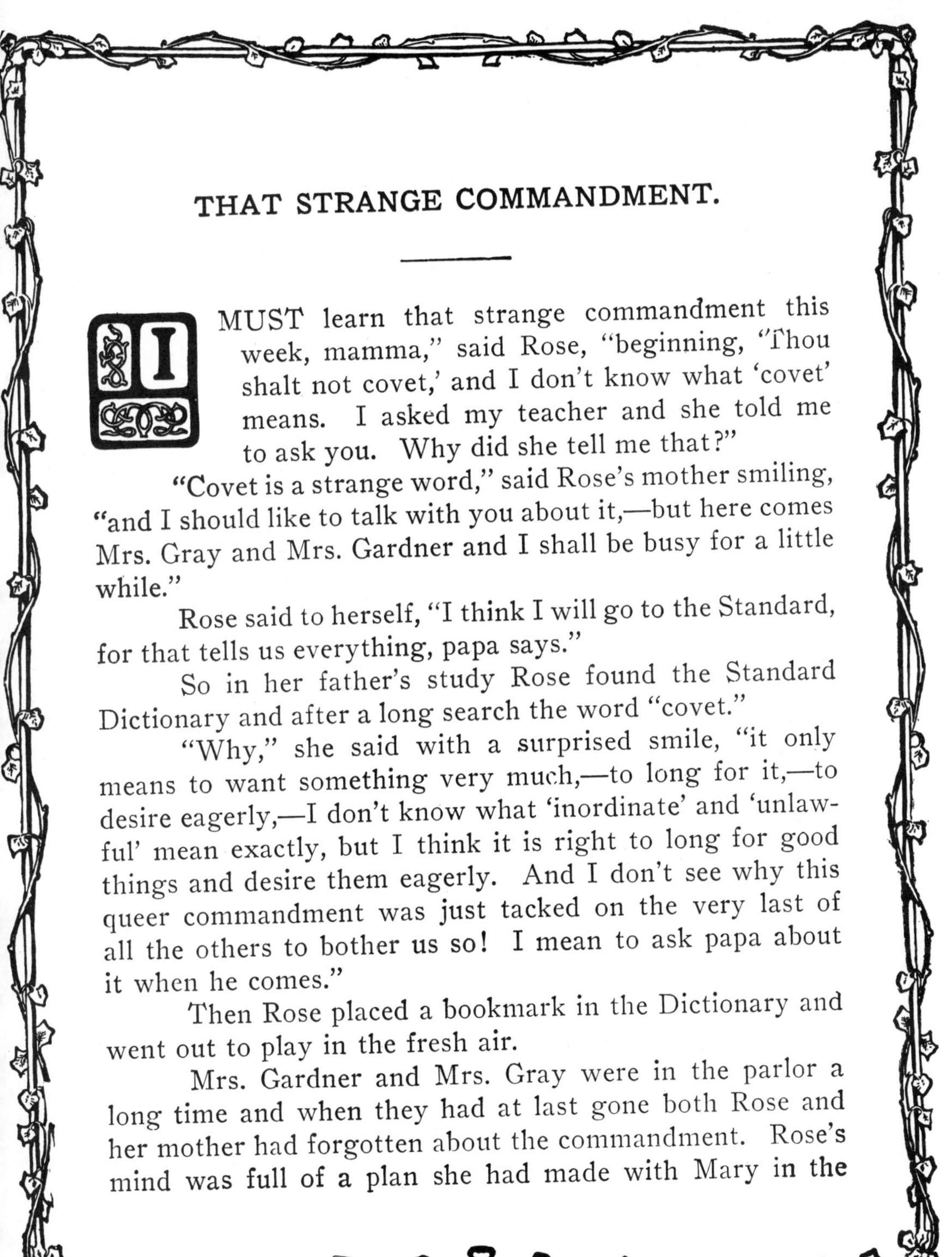

THAT STRANGE COMMANDMENT.

I MUST learn that strange commandment this week, mamma," said Rose, "beginning, 'Thou shalt not covet,' and I don't know what 'covet' means. I asked my teacher and she told me to ask you. Why did she tell me that?"

"Covet is a strange word," said Rose's mother smiling, "and I should like to talk with you about it,—but here comes Mrs. Gray and Mrs. Gardner and I shall be busy for a little while."

Rose said to herself, "I think I will go to the Standard, for that tells us everything, papa says."

So in her father's study Rose found the Standard Dictionary and after a long search the word "covet."

"Why," she said with a surprised smile, "it only means to want something very much,—to long for it,—to desire eagerly,—I don't know what 'inordinate' and 'unlawful' mean exactly, but I think it is right to long for good things and desire them eagerly. And I don't see why this queer commandment was just tacked on the very last of all the others to bother us so! I mean to ask papa about it when he comes."

Then Rose placed a bookmark in the Dictionary and went out to play in the fresh air.

Mrs. Gardner and Mrs. Gray were in the parlor a long time and when they had at last gone both Rose and her mother had forgotten about the commandment. Rose's mind was full of a plan she had made with Mary in the kitchen to send Arthur a box of goodies, which would be a good thing to have at Easter, for the boys at Beechwood School, were many of them to stay for the short vacation. She had this on her mind when she came down to dinner and spoke of it. Both her mother and father were greatly pleased with the plan and said they would help her.

"O, mamma," cried Rose a little later, "I found out what 'covet' means."

"Well," said her mother, "what is it?"

"Why, it means to want something very much,—to long for it,—to desire eagerly; is not that good instead of bad?"

"That depends to whom the something belongs that you want," said mamma.

"Papa, it was your Dictionary that told me, and you say it is always right," said Rose looking surprised.

"Yes, but is that all you found out?"

"It said something about 'inordinate' and 'unlawful,' but I did not know those words."

"We may desire eagerly all the free gifts of God, but not the gifts that he has given to our neighbor. That is an 'inordinate' and 'unlawful' desire. You may long with all your soul for 'the ornament of a meek and quiet spirit,' but not for your Aunt Annie's ruby ring. Do you see?"

A glow as from a ruby spread over Rose's face, for she had often longed for that beautiful and costly ring on Aunt Annie's hand and had hoped that Aunt Annie would say in her will 'My ruby ring to Rose.'"

"Is Aunt Annie my neighbor?" asked Rose.

"To be sure she is," said mamma, "and a very good one, too. We will not steal anything from her with even a wish, will we Rose?"

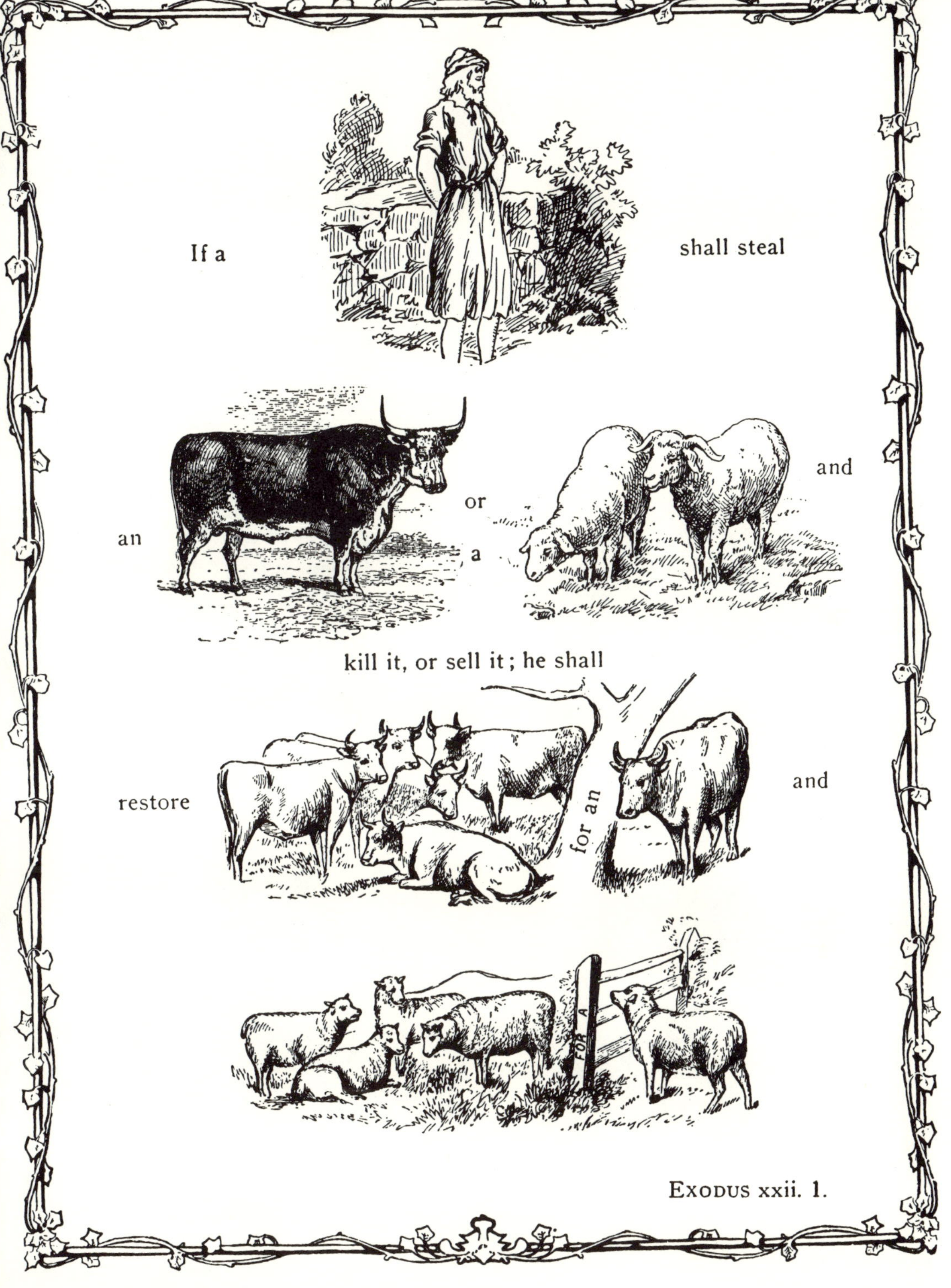

EXODUS xxii. 1.

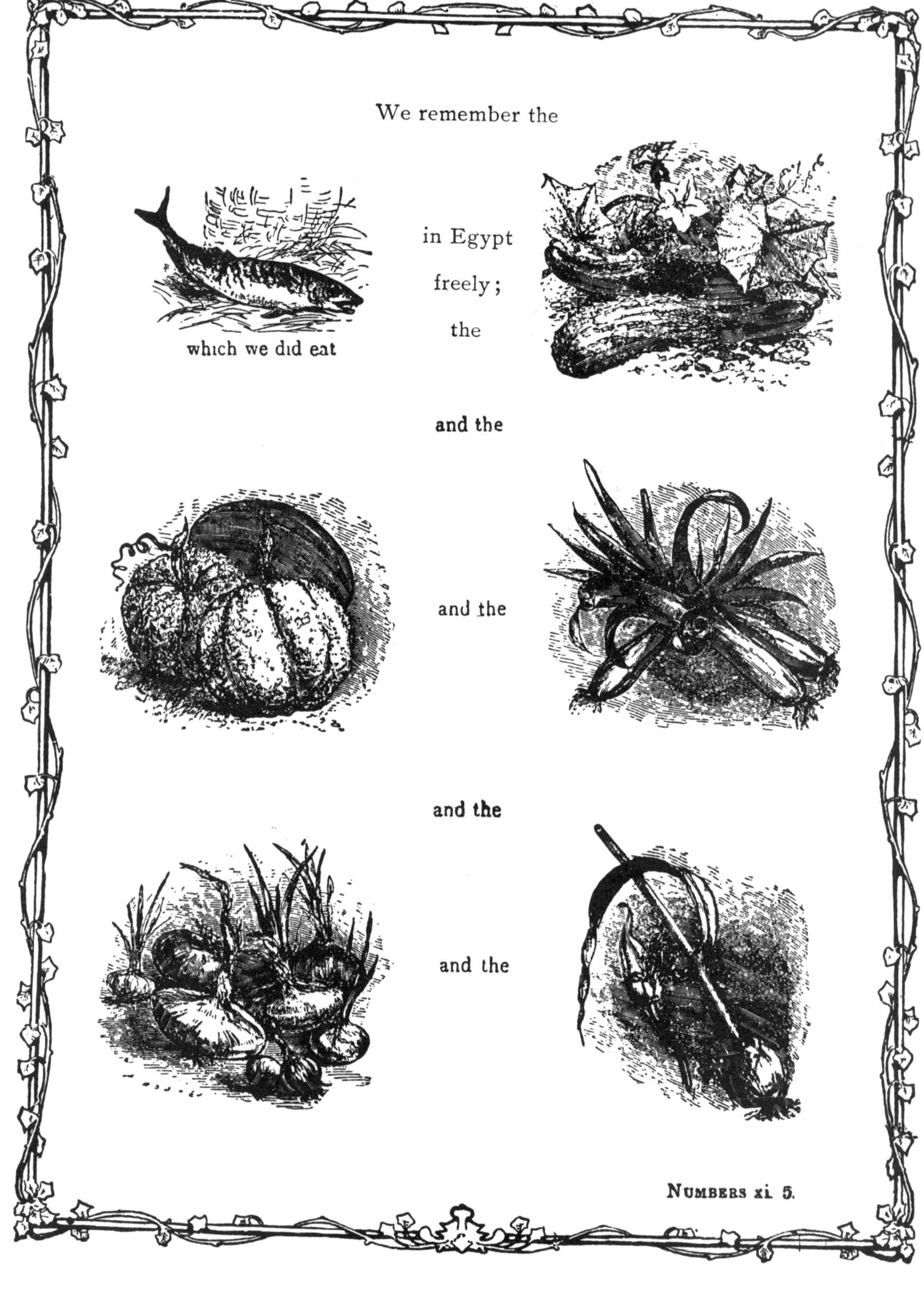
We remember the
which we did eat
in Egypt
freely;
the
and the
and the
and the
and the
Numbers xi. 5.

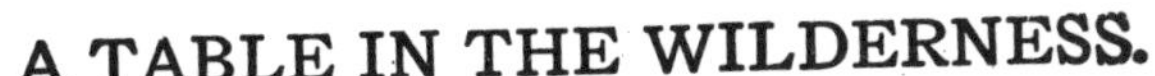

A TABLE IN THE WILDERNESS.

THINK about this for a moment: what if, instead of a dear home, you had only the starry or stormy sky above you each night, or perhaps a little tent that you must roll up and carry with you the next day? Suppose you belonged to a moving nation? That is just what the Israelites were for forty years after they were led out of Egypt. They needed only to cross a little corner of Arabia to come at once into the land of Promise. Their father Jacob and his twelve sons did so and it can easily be done now. It would have taken scarcely a month for this journey, but so wrong-minded were the people of Israel, and so weak was their faith, and so ready were they to disobey the leader God had given them, that they had to be led by many long and painful ways to the land of Canaan.

But all this time God cared for them very tenderly. Do you remember how he made a path for them through the Red Sea when they were in danger, and have you heard how, when they were in a desert land, he sent manna fresh from Heaven to them every night? And then when they longed for the food of Egypt and could not bear the taste of the manna any longer, who but a tender, loving Father would have sent great flocks of quail to cover the ground all around them? Only a loving and powerful God could have been patient with them in all their wilfulness and lead them by day and by night with the pillar of cloud and the pillar of fire all through their journey in the wilderness.

You remember that the Jews were a favored people, and so they are to-day. Wherever they go and however badly they may be treated, yet no nation can ever destroy them. God still watches over them and tries to lead them in the right way. We should never forget that Jesus our Saviour was a Jew.

When you get very tired of oatmeal, or bread and milk, how delightful is the thought of something different. It was just so with the people of Israel. They grew so tired of eating the food in the wilderness that often the smell and the taste of the good food they had had in Egypt came back to them, and they wanted again the crisp, brown fish, the tender cucumber, and the luscious melons. There were also the leeks, the onions, and the garlic, which give a relish to so many other kinds of food. And they loved and longed after all these things.

You do not wonder, do you, that in this great army of "six hundred thousand footmen" there were many who thought of these things and wanted once more to taste the food of Egypt, and to drink the sweet water of the Nile?

This turning back toward Egypt is called "lust" in the Bible and it means turning back toward a state of sin from which the Lord had turned us. Some things grow very dear and beautiful to us as we live in them, but they draw the heart away from goodness and from God and fix it upon self, and the pleasures of this world.

You know Jesus said:

"I am the bread of life," and "whosoever drinketh of the water that I shall give him shall never thirst, but the water that I shall give him shall be in him a well of water, springing up into everlasting life."

This is sometimes called the water of life, and when we have come to know the Lord and he has truly taken us to his heart, then we know just what it is, the true life of God in our spirits.

Let us think of these things whenever false love or "lust" tempts us.

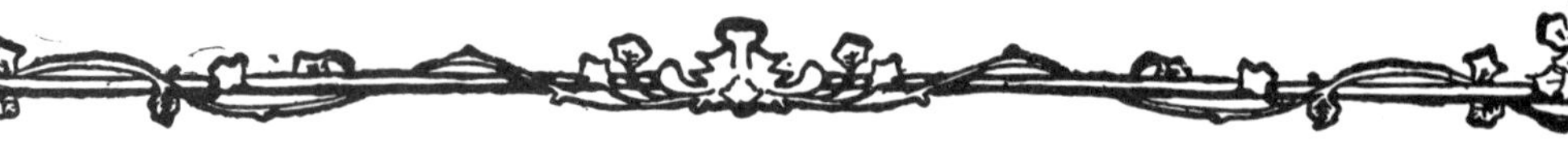

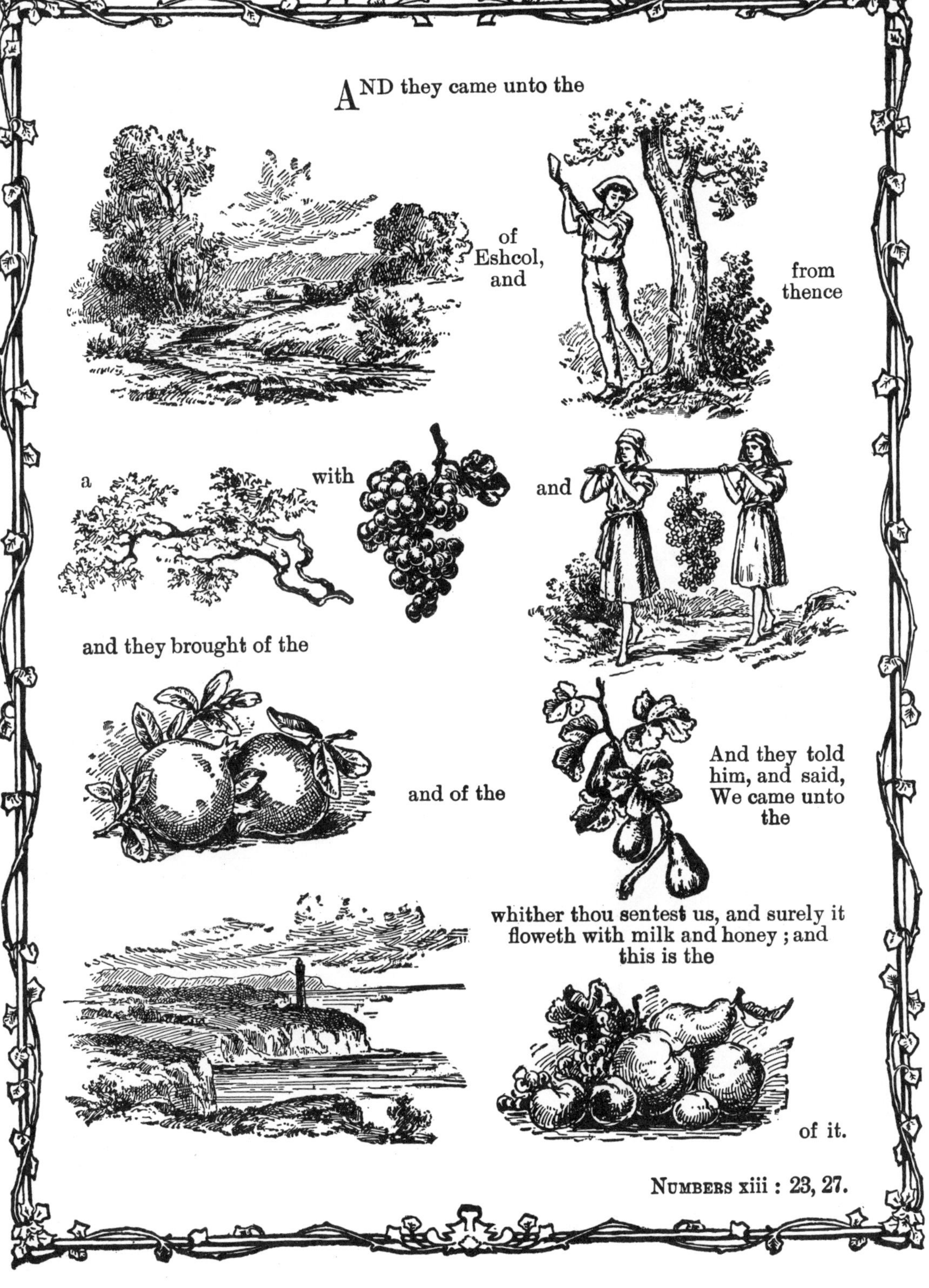
AND they came unto the
of
Eshcol,
and
from
thence
a
with
and
and they brought of the
and of the
And they told
him, and said,
We came unto
the
whither thou sentest us, and surely it
floweth with milk and honey ; and
this is the
of it.
NUMBERS xiii : 23, 27.

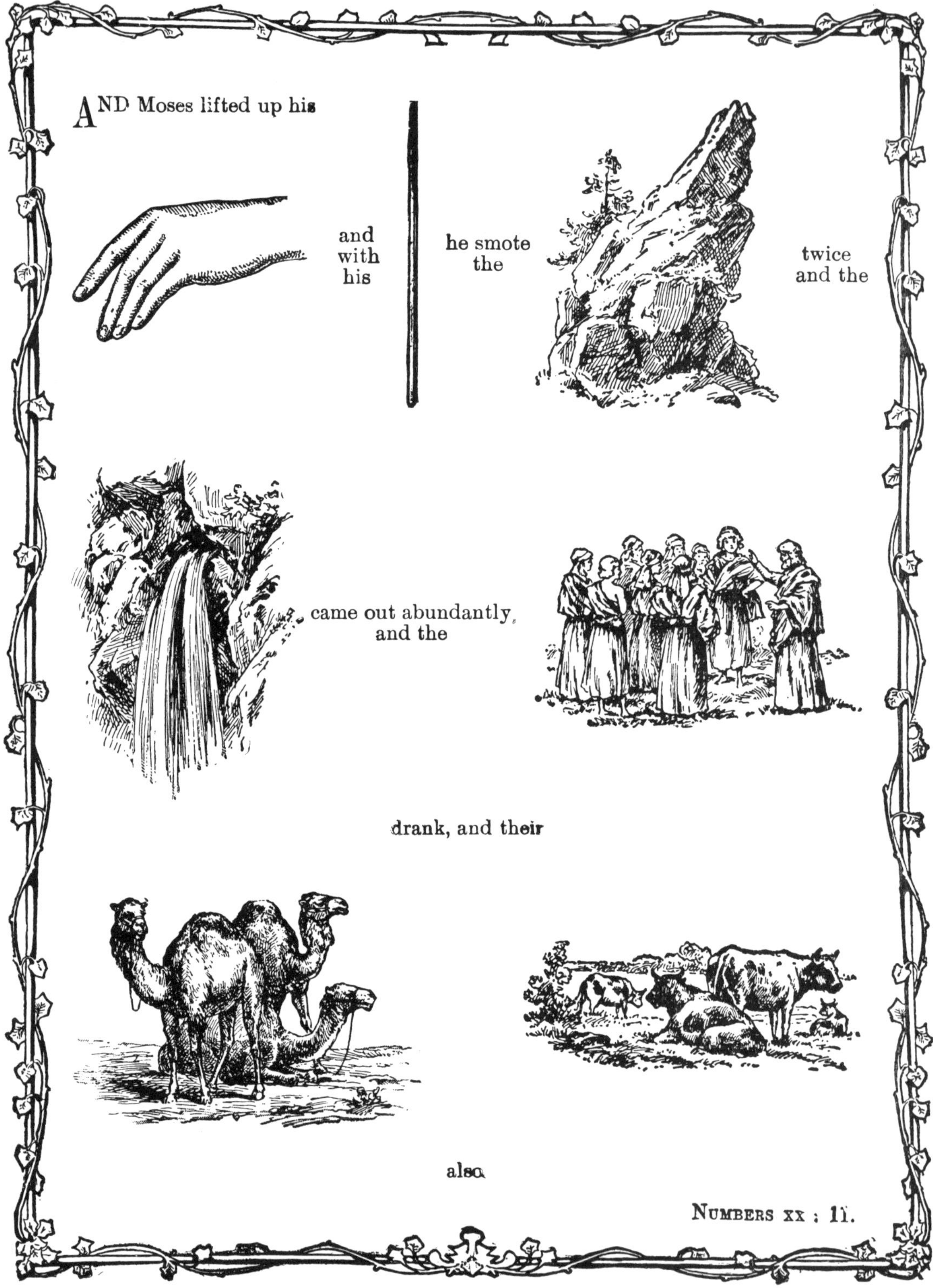
AND Moses lifted up his
and with his
he smote the
twice and the
came out abundantly, and the
drank, and their
also.
NUMBERS XX : 11.

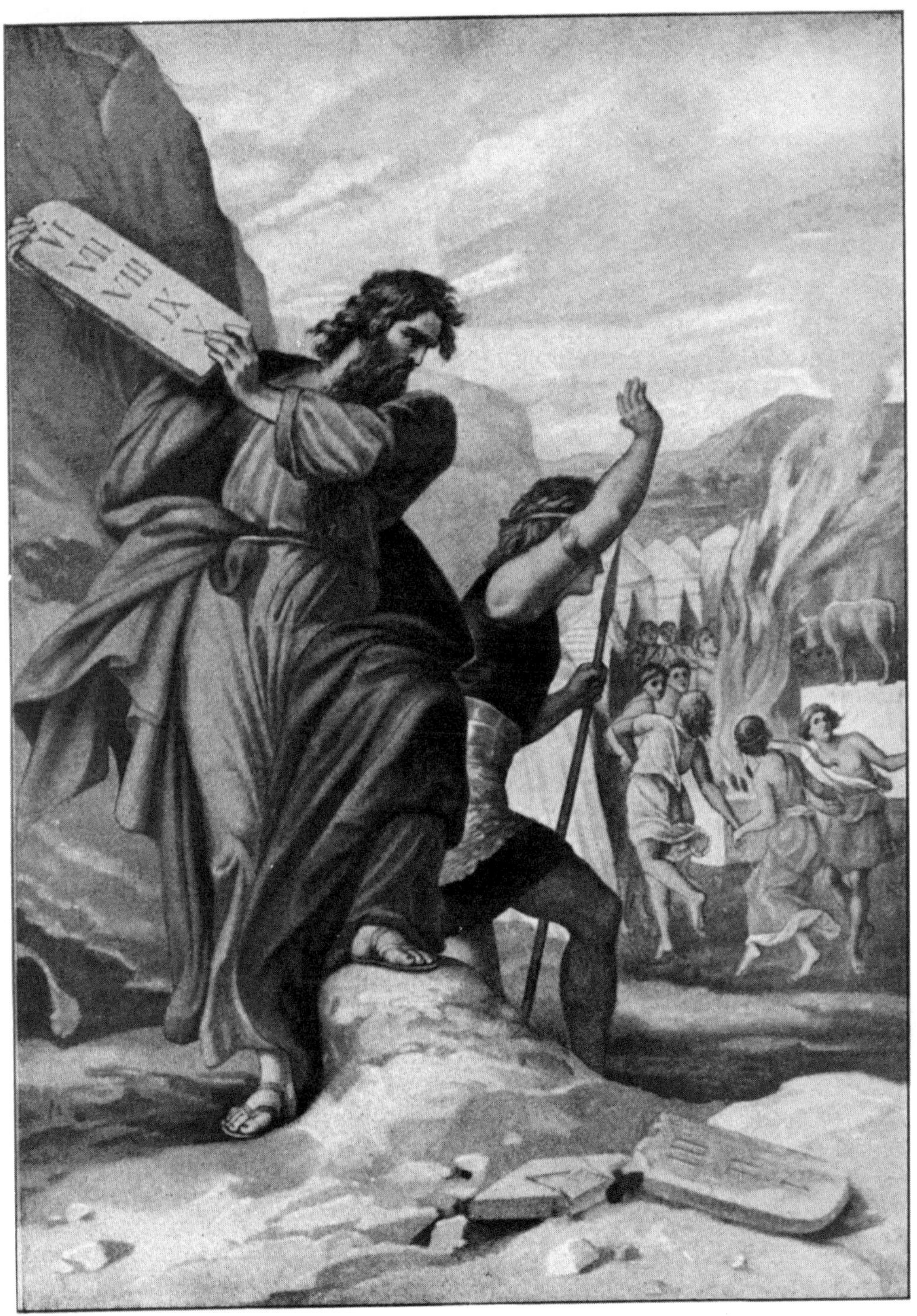

MOSES AND THE GOLDEN CALF.

MOSES AND THE GOLDEN CALF

On pages 71 and 72 you will find the story of the Golden Calf. But why did the Israelites select a calf to adore as their god?

The Egyptians, with whom the Israelites had lived for so many years, had a queer system of religion. They adored many gods; but the greatest and best of all their gods was Osiris. Another name for him was Hapi or Apis, a word that means "hidden." He was so called because the Egyptians said that he hid himself in a young bull or calf that could be found only by its peculiar marks and coloring. These marks were: a black-colored hide, a white triangular spot on its forehead, the hair on its back so arranged as to suggest the shape of an eagle, under its tongue a knot in form of a beetle.

When a calf of this description was found there was great rejoicing among the people. At once they built for him a beautiful house facing toward the east. There they fed him for three months on the purest and best of milk. Then they brought the sacred boat with a gold-lined cabin; they set the calf in it, and amid gorgeous ceremony conveyed him to Memphis. There he was kept in the palace of Osiris, and was the object of the greatest care and veneration. Every year his birthday was celebrated as a national holiday.

The life of the sacred Apis had its limit. If he died before he was twenty-five years old, he was buried with extraordinary funeral pomp; if not, he was killed by the priests and his body sunk into the sea or some well unknown to any but the priests who had sacrificed him. When dead he was called Sarapis. The death of an Apis was always the occasion of great national mourning.

Now, the Israelites had lived for generations in the midst of these people. They had learned all about Osiris, and they were familiar with the ceremonies of his worship. They remembered that it was he who had vanquished Apappus, the dire giant and god of the dread wilderness in which they were then encompassed. Should they not now call upon Osiris to deliver them from this cruel god? Maybe this terrible Jehovah, who had led them out into the desert, was none other than Apappus. So they would invoke the great Osiris to smite him again, and they compelled Aaron to make for them a molten image of the sacred bullock Apis, that they might sacrifice to it and obtain through it their deliverance from the cruel rule of Moses and his God.

This was a very grievous sin on the part of the Israelites, and the Lord punished them severely.

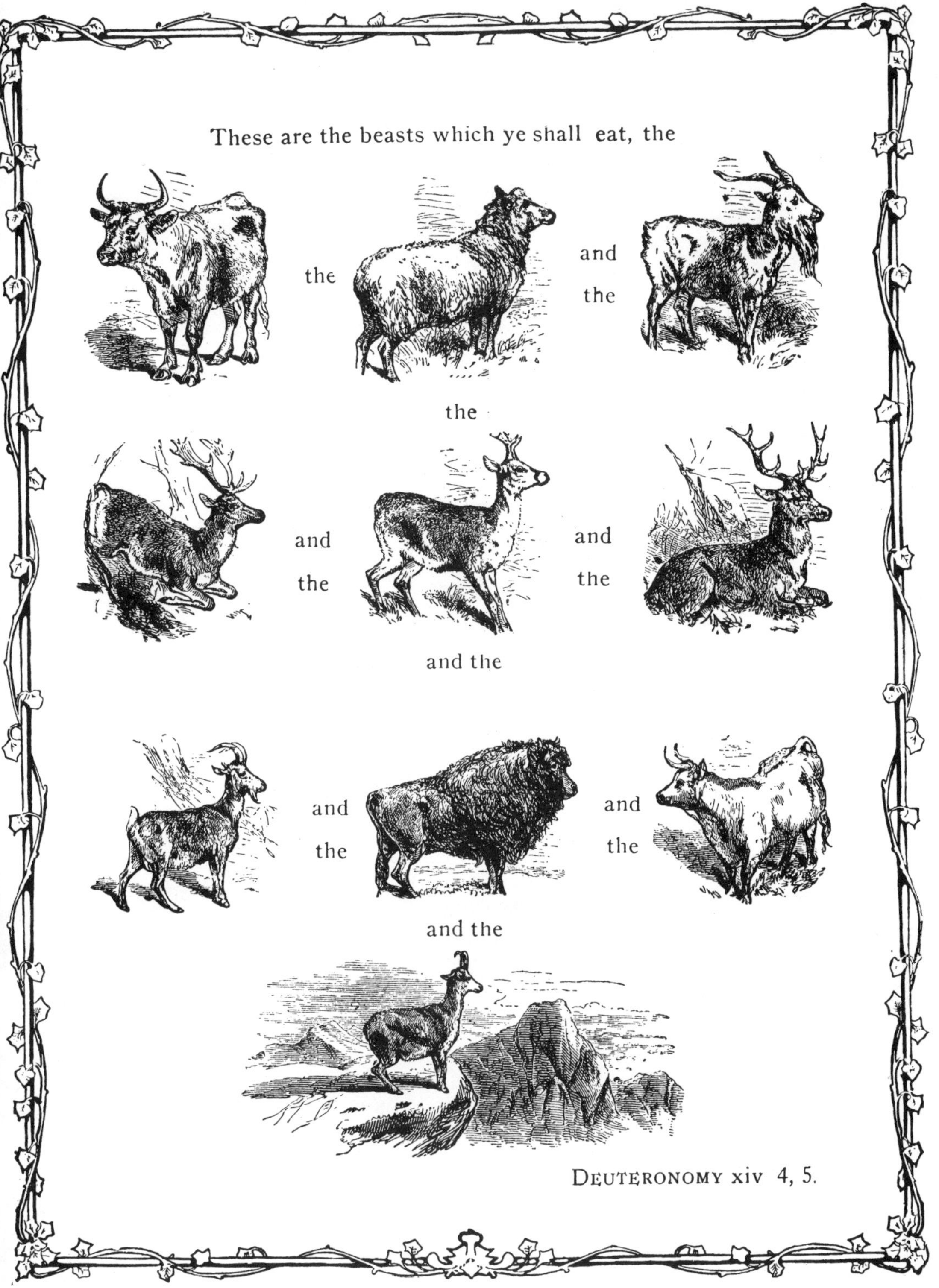

These are the beasts which ye shall eat, the

the

and the

the

and the

and the

and the

and the

and the

and the

DEUTERONOMY xiv 4, 5.

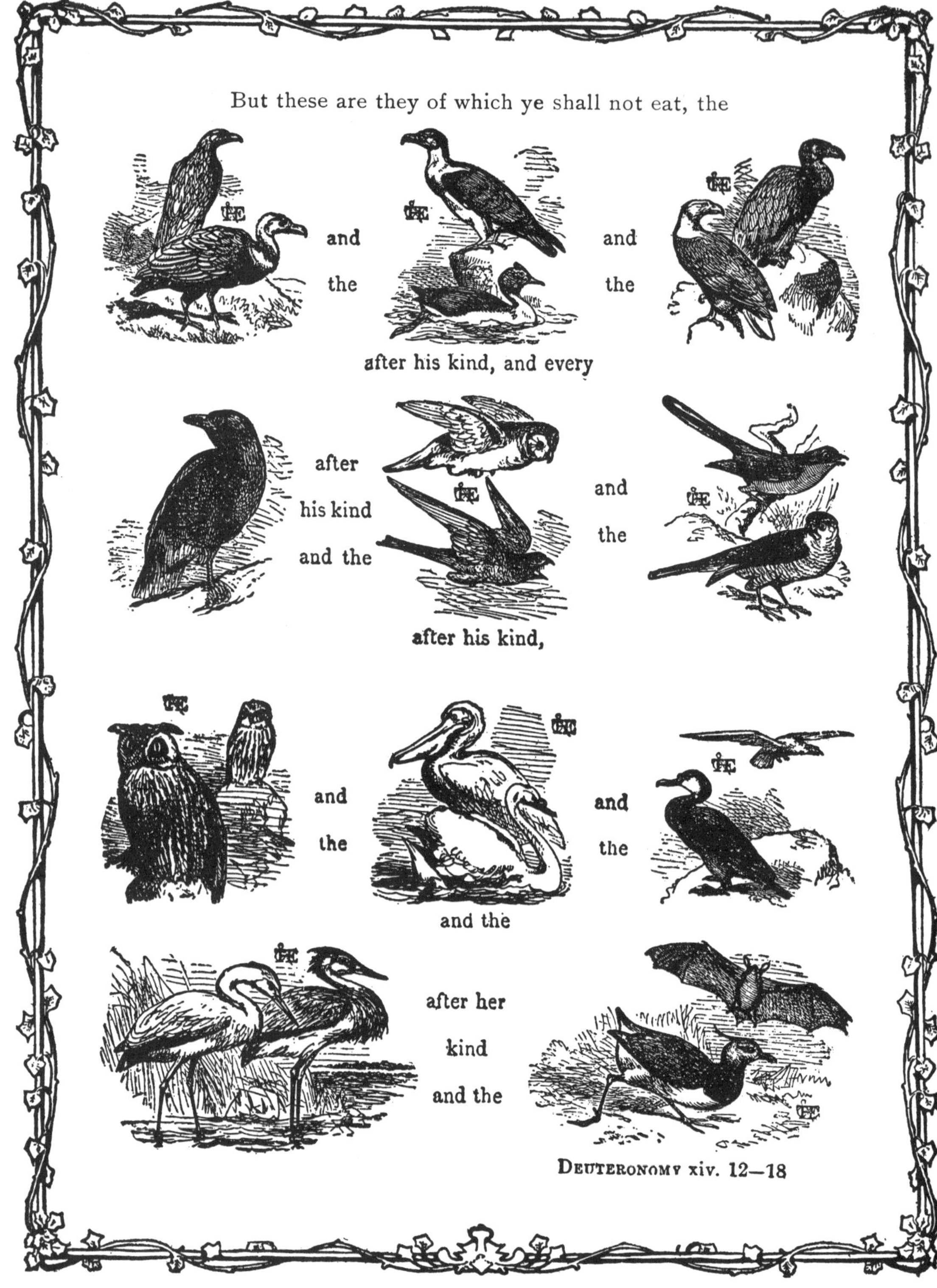
But these are they of which ye shall not eat, the
and
the
and
the
after his kind, and every
after
his kind
and the
and
the
after his kind,
and
the
and
the
and the
after her
kind
and the
DEUTERONOMY xiv. 12—18

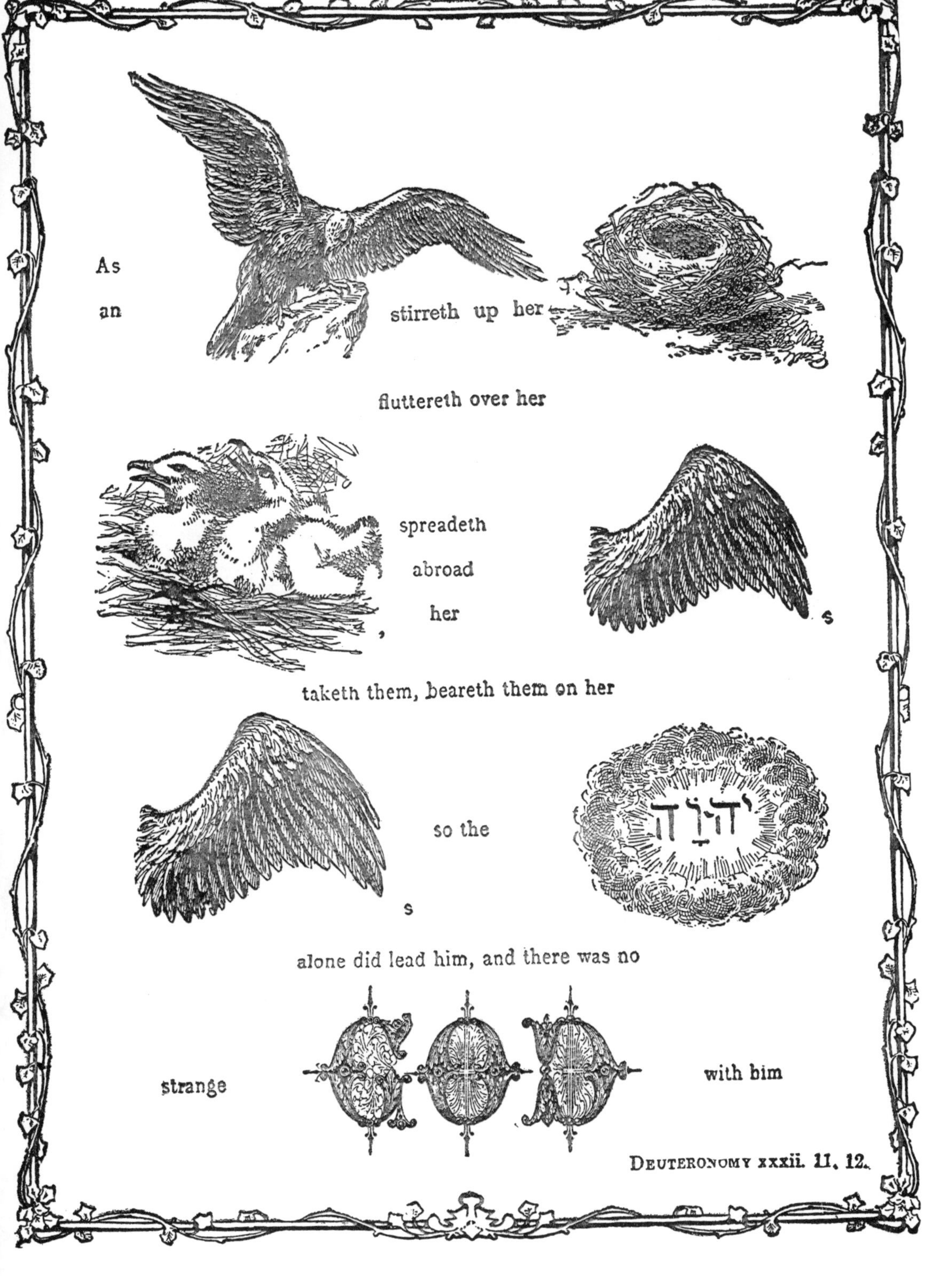
As
an
stirreth up her
fluttereth over her
spreadeth
abroad
her
,
s
taketh them, beareth them on her
so the
יְהֹוָה
s
alone did lead him, and there was no
strange
with him
Deuteronomy xxxii. 11, 12.

A TRUE STORY OF LOVE AND FAITH

"ENTREAT me not to leave thee, or to return from following after thee; for whither thou goest I will go, and where thou lodgest I will lodge; thy people shall be my people, and thy God my God. Where thou diest will I die, and there will I be buried—the Lord do so to me and more also if aught but death part thee and me."

It was a young woman of Moab who spoke these noble and beautiful words to a woman old and sad, and bowed by many sorrows. Years before a man of Bethlehem in Judah took his wife and two sons, because of famine, and went into the land of Moab to dwell for a time. His name was Elimelech, and his wife was called Naomi. Elimelech died in this strange land, and Naomi was left with her two sons, who married wives from among the daughters of Moab. And then came a sad time when the sons died, and Naomi was left alone with her daughters-in-law, Orpah and Ruth. They loved one another and dwelt in peace and union, but the mother's heart turned in her loneliness more and more toward her own kindred, her own land, and above all the God of Israel whom she had loved and served in her happy youth, and whom she still loved, though among a people who knew him not.

The longing desire grew in the heart of Naomi, until she could no longer abide in the land of strangers, and one day she turned her face toward the land of Judah, and Orpah and Ruth said they would go with her.

Naomi bade them return, each to her mother's house, and she kissed them tenderly, while all three women wept as they tried to bid one another a long farewell. Then Ruth, her heart running over with love and faith, spoke the words which have lived, and will always live in the world while love and faith are dear to human hearts.

Again Naomi bade the loving daughters return to their own people, and not seek to follow an old and broken woman upon whom the hand of the Lord had been laid. The daughters again wept aloud, and Orpah kissed her mother-in-law again, and turned to go to her own people. But Ruth, glowing with love and the spirit of self-sacrifice, clung to the older woman. When Naomi saw that Ruth was of a steadfast mind and would not leave her, we may well believe that hope and courage entered into the soul of the sad-hearted woman and she went on her way with a heart lightened and cheered by the love and tenderness of this dear daughter.

Ruth gave up her own people, her own land, and the gods she had been taught to serve. What did she gain?

She gained the undying affection of a lonely woman, the love and respect of all who saw her devotion to duty, and above all else the favor of Israel's God and King! She gained, too, the honor of being an ancestress of the Lord Jesus Christ, and her name will be known as long as he is loved and worshiped on earth.

A good and noble man saw this sweet woman gleaning in the field after the reapers. His heart was drawn to her by her beauty and modest ways, and he made her his honored wife, giving her a name and high position, and a dear child was given her, who became the father of Jesse, the father of David, the great King of Israel, from whom in a direct line "was born Jesus who is called Christ."

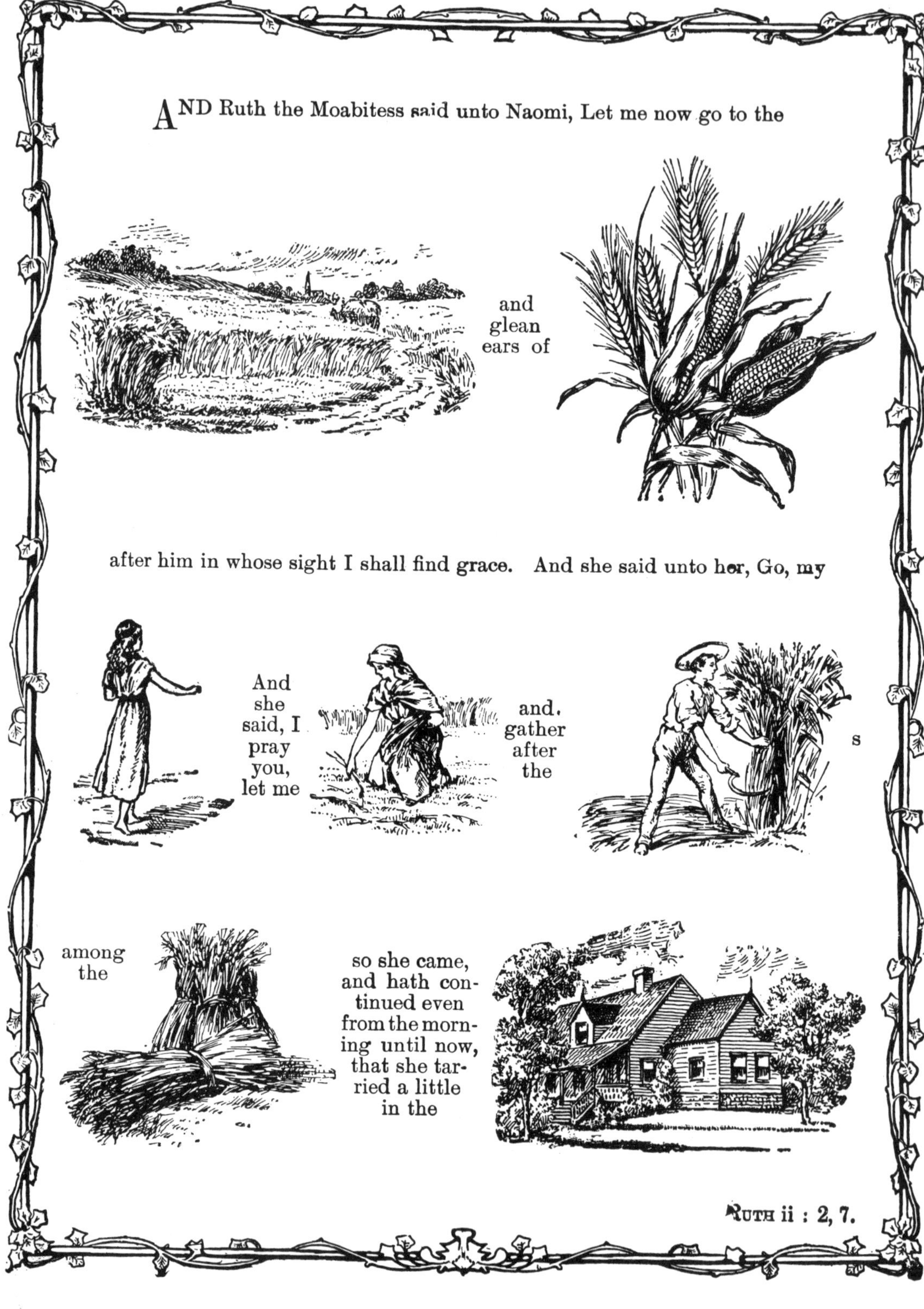

AND Ruth the Moabitess said unto Naomi, Let me now go to the

and glean ears of

after him in whose sight I shall find grace. And she said unto her, Go, my

And she said, I pray you, let me

and gather after the

s

among the

so she came, and hath continued even from the morning until now, that she tarried a little in the

RUTH ii : 2, 7.

DAVID AND GOLIATH

LONG ago when the world was young there lived a clear-eyed, noble boy who feared nothing but evil. He was a shepherd lad, keeping his father's flocks on the wide, grassy plains of Bethlehem. He was the youngest son of Jesse, and had several brothers older than himself. A brave and faithful lad he was,—so brave that when peacefully watching his sheep one day, a lion came out of the rocky gorge not far away, and tried to carry away some of the tender lambs, their young shepherd, thinking not of his own safety, slew the lion, and saved his flock! Another day a hungry bear came seeking food, and young David fearlessly slew him—again saving his flock.

There came a day when there was war between Israel and the Philistines. The armies came in plain sight of each other, and the Philistines sent their champion—the great giant Goliath—to dare any man to come out and fight with him and thus settle the quarrel between the two armies.

Goliath was taller than any man you ever saw. He wore a great helmet of brass on his head, and his body was covered with a coat of mail. He had a big voice and a fierce look, and all the soldiers who heard him were afraid to fight him. Every day the giant came out and taunted the Israelites and called them cowards, and King Saul's heart was full of trouble and dismay.

But one day he was told that a lad had come to the battlefield to bring food to his brothers, who said he would fight the giant! Saul said, "Bring him to me." But when he saw the fair face and slender form of young David, he was much disappointed, and said sadly, "Alas! you are too young and weak to fight a great giant like Goliath." But David, looking the king in the eye, said modestly but bravely, "The Lord who delivered me out of the paw of the lion, and out of the paw of the bear, He will deliver me out of the hand of this Philistine." Then Saul saw that David was not thinking of his own power or strength, but of the power and strength of the great God, and he said, "Go, and the Lord be with thee."

So David went, believing in his faithful young heart that God would humble the pride and wickedness of this powerful giant, and give the victory to His people Israel. He would not wear armor or carry a sword. He wanted all the people to see that God could use a weak boy to conquer evil, and he took only his shepherd's staff and his sling, and went cheerfully to meet the bad, bold giant.

When Goliath saw this fair, ruddy-faced boy coming to meet him, armed only with his shepherd's staff and a sling, he despised him and cursed him by his gods. But David said to him, calmly, "I come to thee in the name of the Lord of hosts; this day will the Lord deliver thee into mine hand." The giant came to meet him in great rage, rattling his armor and waving his sword, but young David, who had picked up a few smooth stones from the side of the brook, only took one of them from his little shepherd's bag, put it carefully in his sling, and threw it with so true an aim, and with such power in his young hand, that it struck the fierce giant squarely in the forehead, and he fell down flat upon his face! When the soldiers of the two armies saw this the Israelites shouted for joy, and the Philistines turned and ran away, for they saw that the God of Israel was fighting for His people.

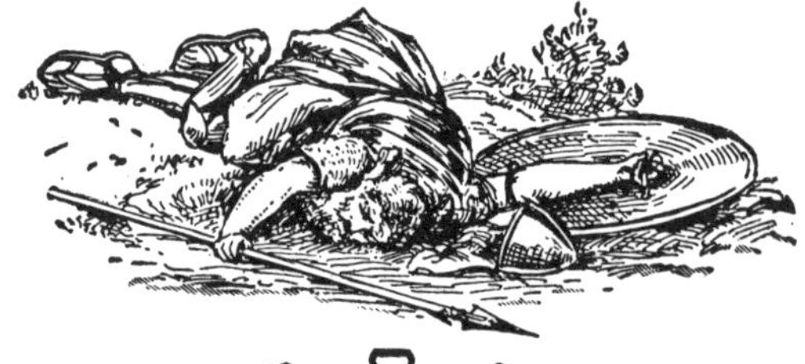

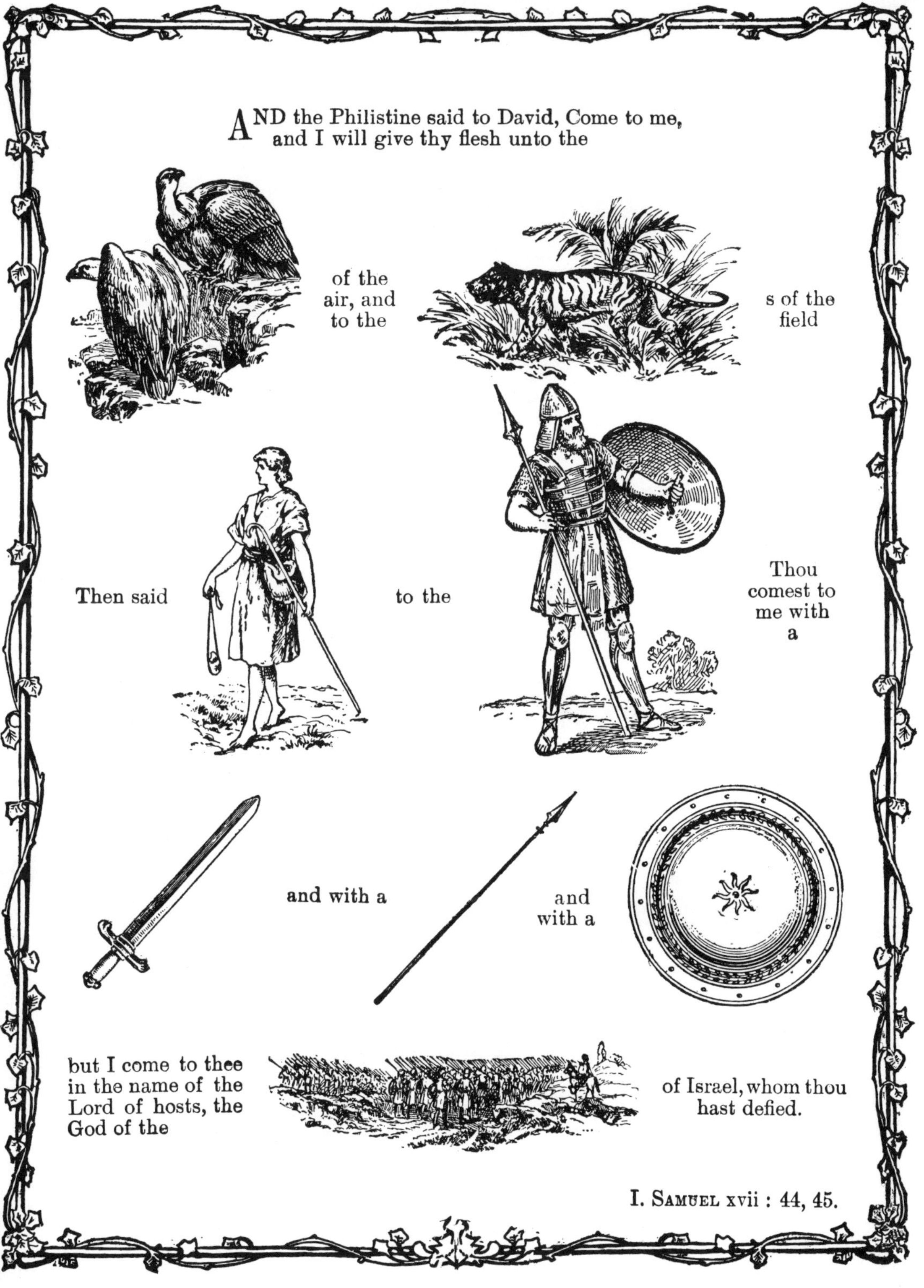
AND the Philistine said to David, Come to me, and I will give thy flesh unto the
of the air, and to the
s of the field
Then said
to the
Thou comest to me with a
and with a
and with a
but I come to thee in the name of the Lord of hosts, the God of the
of Israel, whom thou hast defied.
I. Samuel xvii : 44, 45.

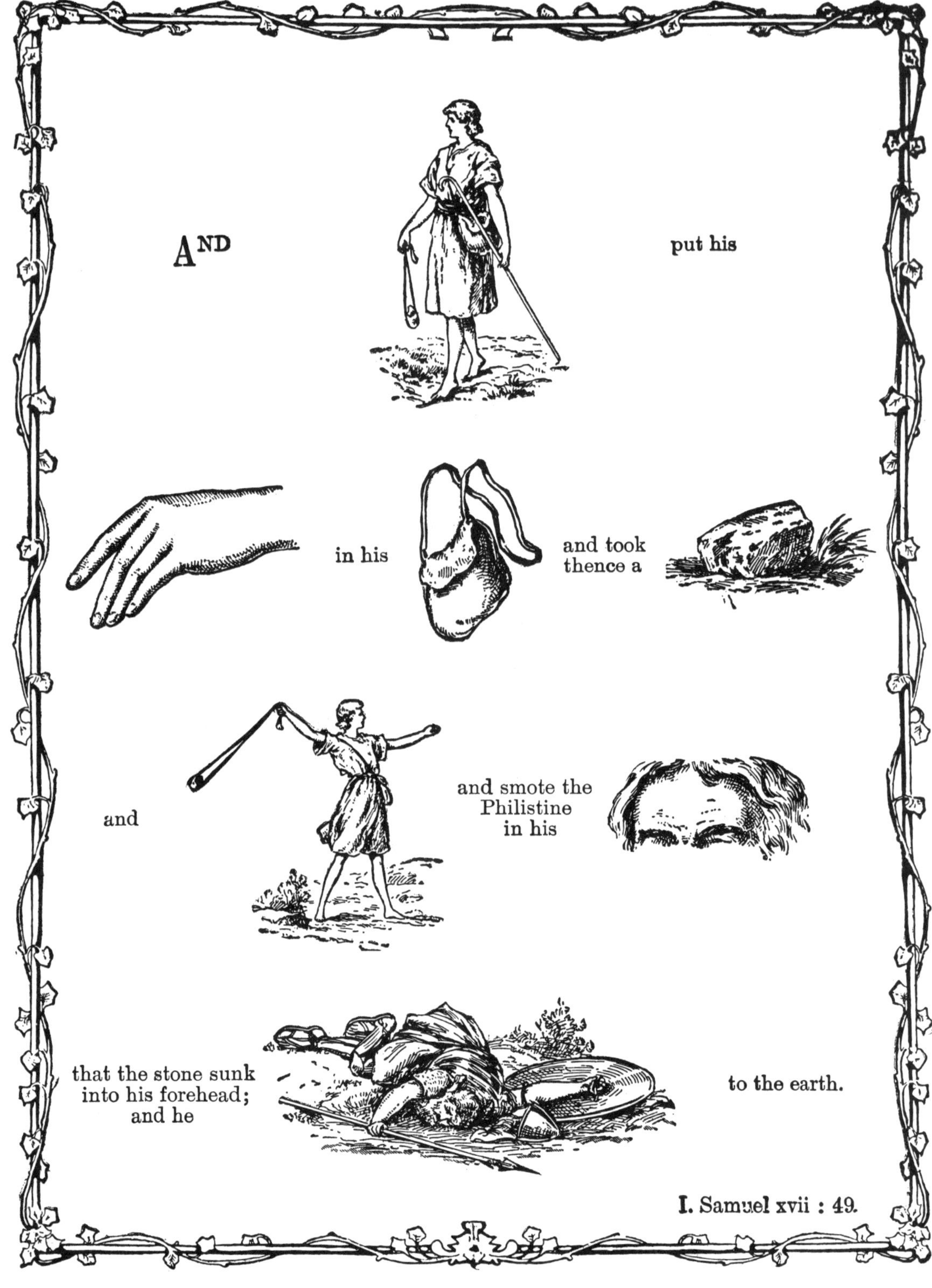
AND
put his
in his
and took
thence a
and
and smote the
Philistine
in his
that the stone sunk
into his forehead;
and he
to the earth.
I. Samuel xvii : 49.

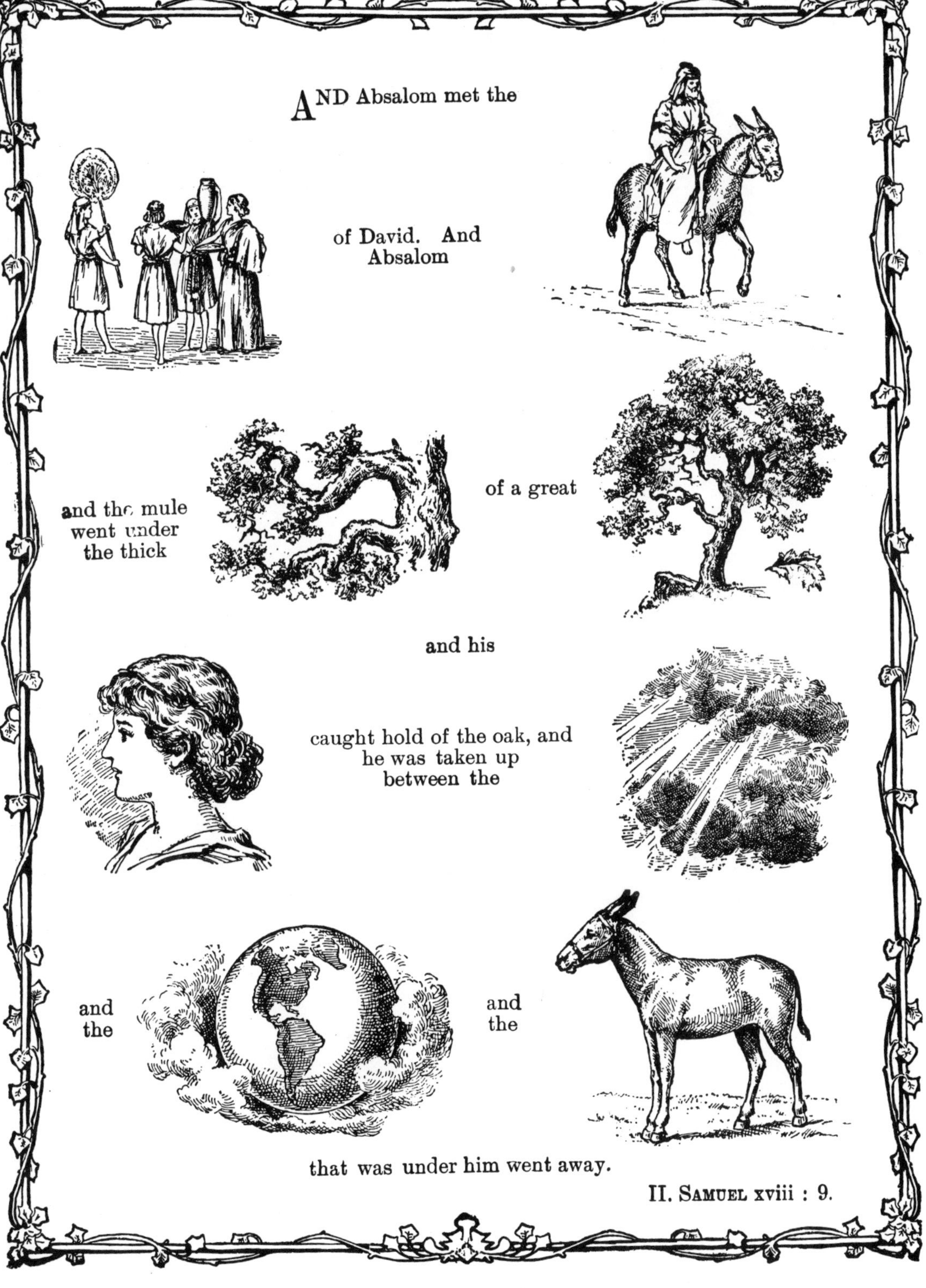
AND Absalom met the
of David. And
Absalom
and the mule
went under
the thick
of a great
and his
caught hold of the oak, and
he was taken up
between the
and
the
and
the
that was under him went away.
II. SAMUEL xviii : 9.

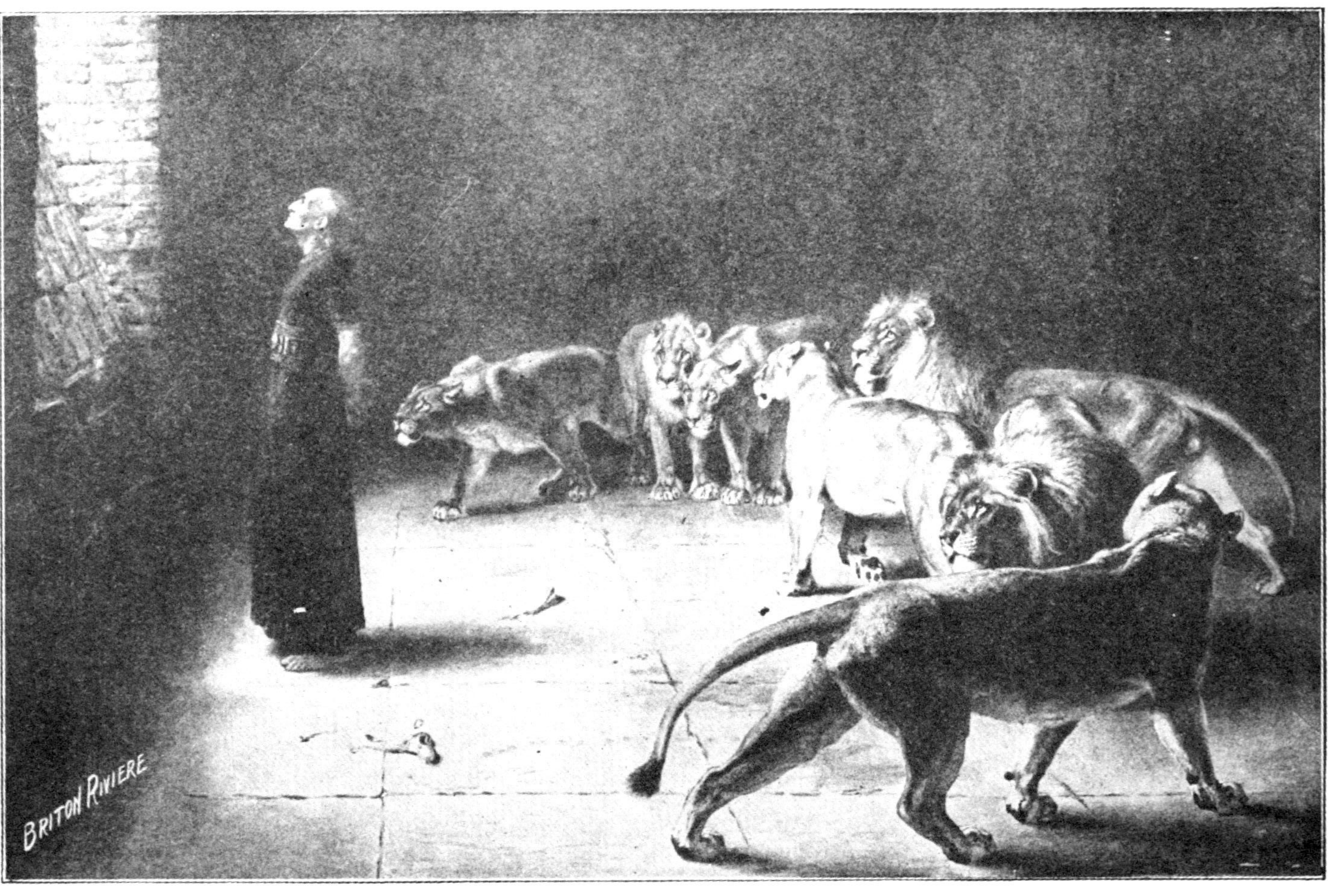

DANIEL'S ANSWER TO THE KING.

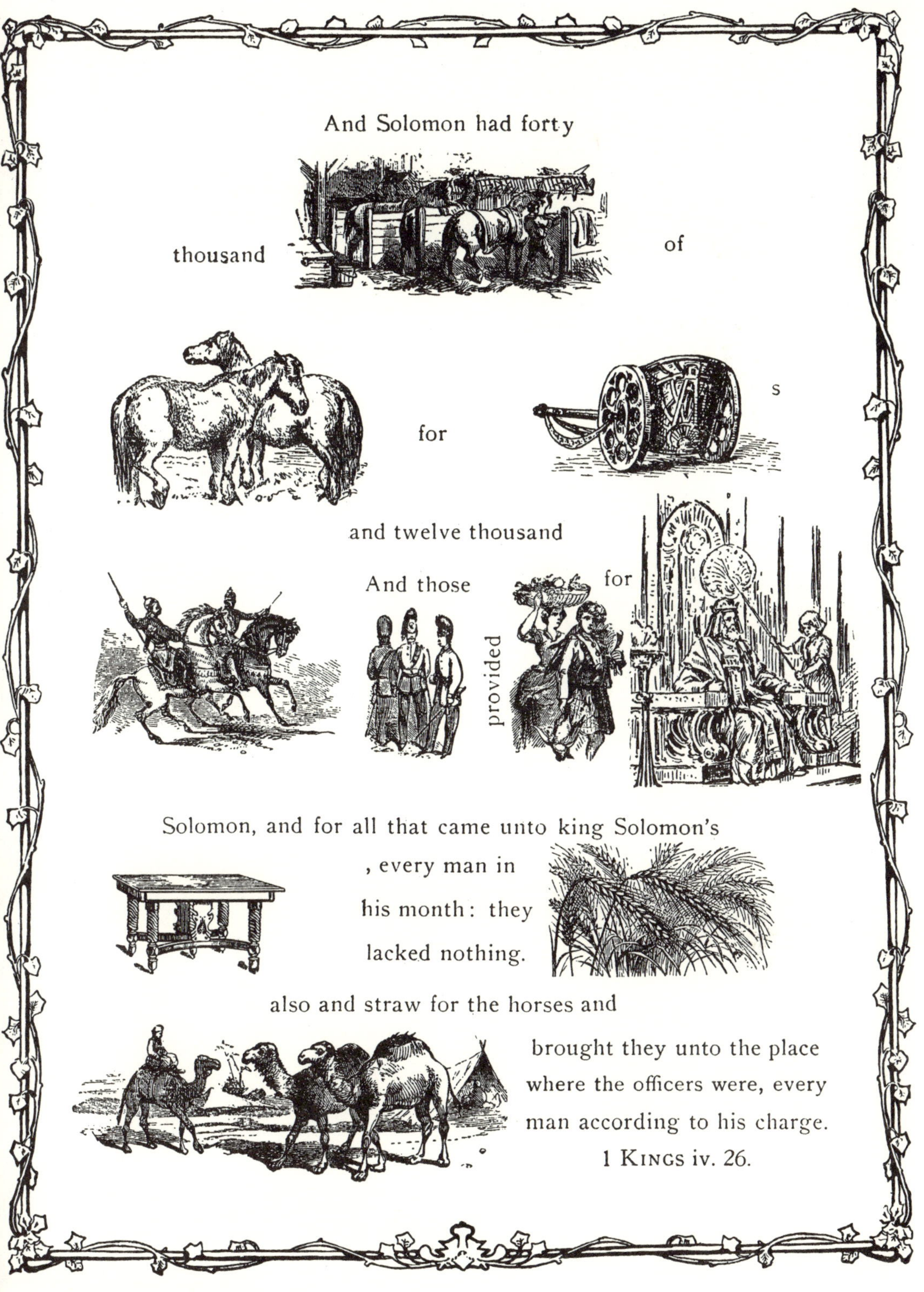

And Solomon had forty

thousand of

for s

and twelve thousand

And those for

provided

Solomon, and for all that came unto king Solomon's

, every man in

his month: they

lacked nothing.

also and straw for the horses and

brought they unto the place
where the officers were, every
man according to his charge.

1 KINGS iv. 26.

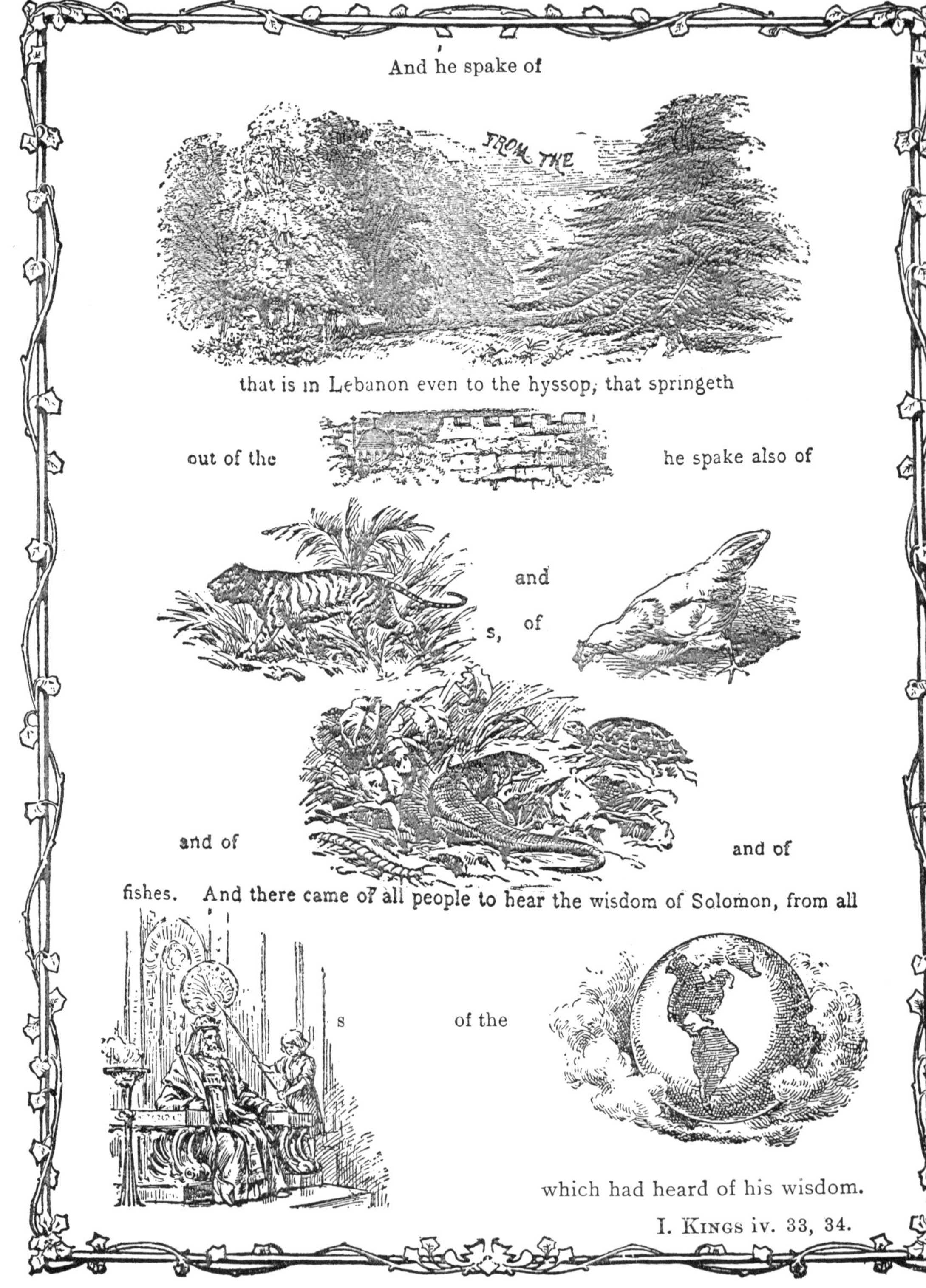
And he spake of
FROM THE
that is in Lebanon even to the hyssop, that springeth
out of the
he spake also of
and
s, of
and of
and of
fishes. And there came of all people to hear the wisdom of Solomon, from all
s
of the
which had heard of his wisdom.
I. Kings iv. 33, 34.

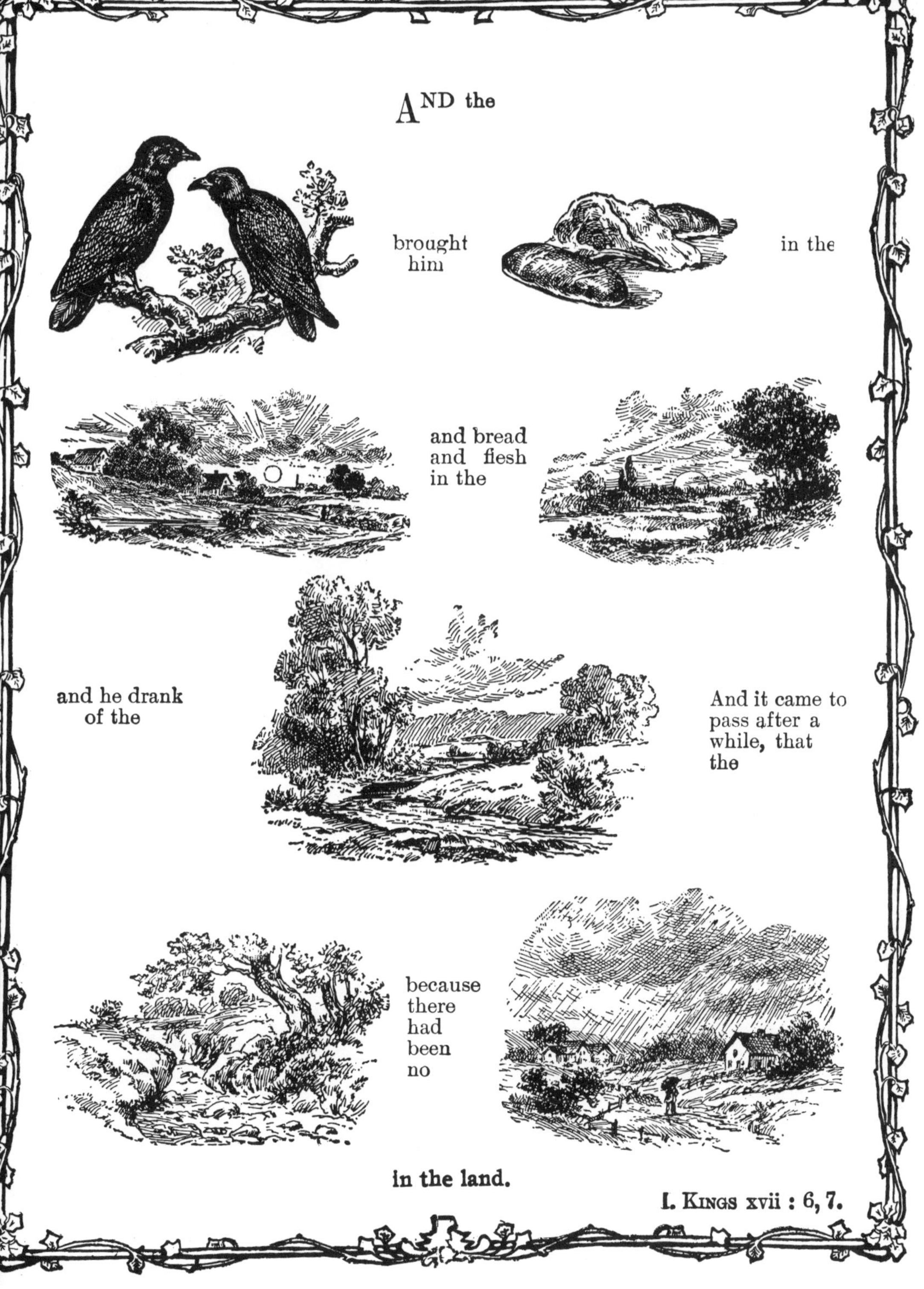

I. Kings xvii : 6, 7.

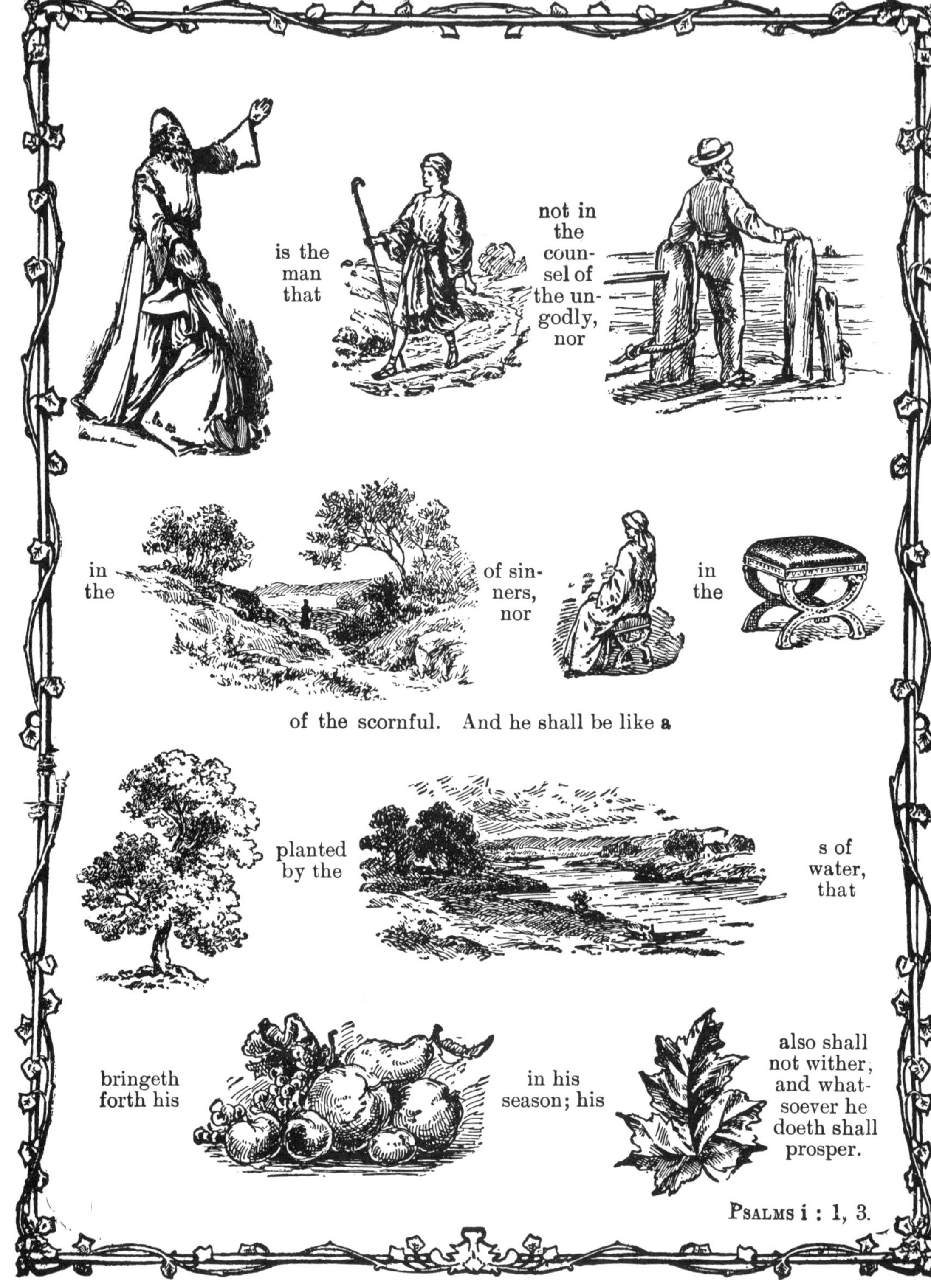
is the man that
not in the counsel of the ungodly, nor
in the
of sinners, nor
in the
of the scornful. And he shall be like a
planted by the
s of water, that
bringeth forth his
in his season; his
also shall not wither, and whatsoever he doeth shall prosper.
Psalms i : 1, 3.

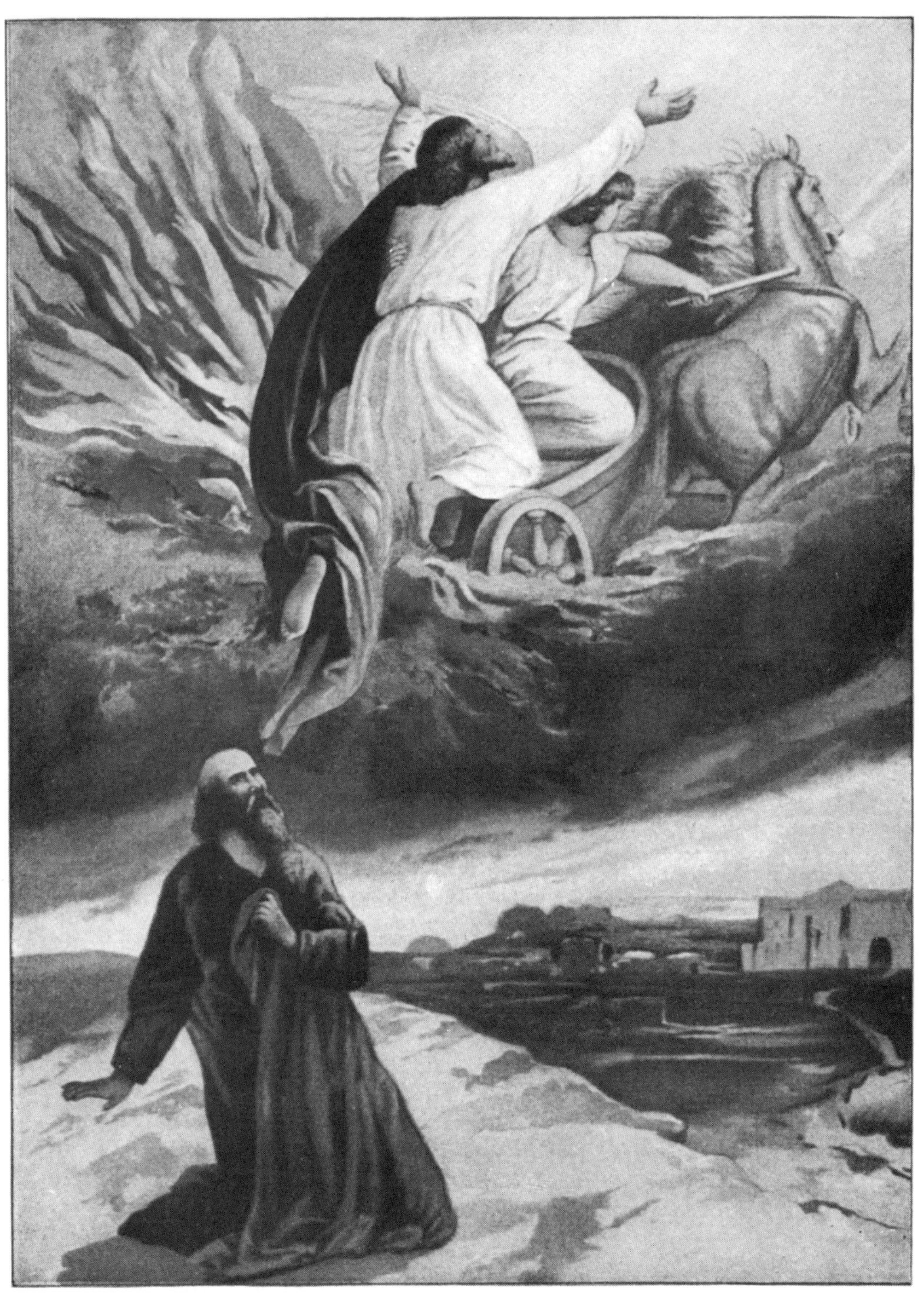

THE TRANSLATION OF ELIAS.

THE TRANSLATION OF ELIAS

Among the stories you may read about the prophets in general, and about Elias in particular. The life of Elias is very interesting. This picture shows how he was taken up into heaven.

God made known to Elias that his labors were coming to an end and that he should be soon removed from this world. The prophet was then at Galgal, where he had founded a school for young prophets whom he taught. After instructing them for the last time, he set out for Bethel, where he had founded another guild of aspirants to the prophetic order. Eliseus, his companion and disciple whom he had requested to stay at Galgal, accompanied him. The young men of the guild at Bethel were curious to find out from Eliseus if it was really so that their master was going to be taken from them. He told them it was so, but he asked them not to speak of the matter.

From there Elias started to visit his school in Jericho; but before leaving he urged Eliseus to remain at Bethel. Eliseus told him he would never separate from him, but would go anywhere he went. The guild at Jericho received them with marks of great joy and veneration. After Elias had confirmed the young candidates in their faith in Jehovah, he wended his way toward the Jordan. Fifty of the young men watched him and Eliseus from a hill top outside the city. They saw them reach the banks of the Jordan and wondered how they would get over. Elias rolled his mantle around his forearm, touched the waters with the hem of it, and the river opened up and made a dry passage for the two. So they crossed over into the hills of Moab. As they were walking and talking, Elias stopped Eliseus and asked him: "What do you want me to leave you when I am taken away from you?" "I want you to leave me," answered Eliseus, "a share in your prophetic spirit double that of the other sons of the prophets." "Your request shall be granted you," said Elias, "if you see me when I am taken up from you."

They were still talking the matter over when a fiery chariot drawn by two horses of fire drove in between them and Elias was rapt up in a whirlwind into the clouds. "My father, my father!" shouted Eliseus; "you the chariot of Israel and the driver thereof!" But Elias was gone. His disciple, bereft, wept and rent his garments. At length he arose and started toward the Jordan. He threw over his arm the mantle which Elias had let fall. When he reached the river he touched the waters with the mantle, but nothing happened. Then he shouted out, in half doubt and half complaint: "Where now is the God of Elias?" and he whacked the waters with the mantle. This time the river opened up, and he passed over.

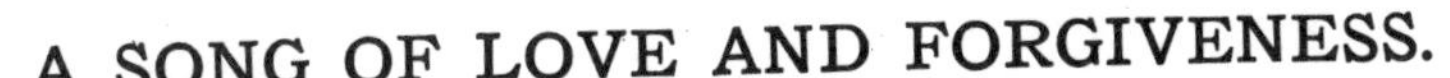

A SONG OF LOVE AND FORGIVENESS.

THIS is a beautiful story of the forgiveness that comes down from Heaven. The story is from the life of David, and at the end of the life of Saul, whom Samuel had anointed king of Israel.

Saul loved himself so much that it made him jealous of others. He was king of Israel and the whole nation looked up to him as their great and wise ruler. He was tall and looked like a king, and he loved to have the people praise him, but he could not do all the great deeds he wanted to do, and the Philistines who came up from the south and spread themselves over his kingdom, made him much trouble.

They brought a giant, Goliath, with them and when he wanted to fight with some Israelite, no man could be found who dared meet him until young David came and said he would go and kill the giant "in the name of the Lord." He did this good deed with a pebble from the brook. David was only a youth and he wore no armor, while Goliath wore a heavy armor and carried great weapons. But God helped David, and the little pebble sped through the air and sank into the giant's forehead and he fell upon his face to the earth.

Then there was a great shout over David. He had won the king's favor and the prize the king had promised, his own daughter for a wife, and also a high place in the kingdom. Now, another shepherd kept the sheep for David's father, and he went to live with Saul. Jonathan, Saul's son, was David's dear friend, but very soon Saul began to be jealous of David. He heard the women sing as David came up from battle with the Philistines;—

"Saul hath slain his thousands;
David his ten thousands."

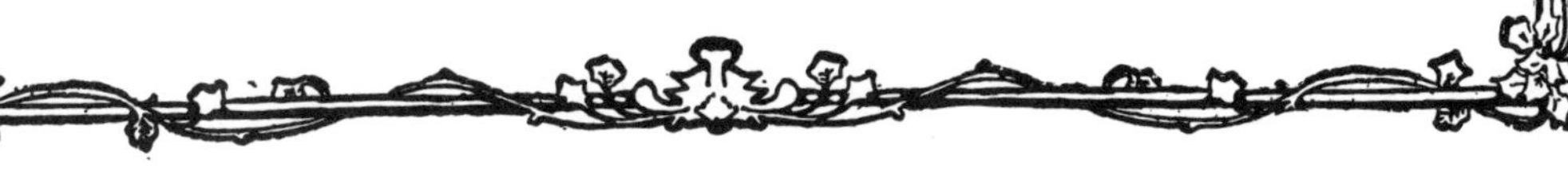

Then Saul was angry and said:

"What more can he have than the kingdom," and Saul eyed David from that day forward.

The next day Saul cast his spear at David twice as he was playing on the harp before him, but God stood by David and saved him from harm, for he was yet to be the king of Israel.

For eight or nine years David had to flee from one cave to another in the wilderness to hide away from Saul's deadly hate and jealousy. Two or three times he found Saul asleep and could have killed him, but his heart was too true and tender.

"Some bade me kill thee, but mine eye spared thee." And he said, "I will not put forth my hand against my lord, for he is the Lord's anointed." And then David said, "I have not sinned against thee, though thou huntest my life to take it."

Then Saul wept and promised to be kind to David for he saw that God was with him, but he did not keep his promise, because the evil spirit was in him.

At last, after several battles, Saul and his three sons lay dead on the battlefield on Mount Gilboa. David was then chasing the enemy who had burned his little camp in the south, and carried away the women and children, but when he came back after conquering them, a man came bringing Saul's crown and bracelet to David and told the story of his death. He thought David would be glad, but instead he wept and fasted until evening. His friend Jonathan had died with his father, and David's heart was distressed.

It was then that his poet soul broke out into a song that you should all know, for it is the most beautiful song of forgiveness in the world. There is a little of it in the pictures that belong with this story.

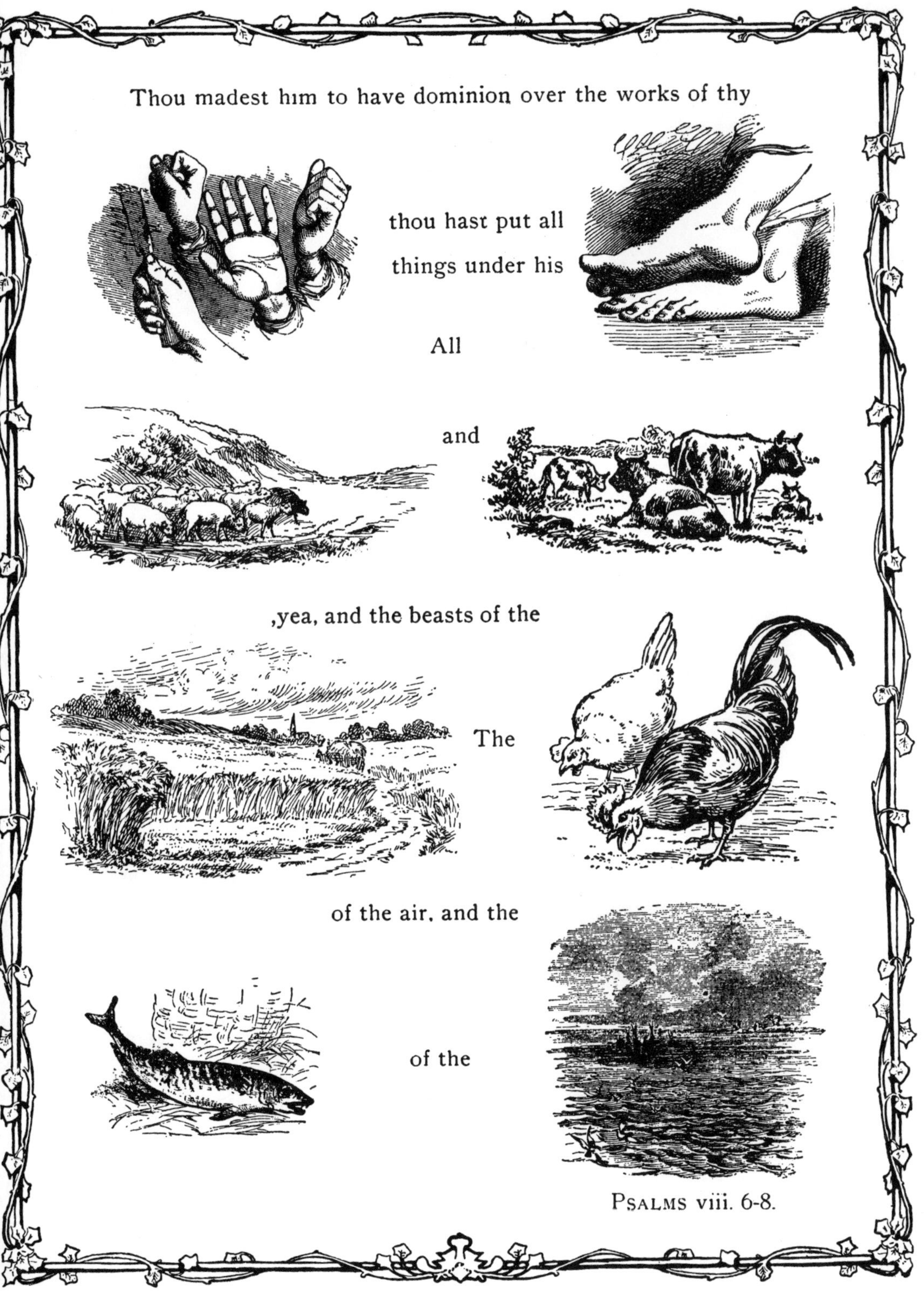

Thou madest him to have dominion over the works of thy

thou hast put all things under his

All

and

,yea, and the beasts of the

The

of the air, and the

of the

PSALMS viii. 6-8.

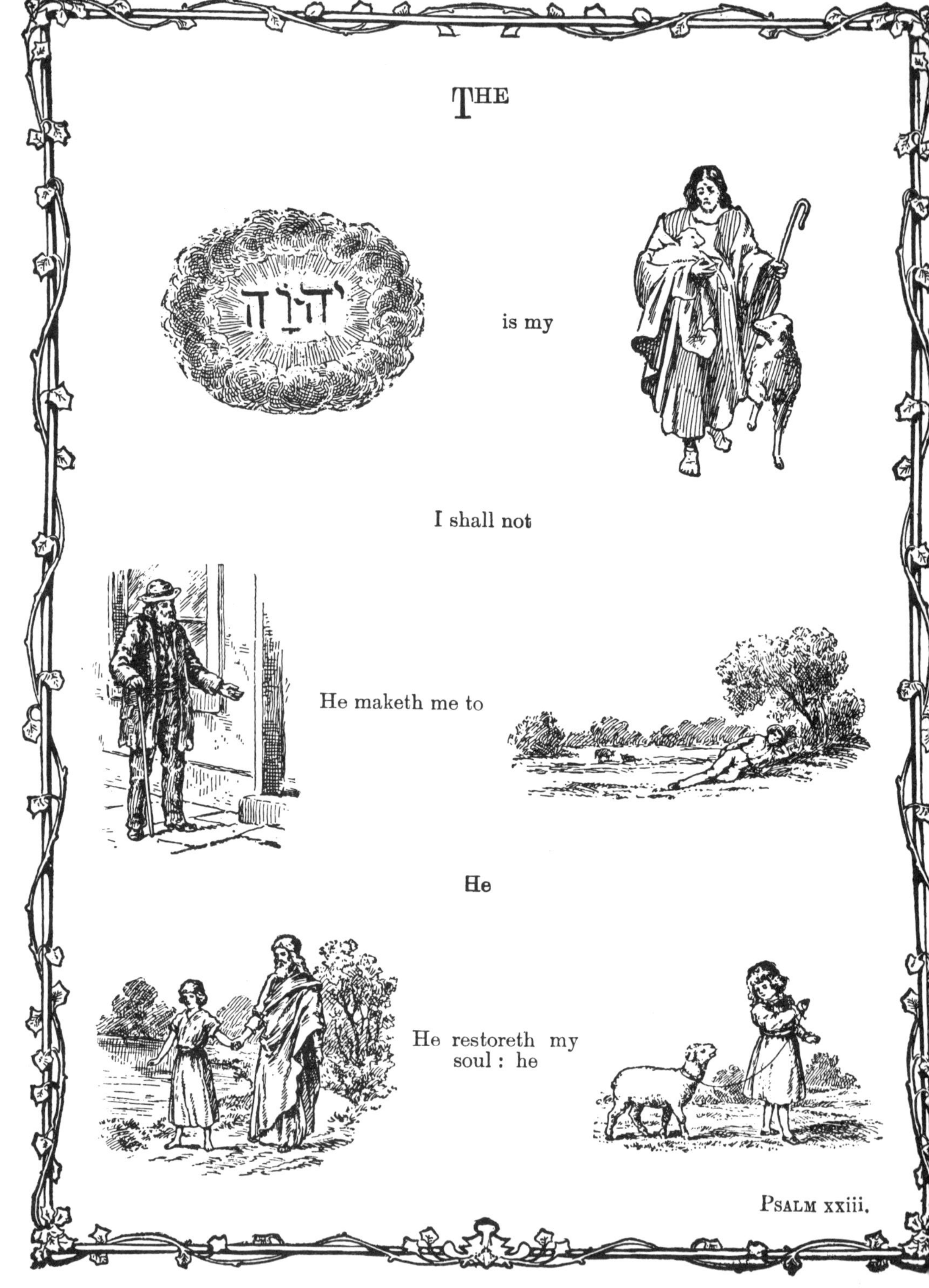
THE
יְהֹוָה
is my
I shall not
He maketh me to
He
He restoreth my soul : he
PSALM xxiii.

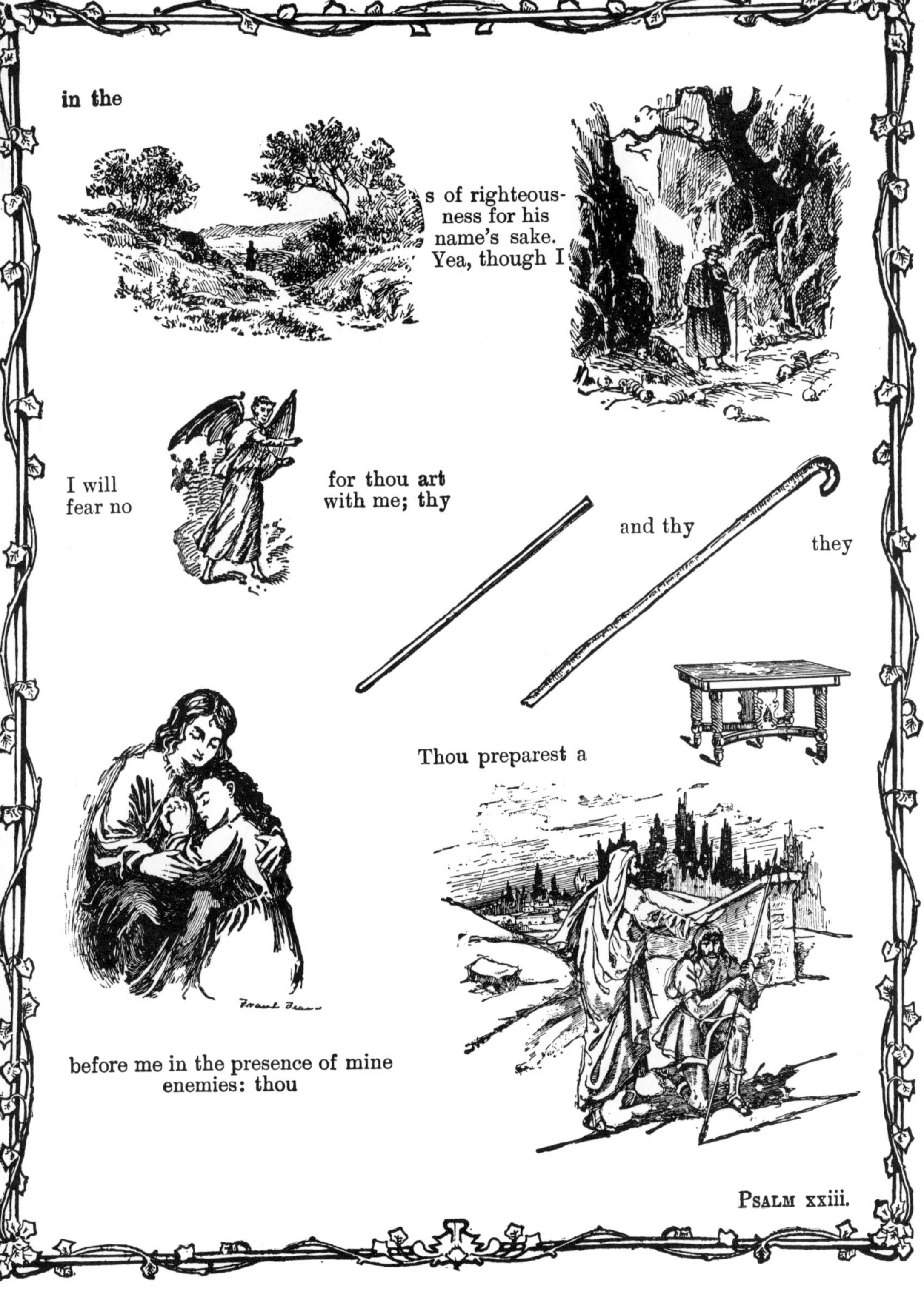

in the

s of righteousness for his name's sake. Yea, though I

I will fear no

for thou art with me; thy

and thy

they

Thou preparest a

before me in the presence of mine enemies: thou

Psalm xxiii.

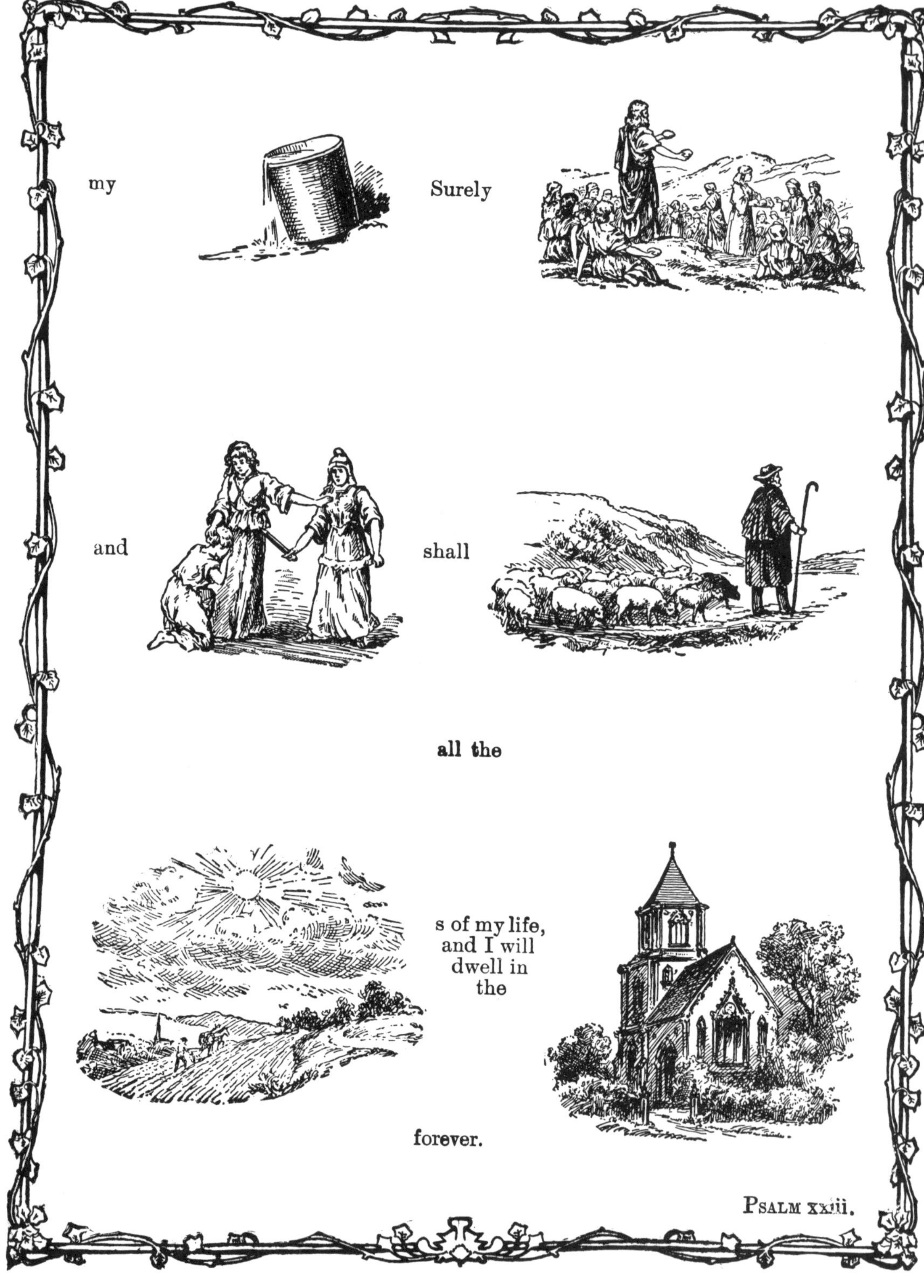
my
Surely
and
shall
all the
s of my life,
and I will
dwell in
the
forever.
Psalm xxiii.

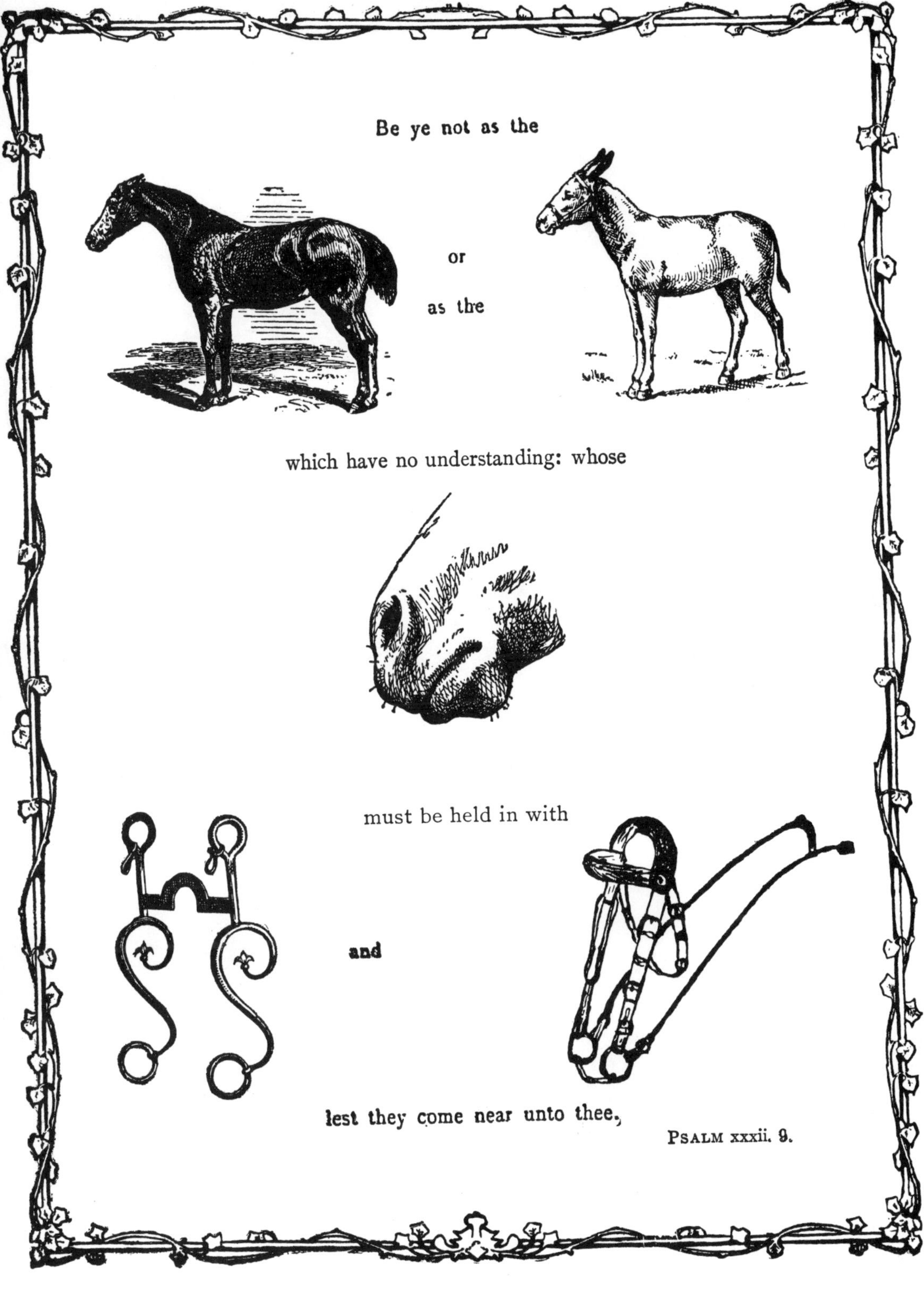
Be ye not as the
or
as the
which have no understanding: whose
must be held in with
and
lest they come near unto thee,
PSALM xxxii. 9.

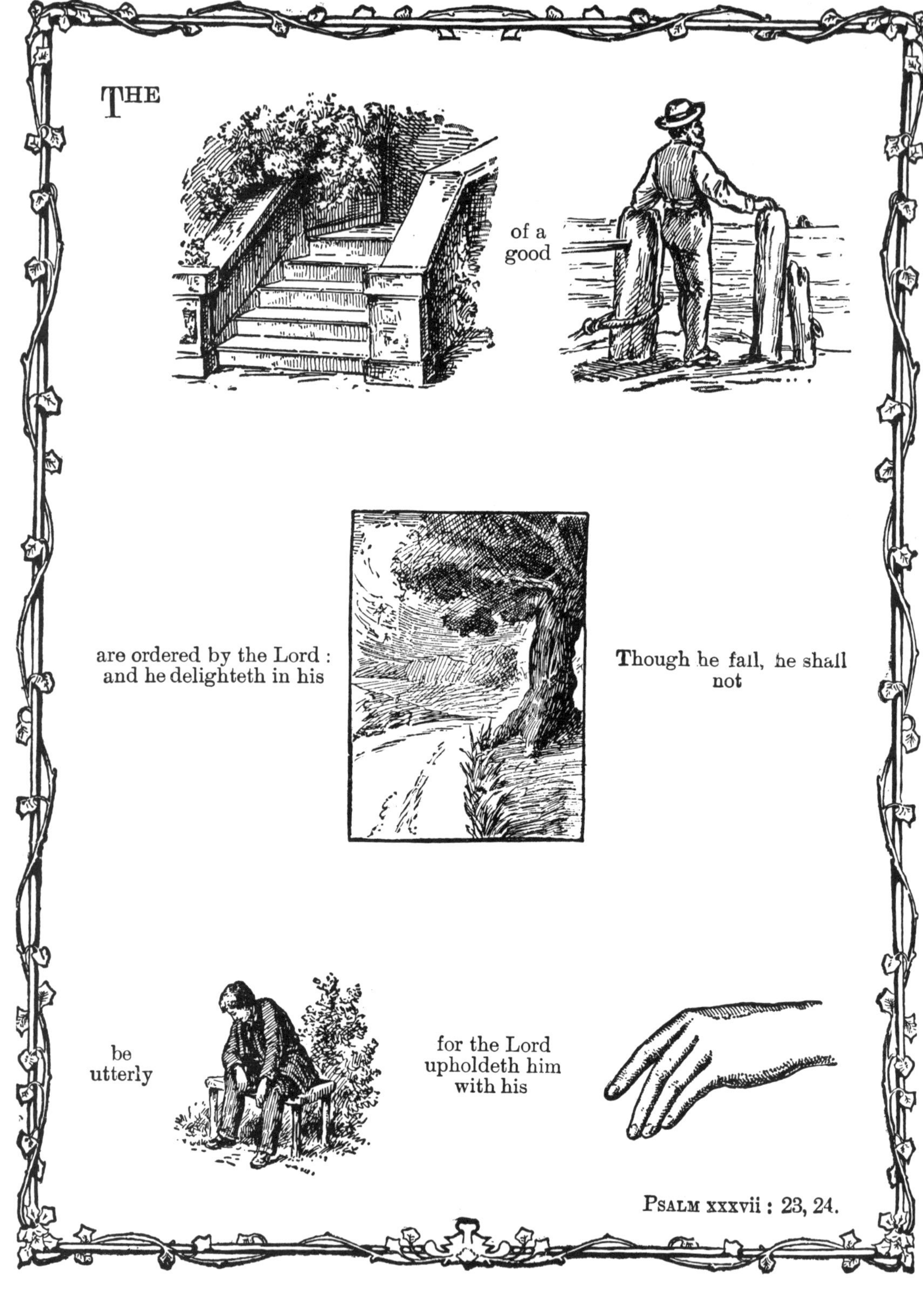

PSALM xxxvii : 23, 24.

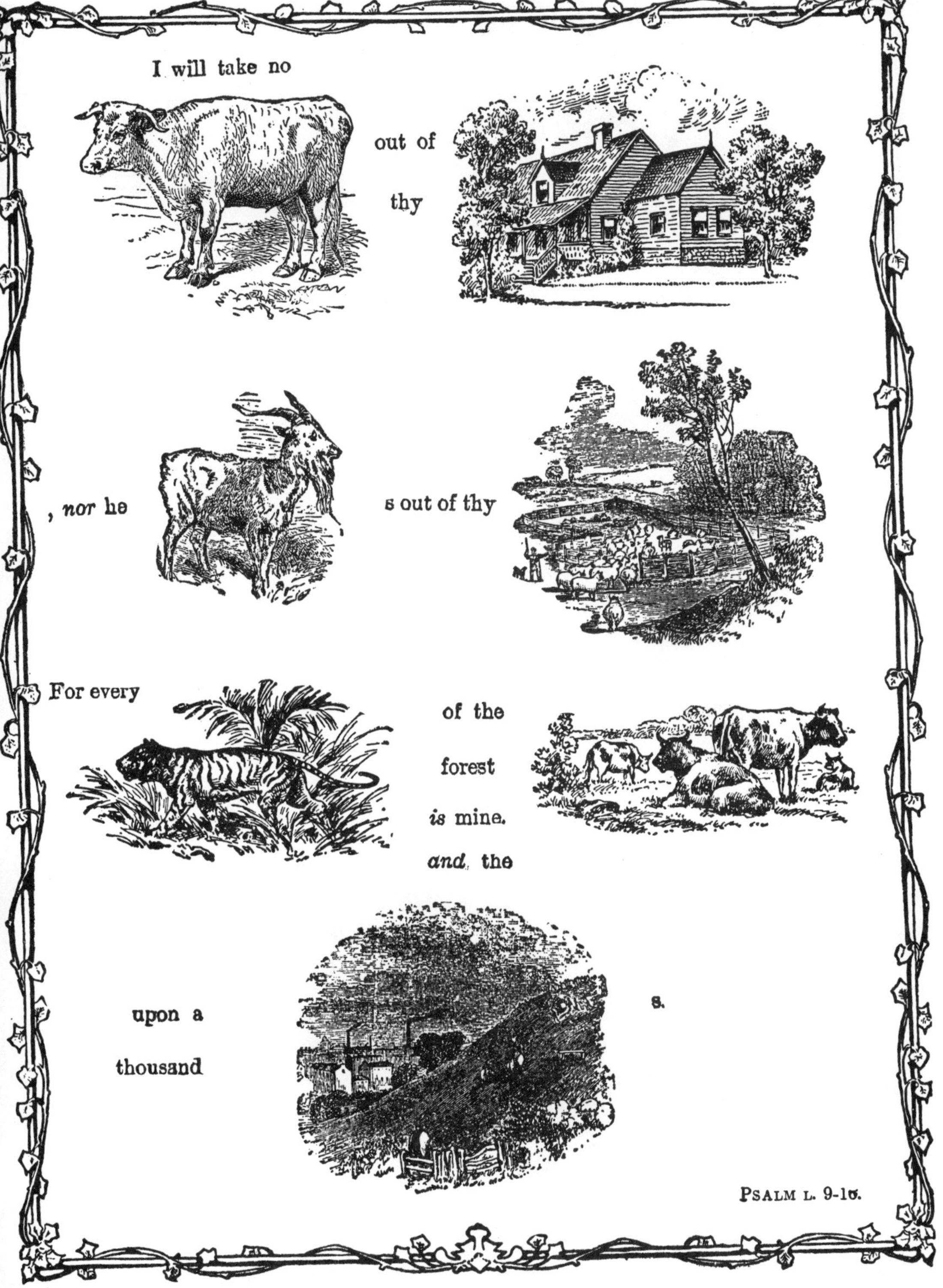
I will take no
out of
thy
, *nor* he
s out of thy
For every
of the
forest
is mine.
and the
upon a
thousand
s.
PSALM L. 9-10.

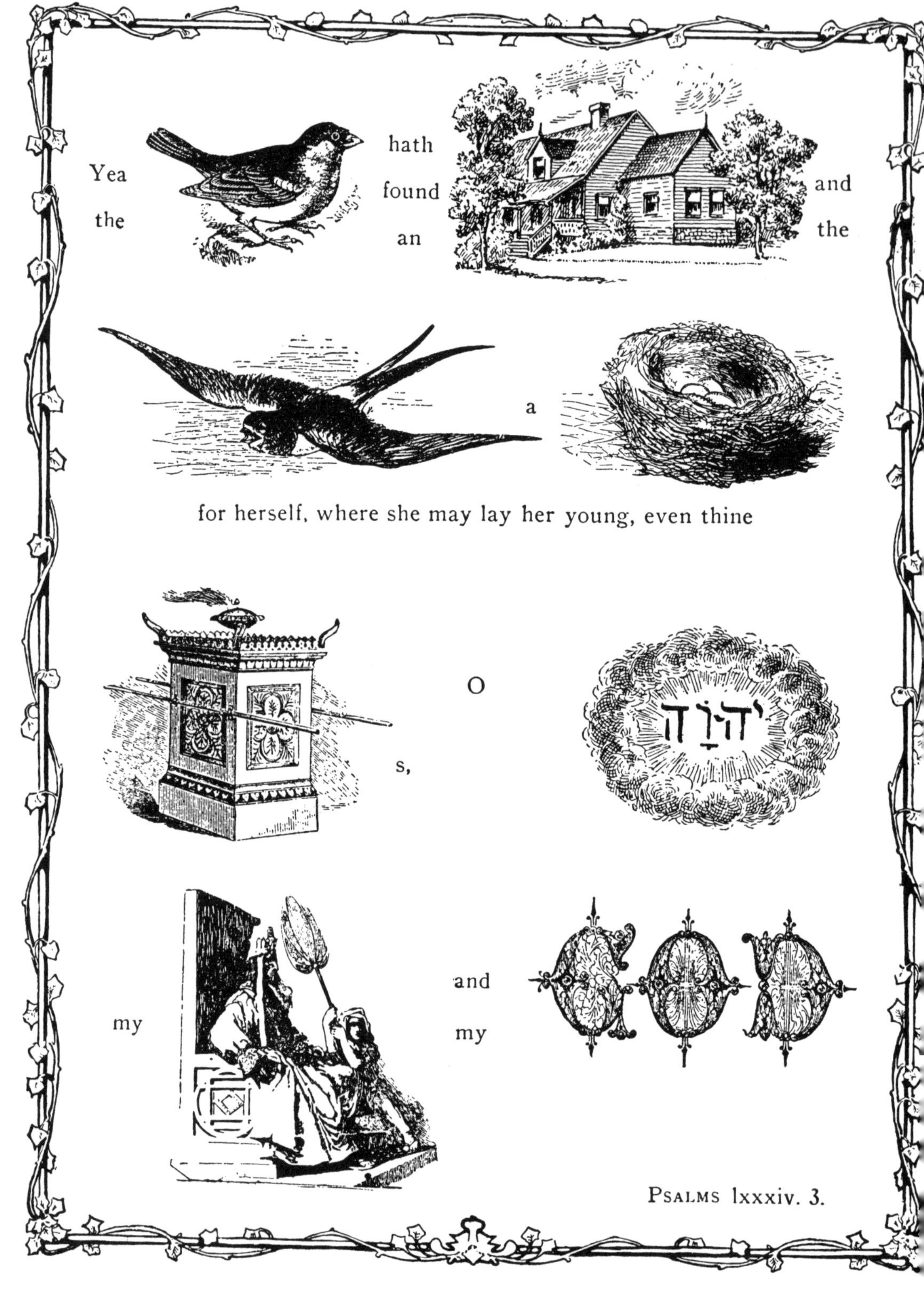

Psalms lxxxiv. 3.

The trees of the Lord are full of sap; the

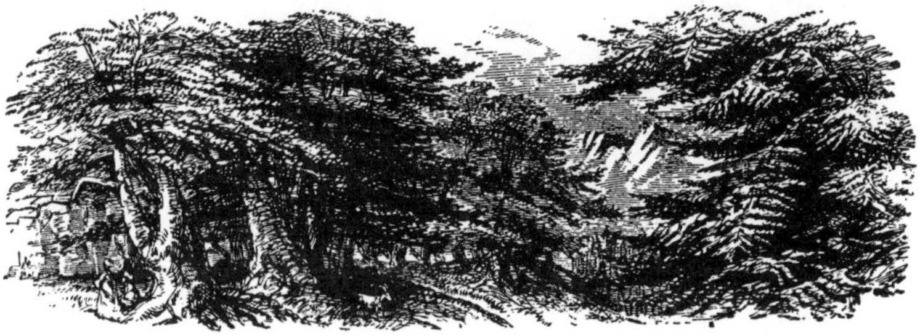

which he hath planted, where the

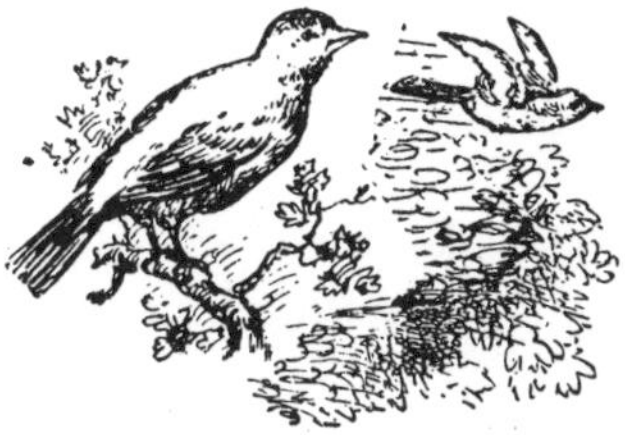

make
their

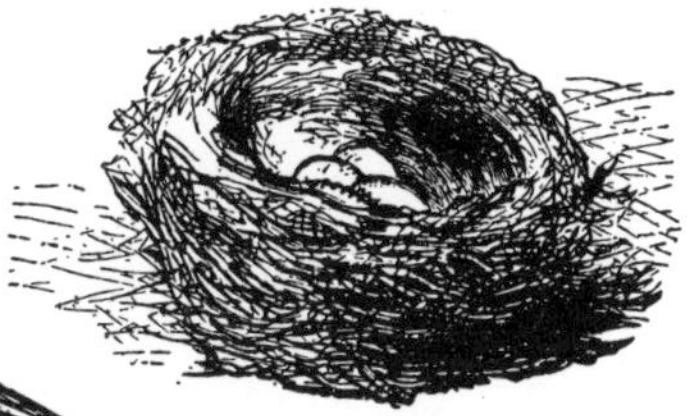

as for the

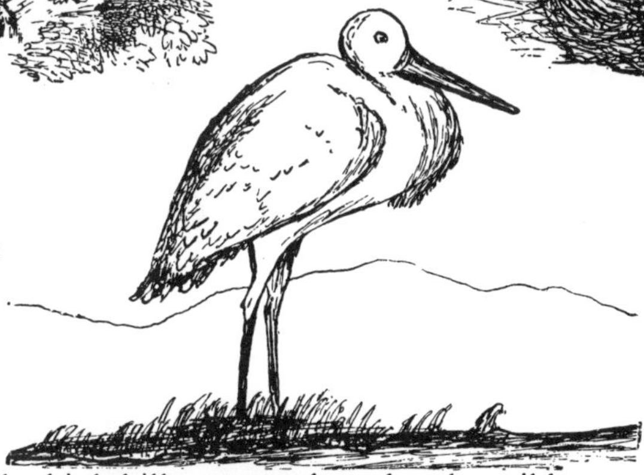

the fir-trees
are her house.

The high hills are a refuge for the wild goats, and the

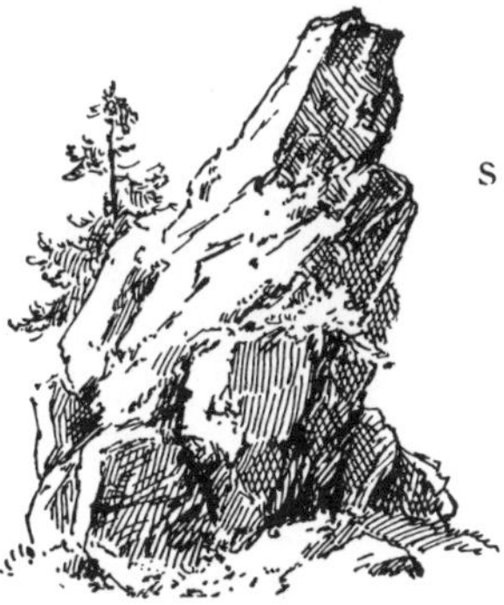

s

for the

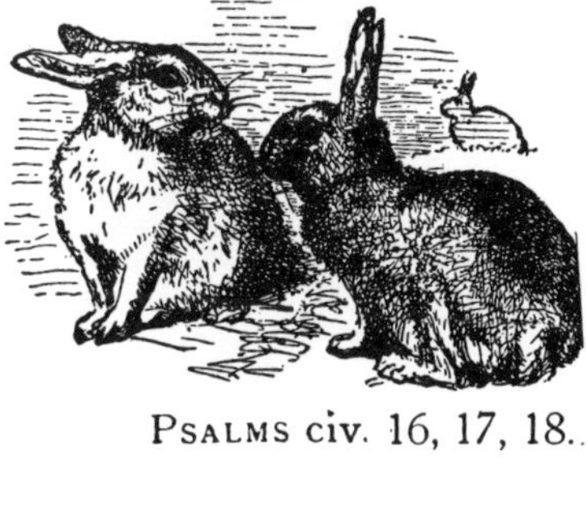

PSALMS civ. 16, 17, 18.

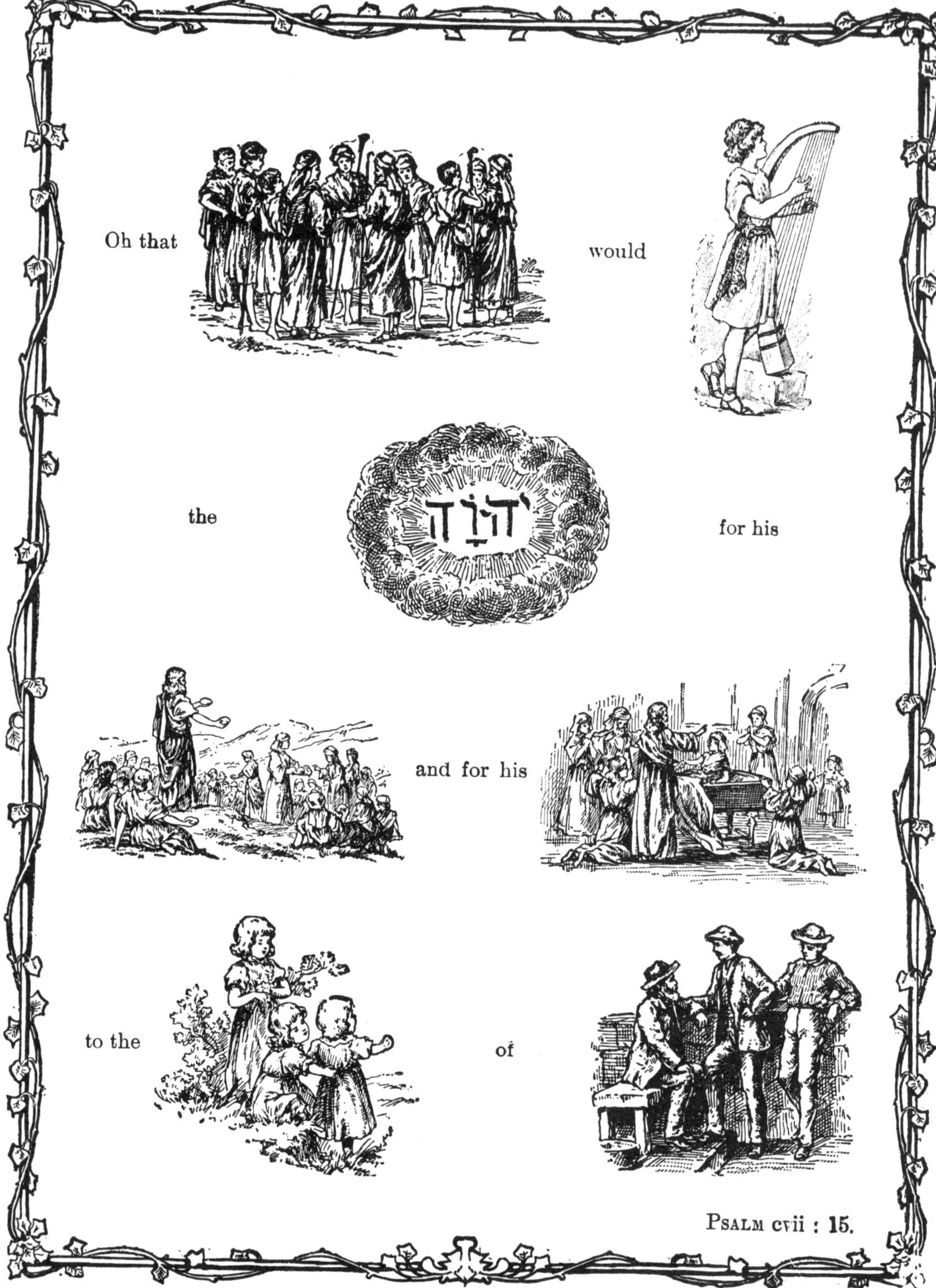

Psalm cvii : 15.

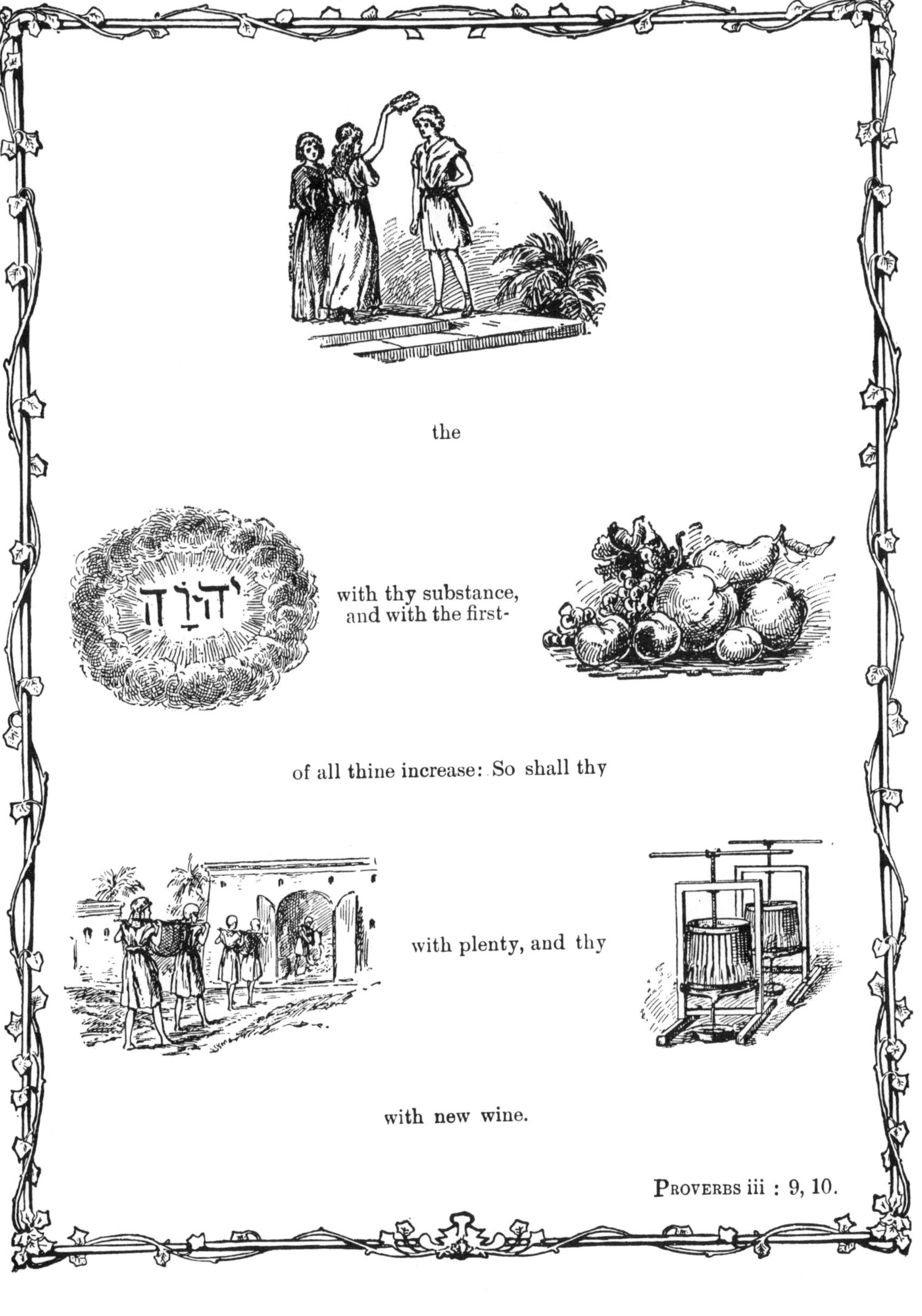

the

with thy substance,
and with the first-

of all thine increase: So shall thy

with plenty, and thy

with new wine.

Proverbs iii : 9, 10.

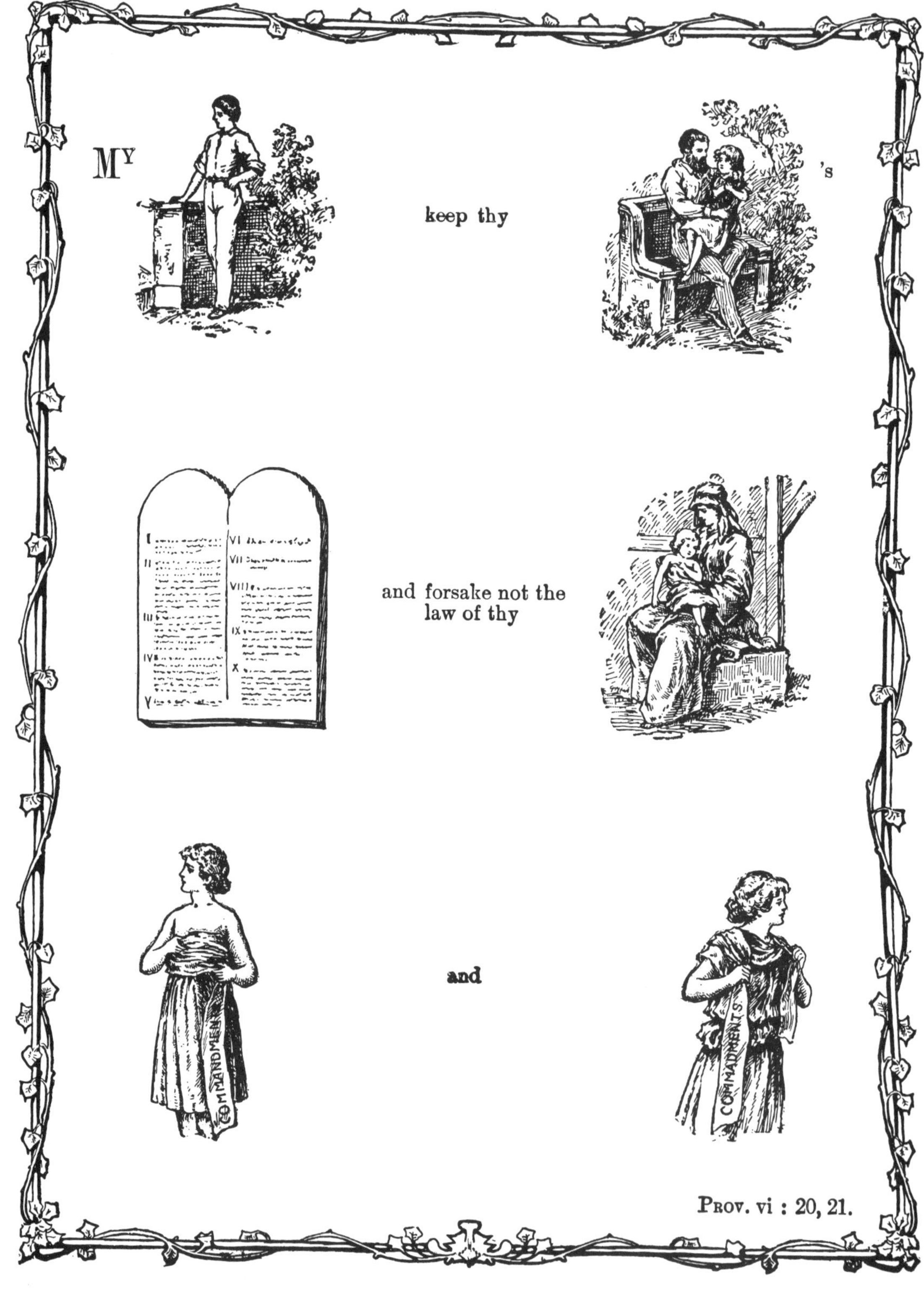
My
keep thy
's
I
II
III
IV
V
VI
VII
VIII
IX
X
and forsake not the
law of thy
and
COMMANDMEN
COMMANDMENTS
Prov. vi : 20, 21.

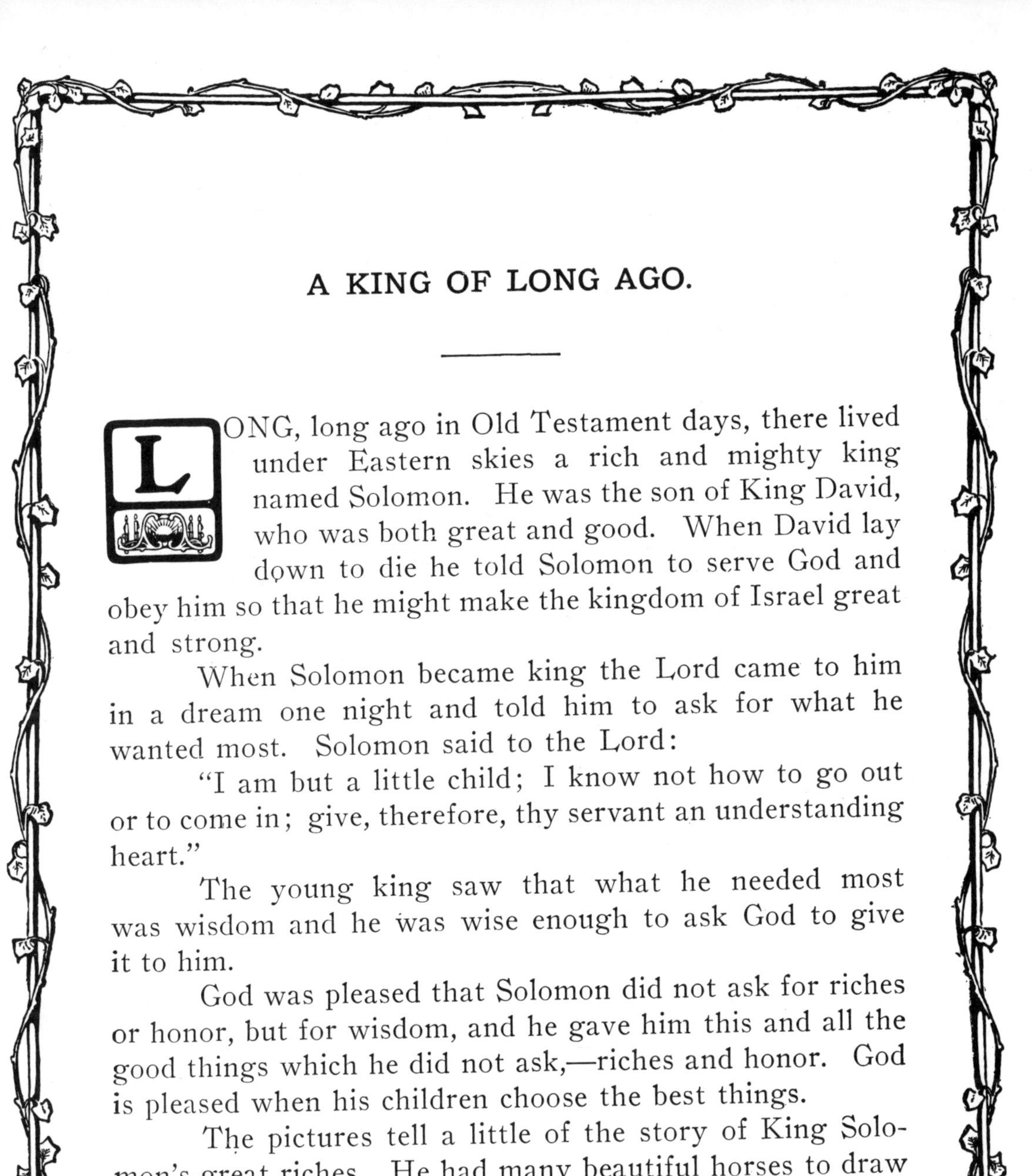

A KING OF LONG AGO.

LONG, long ago in Old Testament days, there lived under Eastern skies a rich and mighty king named Solomon. He was the son of King David, who was both great and good. When David lay down to die he told Solomon to serve God and obey him so that he might make the kingdom of Israel great and strong.

When Solomon became king the Lord came to him in a dream one night and told him to ask for what he wanted most. Solomon said to the Lord:

"I am but a little child; I know not how to go out or to come in; give, therefore, thy servant an understanding heart."

The young king saw that what he needed most was wisdom and he was wise enough to ask God to give it to him.

God was pleased that Solomon did not ask for riches or honor, but for wisdom, and he gave him this and all the good things which he did not ask,—riches and honor. God is pleased when his children choose the best things.

The pictures tell a little of the story of King Solomon's great riches. He had many beautiful horses to draw his chariots, and many other thousands upon which his servants and officers rode. They were not all kept in one place, but were in different cities. In those days horses and chariots were used in war and they were always kept ready for use if the need came. Then also when a great king of the East appeared before his people, it had to be with great show and splendor so as to let the people know that he was very high and powerful.

Do you wonder how food was found for all these thousands of horses? Solomon had officers whose business it was to provide food for the king and for all who came to his table. There were twelve of these officers and each one had his work to do one month in the year. They also had to buy food for the horses—barley and straw—and to see that these things were taken to the cities where the horses were kept. Barley was used in the East instead of oats, which do not grow in that country.

It was not riches alone that God gave to Solomon, but wisdom greater than that of any man in the East. It was wisdom from God and so it was good. Some day when you are older you will read the Proverbs of Solomon, and you will see how wise were his thoughts and his words. But remember that all this wisdom came from God and that it was given to Solomon because he asked for it.

There was something else that Solomon asked of God and that was:

"Largeness of heart, even as the sand that is on the seashore"—and God gave him this also.

A heart that is kind, that loves to be good, and that does not think evil of others, this is a large heart.

King Solomon made many beautiful songs. One of these is in the Bible and it is called the Song of Solomon. It is said that he spoke three thousand Proverbs, or wise sayings, and it was God who gave him all his wisdom.

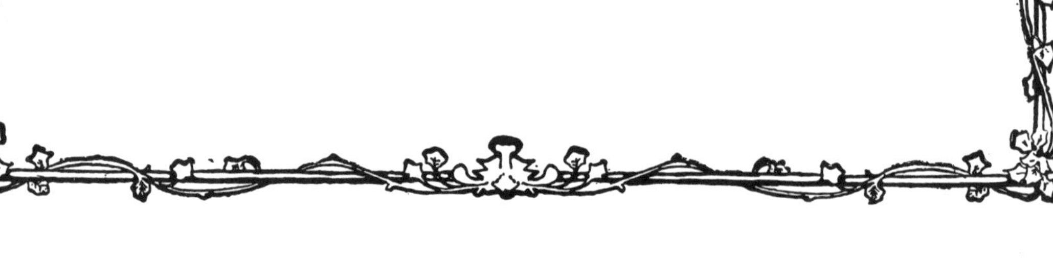

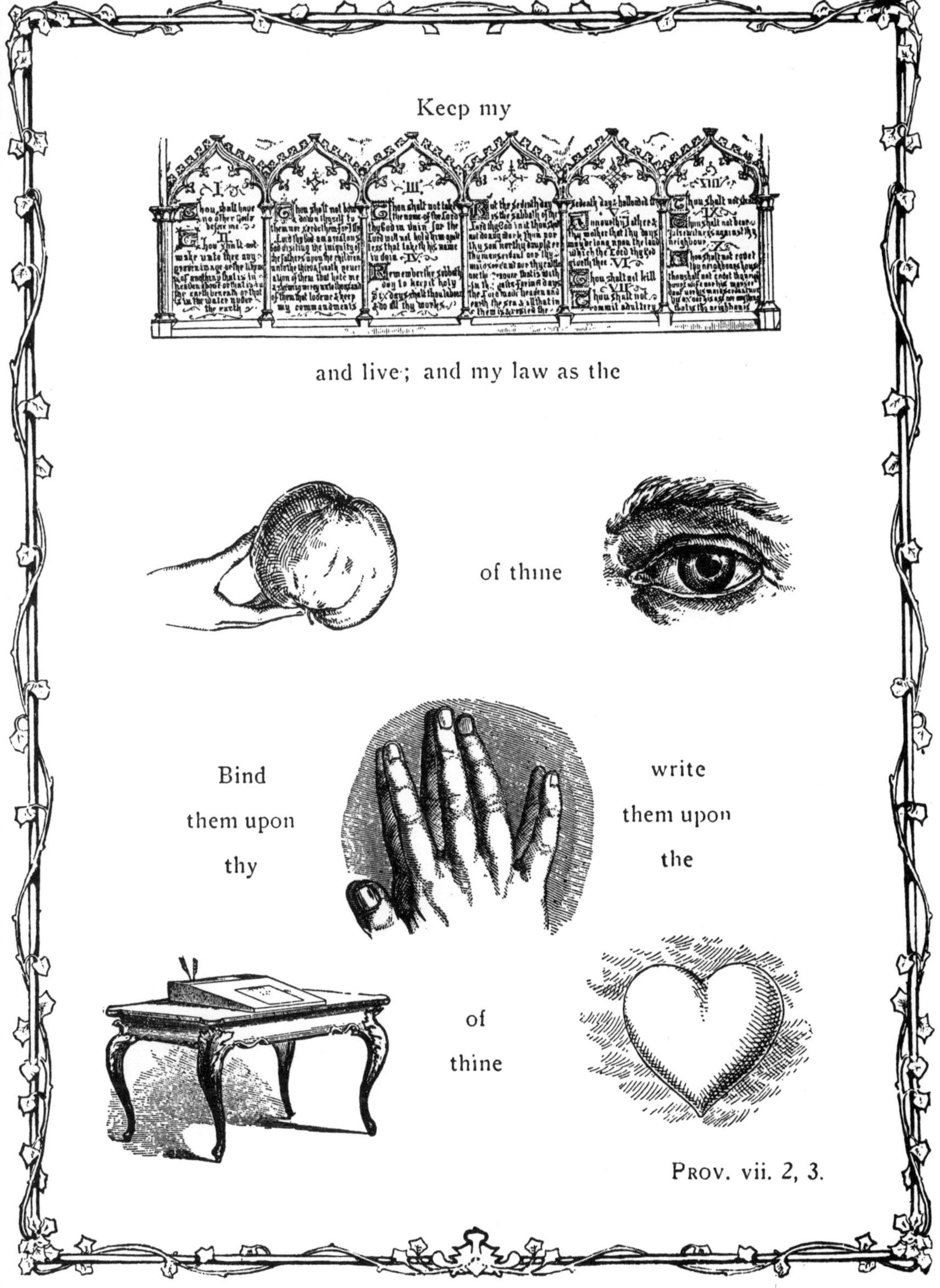
Keep my
and live; and my law as the
of thine
Bind
them upon
thy
write
them upon
the
of
thine
Prov. vii. 2, 3.

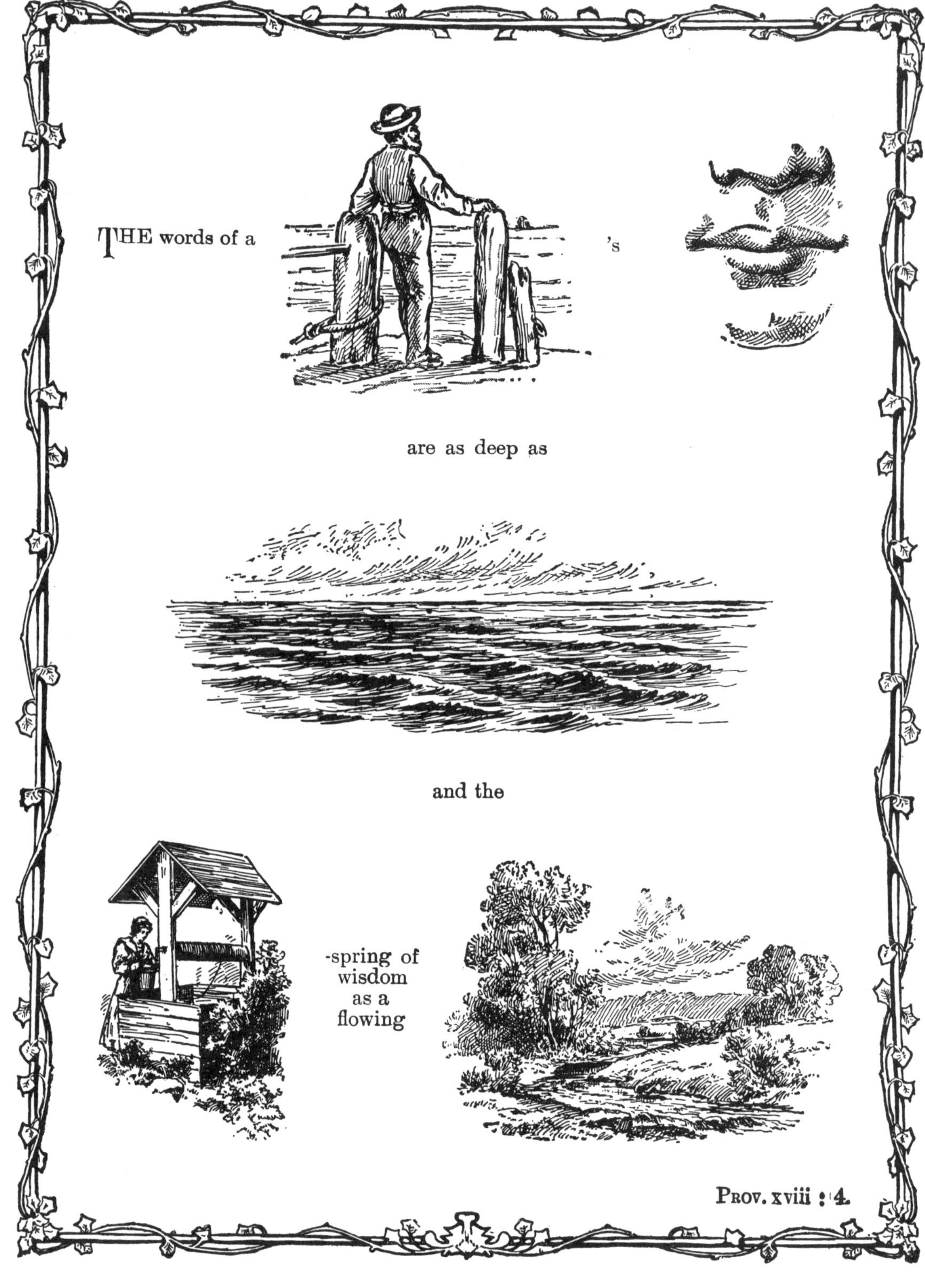
THE words of a
's
are as deep as
and the
-spring of
wisdom
as a
flowing
Prov. xviii : 4.

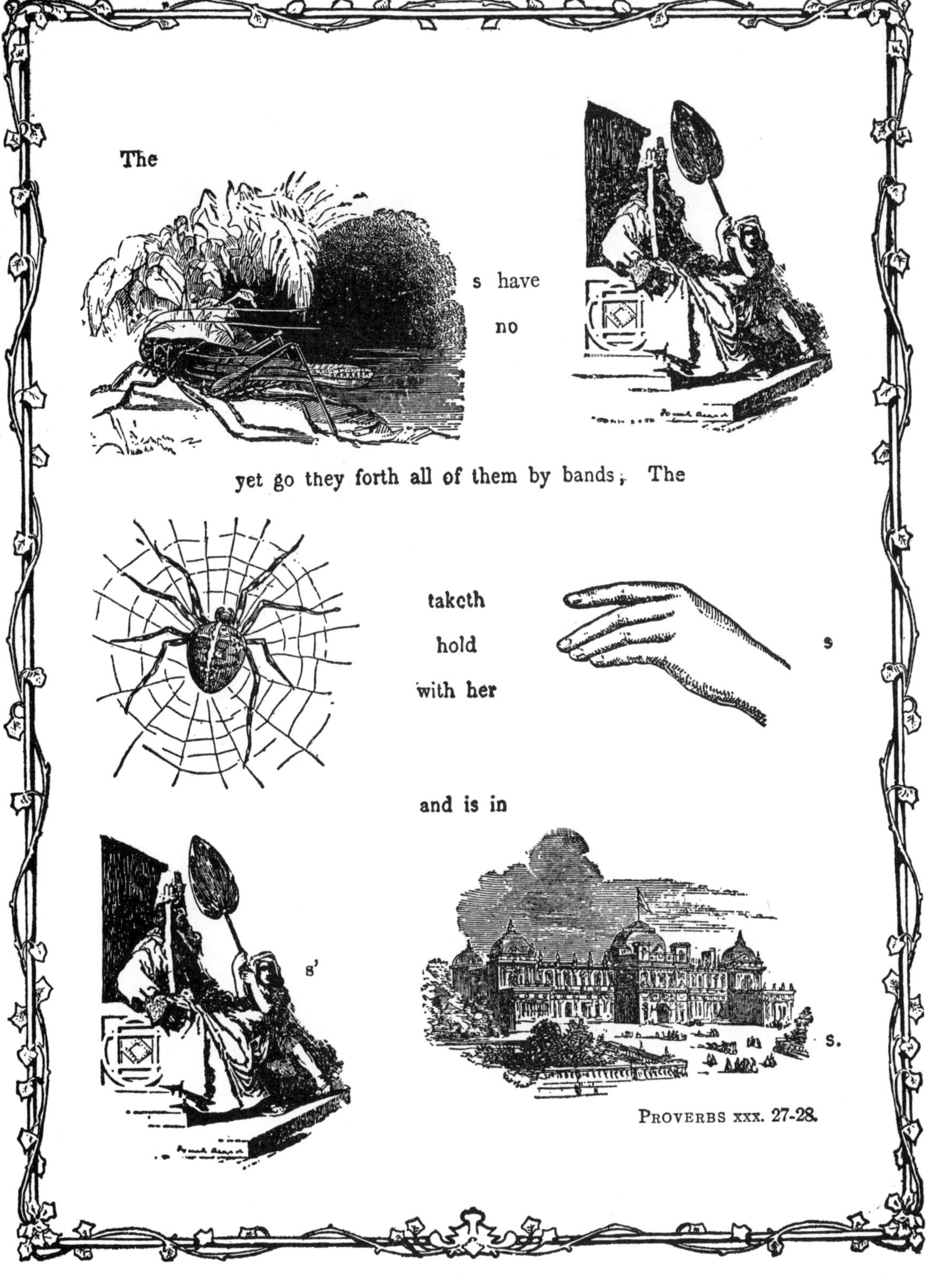

Proverbs xxx. 27-28.

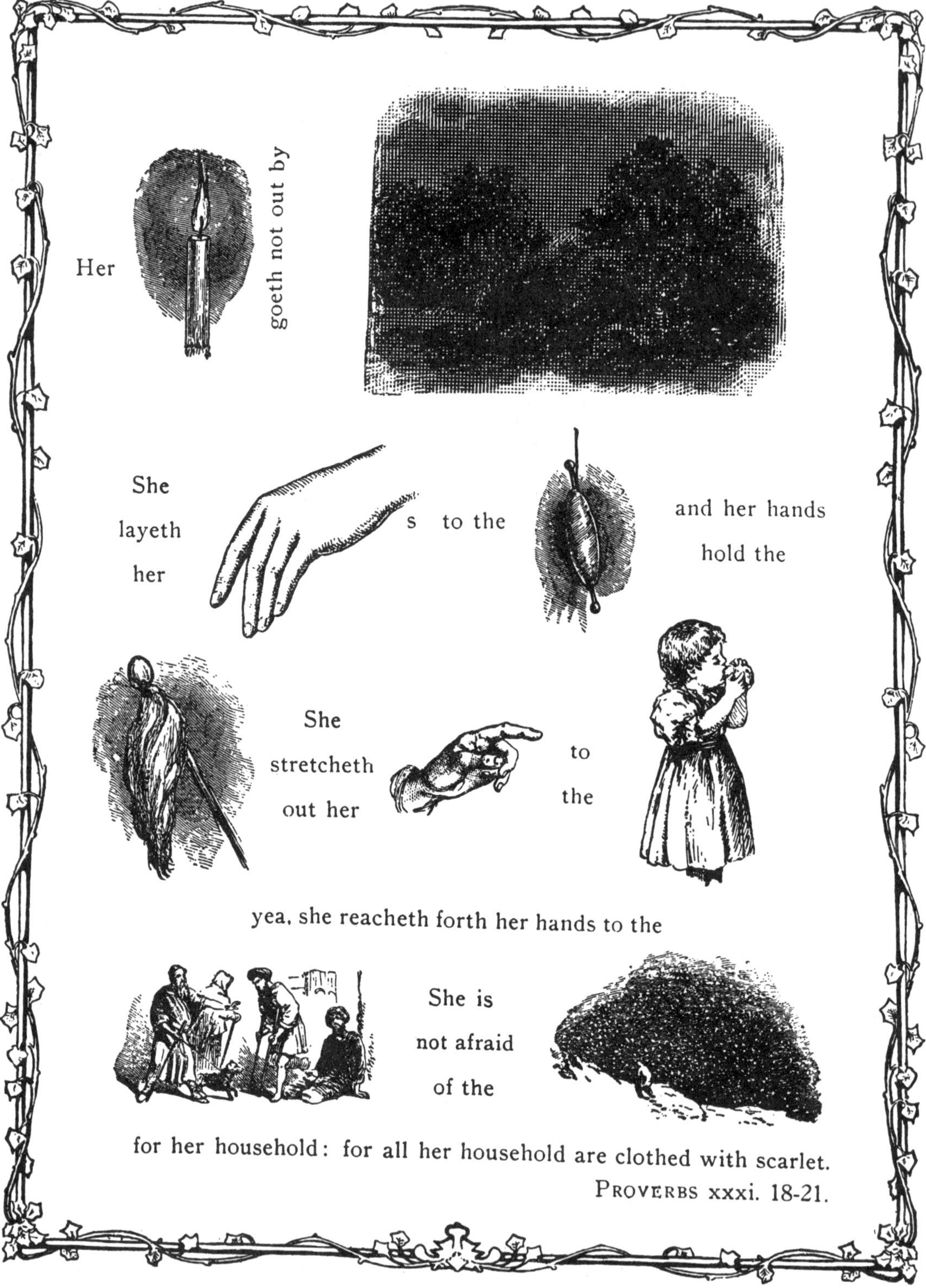
Her
goeth not out by
She
layeth
her
s to the
and her hands
hold the
She
stretcheth
out her
to
the
yea, she reacheth forth her hands to the
She is
not afraid
of the
for her household: for all her household are clothed with scarlet.
PROVERBS xxxi. 18-21.

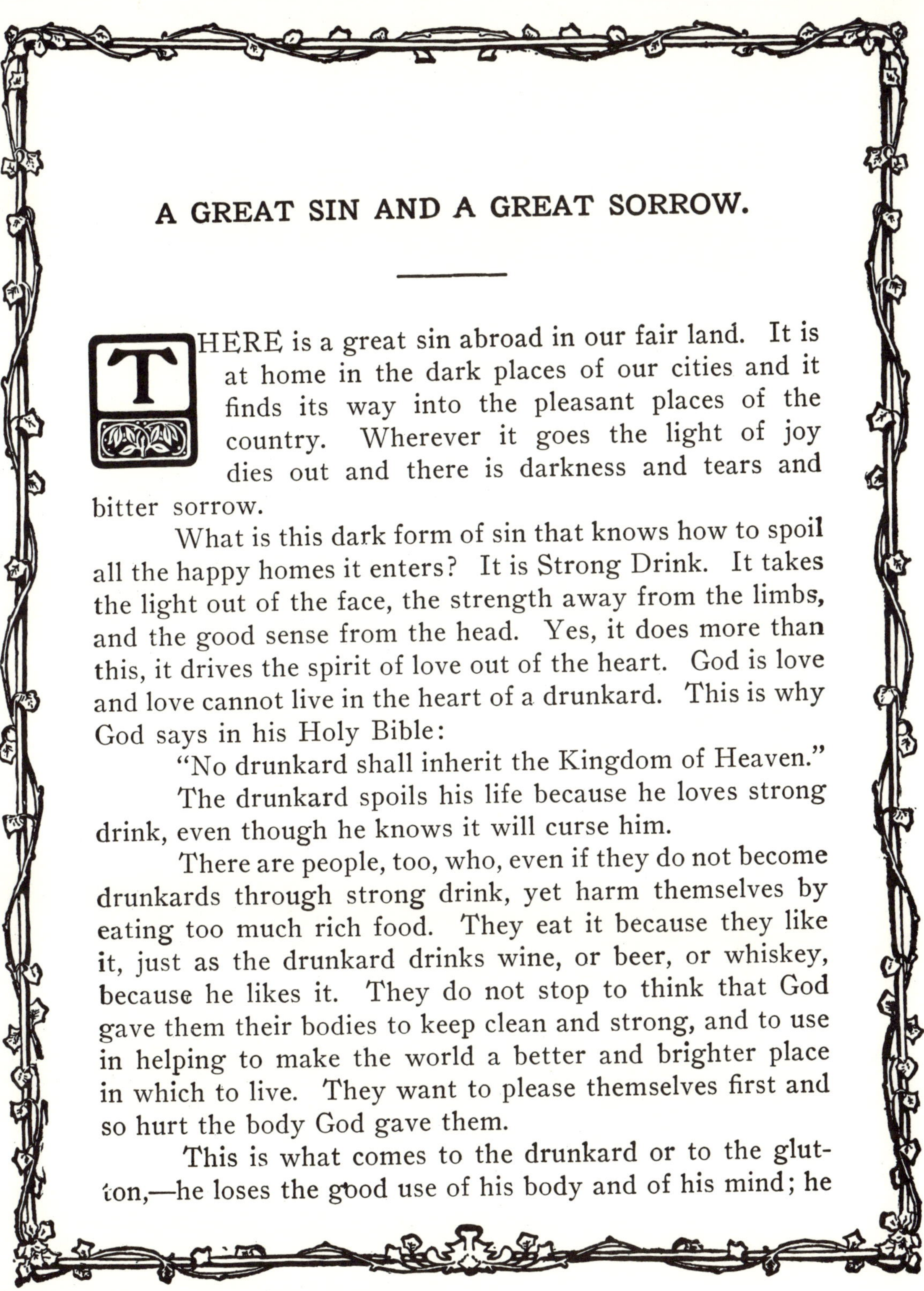

A GREAT SIN AND A GREAT SORROW.

THERE is a great sin abroad in our fair land. It is at home in the dark places of our cities and it finds its way into the pleasant places of the country. Wherever it goes the light of joy dies out and there is darkness and tears and bitter sorrow.

What is this dark form of sin that knows how to spoil all the happy homes it enters? It is Strong Drink. It takes the light out of the face, the strength away from the limbs, and the good sense from the head. Yes, it does more than this, it drives the spirit of love out of the heart. God is love and love cannot live in the heart of a drunkard. This is why God says in his Holy Bible:

"No drunkard shall inherit the Kingdom of Heaven."

The drunkard spoils his life because he loves strong drink, even though he knows it will curse him.

There are people, too, who, even if they do not become drunkards through strong drink, yet harm themselves by eating too much rich food. They eat it because they like it, just as the drunkard drinks wine, or beer, or whiskey, because he likes it. They do not stop to think that God gave them their bodies to keep clean and strong, and to use in helping to make the world a better and brighter place in which to live. They want to please themselves first and so hurt the body God gave them.

This is what comes to the drunkard or to the glutton,—he loses the good use of his body and of his mind; he loses his good name, his friends, and his money, and so he is very likely to come to want and even to go about begging people to give him food to eat or clothing to wear. God never meant one of his children to spoil himself like this.

There is another way in which some people spoil their lives. They love to have an easy time; they want to sleep late in the morning, and rest in easy chairs by glowing fires. Perhaps they are not drunkards or gluttons, but they are what we call lazy people, who will not do their share of the world's work.

God puts all these people in one class and shows us that they lose their place in the world and come to poverty and are unhappy themselves, while at the same time making others unhappy.

The child who loves his own way best and wants pleasure more than he wants to do right is in danger of becoming like these people. God has given each child something to do to make the world better and brighter. He gives us his Book to show us his way and he shows us pictures of wrong-doers so that we will not follow their example.

The self-love which makes drunkards, gluttons, and lazy people is the great sin which causes so much sorrow in the world. If we love God we will do as he says. If we love self we will do as self says, and this will make sorrow for ourselves and for our friends.

But if we turn away from sin we shall save ourselves and those who love us from the sorrow of seeing us lose the good things God meant us to have and spoil the life he gave us to live. Here is a beautiful promise to God:

"I promise thee, sweet Lord,
That I will never cloud the light
Which shines from thee within my soul
And makes my reason bright."

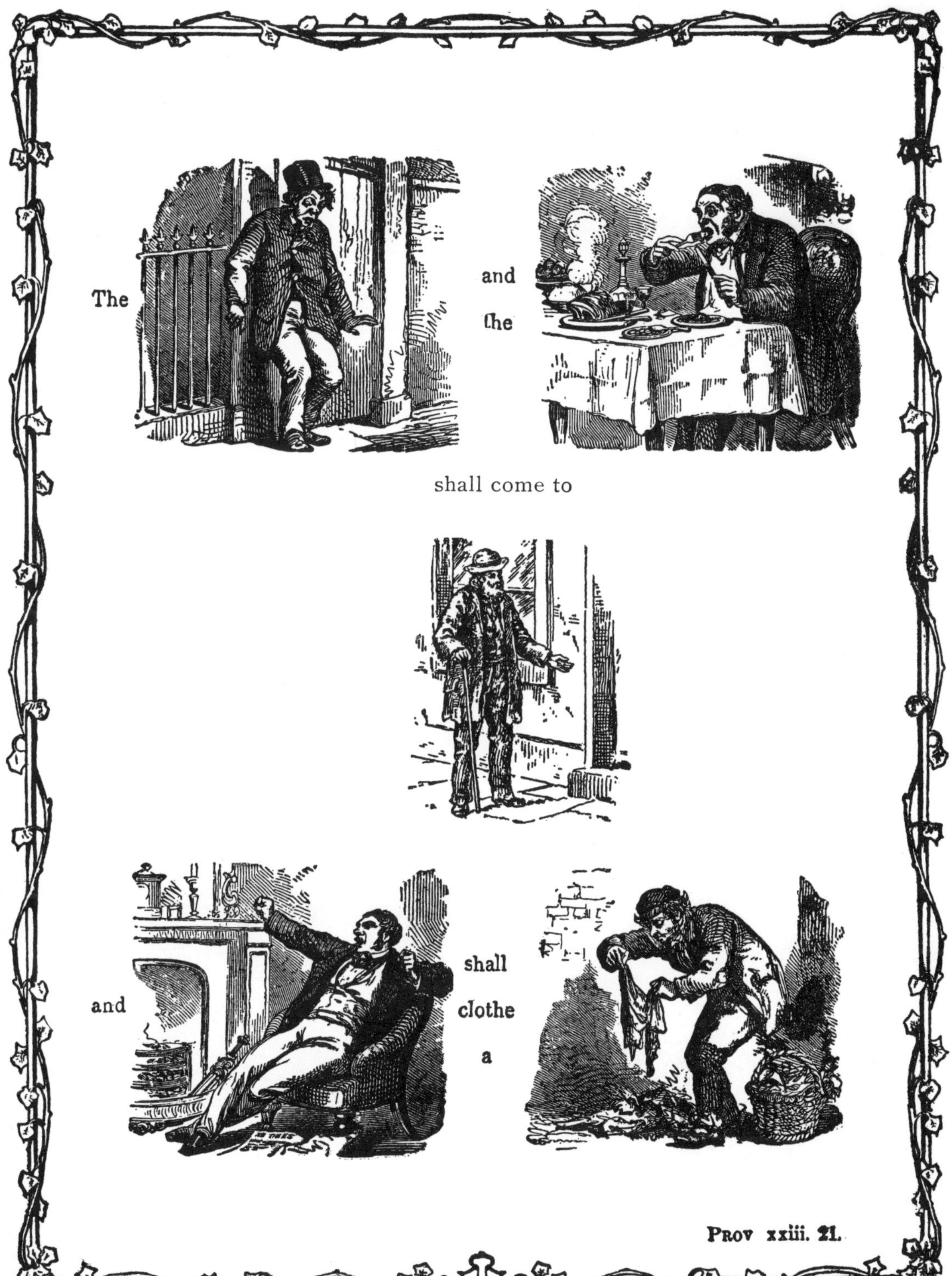
The
and
the
shall come to
and
shall
clothe
a
Prov xxiii. 21.

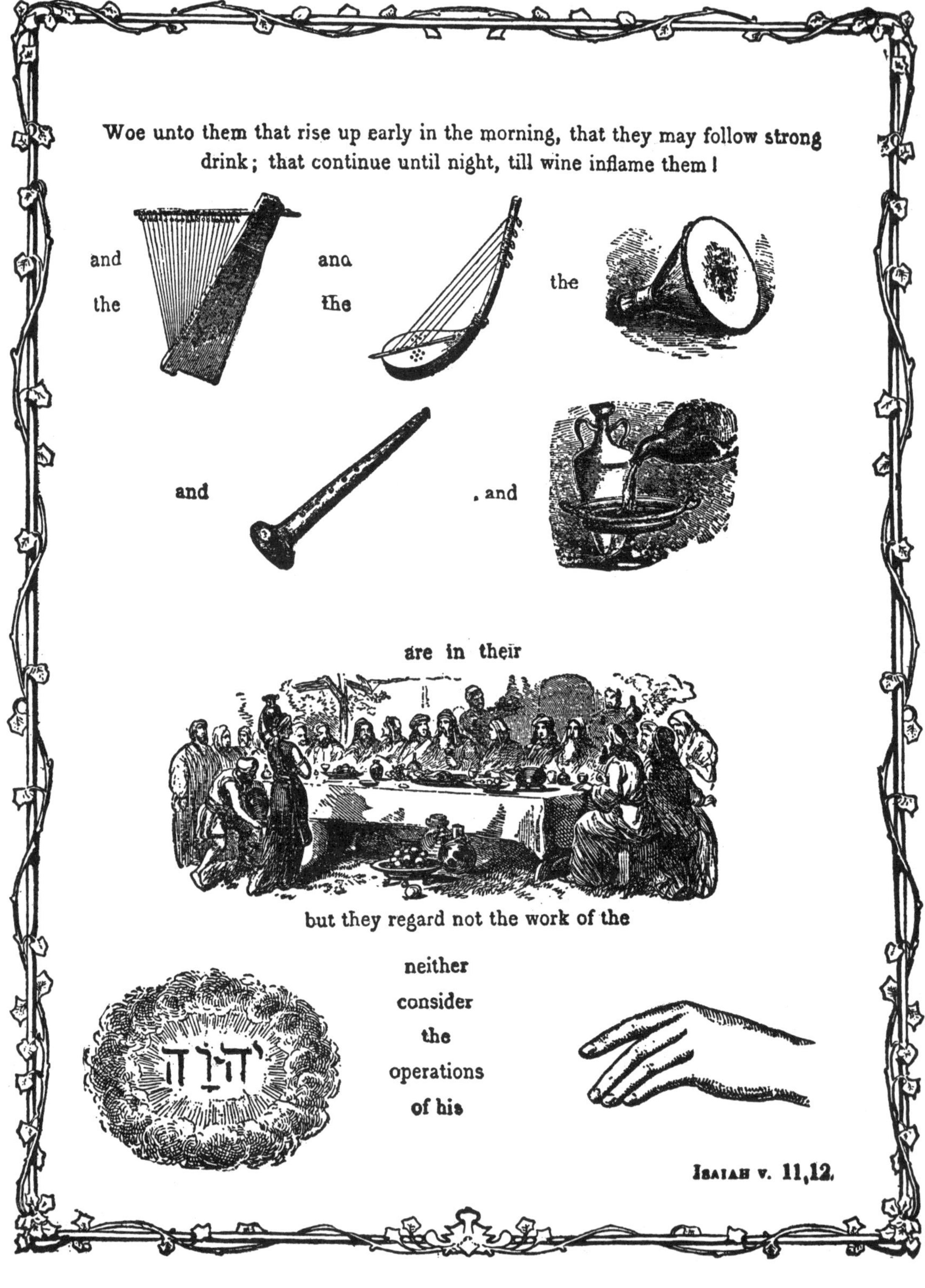
Woe unto them that rise up early in the morning, that they may follow strong drink; that continue until night, till wine inflame them!
and the
ana the
the
and
, and
are in their
but they regard not the work of the
neither consider the operations of his
יהוה
Isaiah v. 11,12.

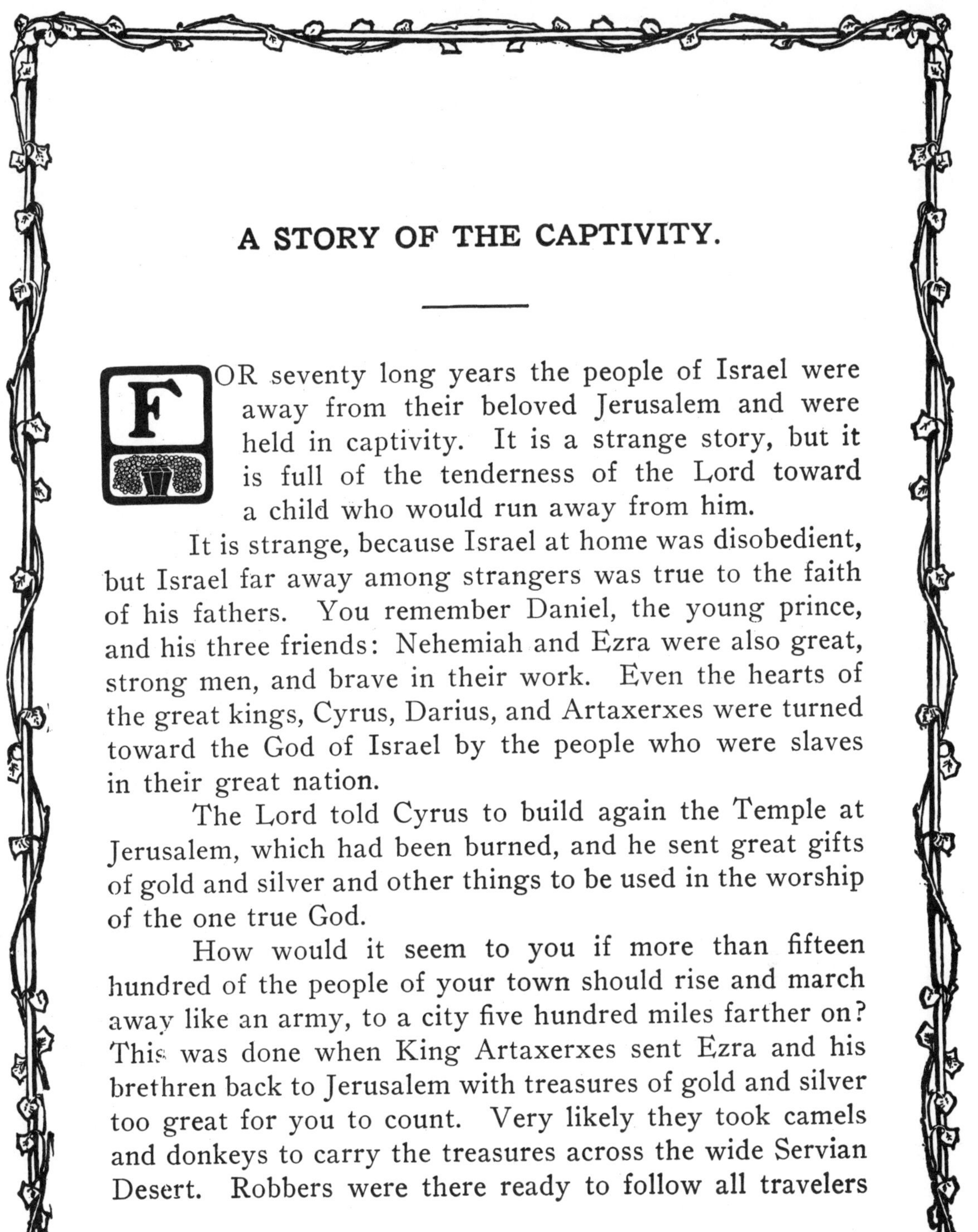

A STORY OF THE CAPTIVITY.

FOR seventy long years the people of Israel were away from their beloved Jerusalem and were held in captivity. It is a strange story, but it is full of the tenderness of the Lord toward a child who would run away from him.

It is strange, because Israel at home was disobedient, but Israel far away among strangers was true to the faith of his fathers. You remember Daniel, the young prince, and his three friends: Nehemiah and Ezra were also great, strong men, and brave in their work. Even the hearts of the great kings, Cyrus, Darius, and Artaxerxes were turned toward the God of Israel by the people who were slaves in their great nation.

The Lord told Cyrus to build again the Temple at Jerusalem, which had been burned, and he sent great gifts of gold and silver and other things to be used in the worship of the one true God.

How would it seem to you if more than fifteen hundred of the people of your town should rise and march away like an army, to a city five hundred miles farther on? This was done when King Artaxerxes sent Ezra and his brethren back to Jerusalem with treasures of gold and silver too great for you to count. Very likely they took camels and donkeys to carry the treasures across the wide Servian Desert. Robbers were there ready to follow all travelers

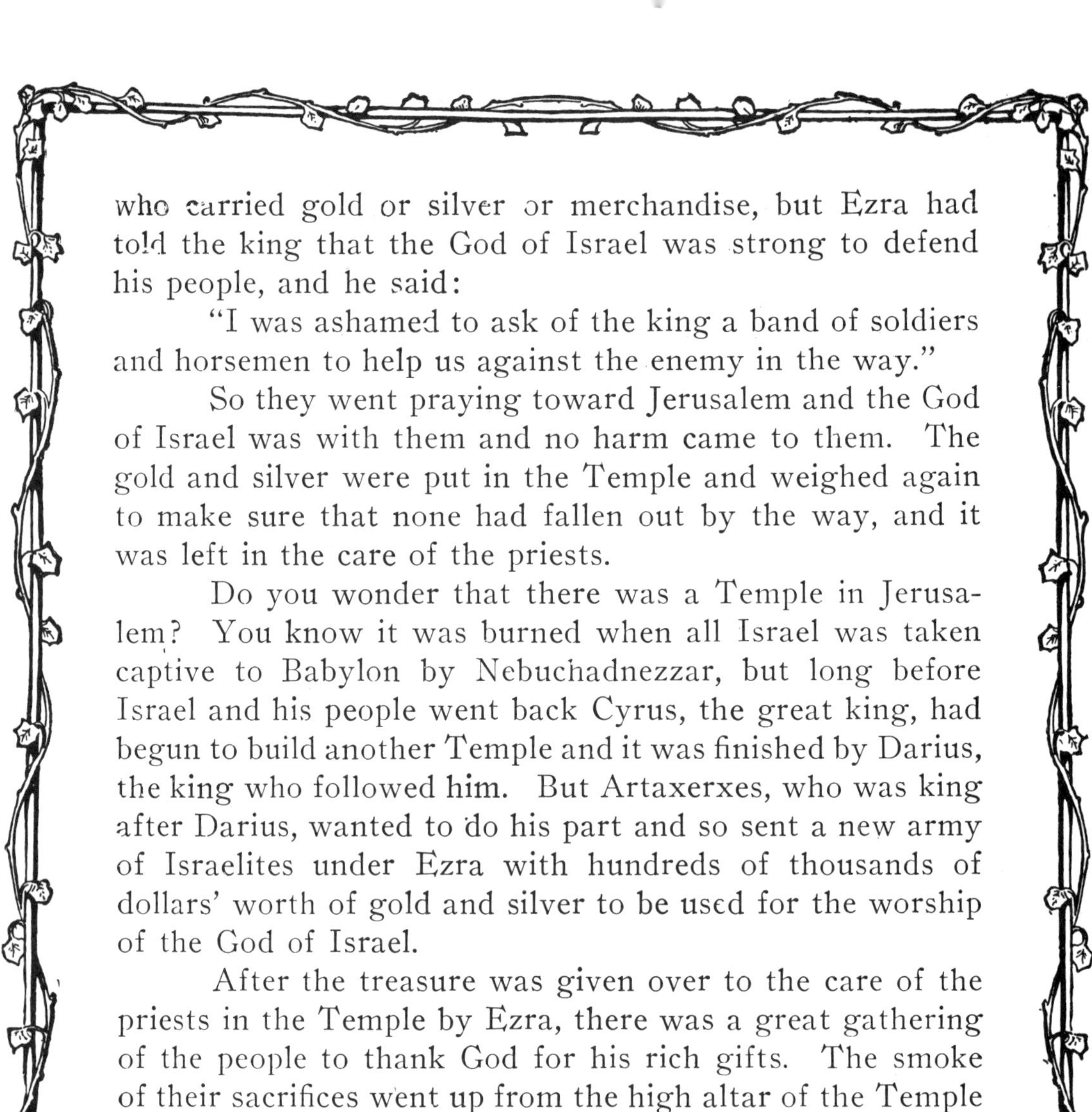

who carried gold or silver or merchandise, but Ezra had told the king that the God of Israel was strong to defend his people, and he said:

"I was ashamed to ask of the king a band of soldiers and horsemen to help us against the enemy in the way."

So they went praying toward Jerusalem and the God of Israel was with them and no harm came to them. The gold and silver were put in the Temple and weighed again to make sure that none had fallen out by the way, and it was left in the care of the priests.

Do you wonder that there was a Temple in Jerusalem? You know it was burned when all Israel was taken captive to Babylon by Nebuchadnezzar, but long before Israel and his people went back Cyrus, the great king, had begun to build another Temple and it was finished by Darius, the king who followed him. But Artaxerxes, who was king after Darius, wanted to do his part and so sent a new army of Israelites under Ezra with hundreds of thousands of dollars' worth of gold and silver to be used for the worship of the God of Israel.

After the treasure was given over to the care of the priests in the Temple by Ezra, there was a great gathering of the people to thank God for his rich gifts. The smoke of their sacrifices went up from the high altar of the Temple and the people sang psalms and rejoiced as they used to in the days of David and Solomon.

Perhaps they sang:

"O, give thanks unto the Lord for he is good,
For his mercy endureth forever."

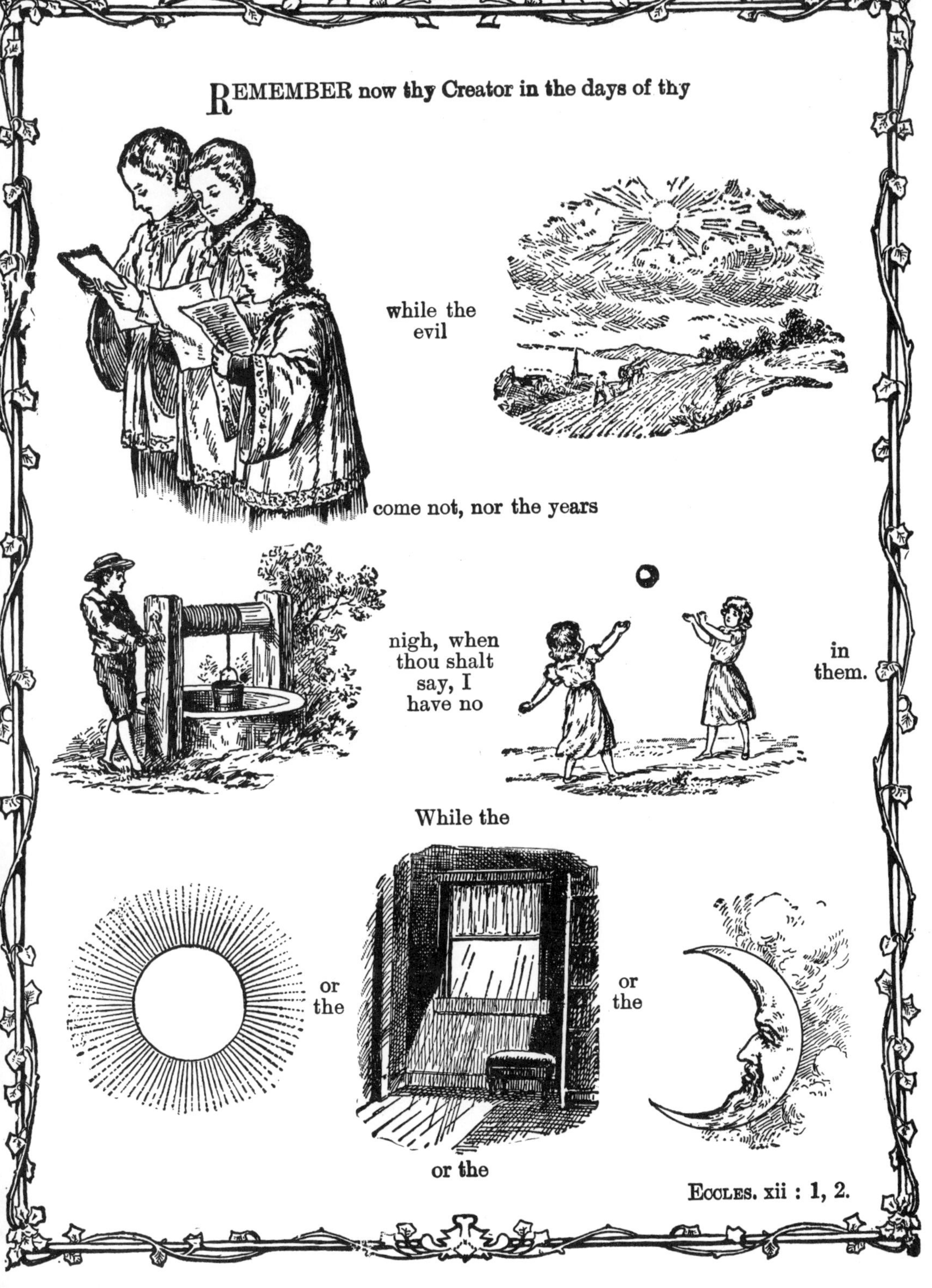
REMEMBER now thy Creator in the days of thy
while the
evil
come not, nor the years
nigh, when
thou shalt
say, I
have no
in
them.
While the
or
the
or
the
or the
Eccles. xii : 1, 2.

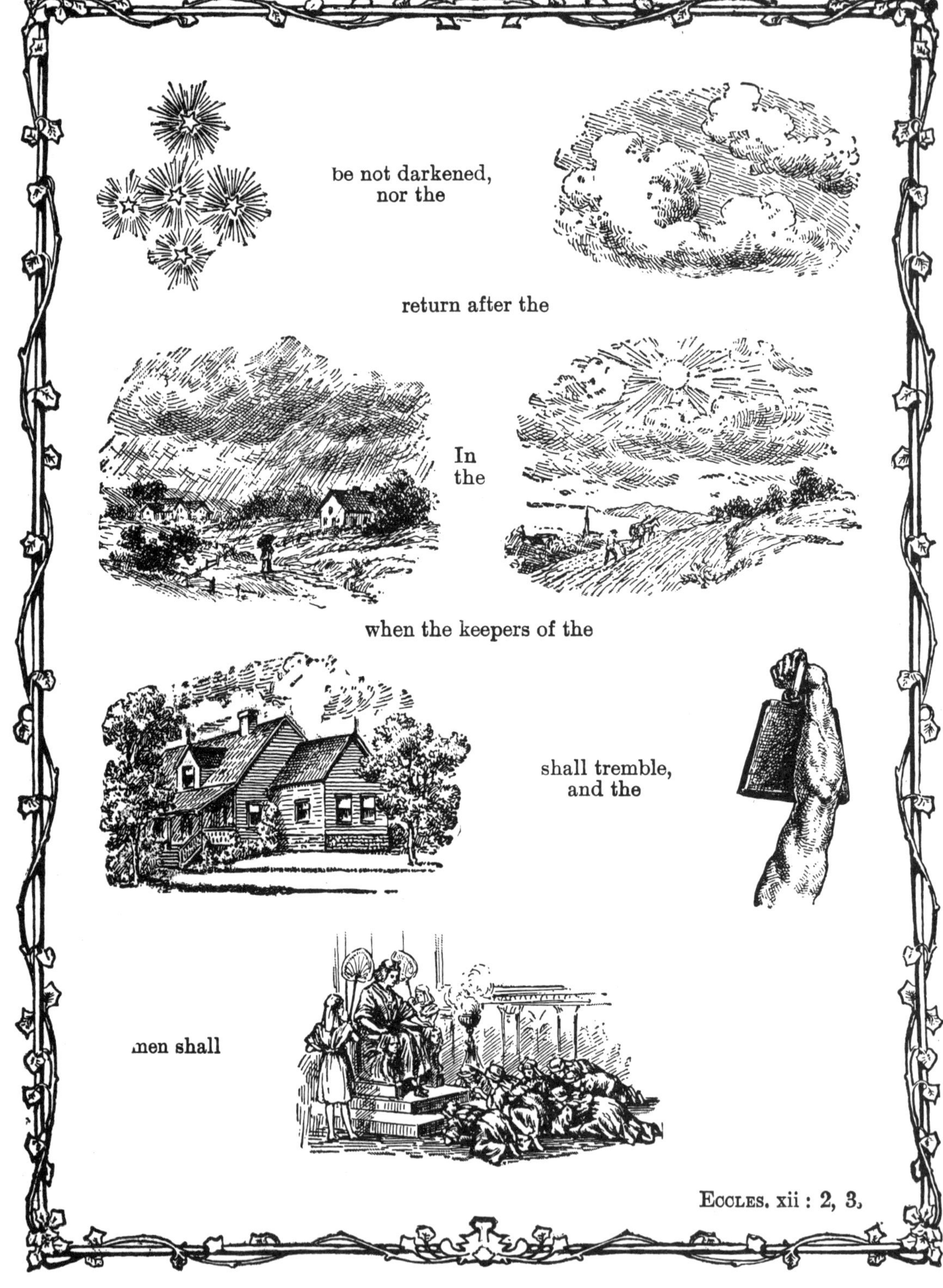

be not darkened,
nor the

return after the

In
the

when the keepers of the

shall tremble,
and the

men shall

Eccles. xii : 2, 3.

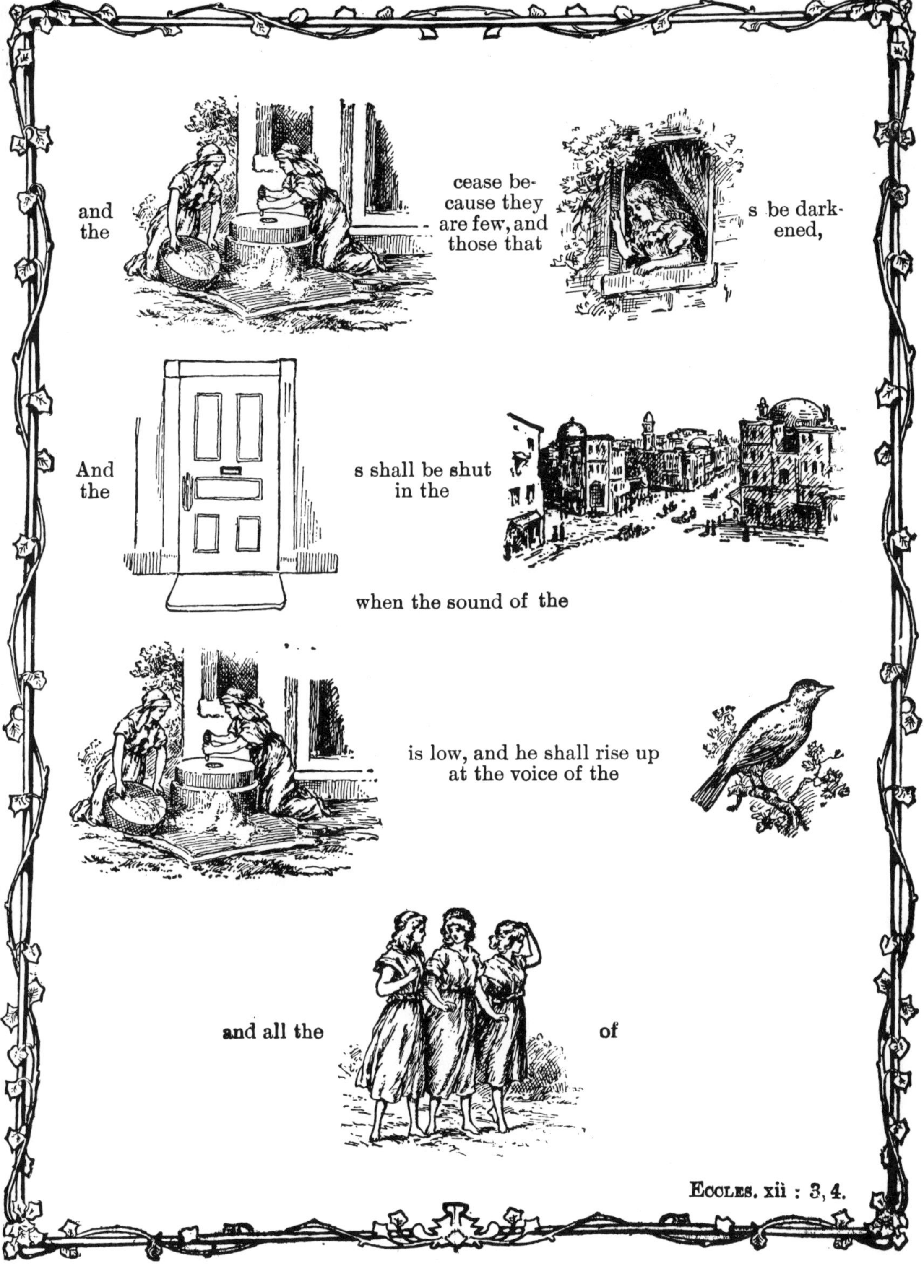
and the
cease because they are few, and those that
s be darkened,
And the
s shall be shut in the
when the sound of the
is low, and he shall rise up at the voice of the
and all the
of
Eccles. xii : 3, 4.

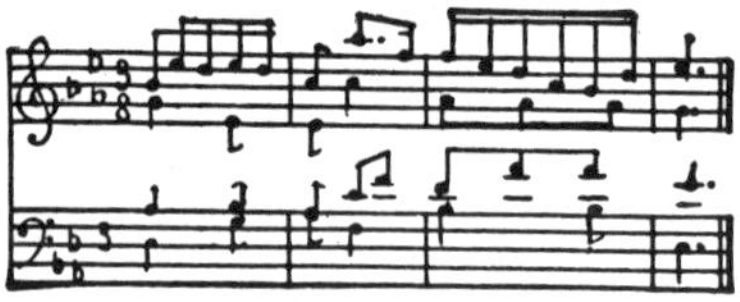

shall be brought low ; Also
when they shall be
afraid of that
which is

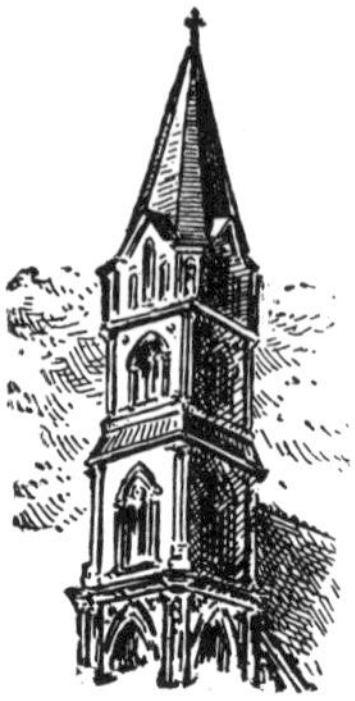

and fears shall be in the

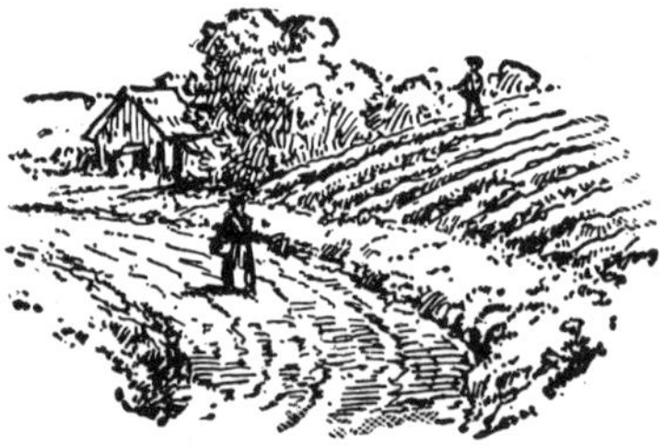

and the

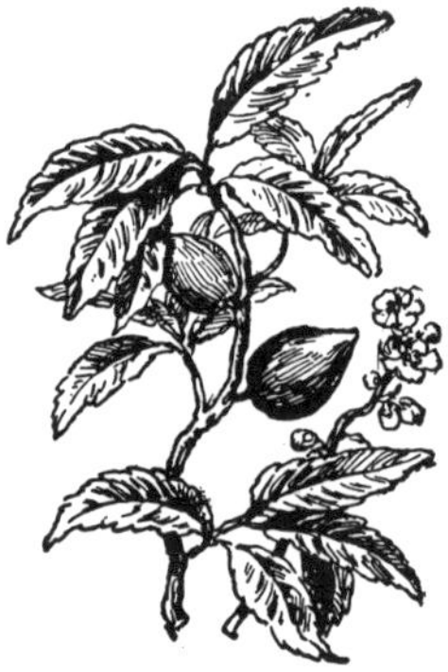

tree shall flourish, and the

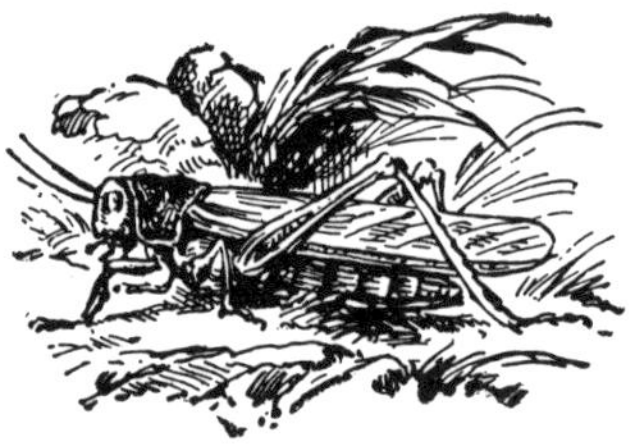

shall be a

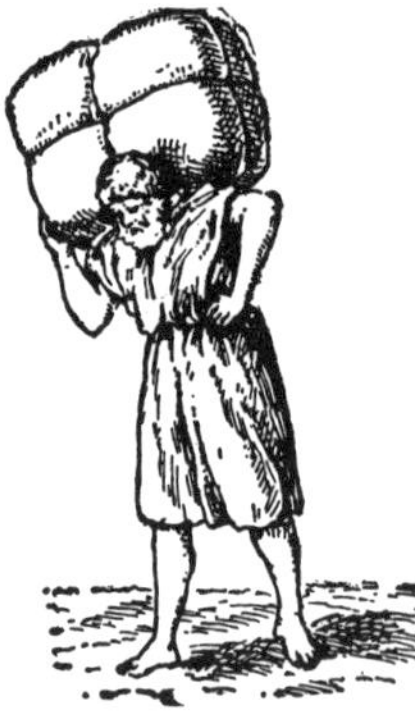

and desire shall fail: because

Eccles. xii : 4, 5.

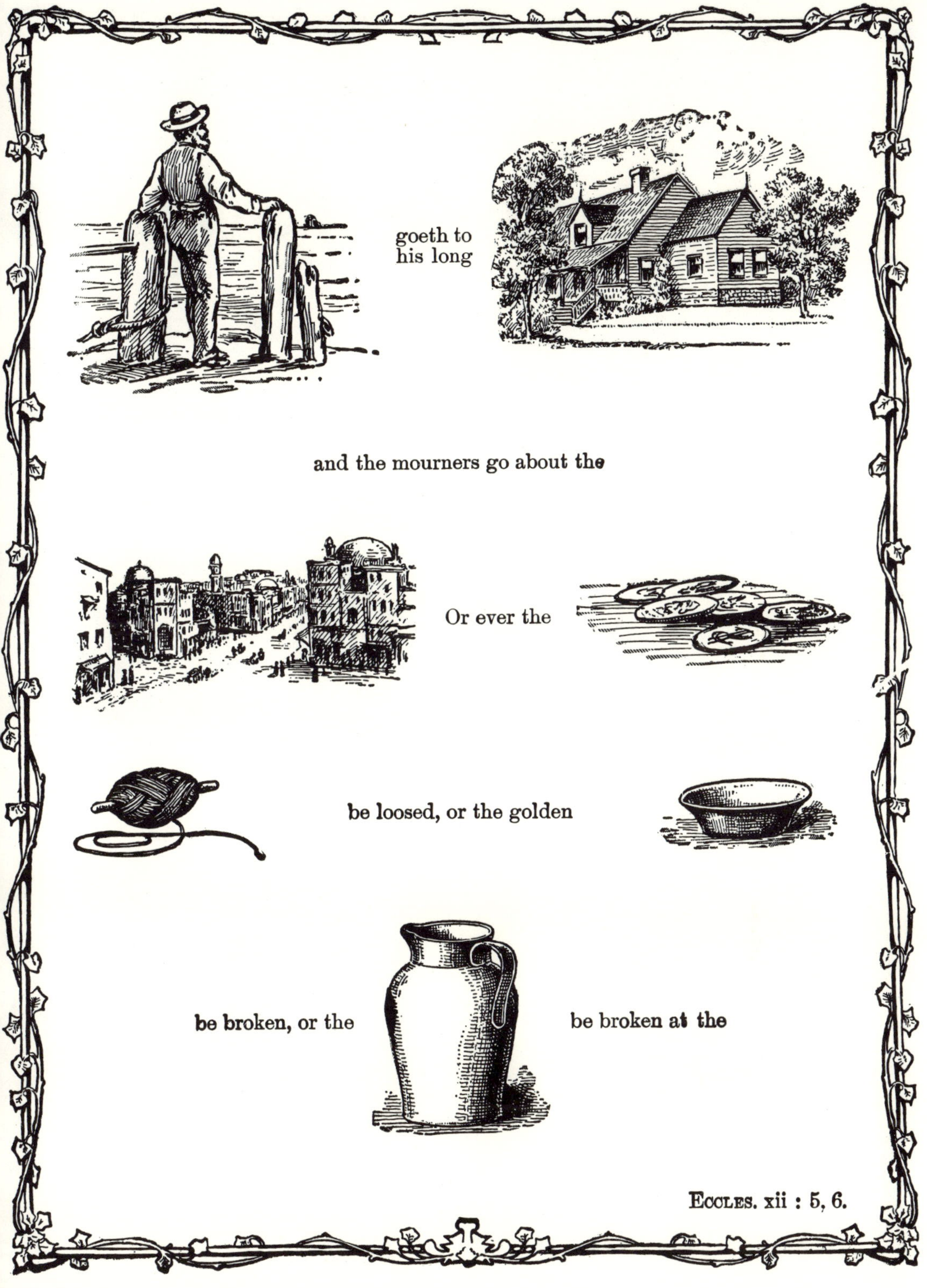

goeth to
his long

and the mourners go about the

Or ever the

be loosed, or the golden

be broken, or the

be broken at the

Eccles. xii : 5, 6.

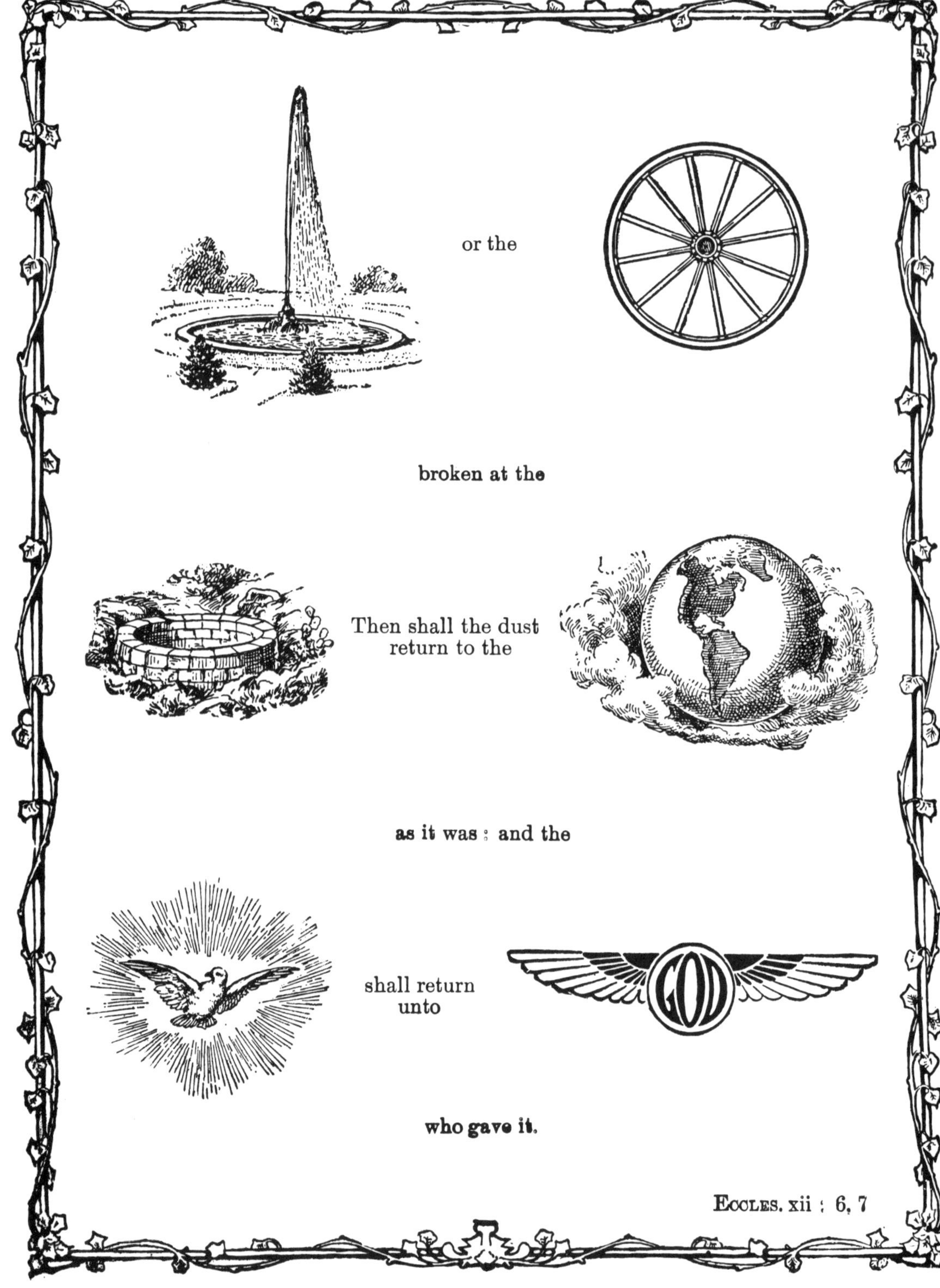
or the
broken at the
Then shall the dust
return to the
as it was : and the
shall return
unto
GOD
who gave it.
Eccles. xii : 6, 7

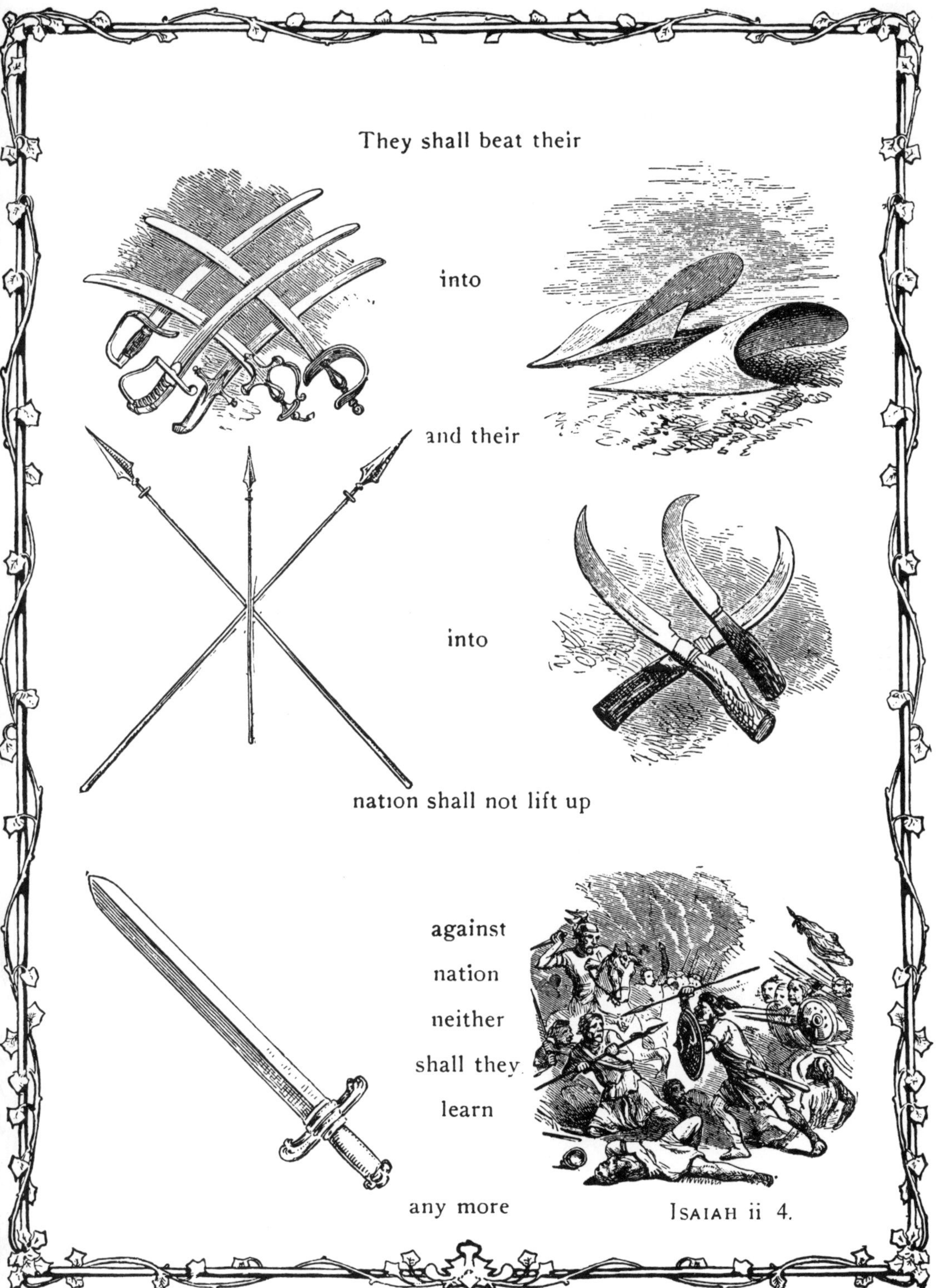
They shall beat their
into
and their
into
nation shall not lift up
against
nation
neither
shall they
learn
any more
ISAIAH ii 4.

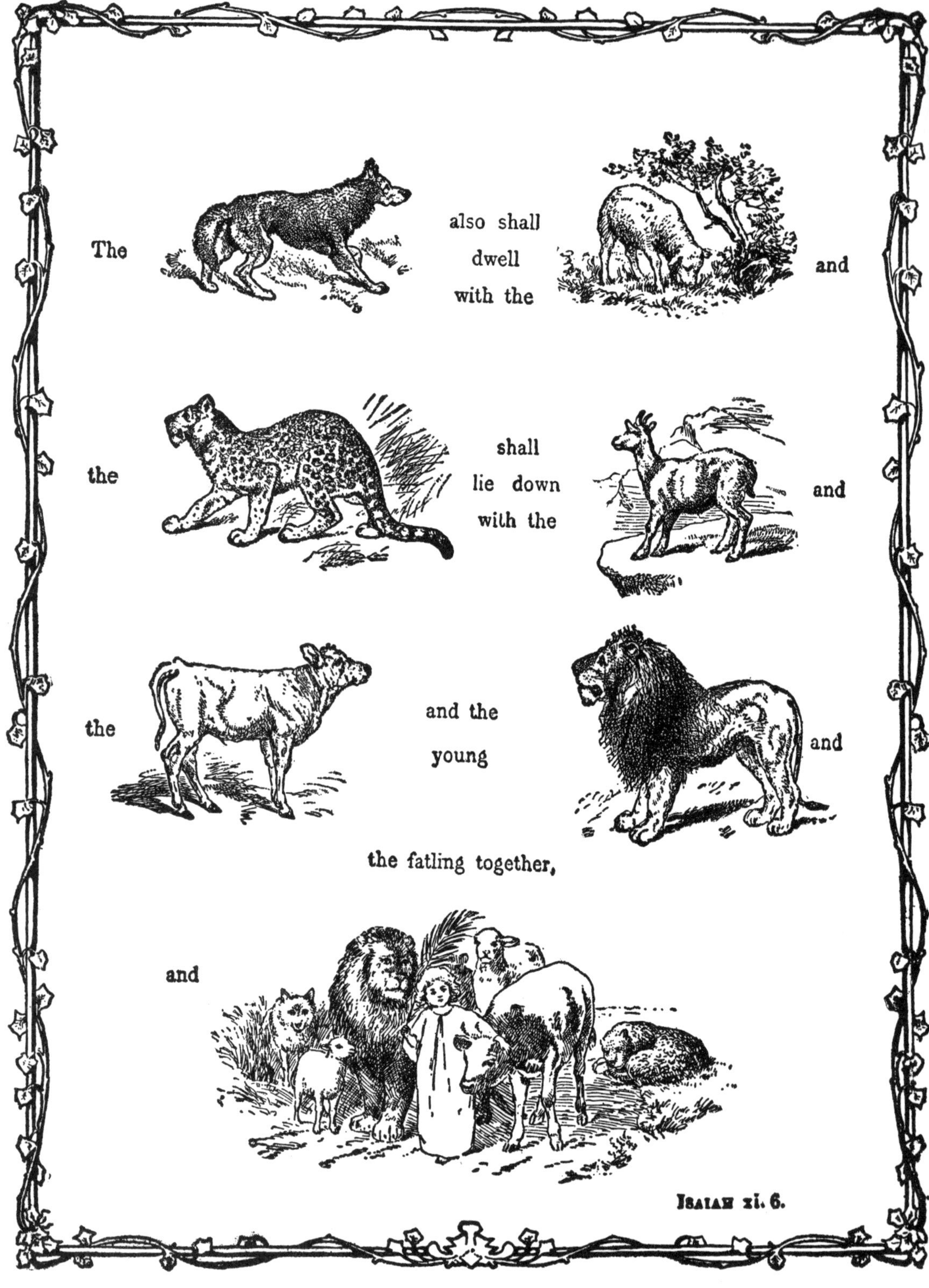
The
also shall
dwell
with the
and
the
shall
lie down
with the
and
the
and the
young
and
the fatling together,
and
Isaiah xi. 6.

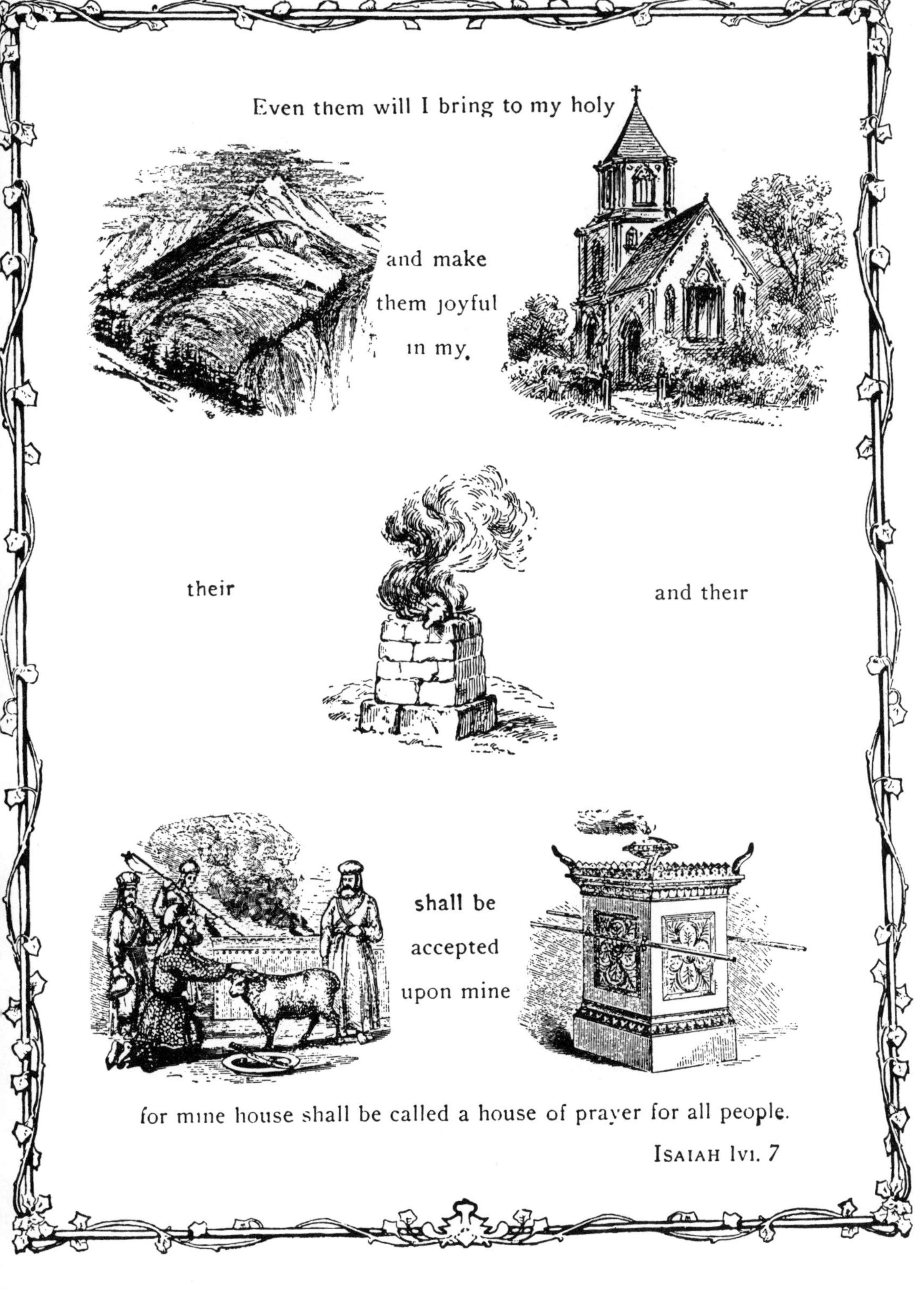

Even them will I bring to my holy

and make them joyful in my.

their

and their

shall be accepted upon mine

for mine house shall be called a house of prayer for all people.

ISAIAH lvi. 7

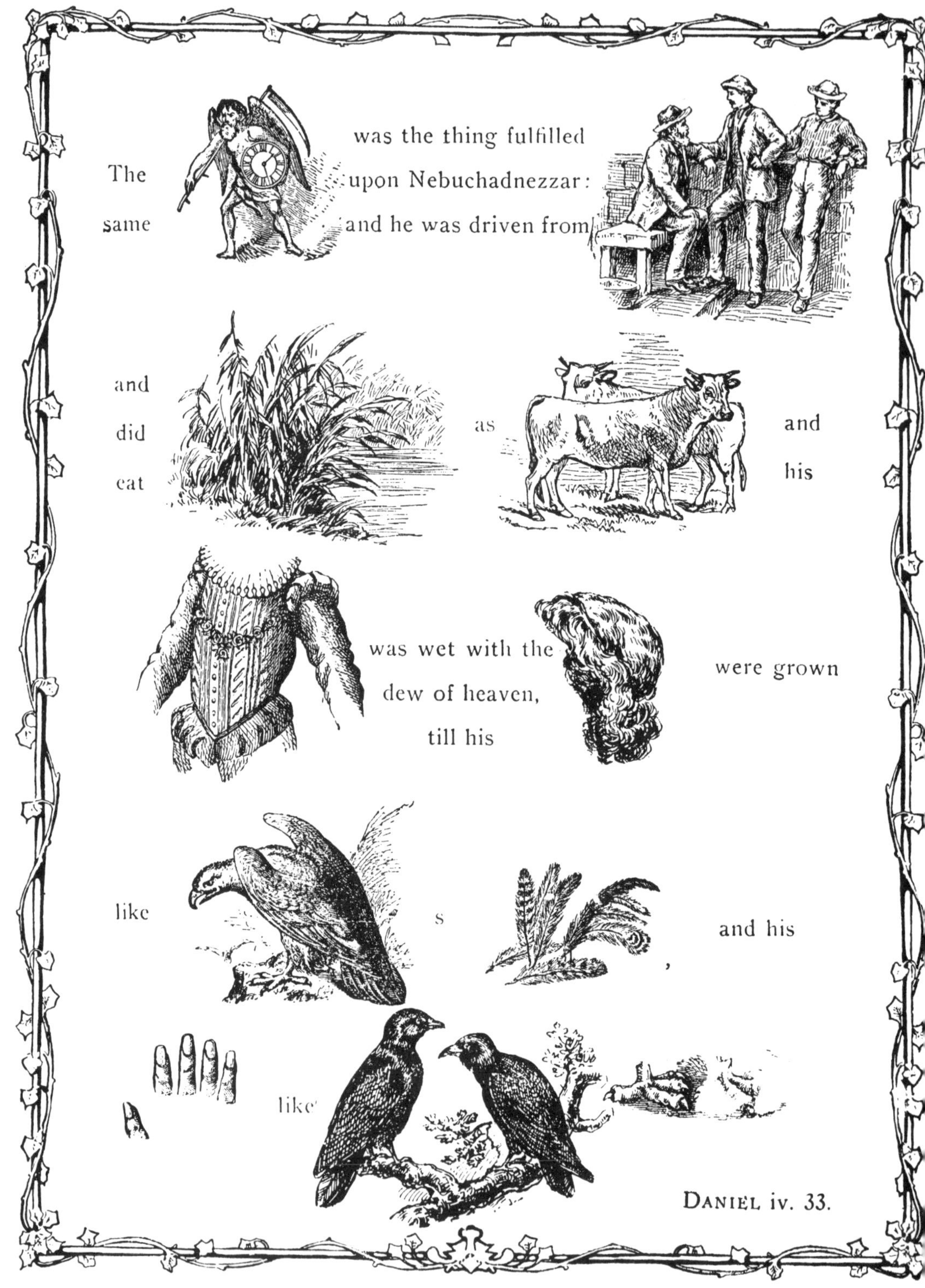

The same was the thing fulfilled upon Nebuchadnezzar: and he was driven from

and did eat as and his

was wet with the dew of heaven, till his were grown

like s , and his

like

DANIEL iv. 33.

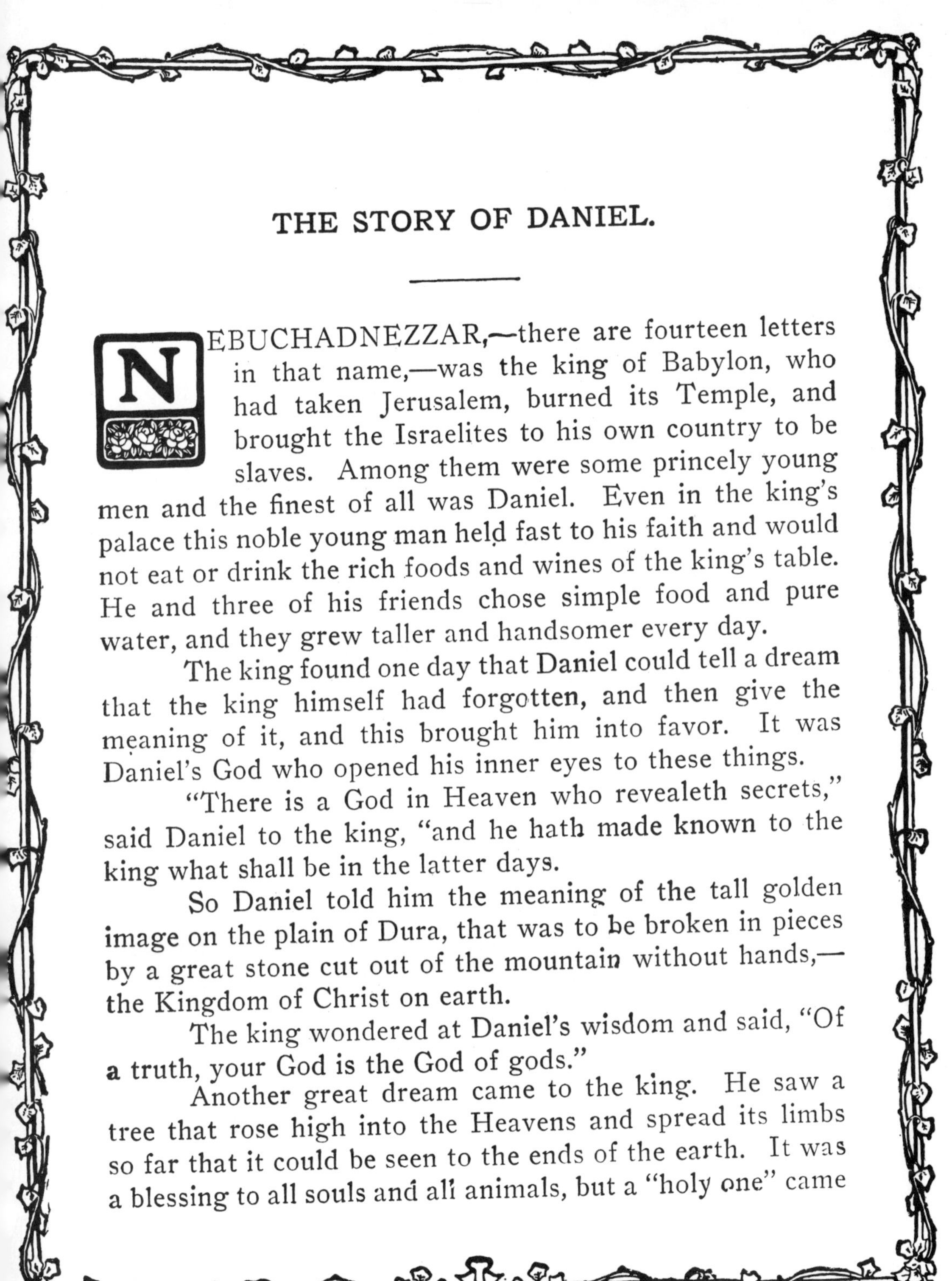

THE STORY OF DANIEL.

NEBUCHADNEZZAR,—there are fourteen letters in that name,—was the king of Babylon, who had taken Jerusalem, burned its Temple, and brought the Israelites to his own country to be slaves. Among them were some princely young men and the finest of all was Daniel. Even in the king's palace this noble young man held fast to his faith and would not eat or drink the rich foods and wines of the king's table. He and three of his friends chose simple food and pure water, and they grew taller and handsomer every day.

The king found one day that Daniel could tell a dream that the king himself had forgotten, and then give the meaning of it, and this brought him into favor. It was Daniel's God who opened his inner eyes to these things.

"There is a God in Heaven who revealeth secrets," said Daniel to the king, "and he hath made known to the king what shall be in the latter days.

So Daniel told him the meaning of the tall golden image on the plain of Dura, that was to be broken in pieces by a great stone cut out of the mountain without hands,—the Kingdom of Christ on earth.

The king wondered at Daniel's wisdom and said, "Of a truth, your God is the God of gods."

Another great dream came to the king. He saw a tree that rose high into the Heavens and spread its limbs so far that it could be seen to the ends of the earth. It was a blessing to all souls and all animals, but a "holy one" came down from Heaven and said, "Hew down the tree." He said it must be cut down to the grass and its roots bound with iron and brass, and "let seven times pass over him." Then the king cried to Daniel, "Because I know the spirit of the holy gods is in thee and no secret troubleth thee, tell me the visions of the dream that I have seen, and the interpretation thereof."

It was hard for Daniel to do this. He did not like to tell the king the meaning of that dream, it was so terrible, but at last he took courage and gave the meaning as God showed it to him. It was a strange meaning. It showed that the mighty king should be driven out from among men to dwell with the beasts of the field, and to be wet with the dew of Heaven until "seven times" had passed over him. The bands around the roots of the tree meant that his kingdom would remain to him after he had learned that God rules over all things.

For a whole year the Lord waited to see the king repent of his sins, but he did not. In that year he had forgotten the dream, and standing on the roof-garden of his palace he looked over the city and said:

"Is not this great Babylon I have built for the royal dwelling place, by the might of my power and for the glory of my majesty!"

Then a voice from Heaven cried, "The kingdom is departed from thee," and that very hour he was driven out from among men and left among the beasts.

You can read the story in the pictures. We do not know how long it was before the king came to his right mind, but at last he looked up to God and knew that God was the ruler of men, and all his friends and riches and honor came back, but he had lost his pride forever.

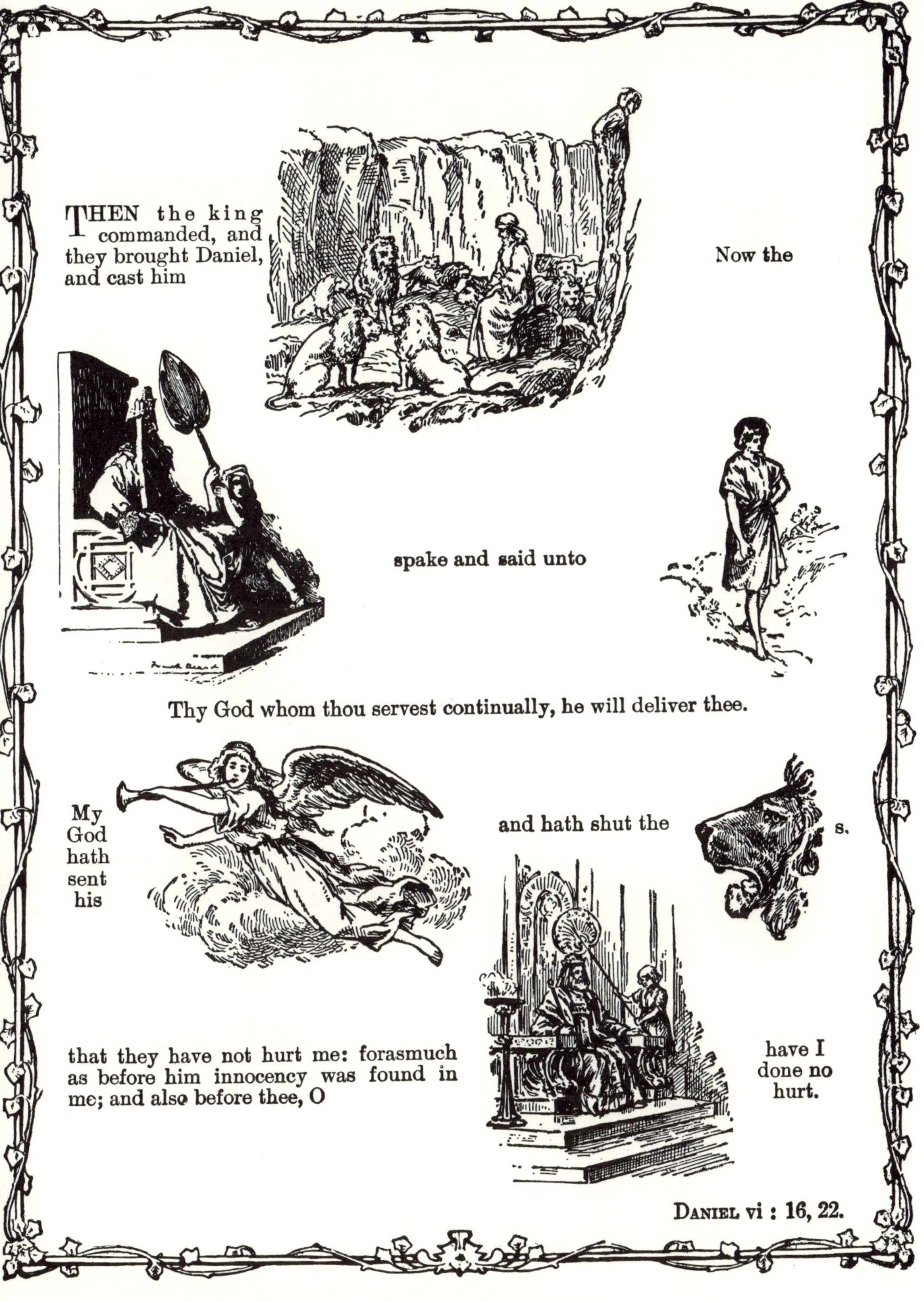

THEN the king commanded, and they brought Daniel, and cast him

Now the

spake and said unto

Thy God whom thou servest continually, he will deliver thee.

My God hath sent his

and hath shut the s.

that they have not hurt me: forasmuch as before him innocency was found in me; and also before thee, O

have I done no hurt.

DANIEL vi : 16, 22.

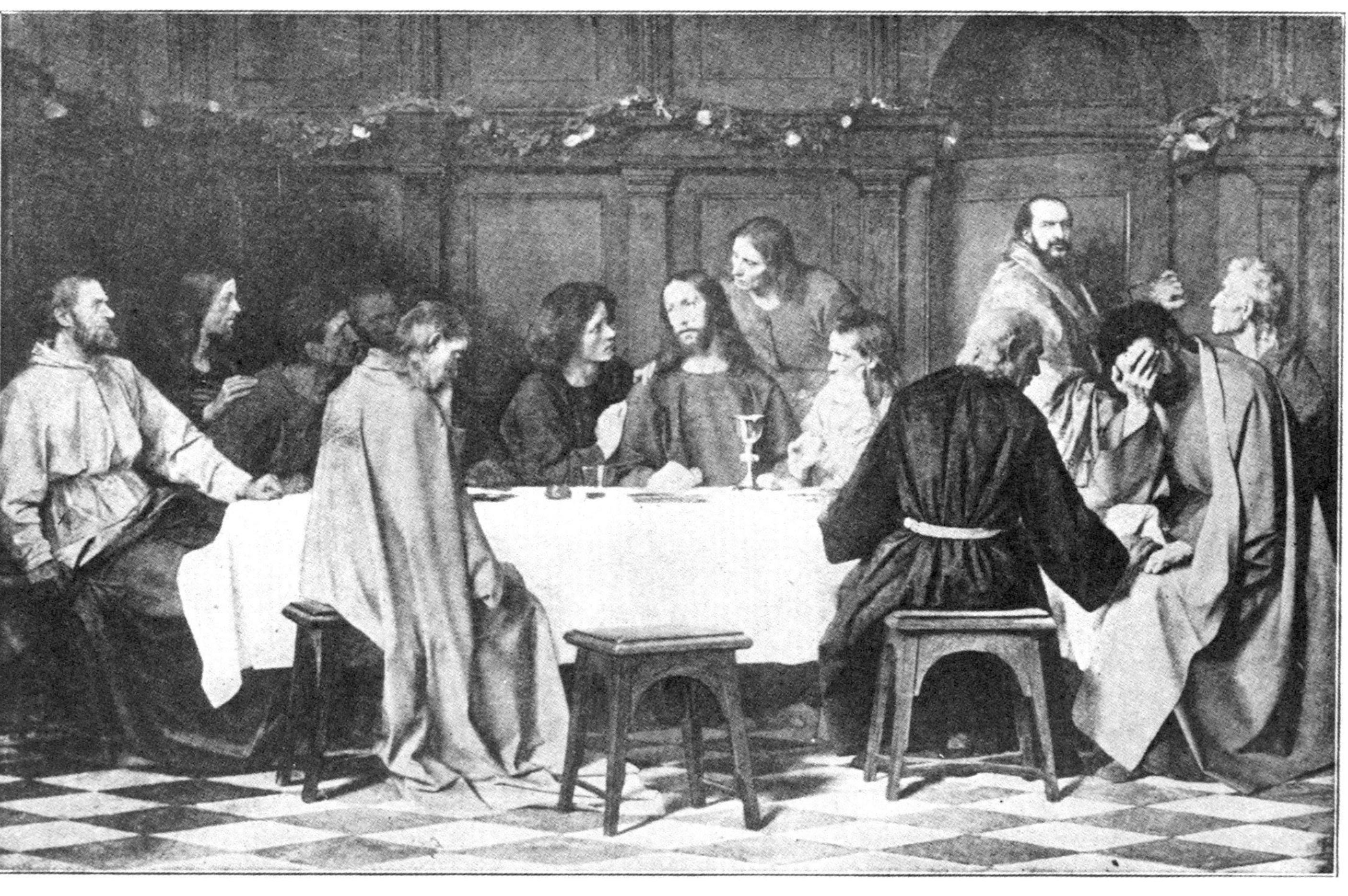

THE LAST SUPPER.

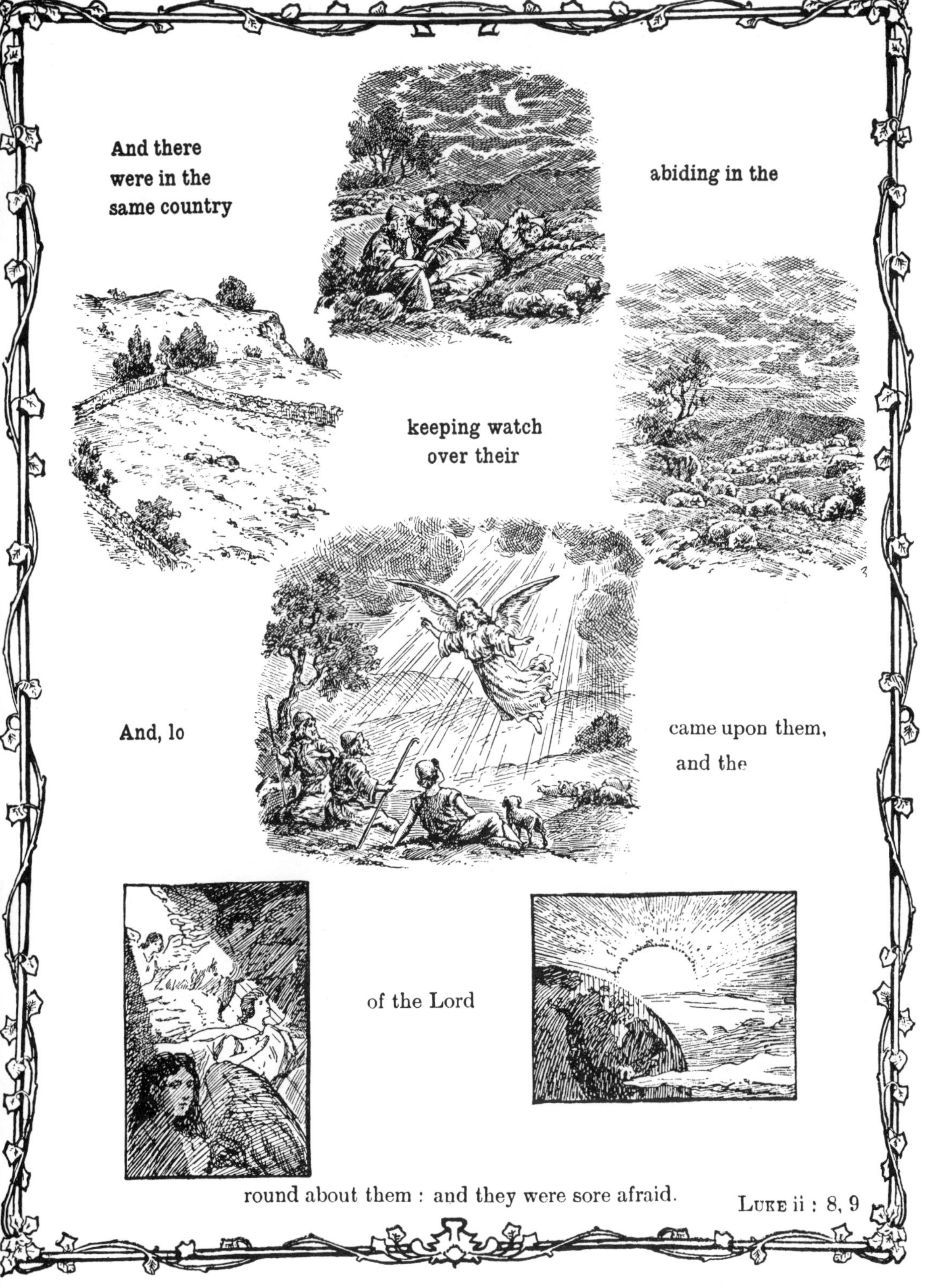

round about them : and they were sore afraid.

LUKE ii : 8, 9

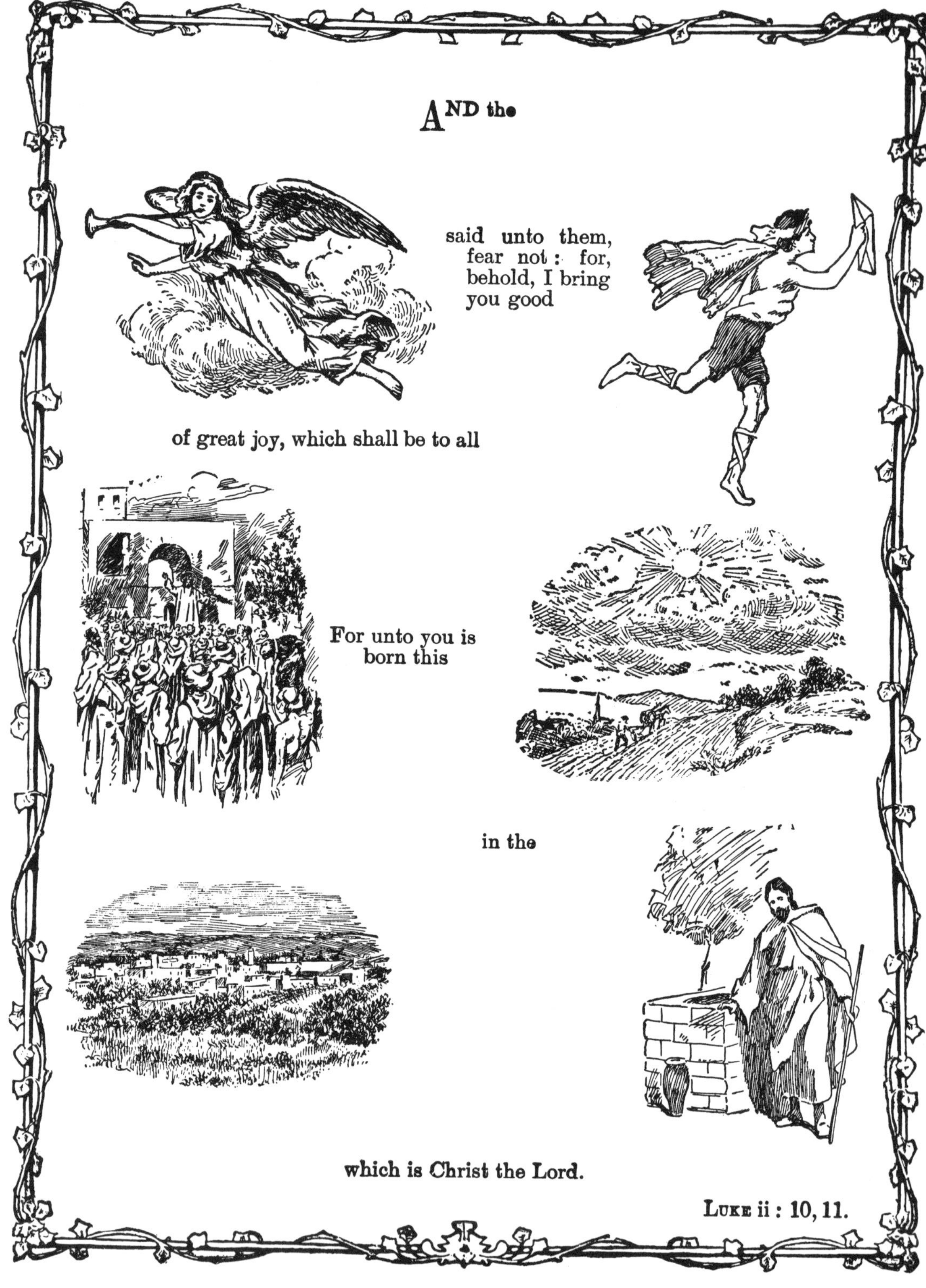

AND the

said unto them, fear not: for, behold, I bring you good

of great joy, which shall be to all

For unto you is born this

in the

which is Christ the Lord.

LUKE ii: 10, 11.

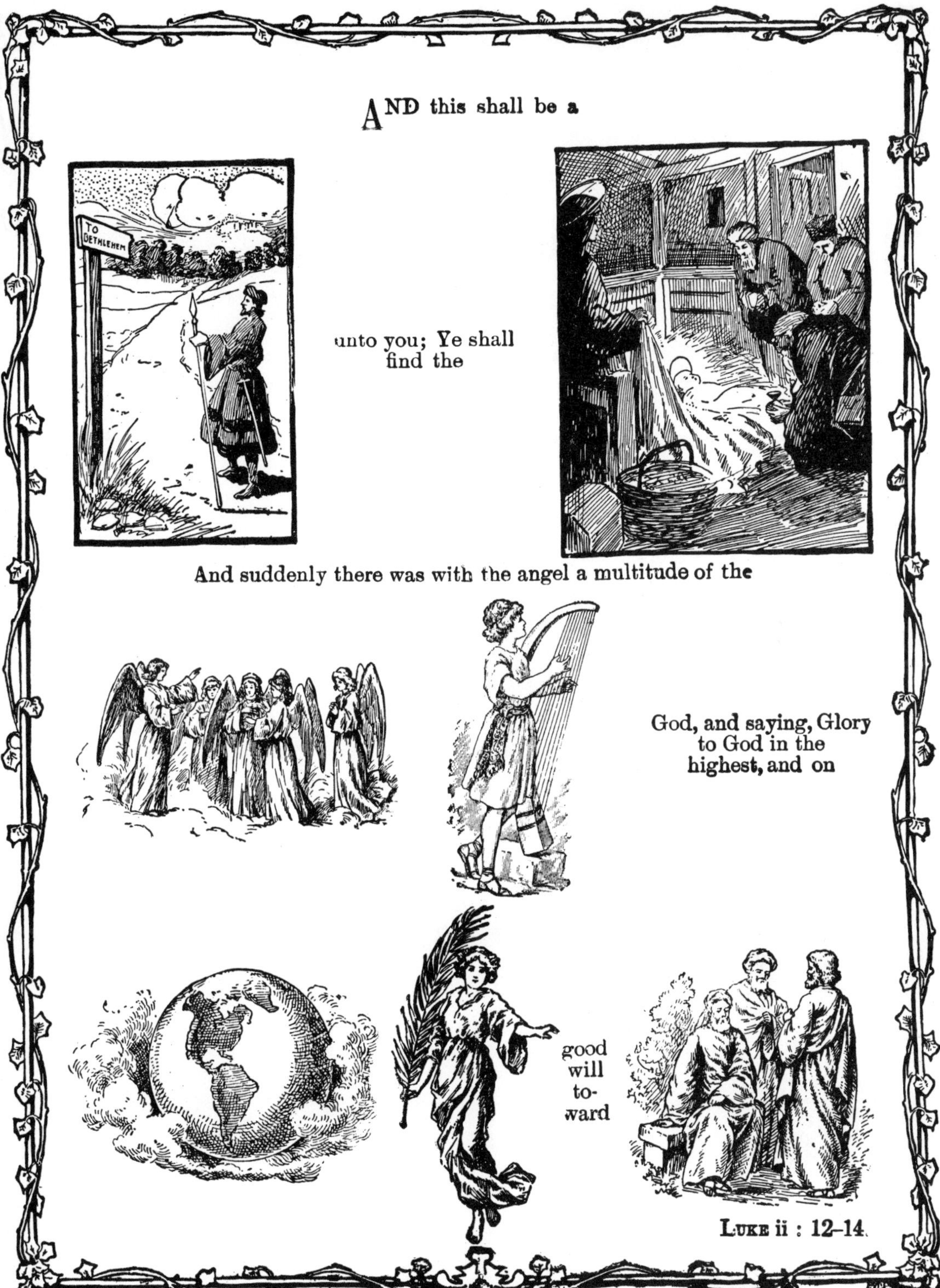
AND this shall be a
TO BETHLEHEM
unto you; Ye shall find the
And suddenly there was with the angel a multitude of the
God, and saying, Glory to God in the highest, and on
good will to-ward
LUKE ii : 12–14.

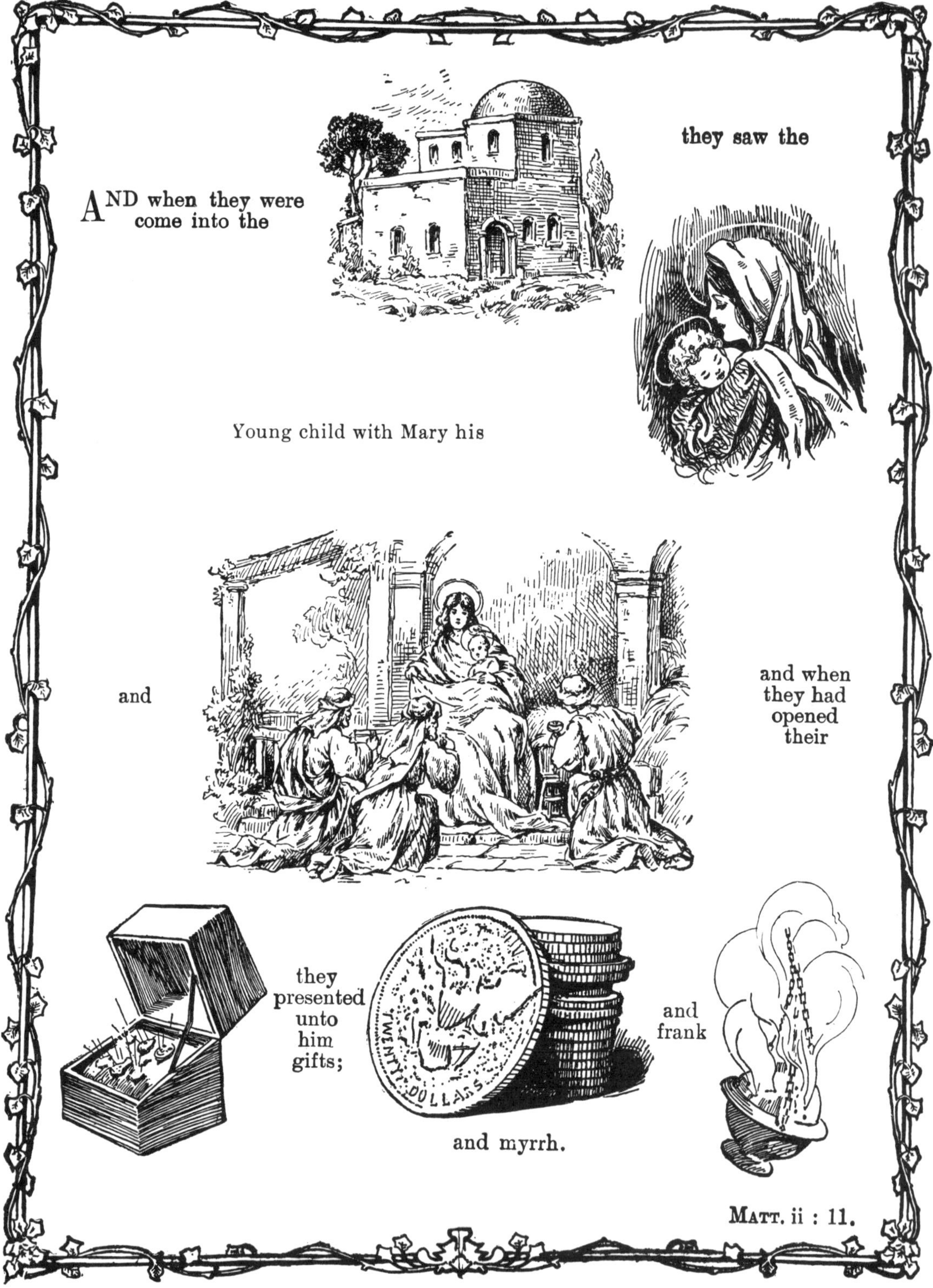

AND when they were come into the

they saw the

Young child with Mary his

and

and when they had opened their

they presented unto him gifts;

and frank

and myrrh.

MATT. ii : 11.

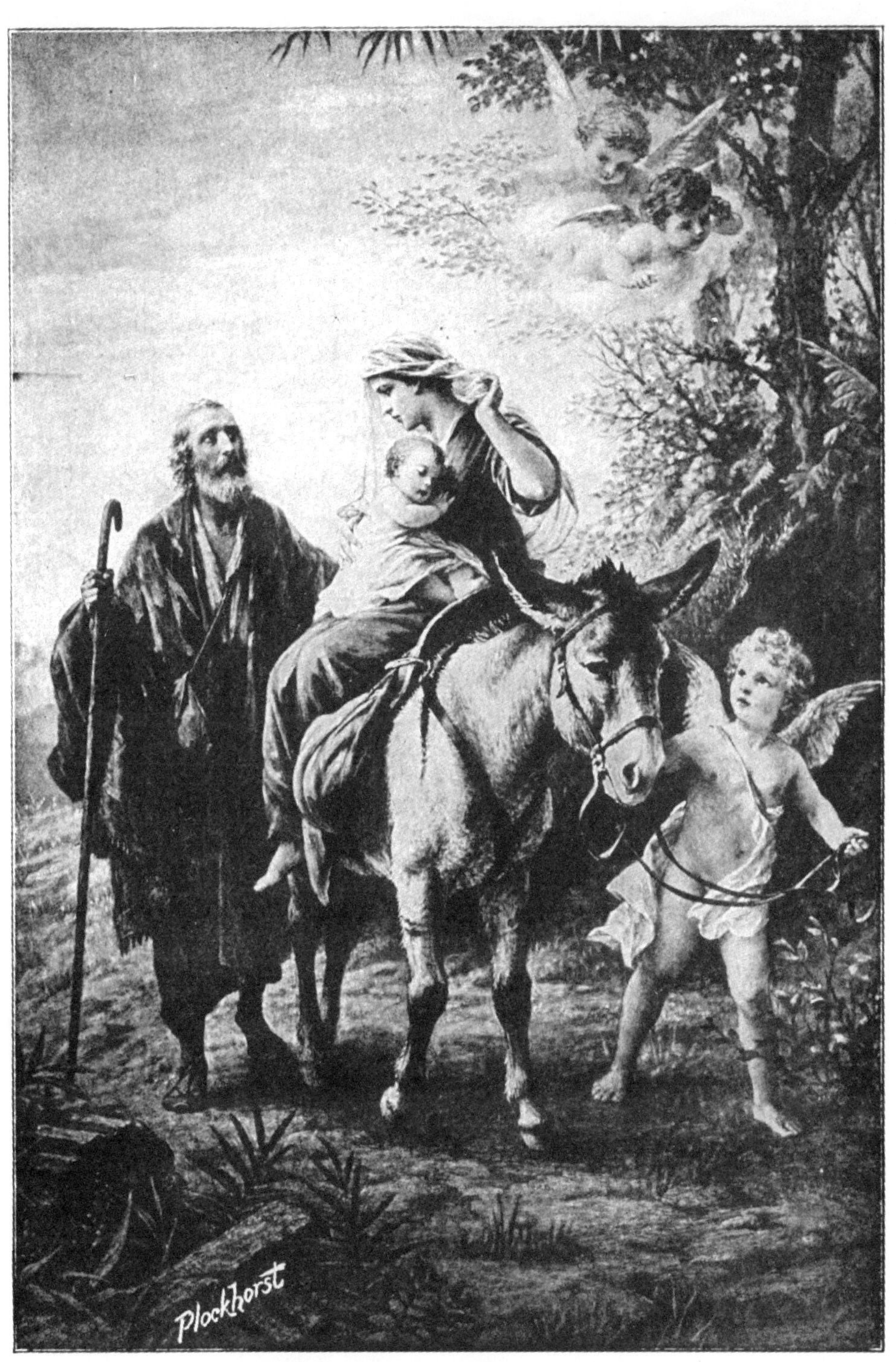

THE FLIGHT INTO EGYPT.

THE FLIGHT INTO EGYPT.

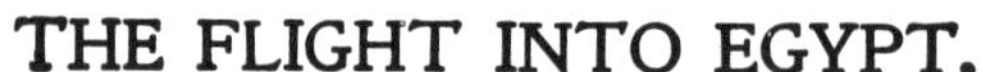

"ARISE! Take the young child quickly: We must flee!" It was Joseph, the carpenter, calling in the still night to Mary, the mother of Jesus. What did it mean?

The Holy Family lingered still in Bethlehem. In the night time an angel of the Lord spoke to Joseph in a dream bidding him take Mary and the Child and fly to Egypt because of the cruel King Herod, who had heard the story of the Wise Men, and feared the little new-born King.

In quiet haste Mary rose and made ready, and soon the three were under the stars, Mary, bearing the precious Babe in tender arms and riding upon the gentle ass, while Joseph hurried along by her side, knowing well that the danger was real, else the Lord would not have sent his angel to warn them. And so it was, for they were scarcely outside the walls of the city when Herod's soldiers came at his command to slay all the children of two years and under, thinking in this way to destroy the Holy Child whom the Wise Men had called King of the Jews.

Egypt lay nearly eighty miles in a straight line from Bethlehem. The road ran along the hill tops, then down to the plains and the seashore. It was the lovely springtime, and in the young mother's fearful heart there was yet a thrill of joy in the thought that her blessed Child was so plainly under the direction of the King of Heaven!

Eighty miles seems but a short journey with our modern ways of travel, but nineteen hundred years ago, and in the land of our Lord, it took many days. The patient ass toiled on, carrying his precious burden, and Joseph, tall and grave, kept faithful watch by day and by night.

And now see how God had made this journey to a strange land and a long stay there possible. Joseph was a poor man, and Mary was a simple maiden of the hills. In all their lives, perhaps, they had never seen so much money as the Wise Men brought, laying it all at the feet of the infant King! They did not know then what it meant, but now they understood that God had sent them the gold and precious things for this very time of need. How they praised him, and how we, too, should praise him, for he is "Our Father," you know,—the Father of Jesus, and our Father, too!

A river ran between the land of Palestine and the land of Egypt, and in a little less than a week, perhaps, from the night when they stole away from Bethlehem, they came to one of the shallow fords of the river and crossed safely over into Egypt.

Here the happy little family stayed on, month after month, for Joseph knew well that he must not return to his own land while King Herod lived. With some of the money which the Wise Men brought he could buy tools such as carpenters used in those days, and take up again his clean, honest toil, making a little home for Mary and the child Jesus,—a home in which love and peace lived.

And so the days went by and another glad spring came, and the little Jesus, growing always stronger and sweeter, made the light and joy of the cottage home. Then again the angel came to Joseph in a dream and said: "Arise, take the young child and his mother and return to thine own country, for they are dead which sought his life."

So Joseph and Mary, with the Holy Child, went gladly back to their own dear home in the hills, and they dwelt there in peace and simple comfort for many happy years

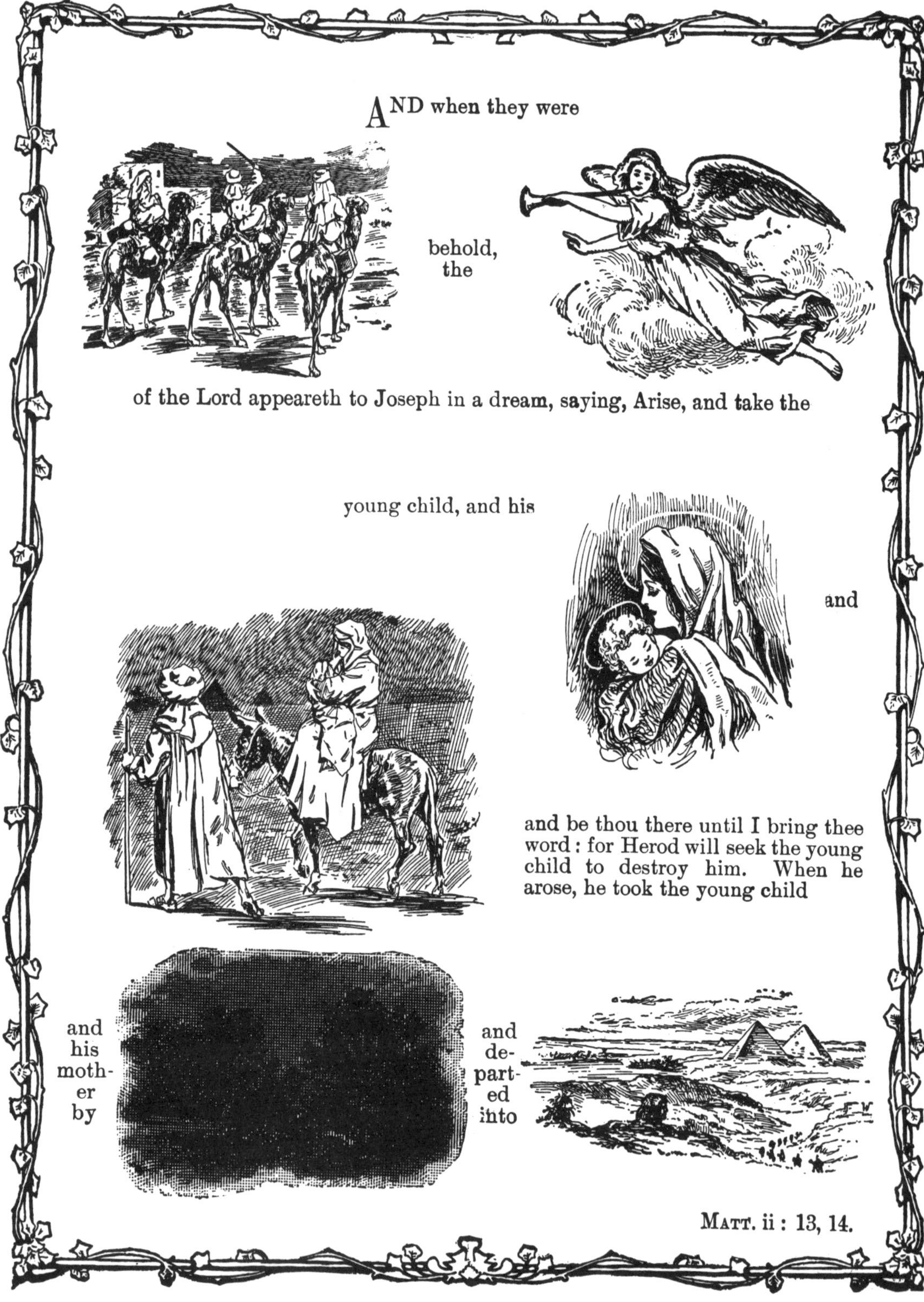

AND when they were

behold, the

of the Lord appeareth to Joseph in a dream, saying, Arise, and take the

young child, and his

and

and be thou there until I bring thee word: for Herod will seek the young child to destroy him. When he arose, he took the young child

and his mother by

and departed into

MATT. ii: 13, 14.

I (Name)......................................FILLED

IN THESE ANSWERS. (Date) ....

1. Where was Jesus born?

....

2. Who were His parents?

....

3. Who told the shepherds of His birth?

....

4. What message did the angel bring?

....

5. How were the shepherds to know the child?

....

6. What song did the angels sing?

....

7. Who visited the baby Jesus after the shepherds?

....

8. What did they bring to Him?

....

9. To what country did Joseph and Mary flee with the babe?

....

10. Why?

....

JESUS AMONG THE DOCTORS.

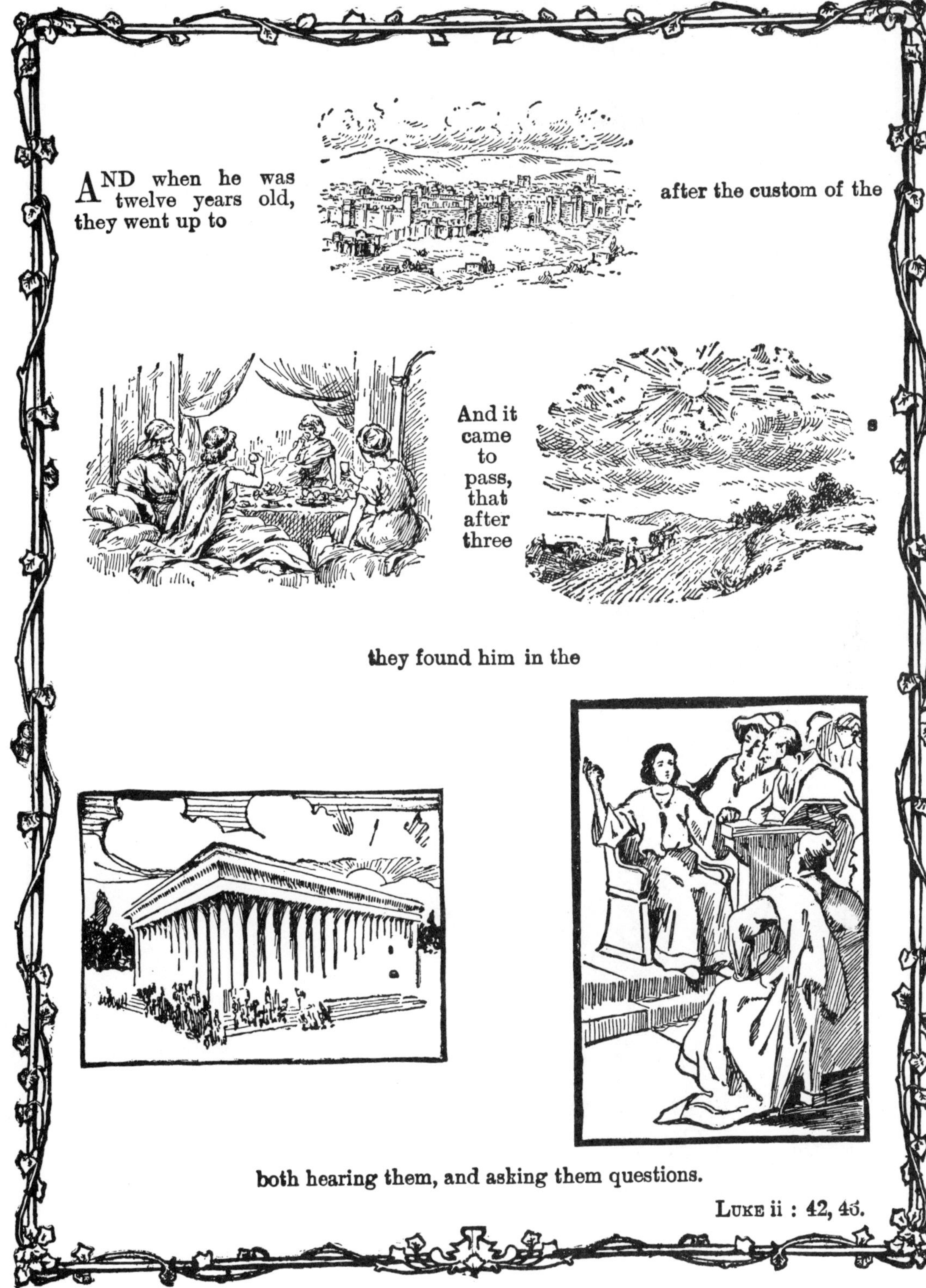

AND when he was twelve years old, they went up to

after the custom of the

And it came to pass, that after three

s

they found him in the

both hearing them, and asking them questions.

LUKE ii : 42, 46.

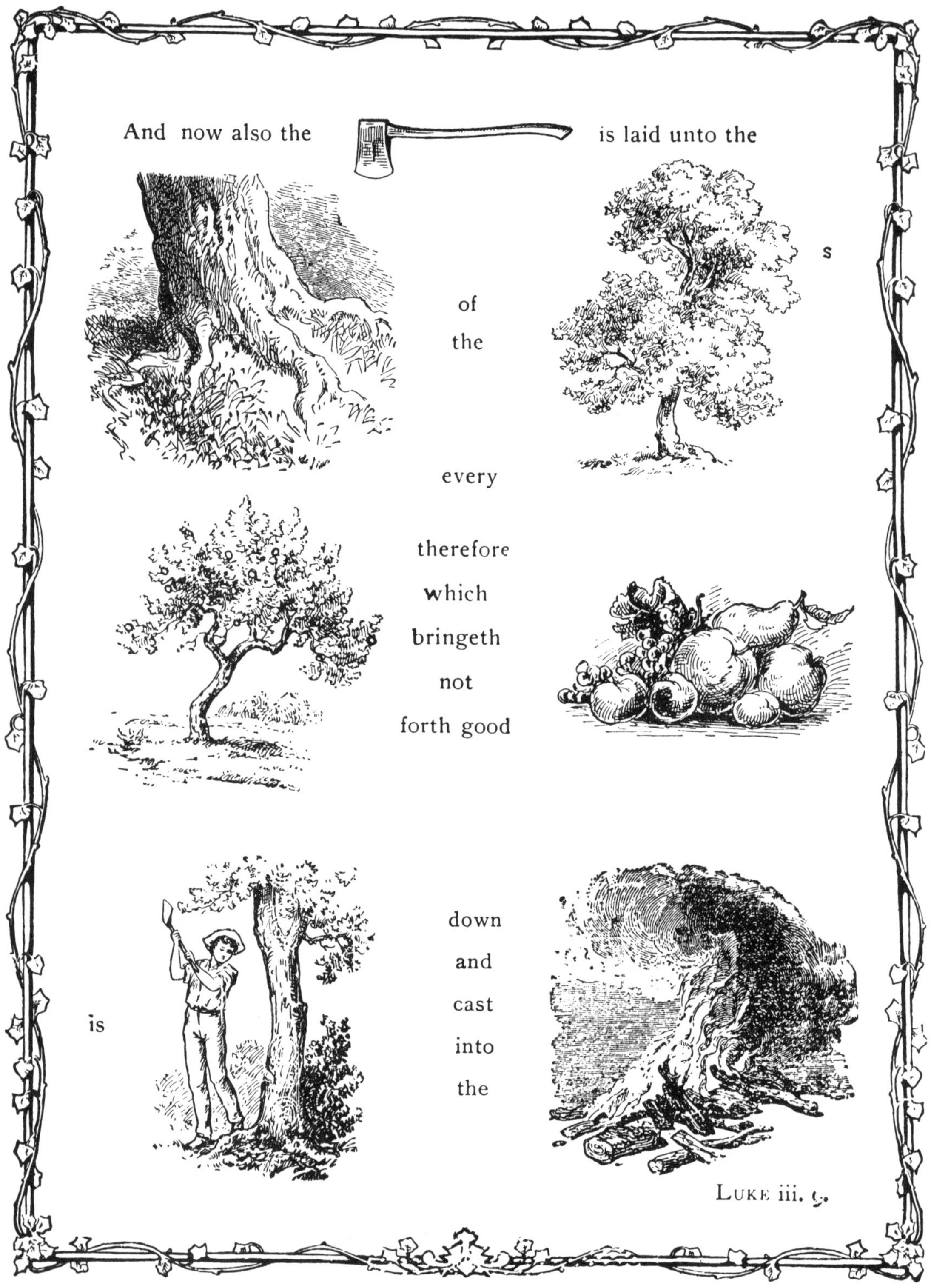
And now also the
is laid unto the
s
of
the
every
therefore
which
bringeth
not
forth good
is
down
and
cast
into
the

LUKE iii. 9.

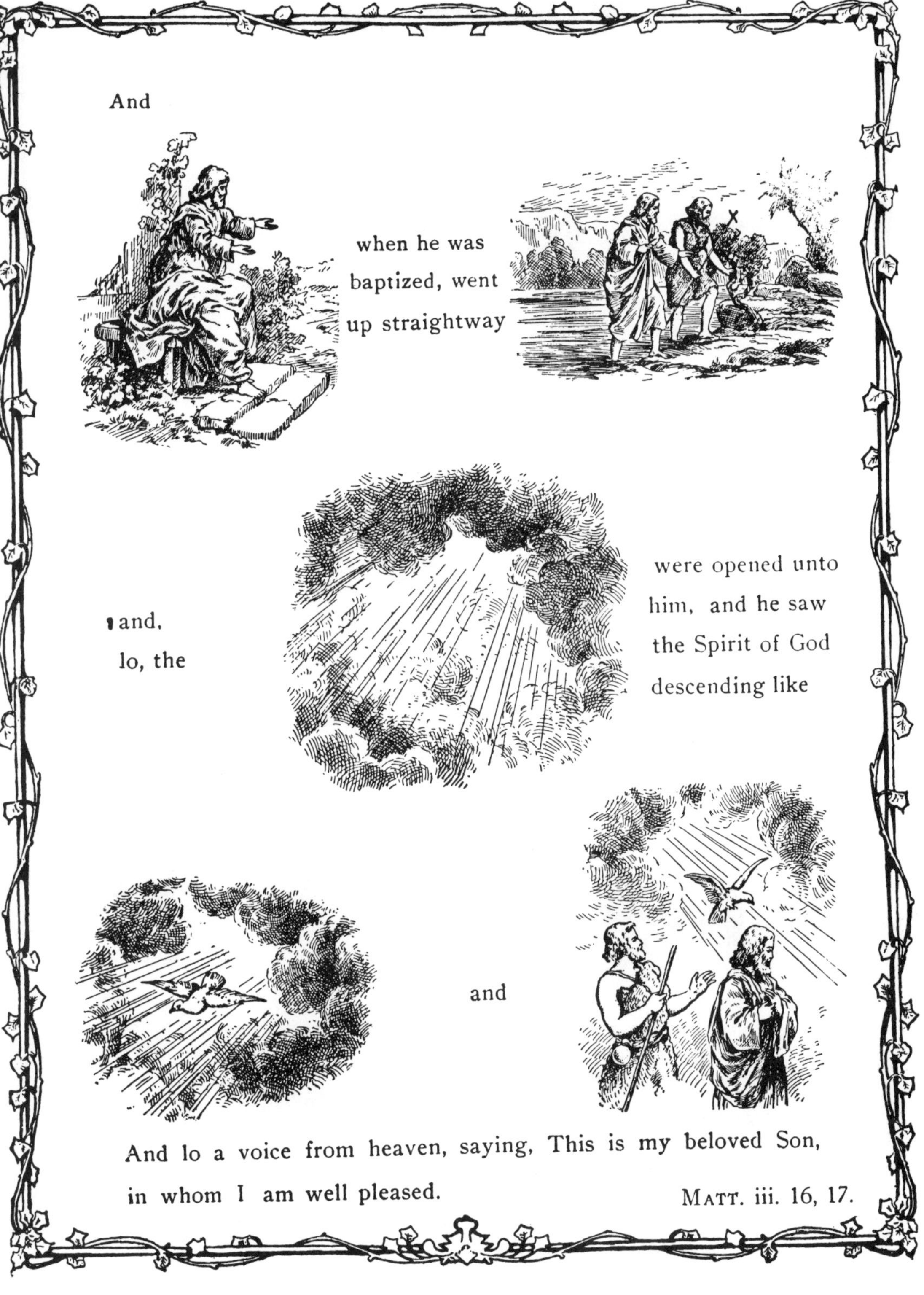

And

when he was baptized, went up straightway

and, lo, the

were opened unto him, and he saw the Spirit of God descending like

and

And lo a voice from heaven, saying, This is my beloved Son, in whom I am well pleased.

MATT. iii. 16, 17.

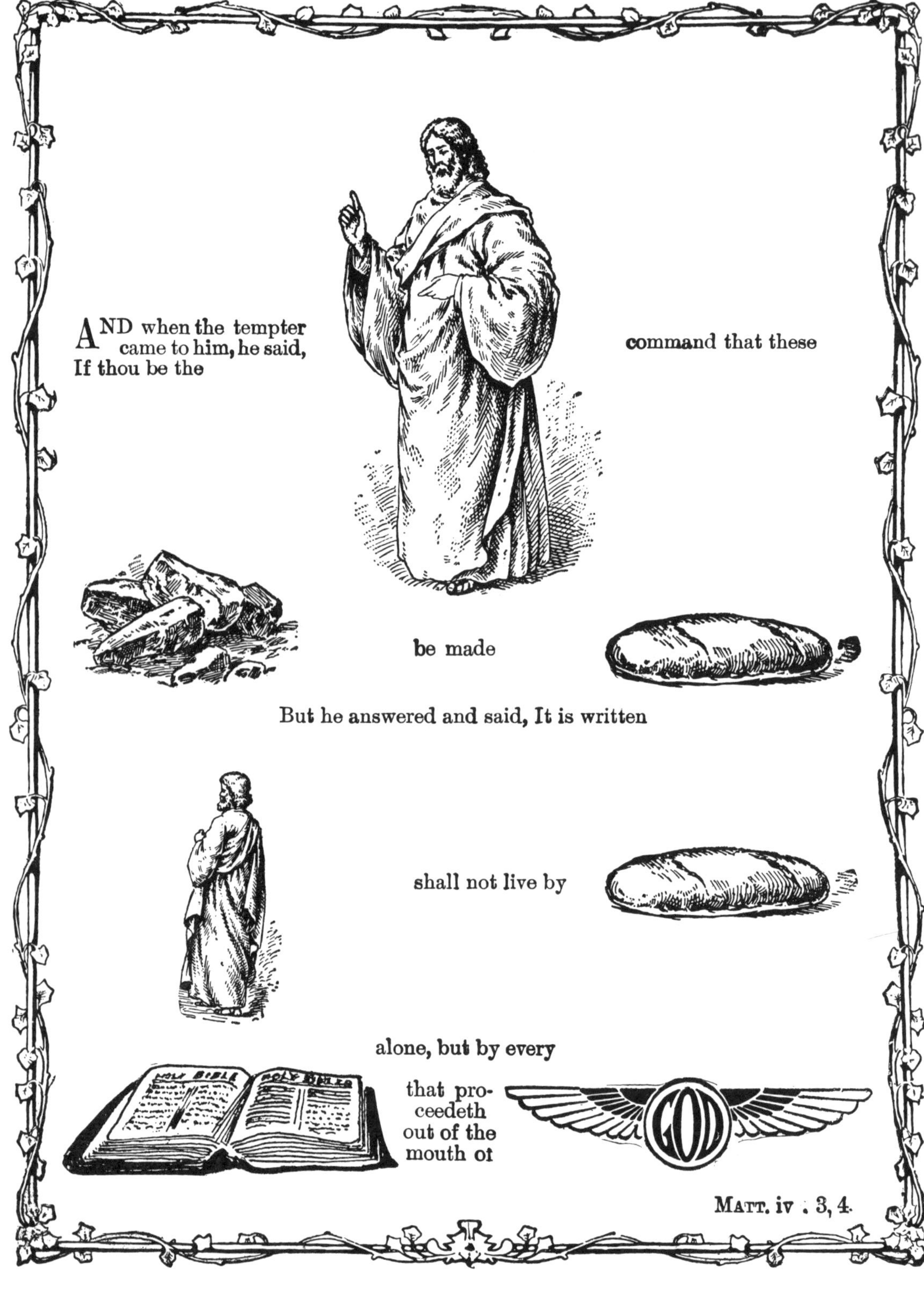

AND when the tempter came to him, he said, If thou be the

command that these

be made

But he answered and said, It is written

shall not live by

alone, but by every

that proceedeth out of the mouth of

MATT. iv . 3, 4.

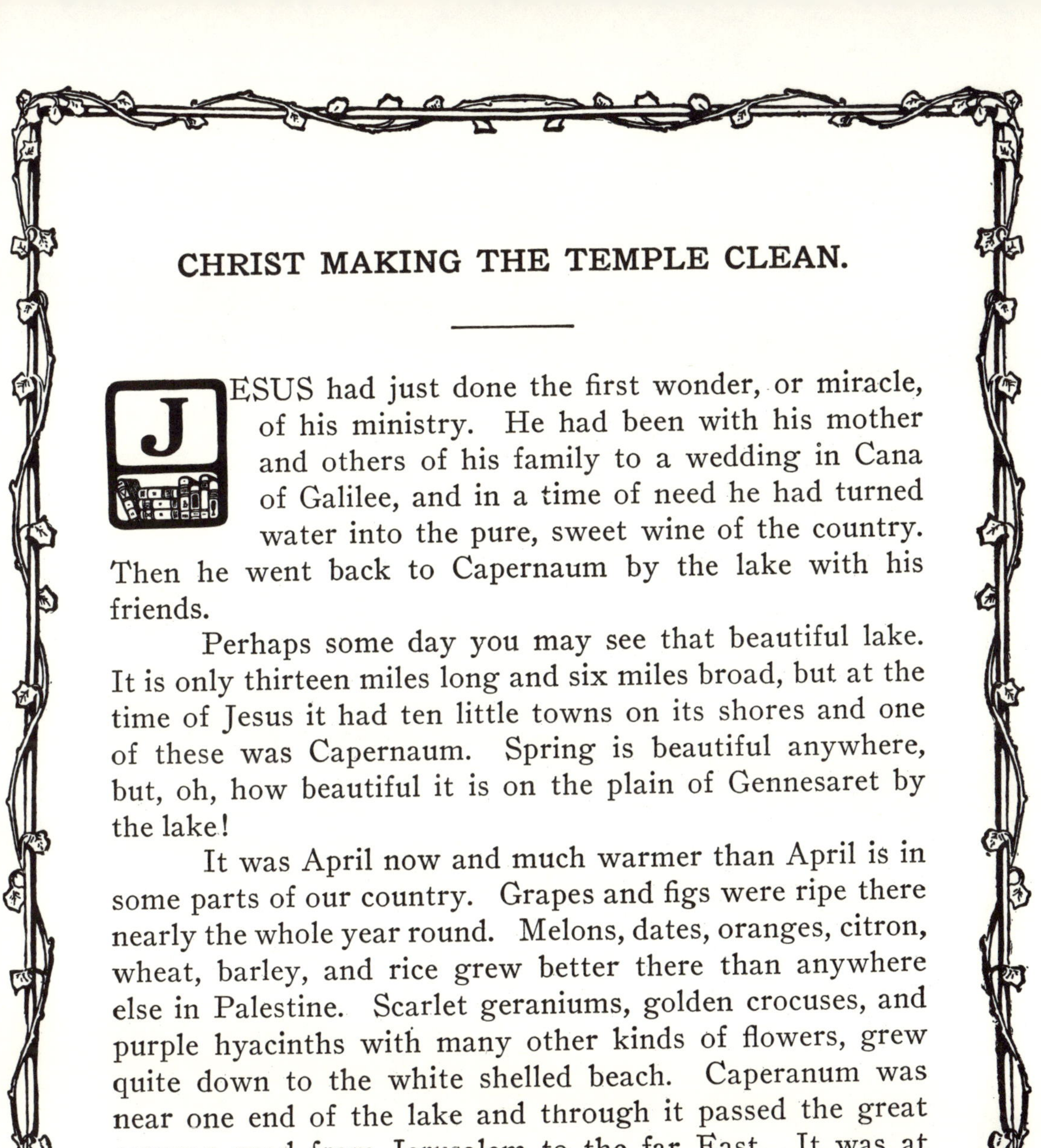

CHRIST MAKING THE TEMPLE CLEAN.

JESUS had just done the first wonder, or miracle, of his ministry. He had been with his mother and others of his family to a wedding in Cana of Galilee, and in a time of need he had turned water into the pure, sweet wine of the country. Then he went back to Capernaum by the lake with his friends.

Perhaps some day you may see that beautiful lake. It is only thirteen miles long and six miles broad, but at the time of Jesus it had ten little towns on its shores and one of these was Capernaum. Spring is beautiful anywhere, but, oh, how beautiful it is on the plain of Gennesaret by the lake!

It was April now and much warmer than April is in some parts of our country. Grapes and figs were ripe there nearly the whole year round. Melons, dates, oranges, citron, wheat, barley, and rice grew better there than anywhere else in Palestine. Scarlet geraniums, golden crocuses, and purple hyacinths with many other kinds of flowers, grew quite down to the white shelled beach. Caperanum was near one end of the lake and through it passed the great caravan road from Jerusalem to the far East. It was at this time a fine city with beautiful buildings, squares, and markets, but now it is a sad ruin, and there is not one city left on the lake.

Jesus went to the home of Peter near the shore, but the Passover, the greatest of all the Jewish feasts, was soon to begin and after a few days he went up to Jerusalem with the company from Capernaum. They went singing glad songs through the sweet spring weather, the blue lake lying on one side and the fresh fields on the other. Through flowery valleys and over grassy plains they went after leaving the lake, and day after day they could see the river Jordan with its fringe of trees not far away.

When they reached the top of the Mount of Olives they burst into a psalm of rejoicing and waved green branches in the air, for there below lay the Holy City, its Temple roof and turrets shining in the sun. They could also see the crowds of people and the herds and flocks for the sacrifice. Jesus knew that the Temple ought to be a very holy place to every Jew, but when he went into it next morning he saw and heard many things that he knew were not right. In the beautiful outer court with its pillars and porches of red and white marble, there were oxen and sheep and doves for sale, and men were buying and selling, and shouting and quarreling so that those who were in the inner courts at prayer were much disturbed. The innocent animals were not to blame, but the men who brought them, as well as the men who sat at the tables changing money were not there to worship God, but to buy and sell, and the priests allowed it to go on.

Jesus picked up some cords and twisted them together and drove the animals and their owners out of the court. He poured out the money from the boxes of the money changers and threw their tables down, saying to those who had cages of doves, "Take these things away. Make not my Father's house a house of merchandise." The people were angry and the more so because they fled before a young countrymen from Galilee whom they thought had no right to send them away, but Jesus was doing his Father's work, and when it was done he went away quietly.

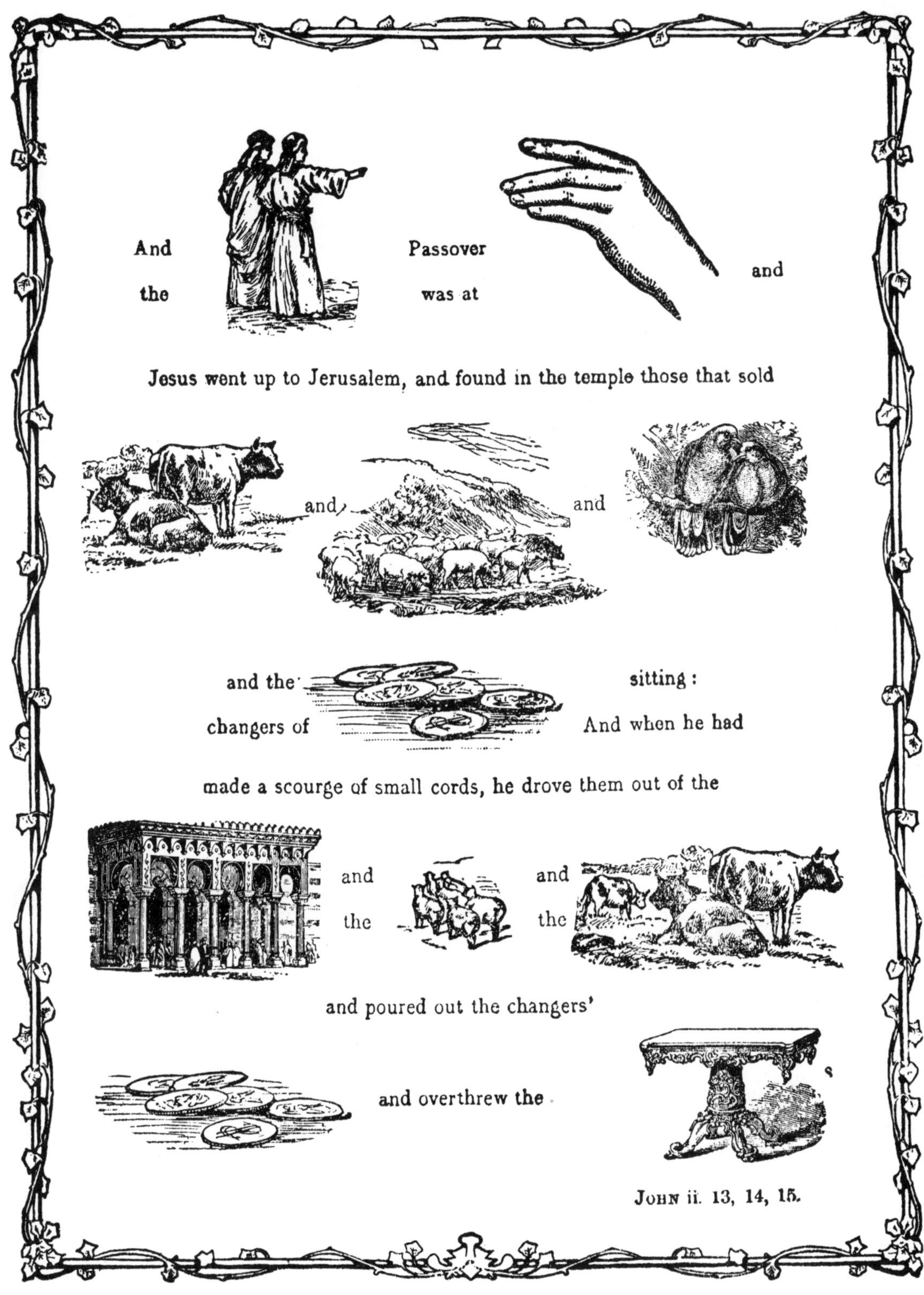

And the Passover was at and

Jesus went up to Jerusalem, and found in the temple those that sold

and and

and the changers of sitting: And when he had

made a scourge of small cords, he drove them out of the

and the and the

and poured out the changers'

and overthrew the

JOHN ii. 13, 14, 15.

I (Name)..............................FILLED

IN THESE ANSWERS. (Date) ....

1. To what feast did Jesus go when 12 years old?

....

2. Where was it held?

....

3. Why did Jesus say some trees ought to be cut down and burned?

....

4. Did He mean that people are like trees?

....

5. Who baptized Jesus and where?

....

6. What two signs did God send at His baptism?

....

7. How many times was Jesus tempted?

....

8. How did He answer the tempter every time?

....

9. Why did the Jews celebrate the Passover?

....

10. What wrong did Jesus find in the Temple and how did He correct it?

....

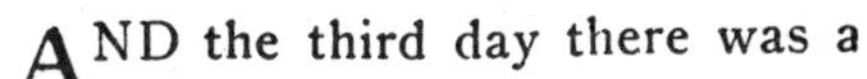

AND the third day there was a

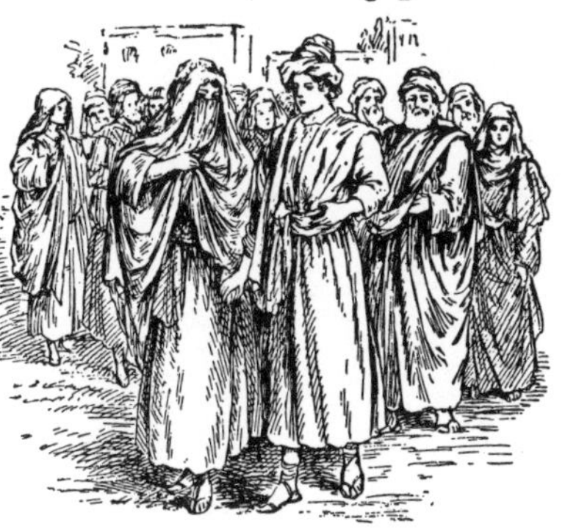

in Cana of Galilee and the

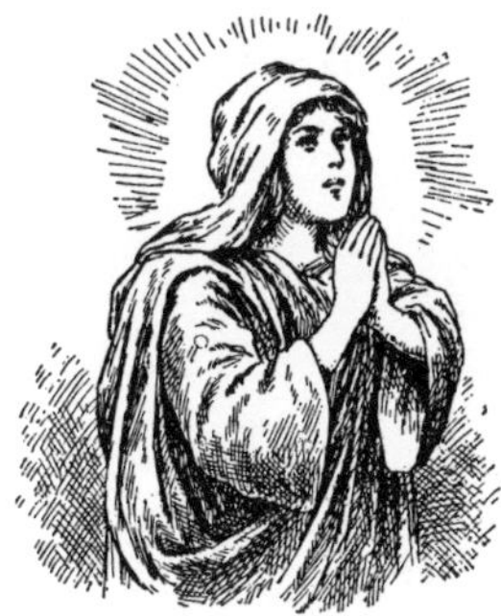

was there: And both Jesus was called, and his disciples, to the marriage. And when they wanted wine, the mother of Jesus saith unto him, They have no wine. Jesus saith unto them, Fill the

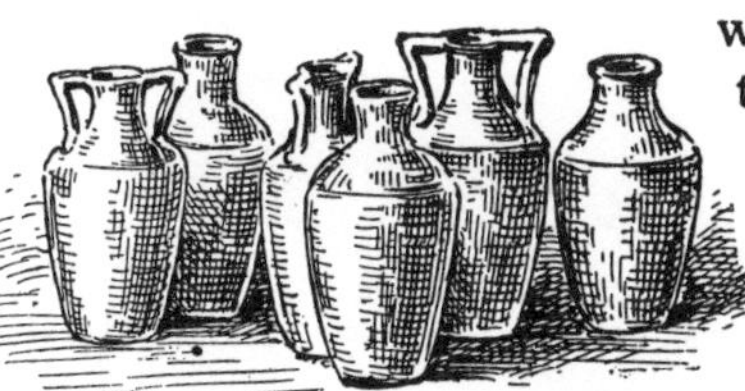

with water. And they filled them up to the brim. And he saith unto them. Draw out now, and bear unto

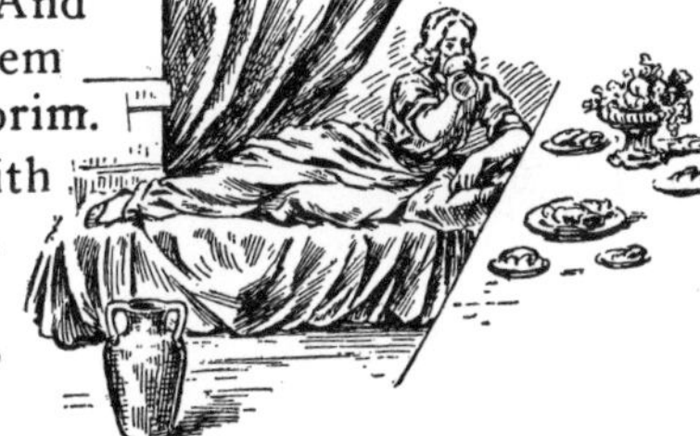

of the feast And they bare it. When the ruler of the feast had tasted the water that was made wine, and knew not whence it was, (but the

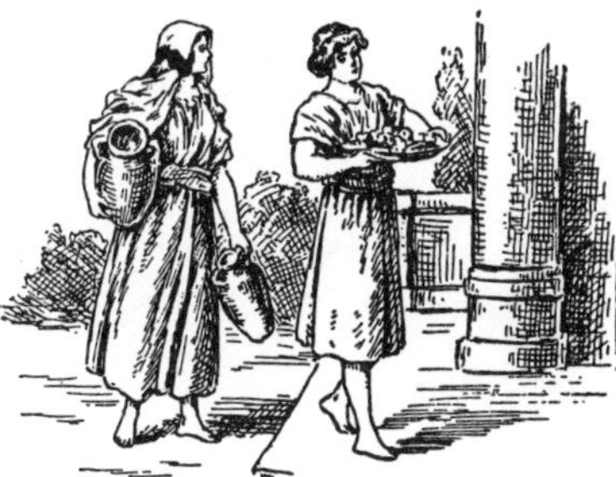

which drew the water knew,) the governor of the feast called the

And saith unto him, Every man at the beginning doth set forth good wine; and when men have well drunk, then that which is worse: but thou hast kept the good wine until now.

John ii: 1-3, 7-10.

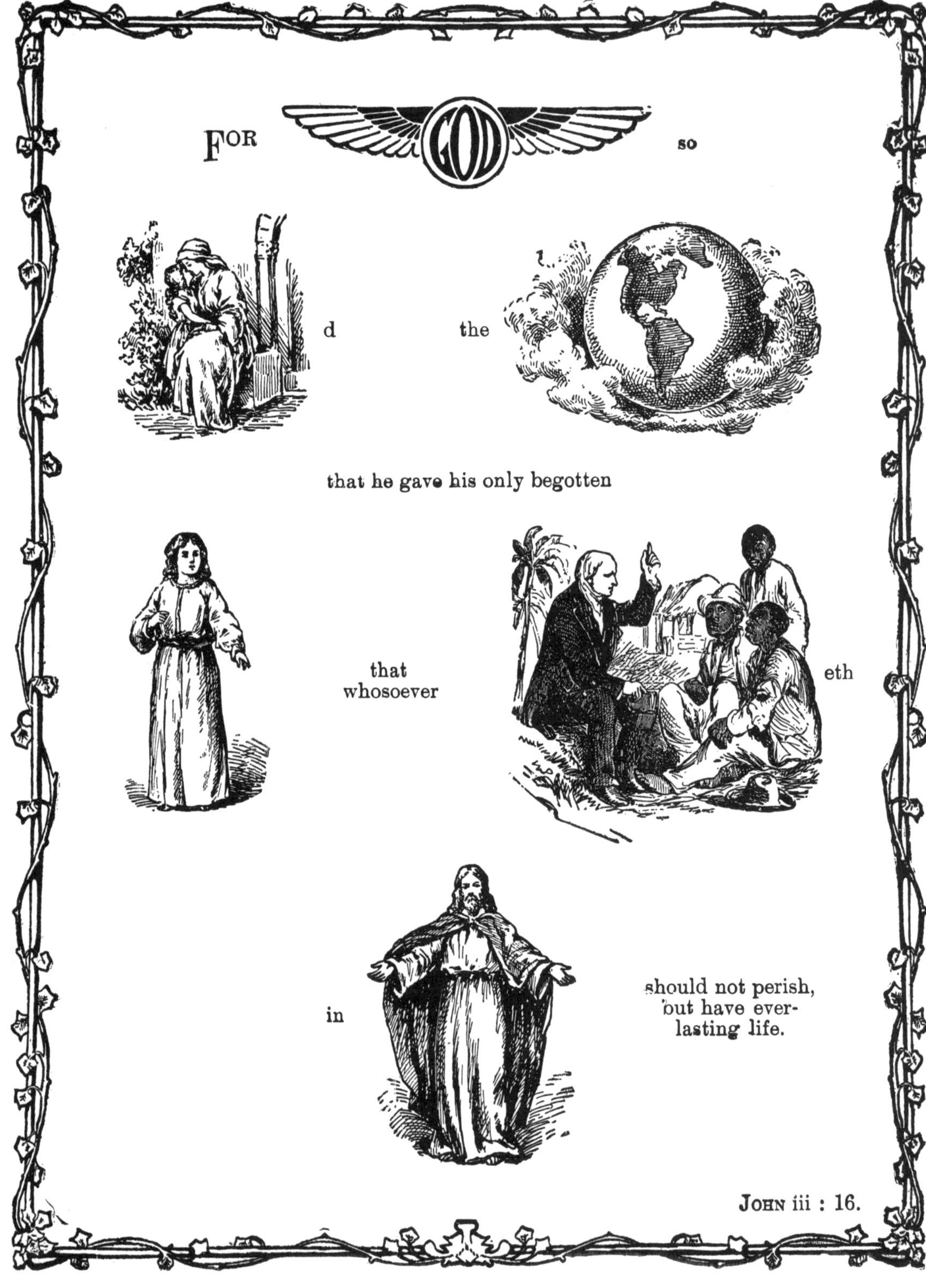
For
GOD
so
d
the
that he gave his only begotten
that
whosoever
eth
in
should not perish,
but have ever-
lasting life.
John iii : 16.

"FISHERS OF MEN."

"FEAR not, from henceforth thou shalt catch men."

Jesus spoke these words to Peter one lovely morning, standing on the shore of the blue Sea of Galilee. He had been teaching the people who flocked in crowds about him, and while he was still speaking two fishing boats came to the shore. The fishermen were tired, for they had toiled all night and had caught nothing. They began at once to take the nets from their boats, and to wash the sand and pebbles out of them in order to get them ready for the next night's work.

By this time the people had crowded down upon the water's edge, so that Jesus stepped into Peter's boat and asked him to push it out a little way from the shore. Peter gladly did so, and from the boat Jesus went on speaking to the people, and they listened eagerly to every word he said. When he was done he sent them away, and then told Peter, and Andrew, his brother, to push the boat out into the deep water, and let the nets down again. Peter thought in his heart that this would do no good, but he said, "At thy word I will let down the nets." Peter knew that Jesus was a great Teacher, but he did not know that he was a great Wonder-worker.

Out into the blue lake Peter rowed again, and this time, though it was morning, when the fish are not easily caught, the nets filled so quickly and were so heavy that the fishermen had to make signs to James and John, their partners in fishing, to bring their boats and help carry the load. When Peter saw this he knew that Jesus could do mighty works, and as soon as he came to the shore he ran and knelt down before him, and said, "Depart from me, for I am a sinful man, O Lord." Peter meant by this that he was not worthy to be a disciple because he had doubted the power of Jesus, and then Jesus told him not to be afraid, for he would make him a fisher of men.

Peter and Andrew and James and John, all fishermen, had been called to be the disciples of Jesus. A disciple is a learner, and Jesus wanted these fishermen to learn from him all that he could teach them, so that they might become teachers. These were among the very first disciples. Jesus was not looking for men who had much money or great learning or rich friends to become his followers. He wanted men with simple hearts, who, for love of him, would be willing to help other people to know and love him too. This is what he meant when he said, "Follow me, and I will make you fishers of men."

It is the same now as in those days. Anyone who truly follows Jesus will become a fisher of men. He will want other people to know and love Jesus so much that he will be making plans to "catch" them just as a good fisherman does who is eager to catch fish. You do not need to be a preacher and stand in a pulpit to be a fisher of men, nor do you have to be a missionary and go far away to some strange country. Just the place in which you are, just that which is given you to do at the time, is *your* place and *your* opportunity to do the kind of fishing Jesus wants done. The boy or the girl in the home, at school, on the playground, anywhere, everywhere, may be a true follower of Jesus, and therefore a real fisher of men.

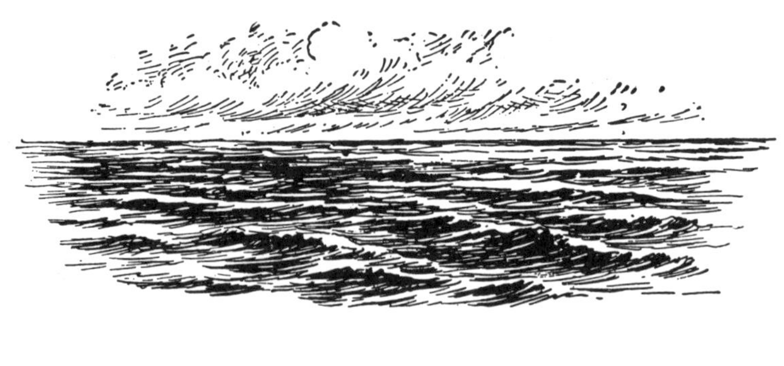

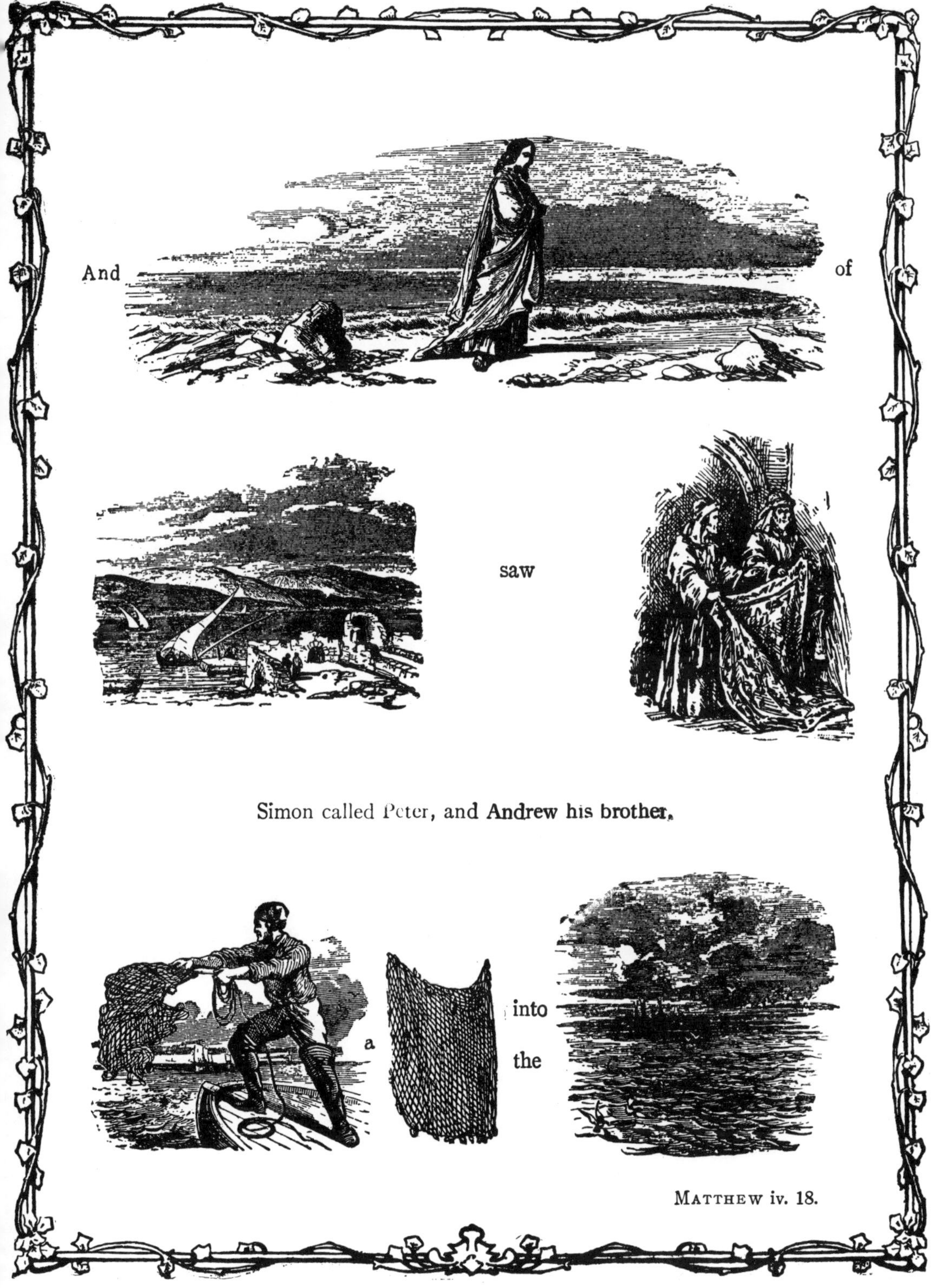

MATTHEW iv. 18.

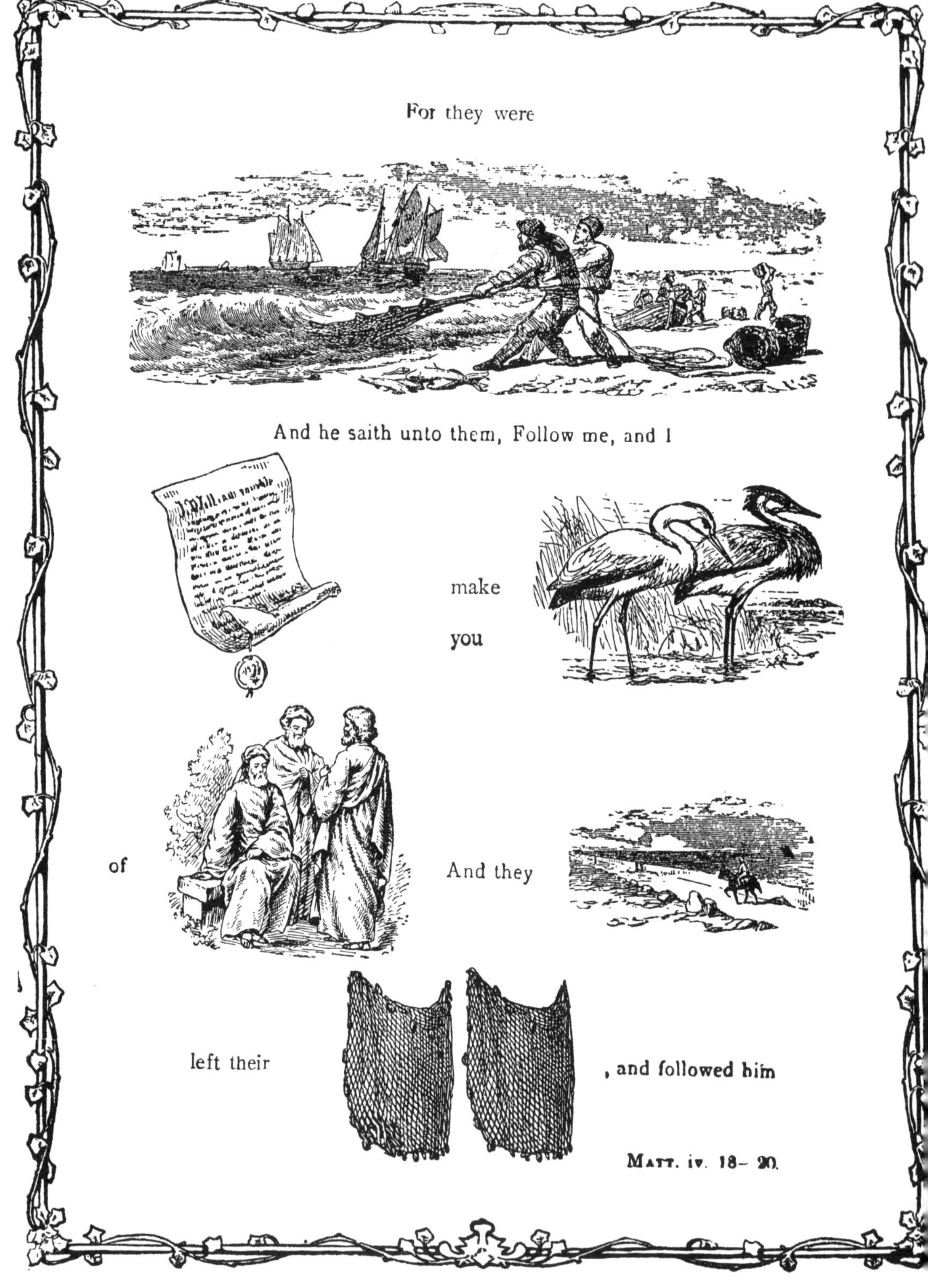

For they were

And he saith unto them, Follow me, and I

make

you

of

And they

left their

, and followed him

MATT. iv. 18– 20.

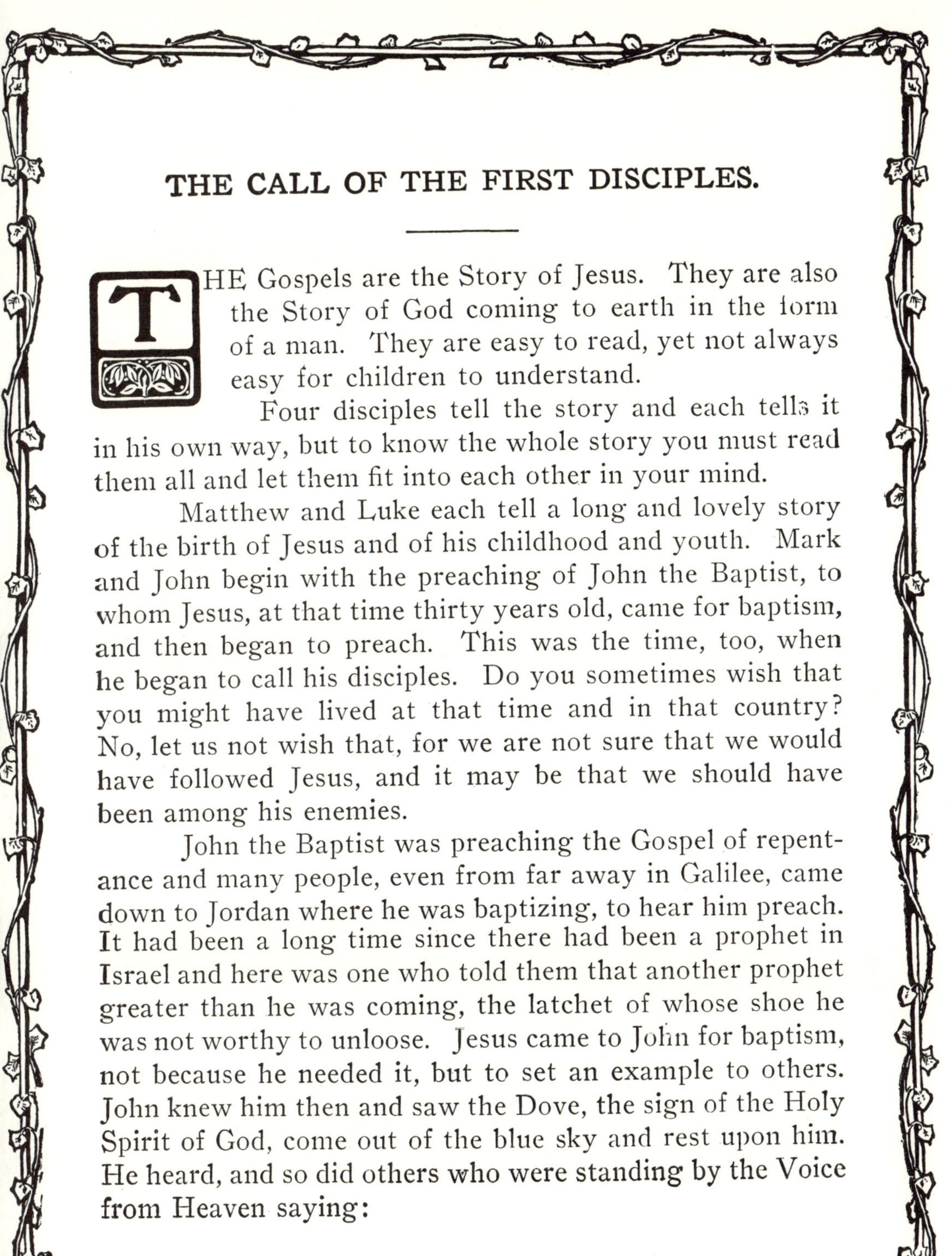

THE CALL OF THE FIRST DISCIPLES.

THE Gospels are the Story of Jesus. They are also the Story of God coming to earth in the form of a man. They are easy to read, yet not always easy for children to understand.

Four disciples tell the story and each tells it in his own way, but to know the whole story you must read them all and let them fit into each other in your mind.

Matthew and Luke each tell a long and lovely story of the birth of Jesus and of his childhood and youth. Mark and John begin with the preaching of John the Baptist, to whom Jesus, at that time thirty years old, came for baptism, and then began to preach. This was the time, too, when he began to call his disciples. Do you sometimes wish that you might have lived at that time and in that country? No, let us not wish that, for we are not sure that we would have followed Jesus, and it may be that we should have been among his enemies.

John the Baptist was preaching the Gospel of repentance and many people, even from far away in Galilee, came down to Jordan where he was baptizing, to hear him preach. It had been a long time since there had been a prophet in Israel and here was one who told them that another prophet greater than he was coming, the latchet of whose shoe he was not worthy to unloose. Jesus came to John for baptism, not because he needed it, but to set an example to others. John knew him then and saw the Dove, the sign of the Holy Spirit of God, come out of the blue sky and rest upon him. He heard, and so did others who were standing by the Voice from Heaven saying:

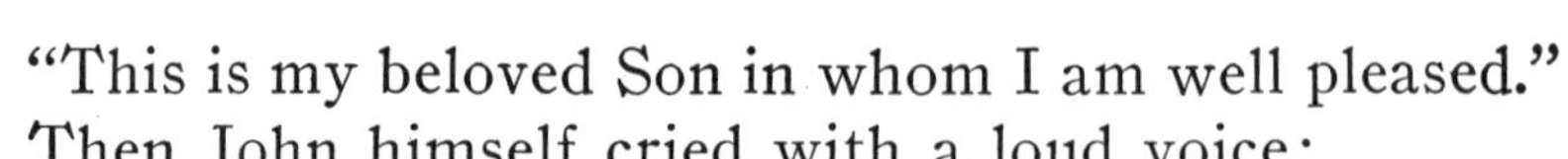

"This is my beloved Son in whom I am well pleased."

Then John himself cried with a loud voice:

"Behold the Lamb of God who taketh away the sin of the world."

Then Jesus went away into the wilderness and was tempted by the evil spirit, while he fasted for forty days. But the evil one could not gain a victory over Jesus for he was the Lord over all.

When Jesus came up out of the wilderness, strong in the Spirit, he came back to the river Jordon where John was baptizing. The spring was in the land and fresh green leaves and lovely wild flowers were making it beautiful. John had two disciples named Andrew and John. They were fishermen of Galilee. As they stood with him Jesus passed by and John cried again:

"Behold the Lamb of God."

Then these two disciples left John and followed Jesus. He said to them, "Whom seek ye?" And they said:

"Rabbi (teacher), where dwellest thou?" And he said:

"Come and see."

He led them to his tent and they listened to him as he talked of the things of the Kingdom of Heaven. It was late in the day, but it was morning in their hearts. Andrew was eager to find his brother, Simon Peter, and when he found him he cried:

"We have found the Messiah!"

Jesus was glad to see Simon Peter, and he said:

"Thou art Simon the son of Jona: thou shalt be called Cephus (Peter), which is by interpretation a stone.

Then they went away to Galilee and again Jesus called Peter and Andrew from their father's boat to follow him.

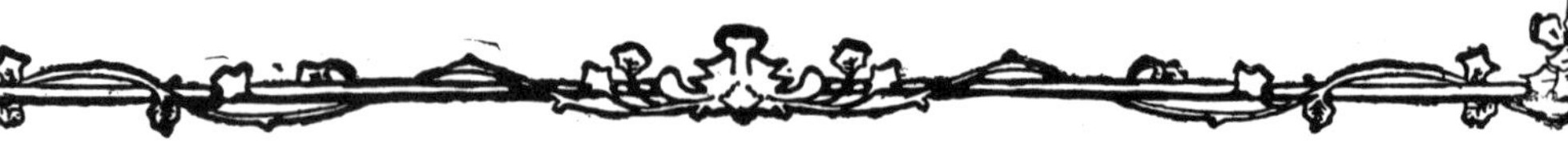

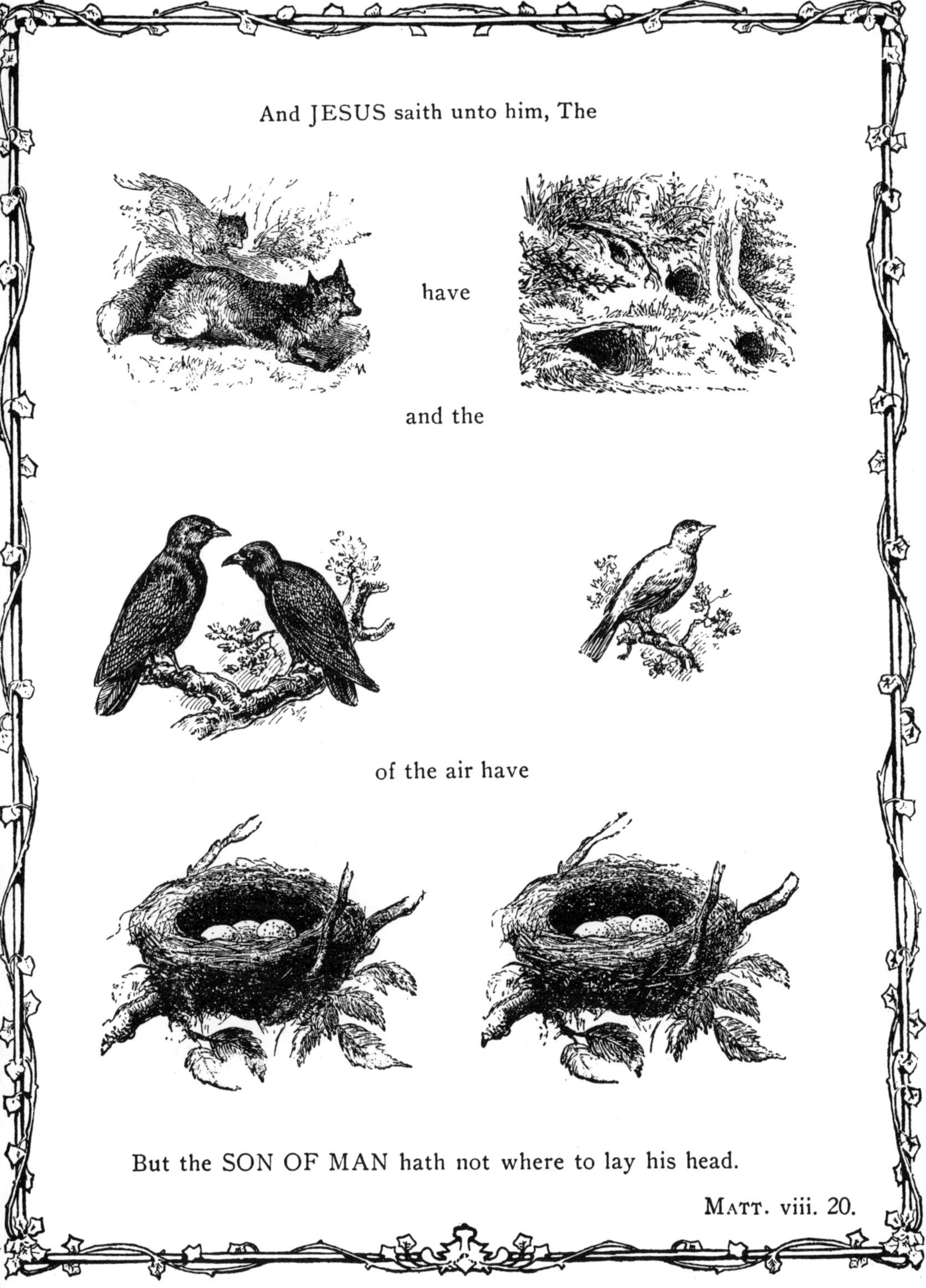

And JESUS saith unto him, The

have

and the

of the air have

But the SON OF MAN hath not where to lay his head.

MATT. viii. 20.

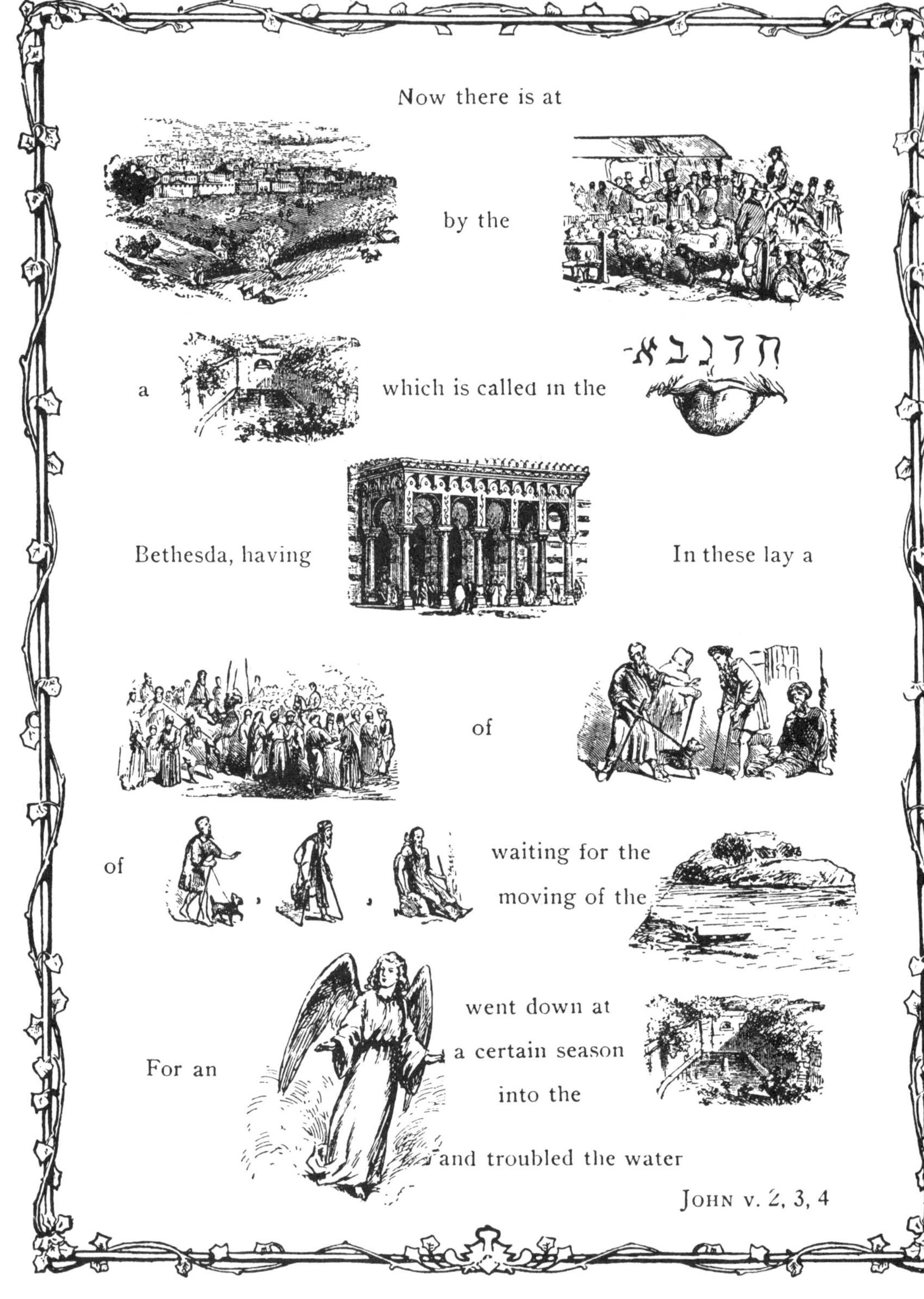
Now there is at
by the
a
which is called in the
Bethesda, having
In these lay a
of
of
waiting for the
moving of the
For an
went down at
a certain season
into the
and troubled the water
JOHN v. 2, 3, 4

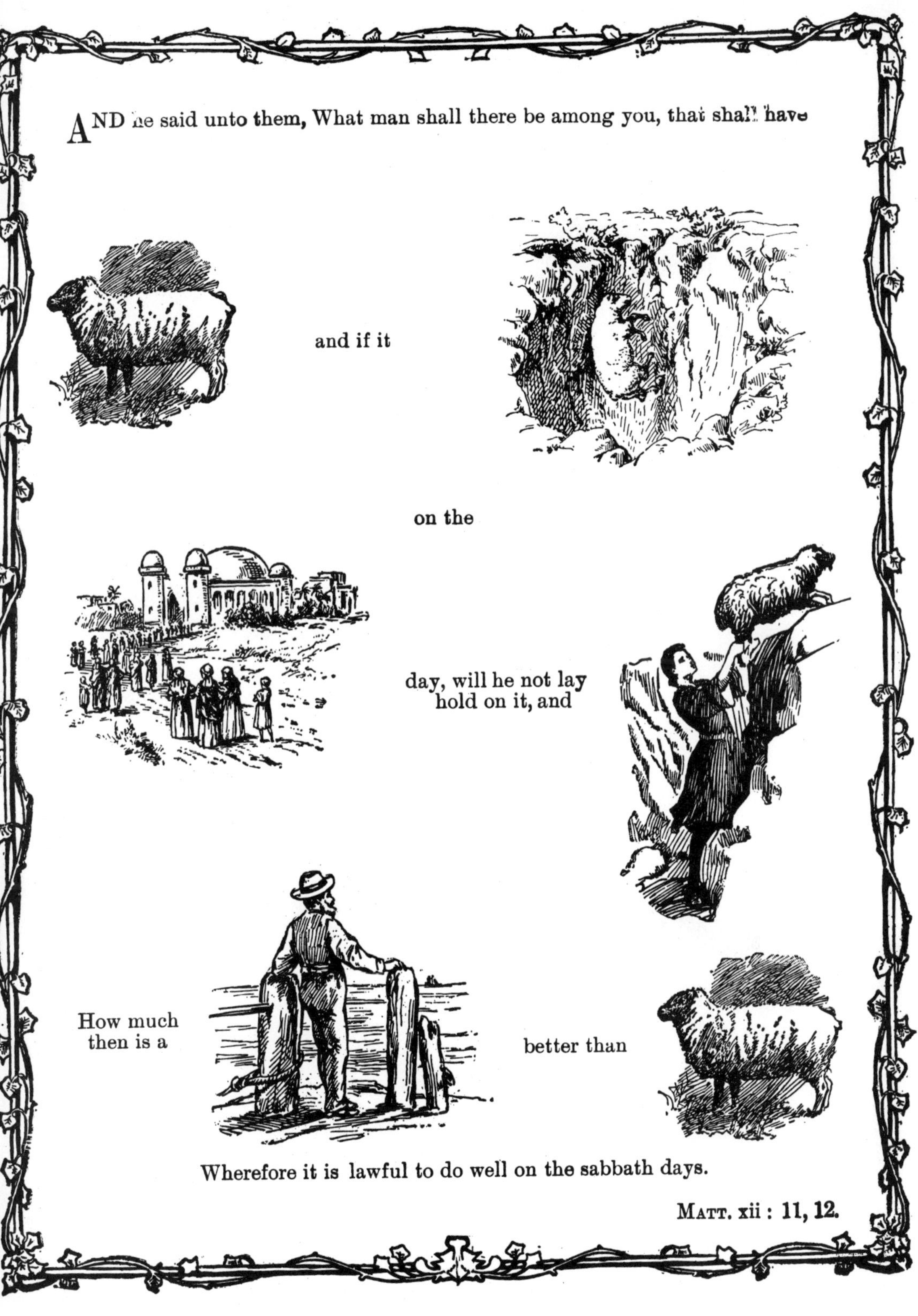
AND he said unto them, What man shall there be among you, that shall have
and if it
on the
day, will he not lay hold on it, and
How much then is a
better than
Wherefore it is lawful to do well on the sabbath days.
MATT. xii : 11, 12.

I (Name).....................................FILLED IN THESE ANSWERS. (Date) ....

1. What was Jesus' first miracle?

....

2. When and where was it performed?

....

3. What is the most precious verse in the Bible?

....

4. How much did God love the world?

....

5. What two disciples did Jesus call from their fishing?

....

6. For what purpose did he want them to follow Him?

....

7. Did Jesus have any home?

....

8. Where was the pool of Bethesda?

....

9. Who did Jesus heal at the pool?

....

10. What did Jesus say was right to do on the Sabbath?

....

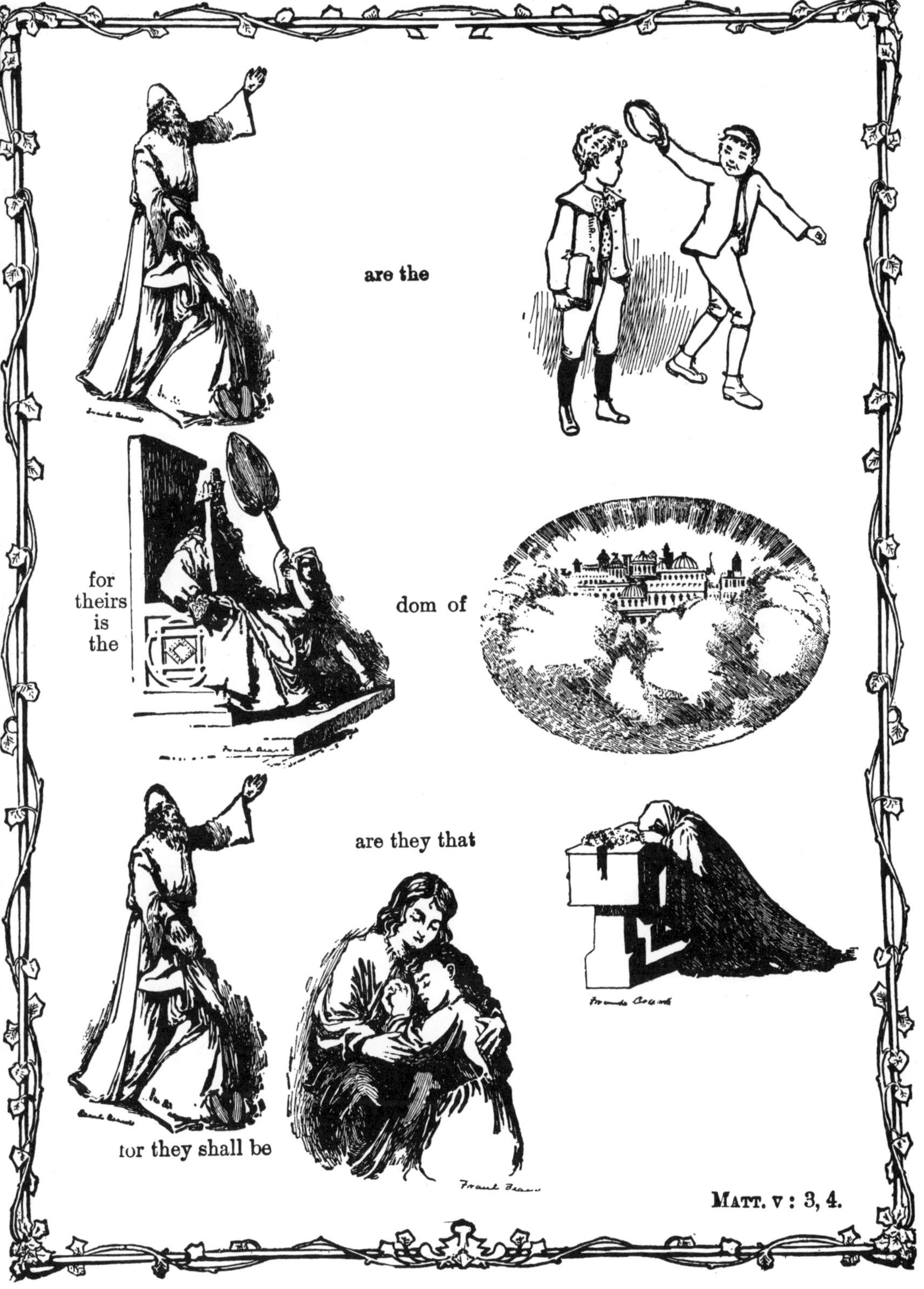
are the
for
theirs
is
the
dom of
are they that
tor they shall be
Matt. v : 3, 4.

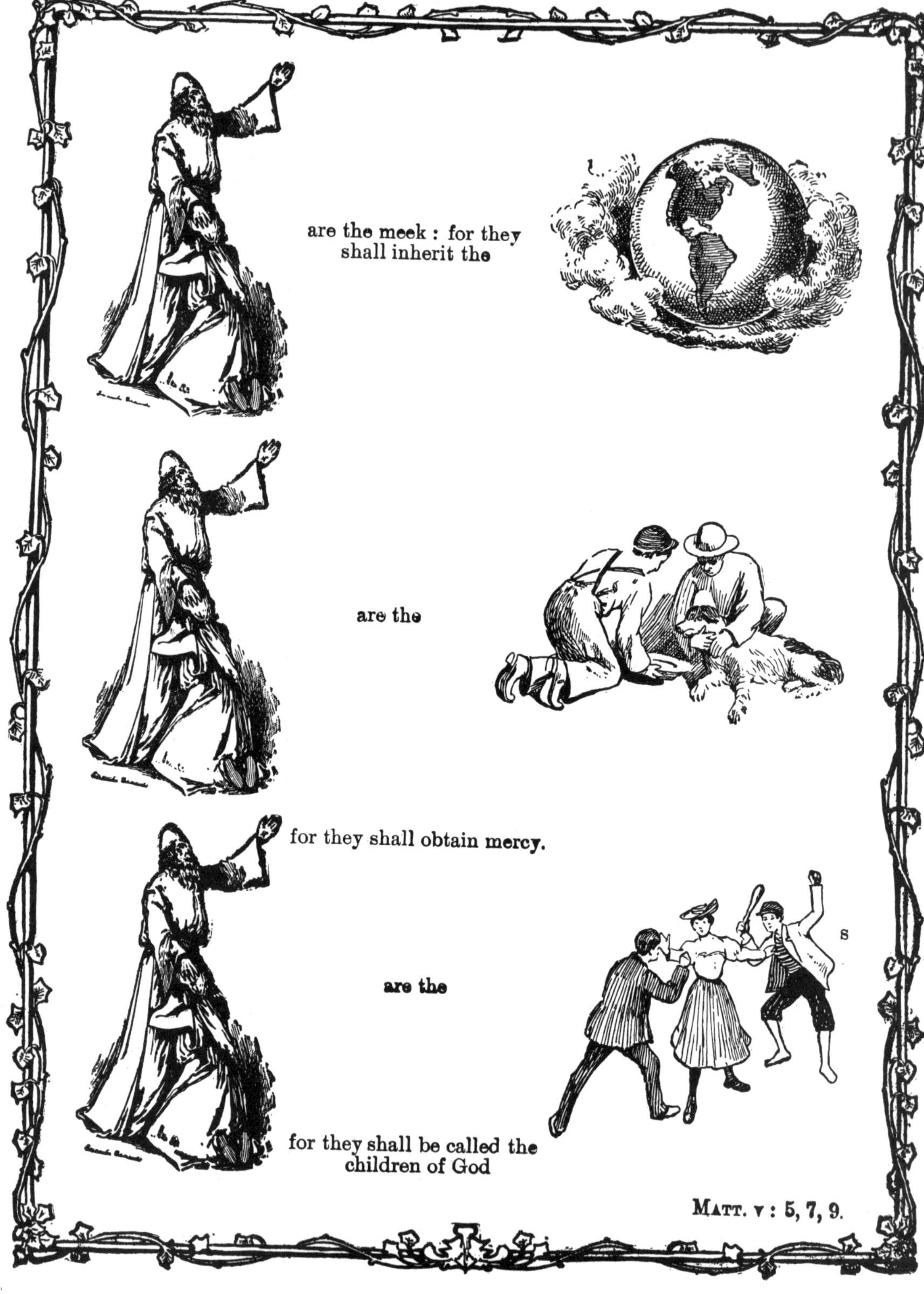

are the meek : for they shall inherit the

are the

for they shall obtain mercy.

s

are the

for they shall be called the children of God

Matt. v : 5, 7, 9.

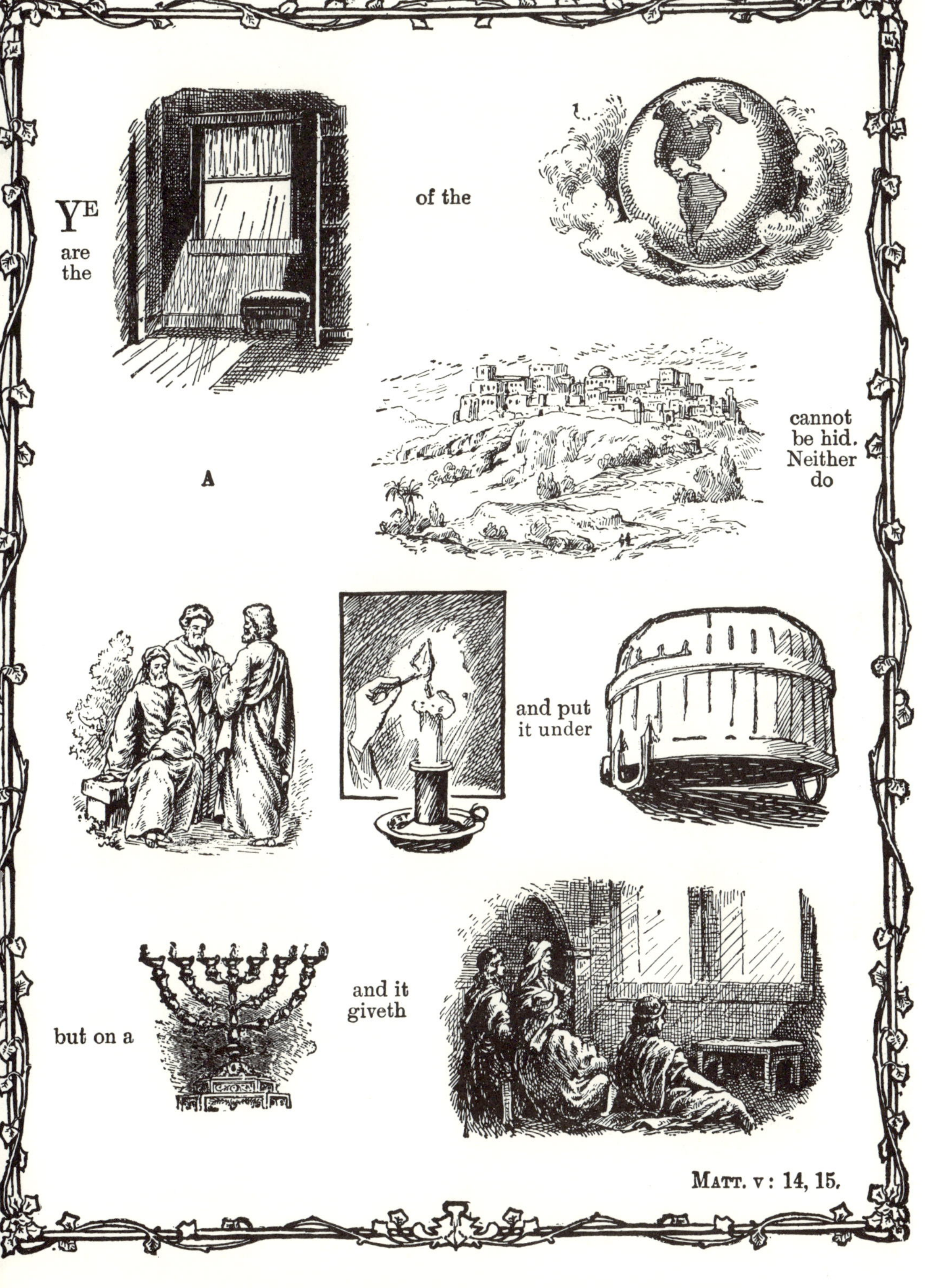
YE
are
the
of the
A
cannot
be hid.
Neither
do
and put
it under
but on a
and it
giveth
MATT. v: 14, 15.

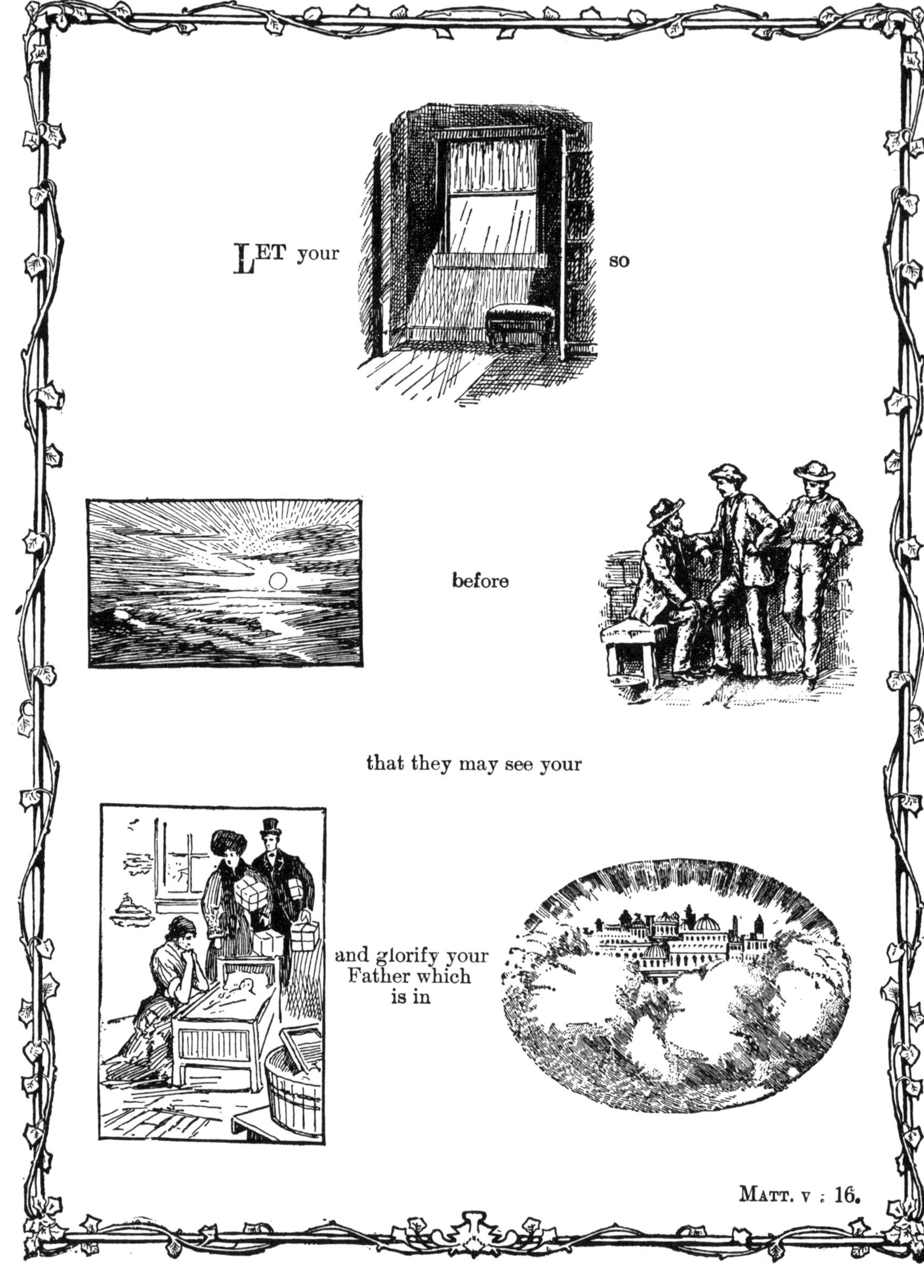

LET your so

before

that they may see your

and glorify your
Father which
is in

MATT. v : 16.

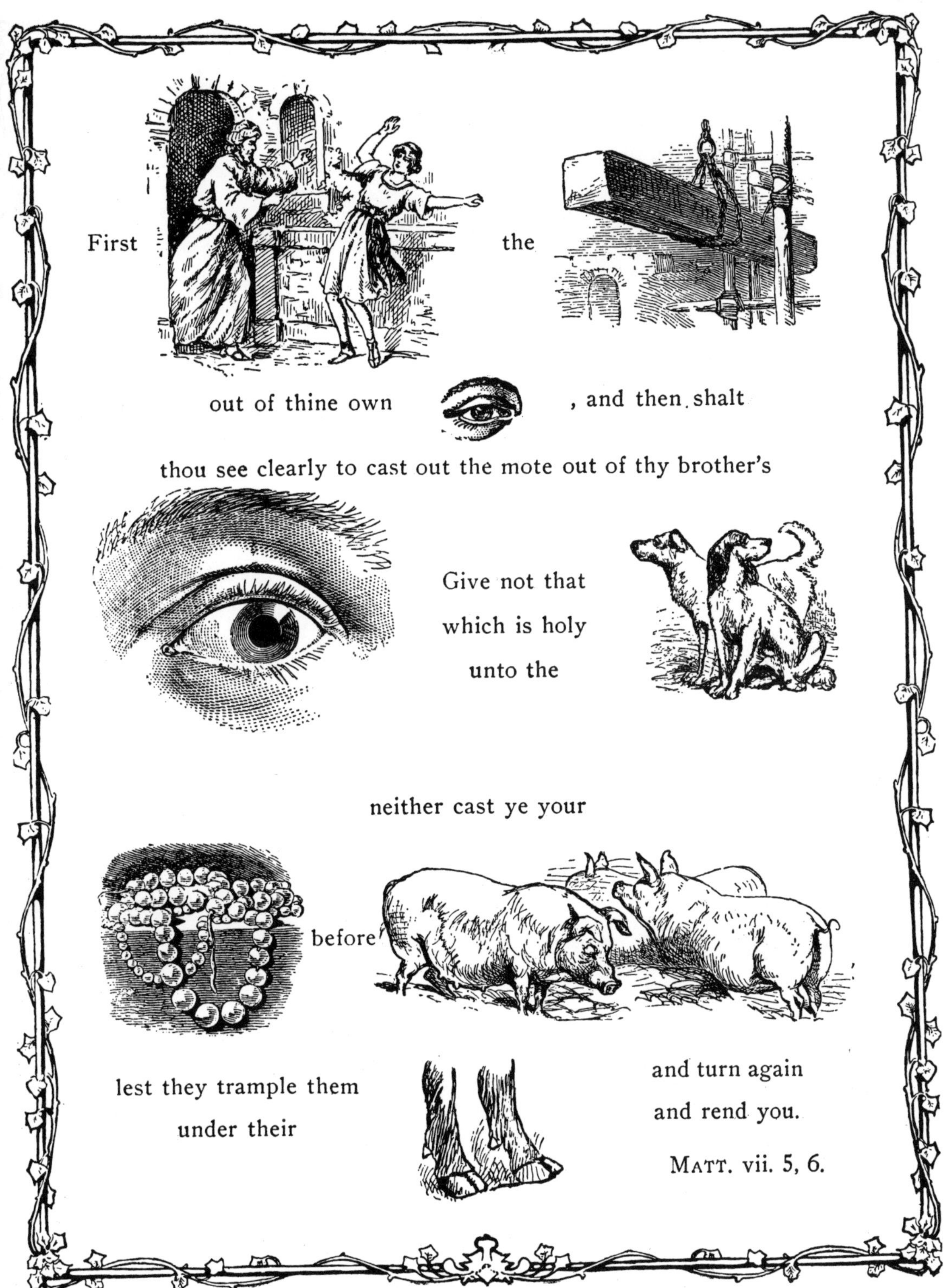

First [picture] the [picture] out of thine own [picture], and then shalt thou see clearly to cast out the mote out of thy brother's [picture]

Give not that which is holy unto the [picture]

neither cast ye your [picture] before [picture]

lest they trample them under their [picture] and turn again and rend you.

MATT. vii. 5, 6.

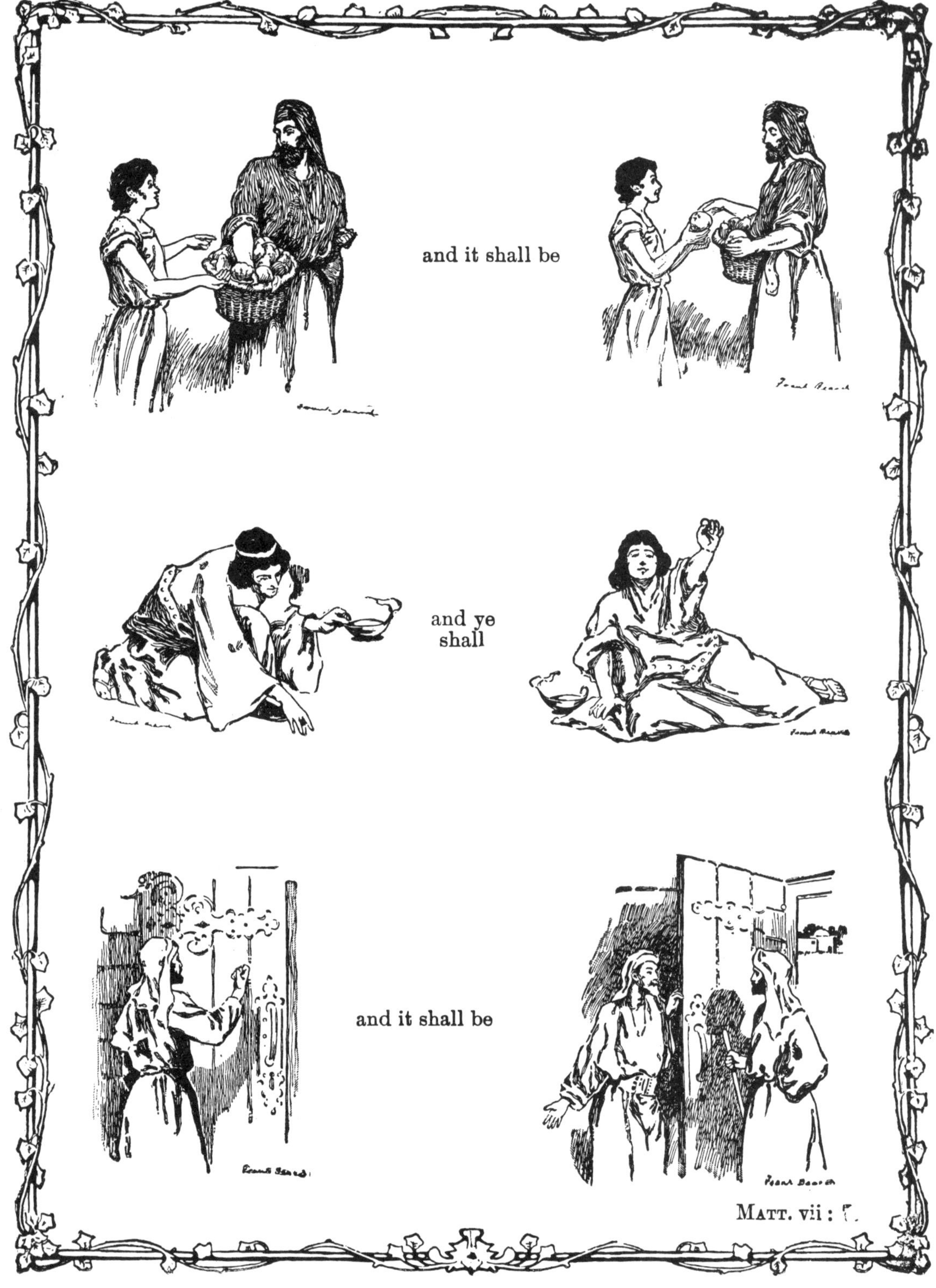
and it shall be
and ye
shall
and it shall be
Matt. vii : 7

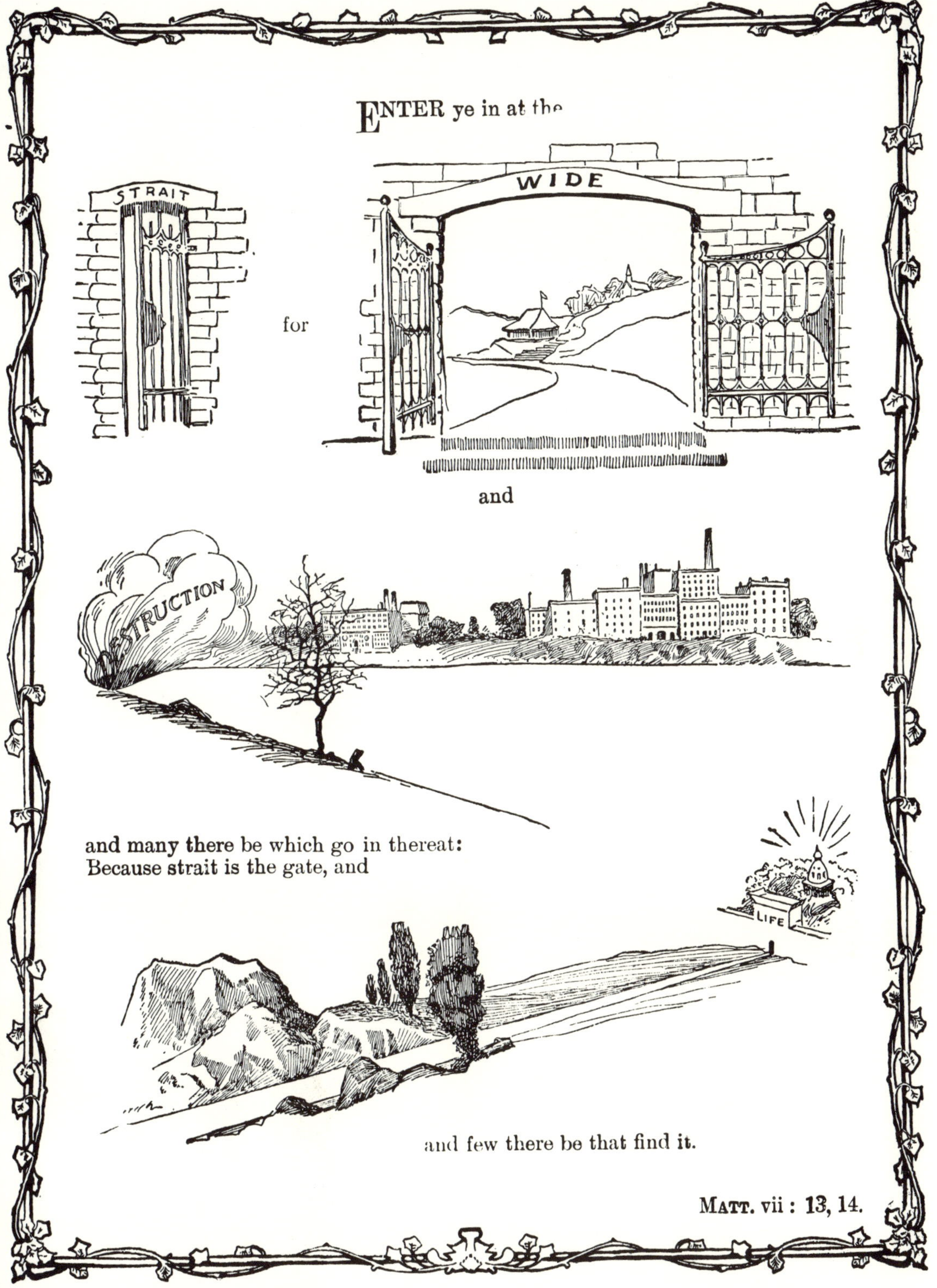
ENTER ye in at the
STRAIT
for
WIDE
and
STRUCTION
and many there be which go in thereat:
Because strait is the gate, and
LIFE
and few there be that find it.
MATT. vii : 13, 14.

I (Name)................................FILLED

IN THESE ANSWERS. (Date) ....

1. Where are the Beatitudes found?

....

2. Of what great sermon are they the beginning?

....

3. Why are Jesus' followers the light of the world?

....

4. Are you one of His and do your friends know it?

....

5. Why should we let our light shine?

....

6. What must we do before we can correct the faults of others?

....

7. What are we promised if we ask; seek; knock?

....

8. How do we know these promises are true?

....

9. To where does the straight gate and narrow way lead?

....

10. To where does the wide gate and broad way lead and why?

....

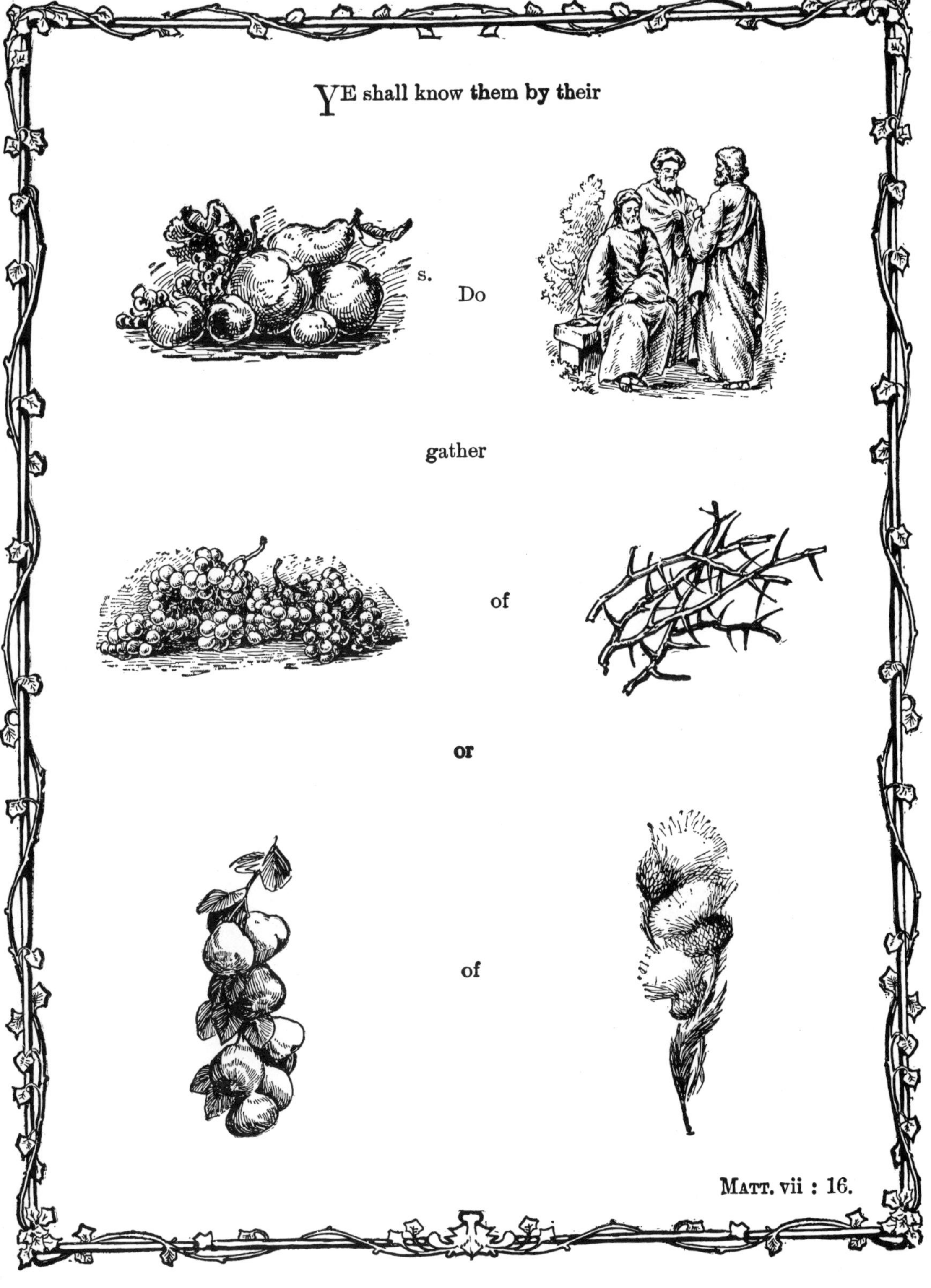
YE shall know them by their
s. Do
gather
of
or
of
Matt. vii : 16.

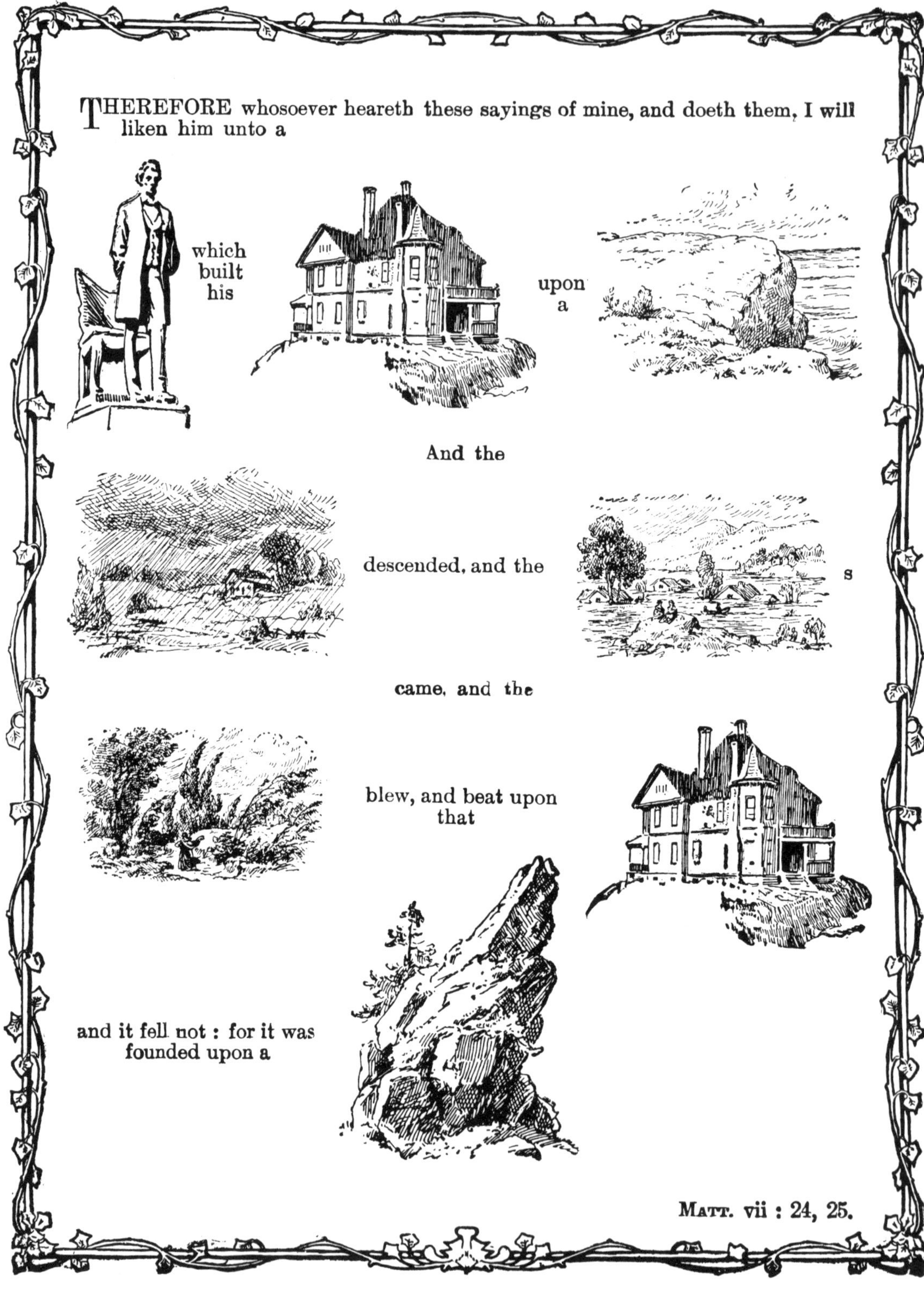

THEREFORE whosoever heareth these sayings of mine, and doeth them, I will liken him unto a

which built his

upon a

And the

descended, and the

s

came, and the

blew, and beat upon that

and it fell not : for it was founded upon a

MATT. vii : 24, 25.

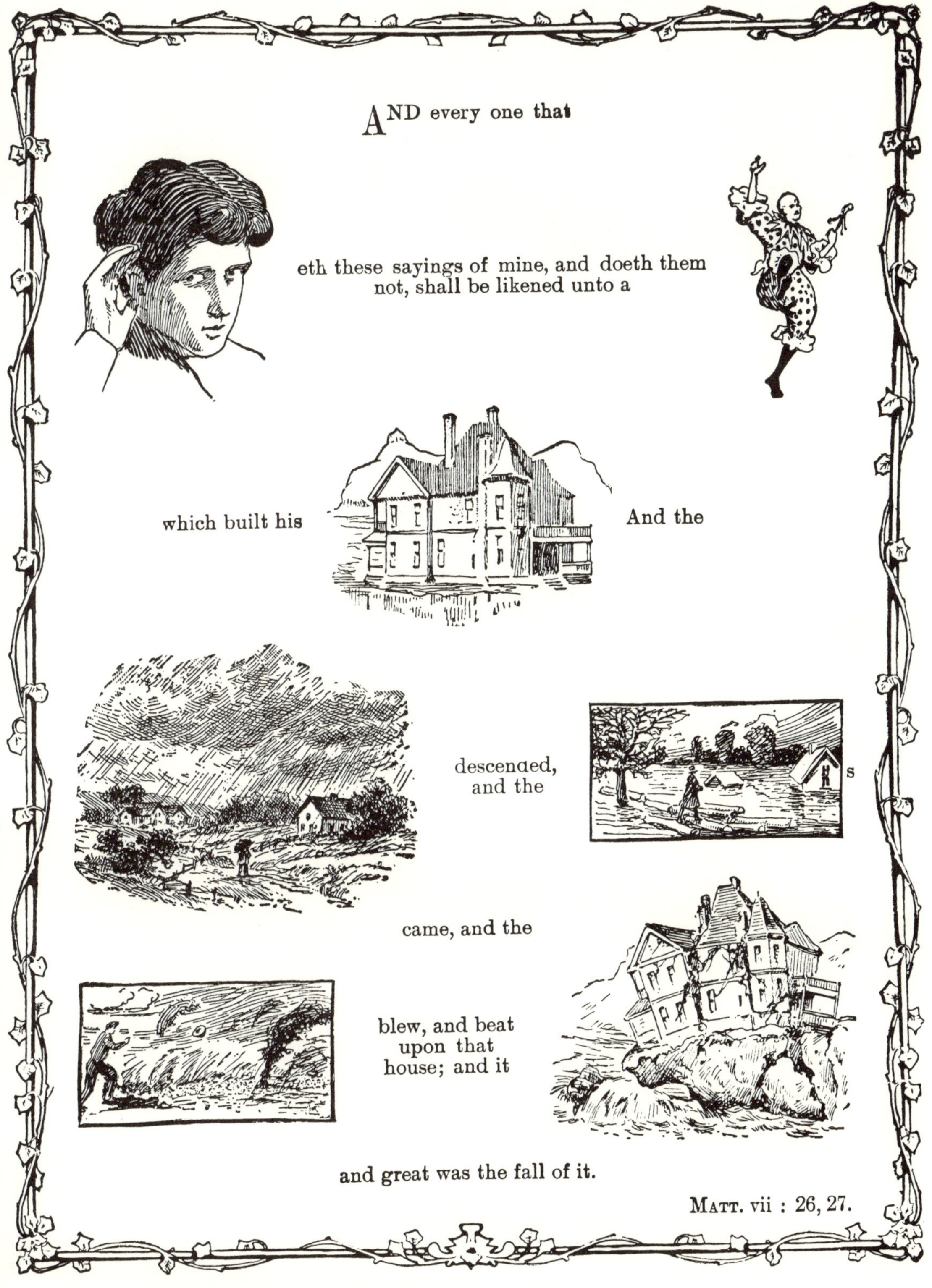
AND every one that
eth these sayings of mine, and doeth them not, shall be likened unto a
which built his
And the
descenaed, and the
s
came, and the
blew, and beat upon that house; and it
and great was the fall of it.
MATT. vii : 26, 27.

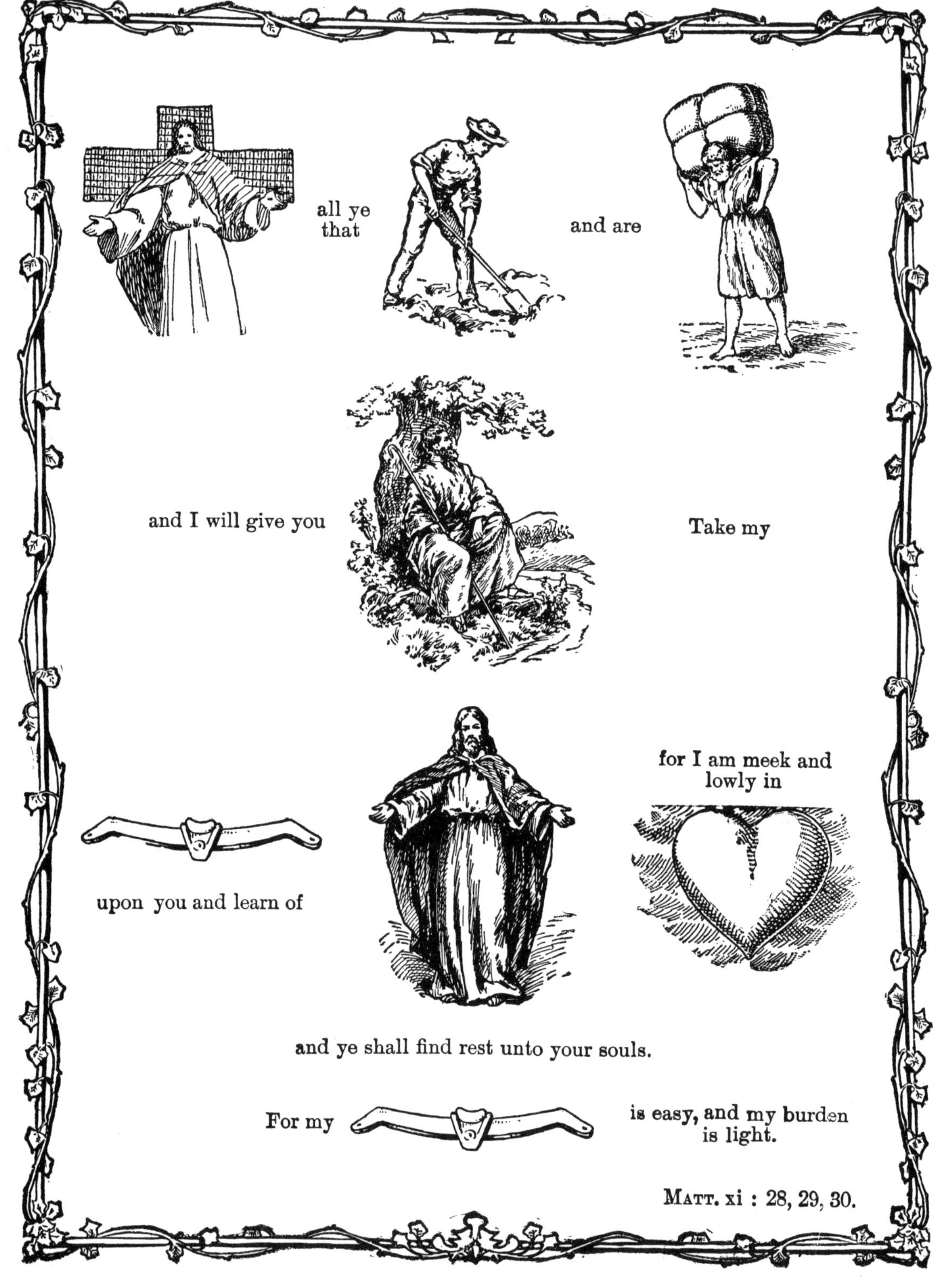
all ye
that
and are
and I will give you
Take my
for I am meek and
lowly in
upon you and learn of
and ye shall find rest unto your souls.
For my
is easy, and my burden
is light.
Matt. xi : 28, 29, 30.

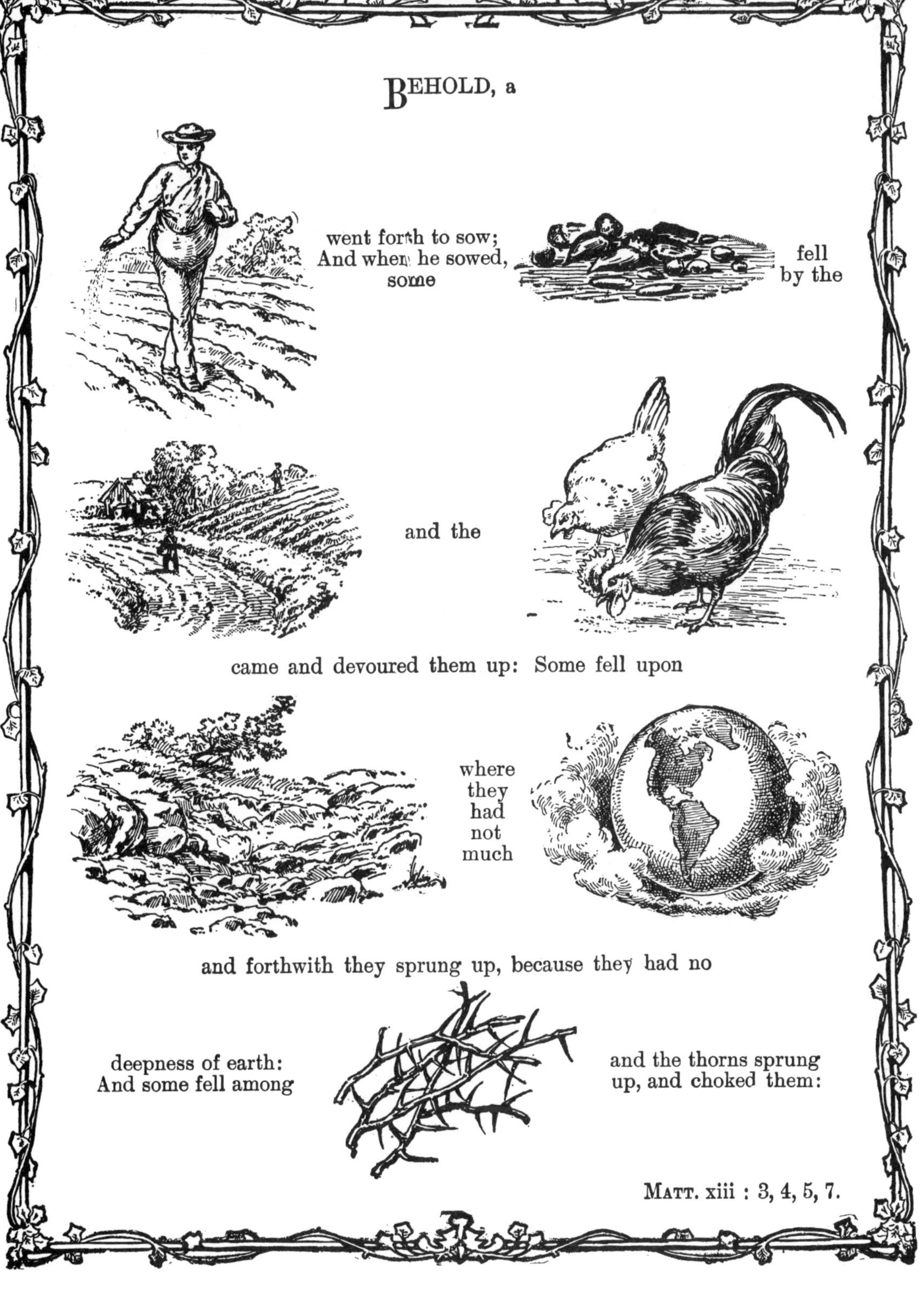

BEHOLD, a

went forth to sow;
And when he sowed,
some

fell
by the

and the

came and devoured them up: Some fell upon

where
they
had
not
much

and forthwith they sprung up, because they had no

deepness of earth:
And some fell among

and the thorns sprung
up, and choked them:

MATT. xiii : 3, 4, 5, 7.

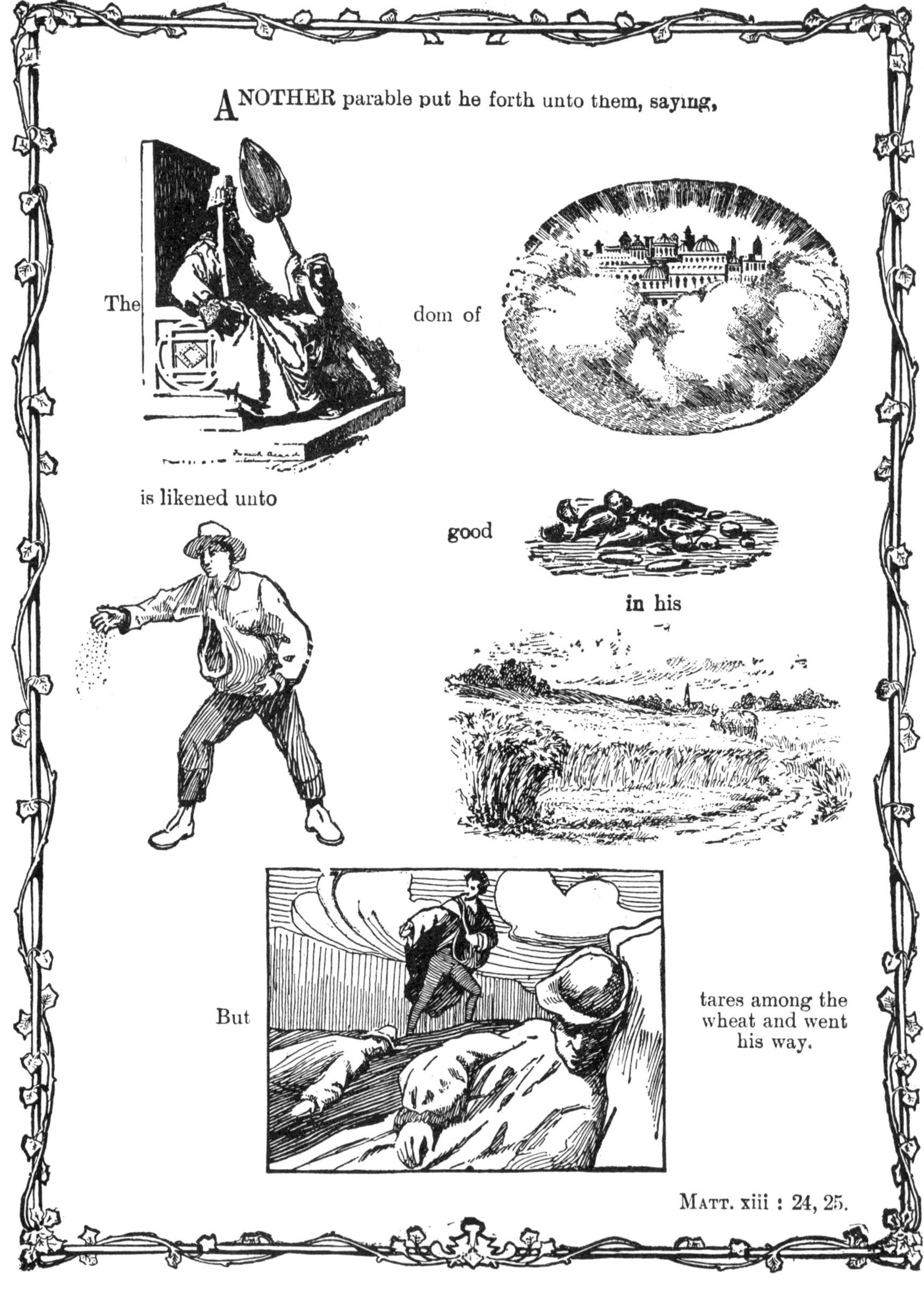
ANOTHER parable put he forth unto them, saying,
The
dom of
is likened unto
good
in his
But
tares among the wheat and went his way.
Matt. xiii : 24, 25.

I (Name).............................FILLED

IN THESE ANSWERS. (Date) ....

1. What was Jesus' favorite method of teaching?

....

2. How did Jesus say people would be known?

....

3. Where did the wise man build his house?

....

4. Where did the foolish man build his?

....

5. Why was one man wise and the other foolish?

....

6. Who does Jesus invite to Him for rest?

....

7. What does Jesus say His service is like?

....

8. How many kinds of soil in the parable of the sower?

....

9. What is meant by the Kingdom of Heaven?

....

10. Who sowed the tares in the wheat?

And there arose a great storm of wind, and the waves beat into the ship, so that it was now full. And he was in

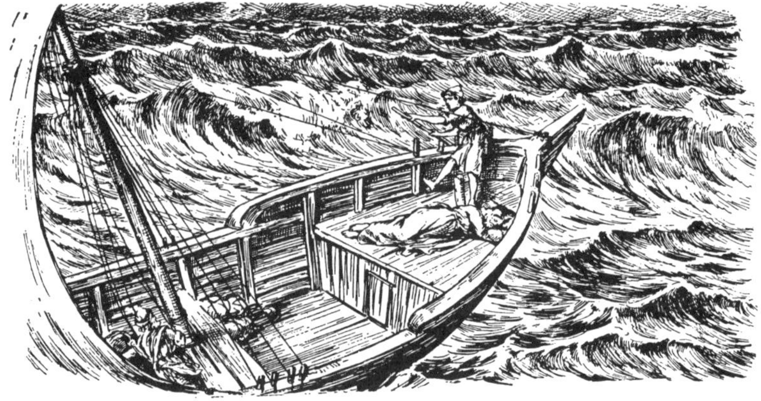

asleep on a pillow: and they

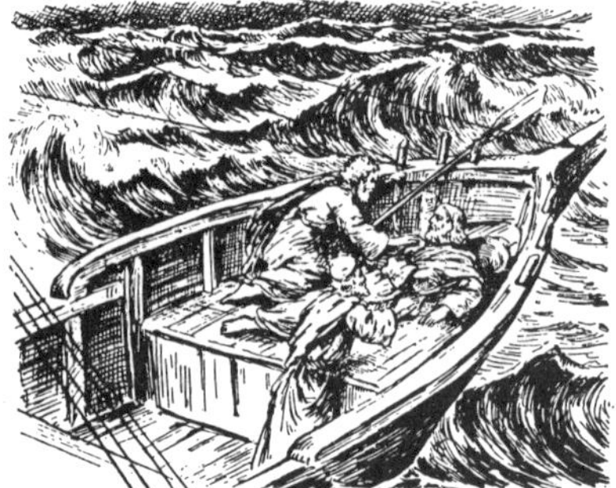

and say unto him, Master, carest thou not that we perish? And

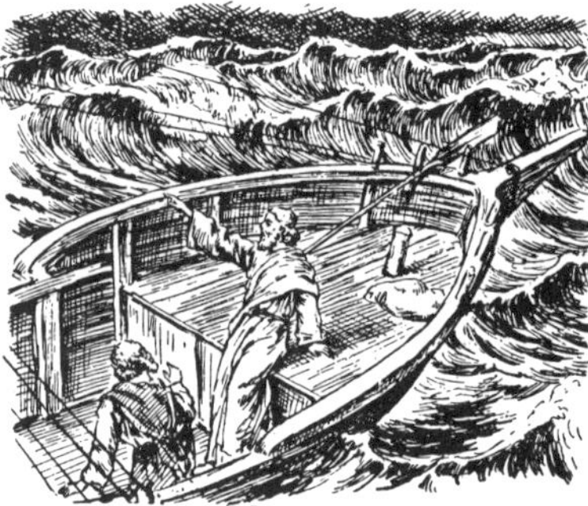

and rebuked the wind, and said unto the

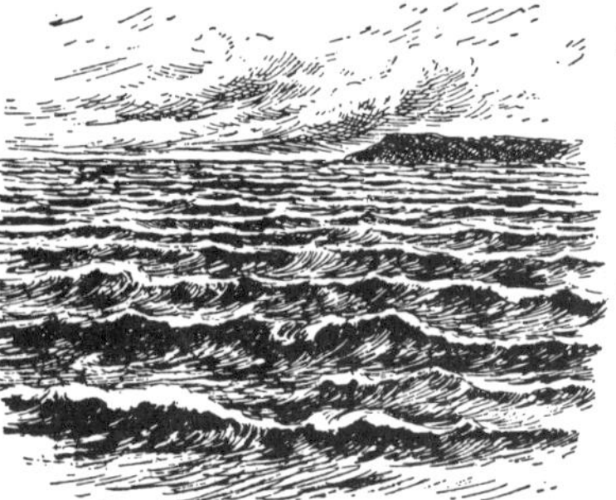

Peace be still. And the wind ceased, and there was a great

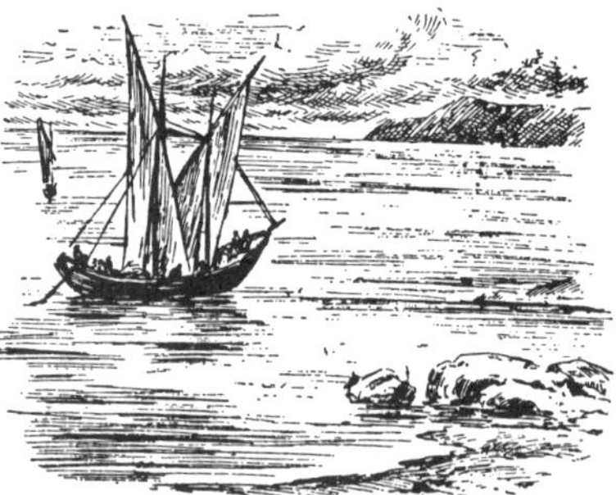

And he said unto them, Why are ye so fearful? how is it that ye have no faith? And they feared exceedingly, and said one to another, What manner of man is this, that even the wind and the sea obey him?

MARK IV. 37-41.

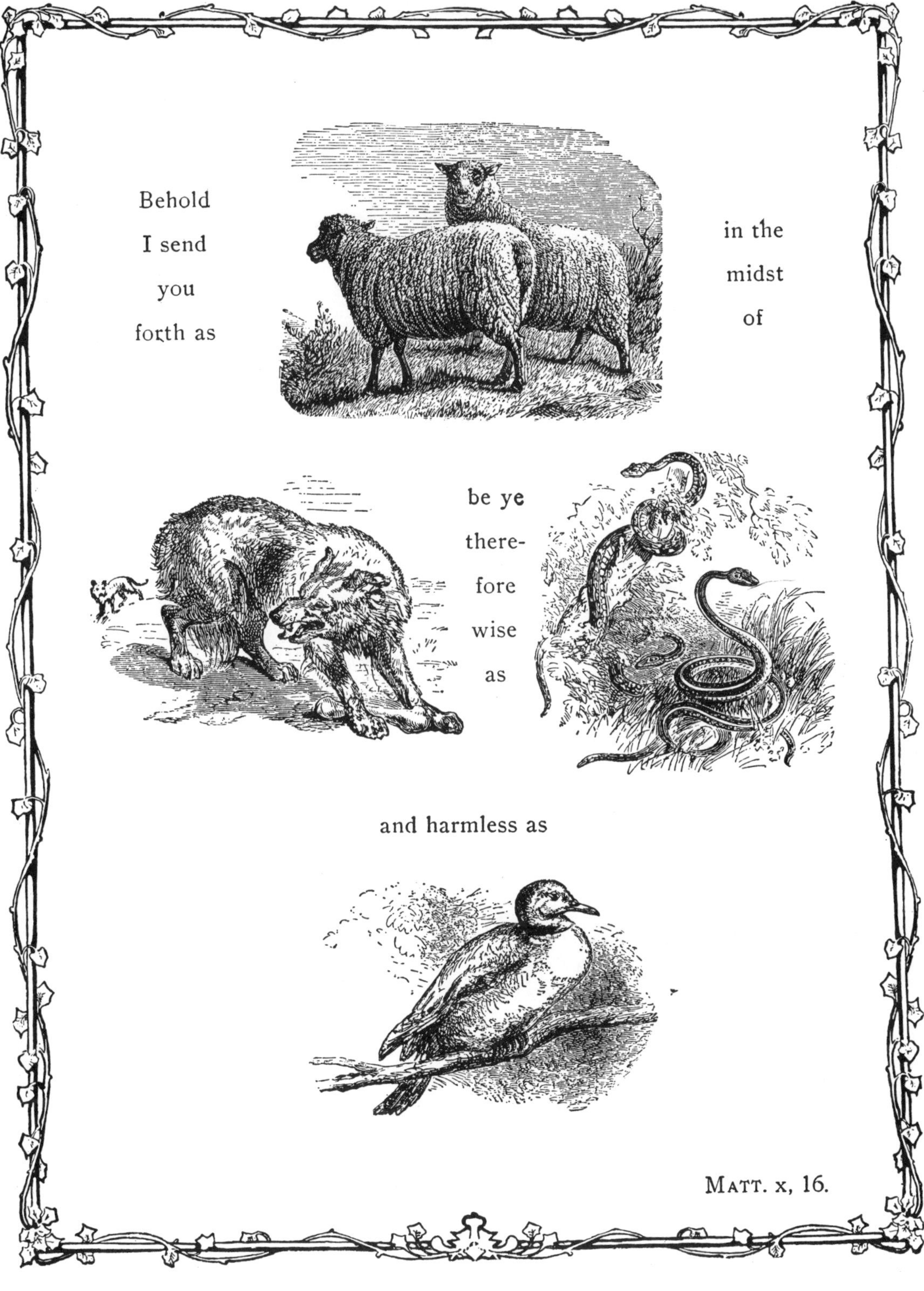
Behold
I send
you
forth as
in the
midst
of
be ye
there-
fore
wise
as
and harmless as
Matt. x, 16.

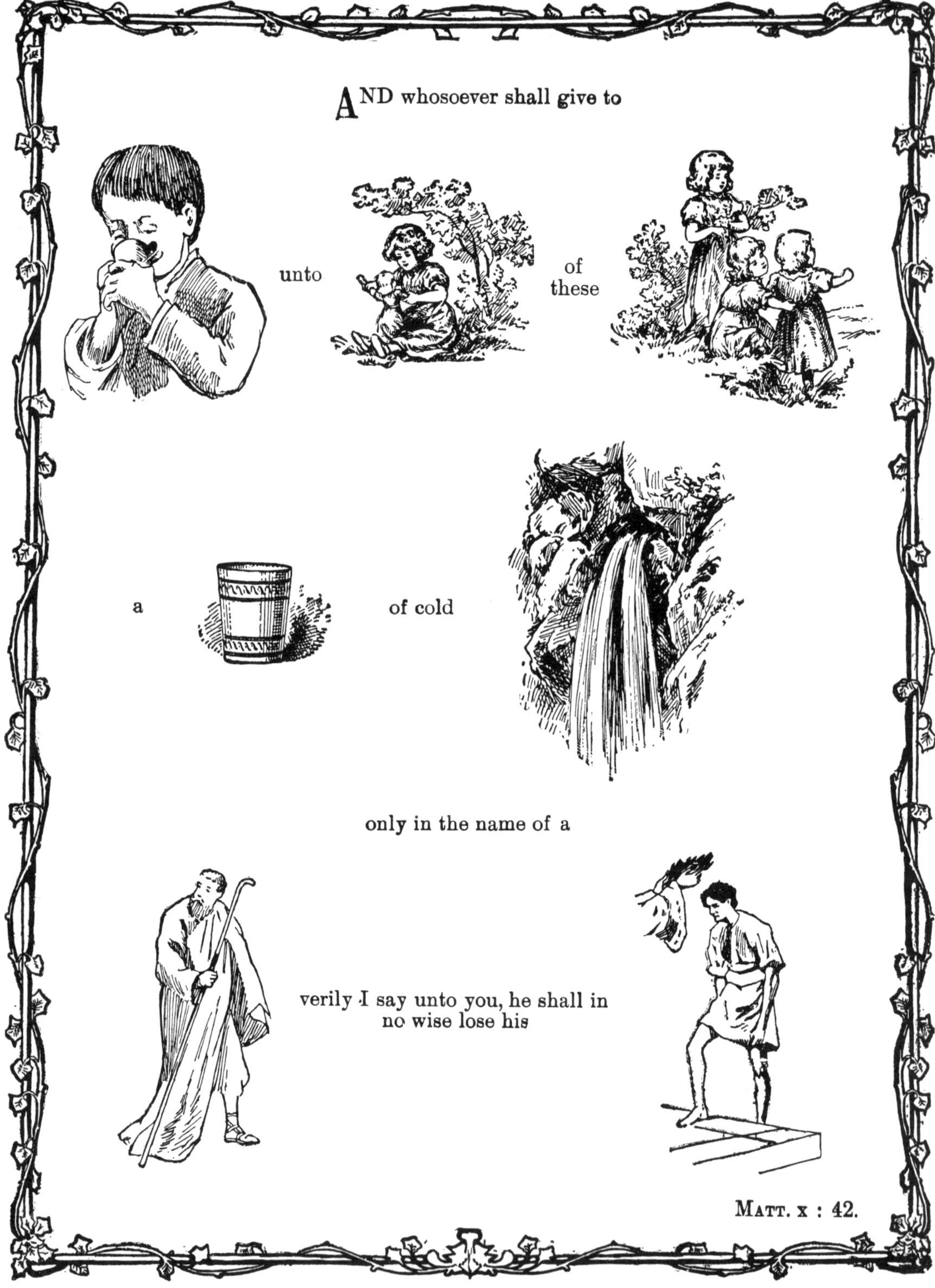
AND whosoever shall give to
unto
of
these
a
of cold
only in the name of a
verily I say unto you, he shall in
no wise lose his
MATT. x : 42.

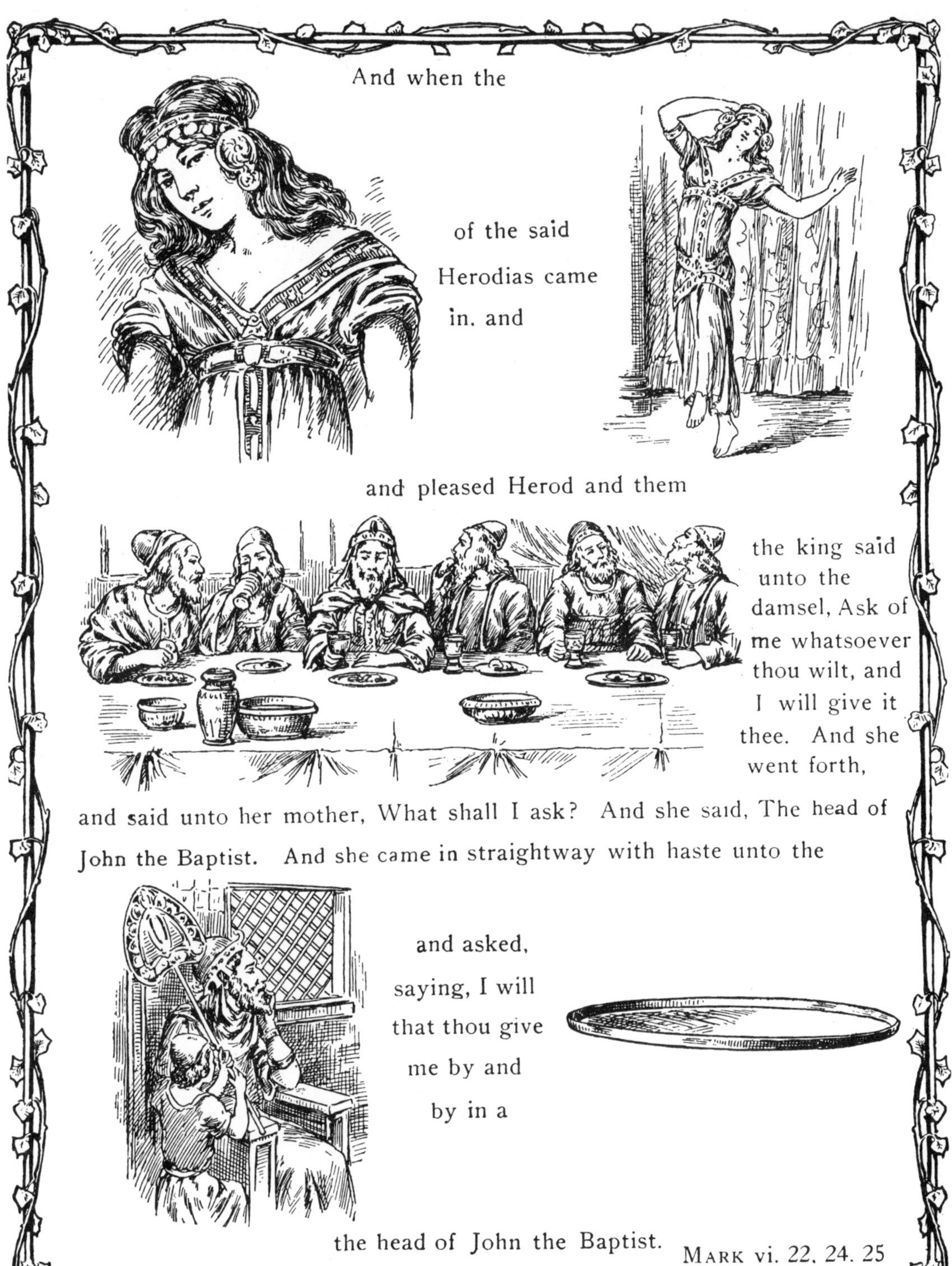

And when the

of the said Herodias came in, and

and pleased Herod and them

the king said unto the damsel, Ask of me whatsoever thou wilt, and I will give it thee. And she went forth,

and said unto her mother, What shall I ask? And she said, The head of John the Baptist. And she came in straightway with haste unto the

and asked, saying, I will that thou give me by and by in a

the head of John the Baptist. MARK vi. 22, 24, 25

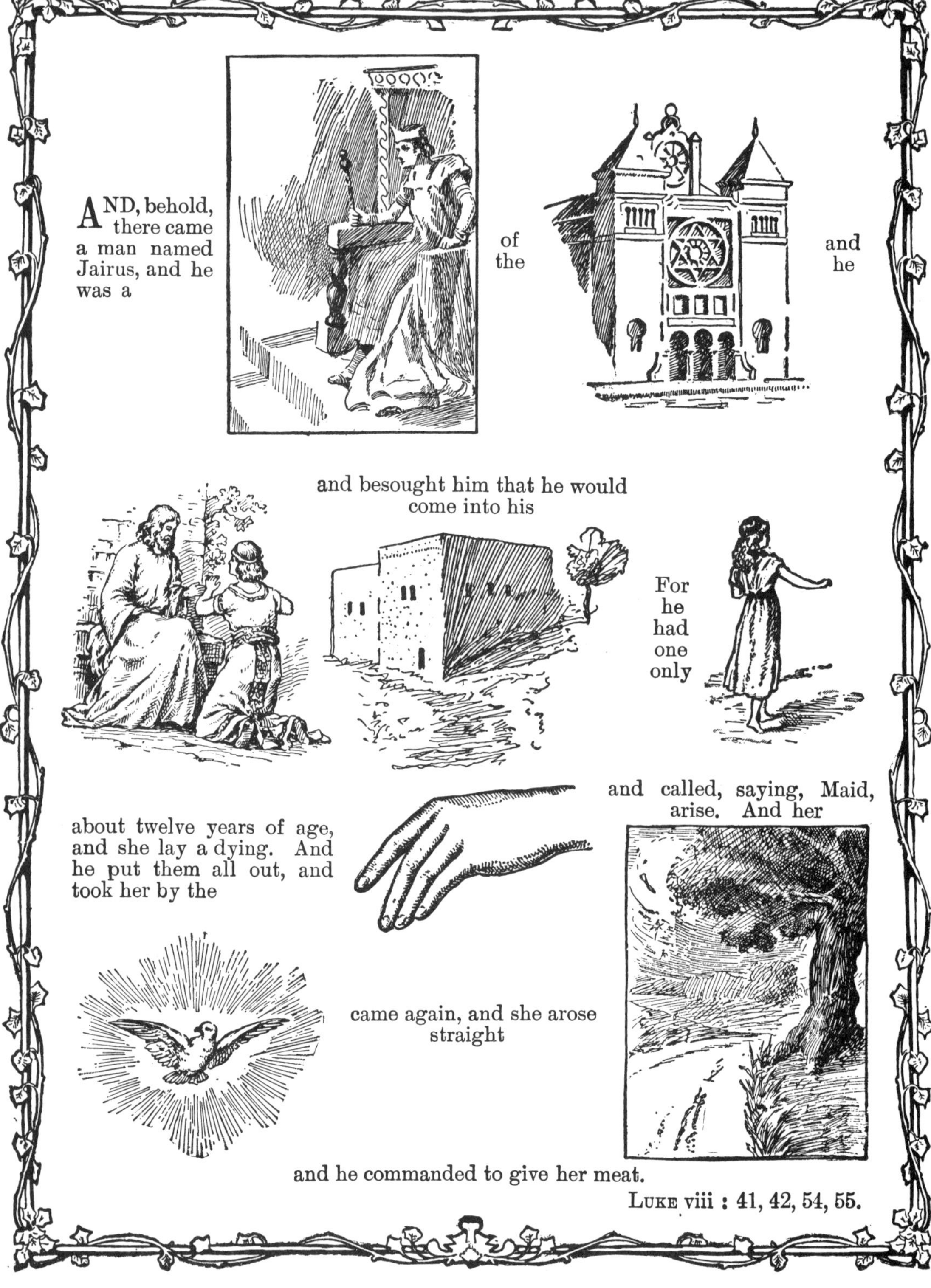

AND, behold, there came a man named Jairus, and he was a

of the

and he

and besought him that he would come into his

For he had one only

about twelve years of age, and she lay a dying. And he put them all out, and took her by the

and called, saying, Maid, arise. And her

came again, and she arose straight

and he commanded to give her meat.

LUKE viii : 41, 42, 54, 55.

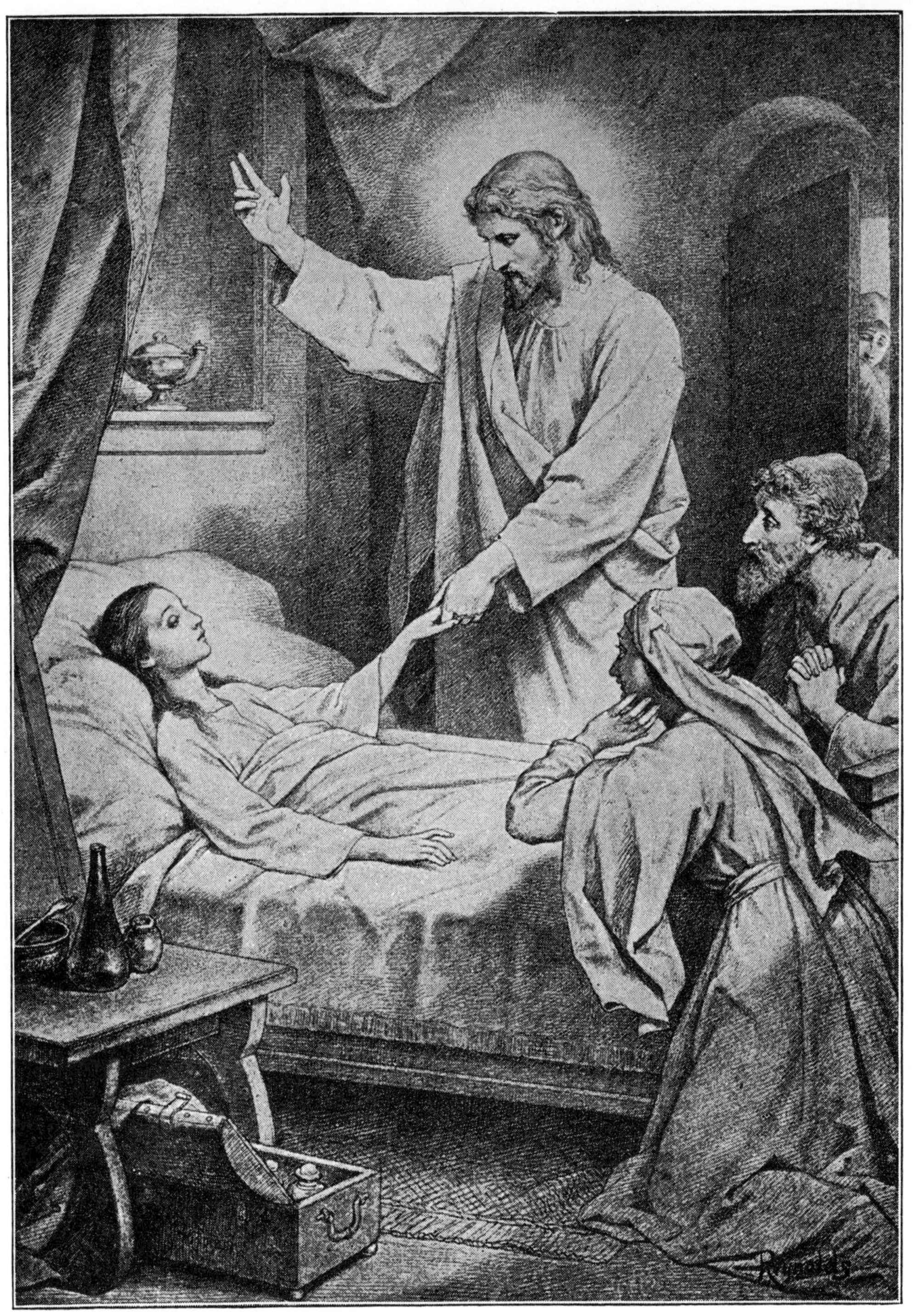

RAISING OF JAIRUS' DAUGHTER.

THE RAISING OF JAIRUS' DAUGHTER.

A GREAT crowd was waiting to welcome Jesus when Peter's boat, bearing the Master and his disciples, came in sight of the landing place at Capernaum. The sharp-pointed, red sail was lowered, and the curious, kindly people pressed close to Jesus to welcome him back to their town. They were proud and pleased to have him among them, for at this time the friends of Jesus were many, and if he had any enemies they wisely held their peace.

But now, pressing through the crowd, with a look of pain on his fine face, came Jairus, one of the great men of the church and town. The people made place for him with looks of pity, for many of them knew that his little girl was lying at the point of death in his home. They looked on with astonishment when they saw the great man come, bending low before Jesus, and heard him say in a voice full of trouble, "My little daughter is dying. Come, I pray thee, and lay thy hand upon her, that she may live." Jairus knew that Jesus had done many wonderful works, and now in his time of great distress he came to him for help.

Turning away from the seashore, Jesus went with Jairus toward his fine house, which was just a little distance from the town. His disciples and a crowd of eager people followed him, and they pressed upon him so that he could not move quickly. Then, too, a poor sick woman made herself known to Jesus and begged his help and pity, and did not beg in vain. But while Jesus and Jairus were thus held, a servant came running from the house of Jairus to say that the child was dead, and that he need not trouble the Master to come any farther. Jesus heard the words, and, looking upon Jairus, said, "Fear not; only believe." What hope and cheer these words must have brought to the heart of the unhappy father!

When Jairus came, bringing the Healer, to his beautiful house. he found the door wide open, and many hired mourners had already gathered there. They sat on the floor, the women with their hair falling over their eyes and dust on their heads, and men with garments torn to show their grief—all weeping and wailing loudly. This was the custom in that country when one was dead in a house, and all the time the mournful sound of flutes told those who passed by that the death angel had entered the home.

Jesus told Jairus to send all these people away, for well he knew that the mourning was only a show, without any real grief in their hearts. And when all were gone, except the father and mother of the dear child, he took them, with Peter and James and John, into the little darkened room where lay the silent form of the sweet girl, only twelve years of age. Jesus took the little cold hand into his own, warm and throbbing with life, and saying only two words, "Talitha cumi," which means "Little maid, I say unto thee, arise,"—straightway the spirit of life came back. The child opened her eyes, rose up, and was again her bright, sweet self!

We may never know what she said or felt, or what the glad father and mother felt in their hearts, but it is easy to believe that they fell down at Jesus' feet and thanked him with tears of joy and love, and that ever afterward they loved and trusted the great Healer. And the little girl—did she not owe her life to the One who had called it back, and would it not be her highest joy to pay her debt in love and glad service?

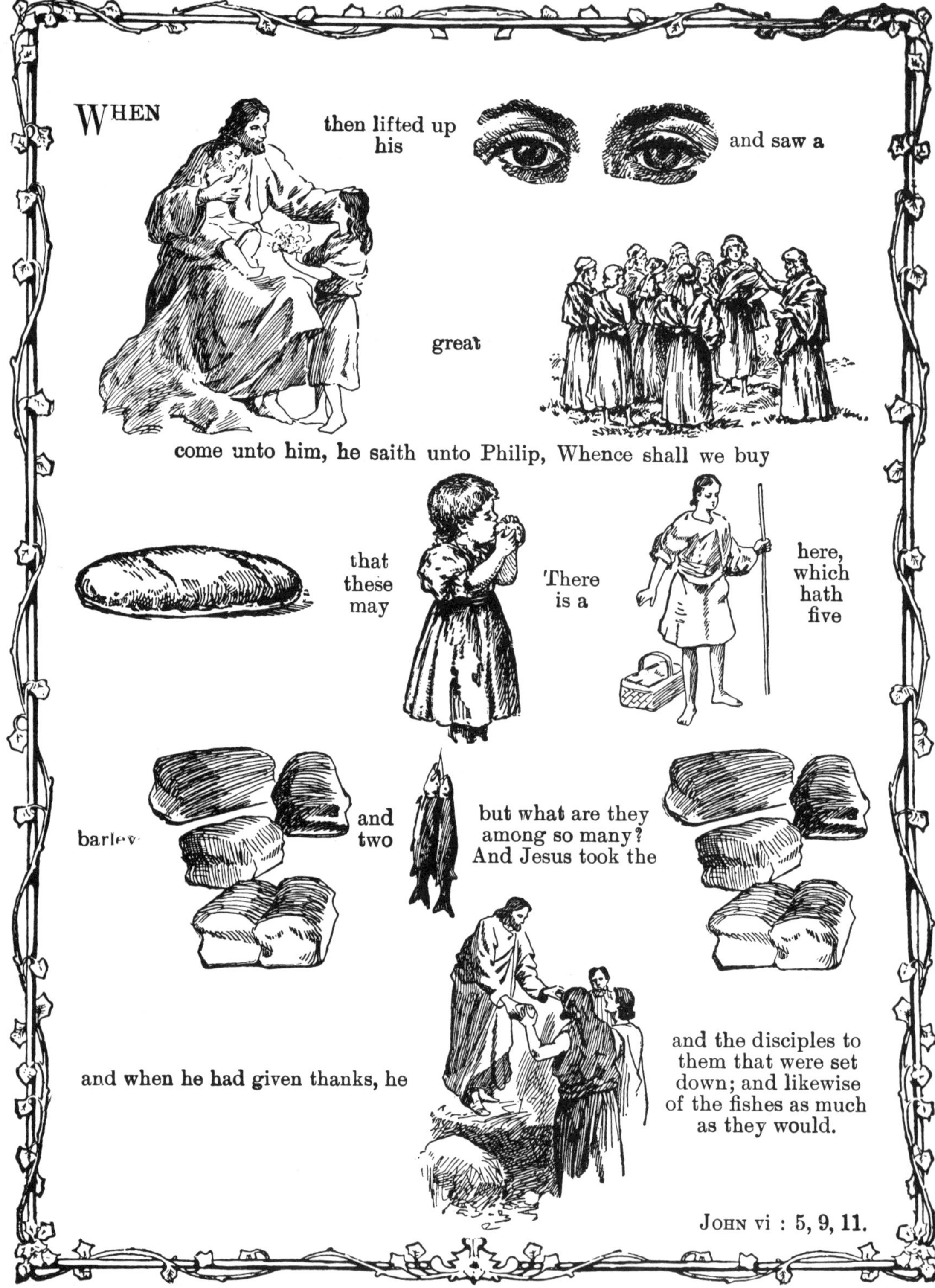
WHEN
then lifted up his
and saw a
great
come unto him, he saith unto Philip, Whence shall we buy
that these may
There is a
here, which hath five
barley
and two
but what are they among so many? And Jesus took the
and when he had given thanks, he
and the disciples to them that were set down; and likewise of the fishes as much as they would.
JOHN vi : 5, 9, 11.

FEEDING THE MULTITUDE.

DEAREST Children, when we are tired, and perhaps lessons are to be learned, or errands to be done for mother or father, or even little baby brother needs a playmate, it may help us to do whatever is before us if we remember how patient Jesus always was, and how his disciples labored even when weary, to help the people and to work with Jesus.

One time when Jesus and the disciples had worked very hard and all felt weary, Jesus said, "Come, my dear brothers, we will cross the sea in a ship all alone, and reach a quiet place where we can have sweet rest." The disciples gladly went, for they longed for the promised rest. But many people saw the ship depart, and not knowing that Jesus and the disciples went away to be alone, they followed on foot, walking around on the land, and hurried so as to be there when the ship landed.

Jesus was surprised when they came ashore not to find the quiet spot which he sought, but a gathering of thousands of people, who had come to be healed and helped.

He did not tell them that he and his disciples had worked hard and must rest; he smiled sweetly, and patiently spent the remainder of the day talking gently to those who needed counsel, and healing those who were ill. The little children gathered about him, knowing Jesus could soothe all their sorrows, and when evening came there was not a troubled heart in all the gathering.

At length the disciples came to Jesus and said, "It is growing late and these people have no food. Shall we not send them to the villages that they may be fed?" But Jesus answered, "No, they walked so far to be with us, that I fear they are too weary to go to the villages. The little children could not wait so long or walk so far—all of these dear followers must be fed here." The disciples in surprise replied, "Master, there are thousands here and no one has brought food except a little lad, and he has only five barley loaves and two small fishes."

Jesus was glad to hear of the little lad who had the loaves and fishes and asked them to bring the boy to him. The little boy was very happy to be called close to Jesus' side, and although he was hungry and did not know what Jesus intended to do, he quickly gave him his little luncheon, for, trusting Jesus, no sacrifice was too great to make for his dear sake. But Jesus, who never fails us, surprised the little boy as well as the people gathered there, by making the five loaves and the two fishes feed them all, for as quickly as he gave food to one, more food appeared for another, and soon they were all supplied with plenty to eat, and were seated on the soft, green grass, eating and resting, and not forgetting to have thankful hearts for the blessing they had received.

After the people had eaten, and all were satisfied, Jesus told his disciples to gather up what was left, and they quickly did so, filling twelve baskets with the fragments.

No crumbs were left on the beautiful velvety grass—all was left as clean as if no one had feasted there. Everybody looked satisfied and happy and peace reigned in the hearts of all.

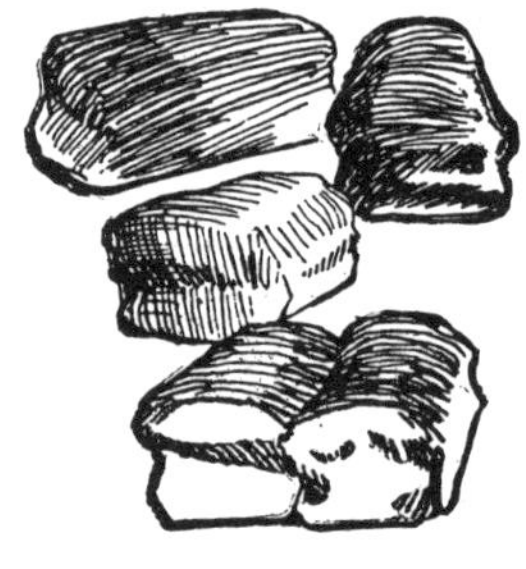

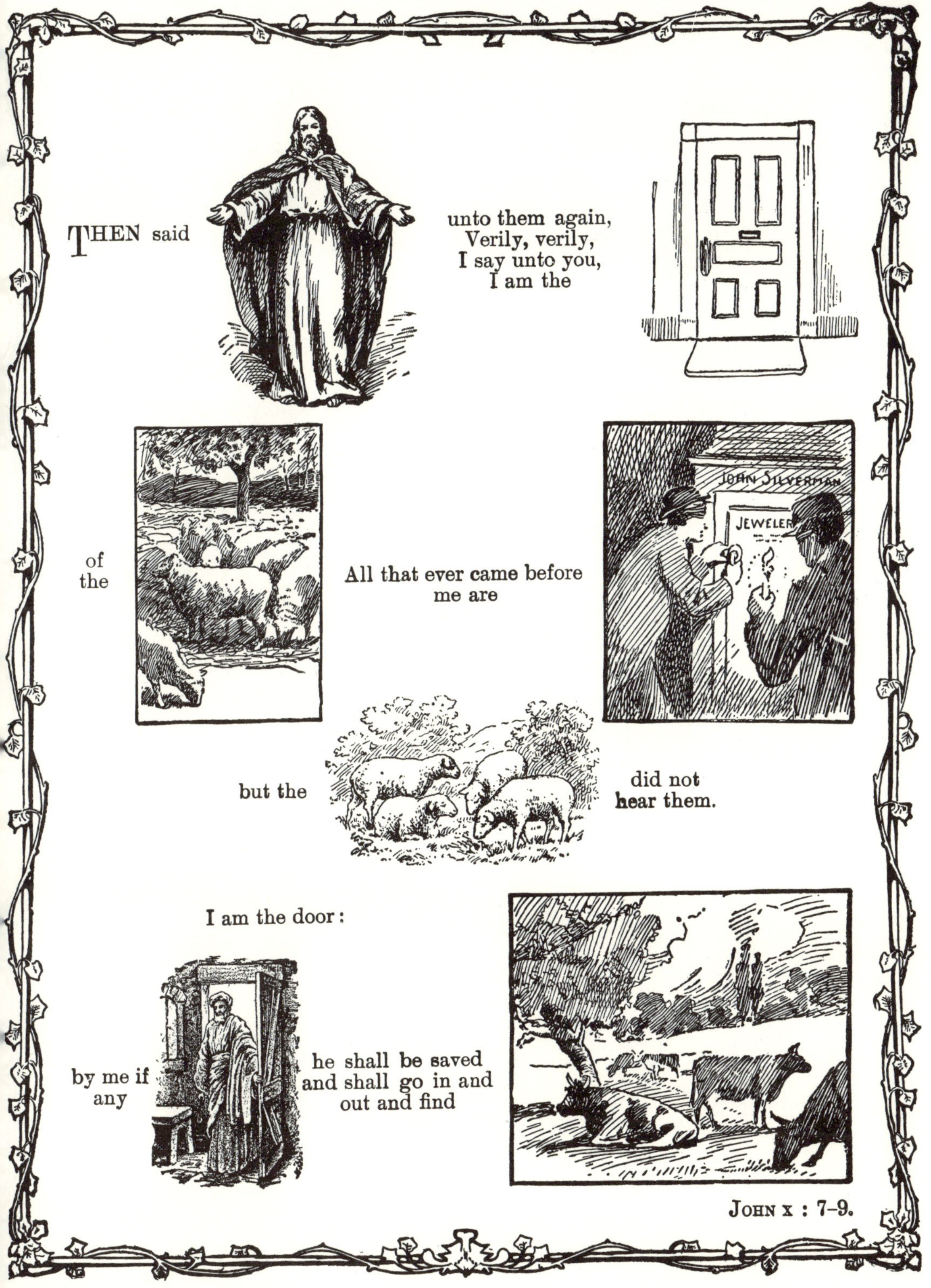

THEN said unto them again,
Verily, verily,
I say unto you,
I am the

of the

All that ever came before
me are

but the did not
hear them.

I am the door:

by me if
any

he shall be saved
and shall go in and
out and find

JOHN x : 7–9.

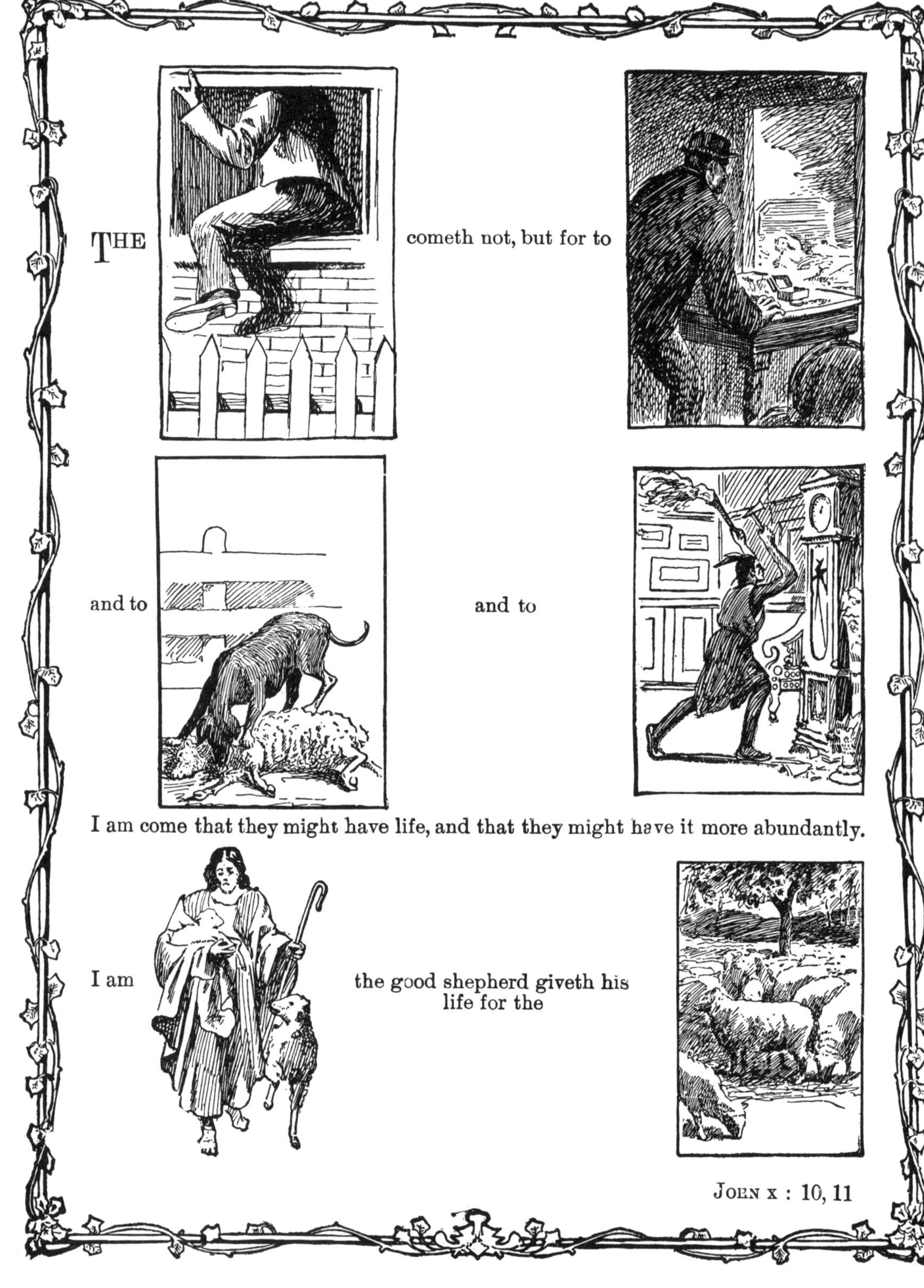

THE cometh not, but for to

and to and to

I am come that they might have life, and that they might have it more abundantly.

I am the good shepherd giveth his life for the

JOHN x : 10, 11

I (Name)..............................FILLED

IN THESE ANSWERS. (Date) ....

1. Why was Jesus able to calm the storm?

....

2. Why would Jesus' disciples be like sheep among wolves where He sent them?

....

3. For how small a favor did Jesus promise a reward?

....

4. What did Salome ask of the king and who told her what to ask?

....

5. Who was Jairus and why did he come to Jesus?

....

6. What did Jesus do for him?

....

7. How many people did the five loaves and two fishes feed?

....

8. Where did Jesus get the loaves and fishes?

....

9. Why did Jesus say He came into the world?

....

10. Who is called the good shepherd?

....

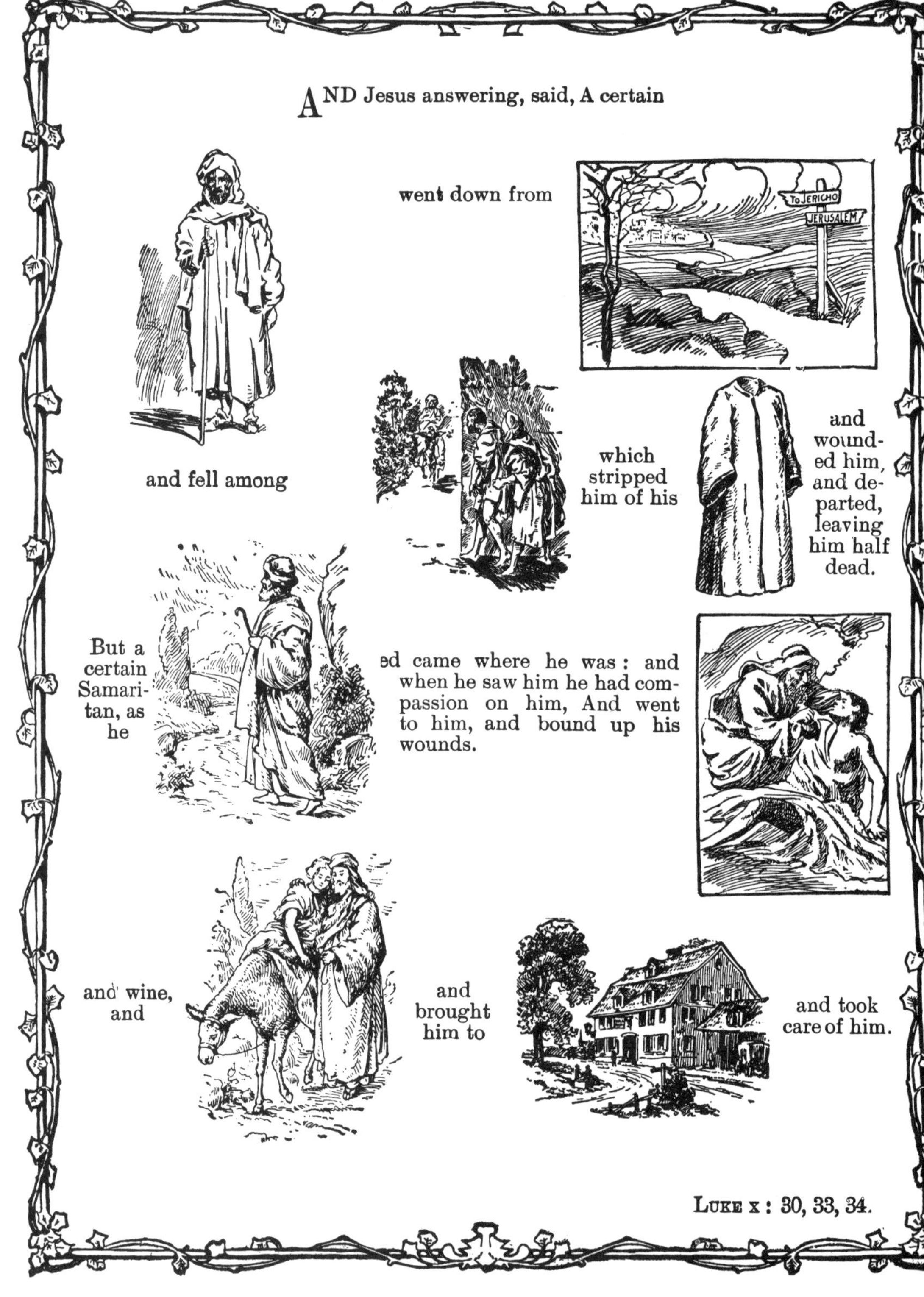
AND Jesus answering, said, A certain
went down from
To JERICHO
JERUSALEM
and fell among
which stripped him of his
and wounded him, and departed, leaving him half dead.
But a certain Samaritan, as he
ed came where he was: and when he saw him he had compassion on him, And went to him, and bound up his wounds.
and wine, and
and brought him to
and took care of him.
LUKE x: 30, 33, 34.

Now it came to pass, as they went, that he entered into a certain village: and a certain woman named Martha received him into her

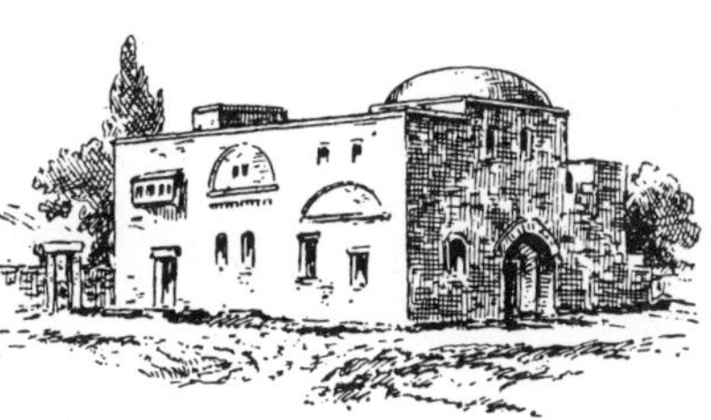

And she had a sister called Mary, which also sat at Jesus' feet, and heard his word. But Martha was cumbered about much serving, and came to

him, and said, Lord, dost thou not care that my

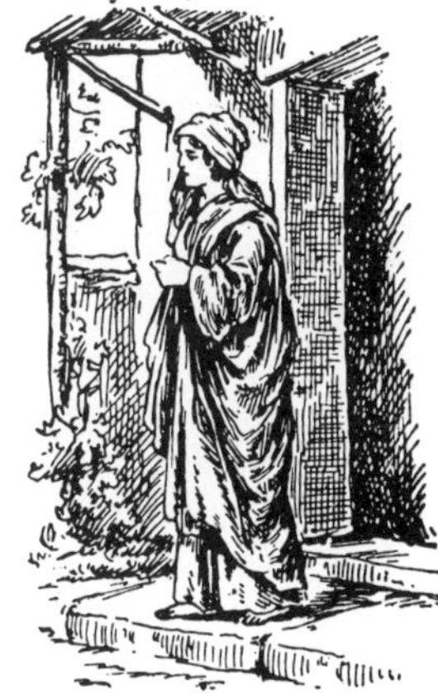

hath left me to

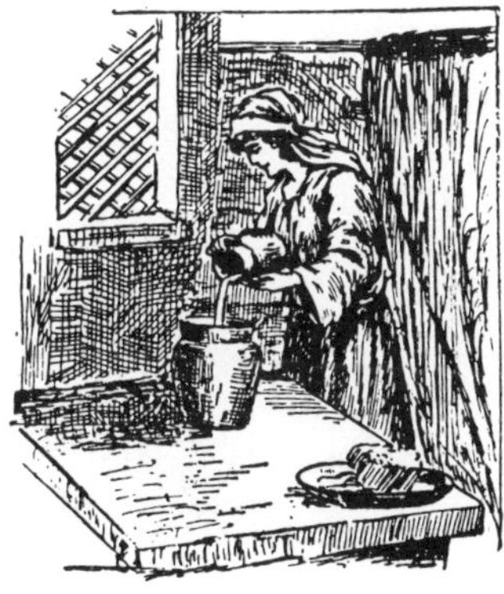

alone? bid her therefore that she help me. And

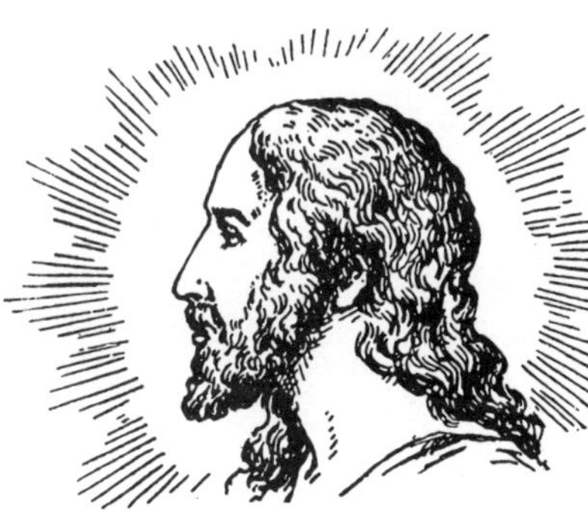

answered and said unto her, Martha, Martha, thou art careful and troubled about many things: But one thing is needful; and

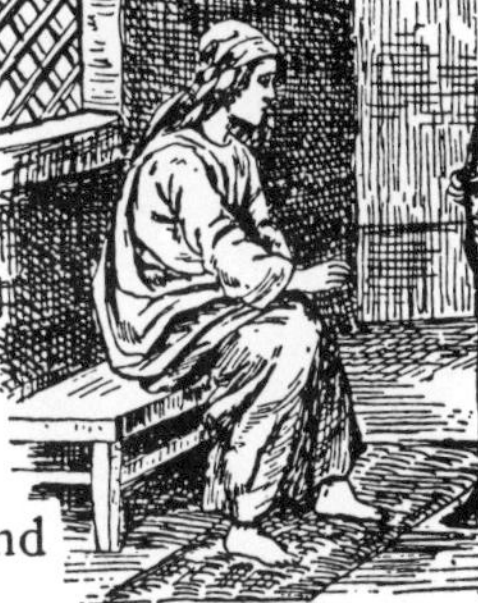

hath chosen that good part, which shall not be taken away from her.

LUKE x. 38-42.

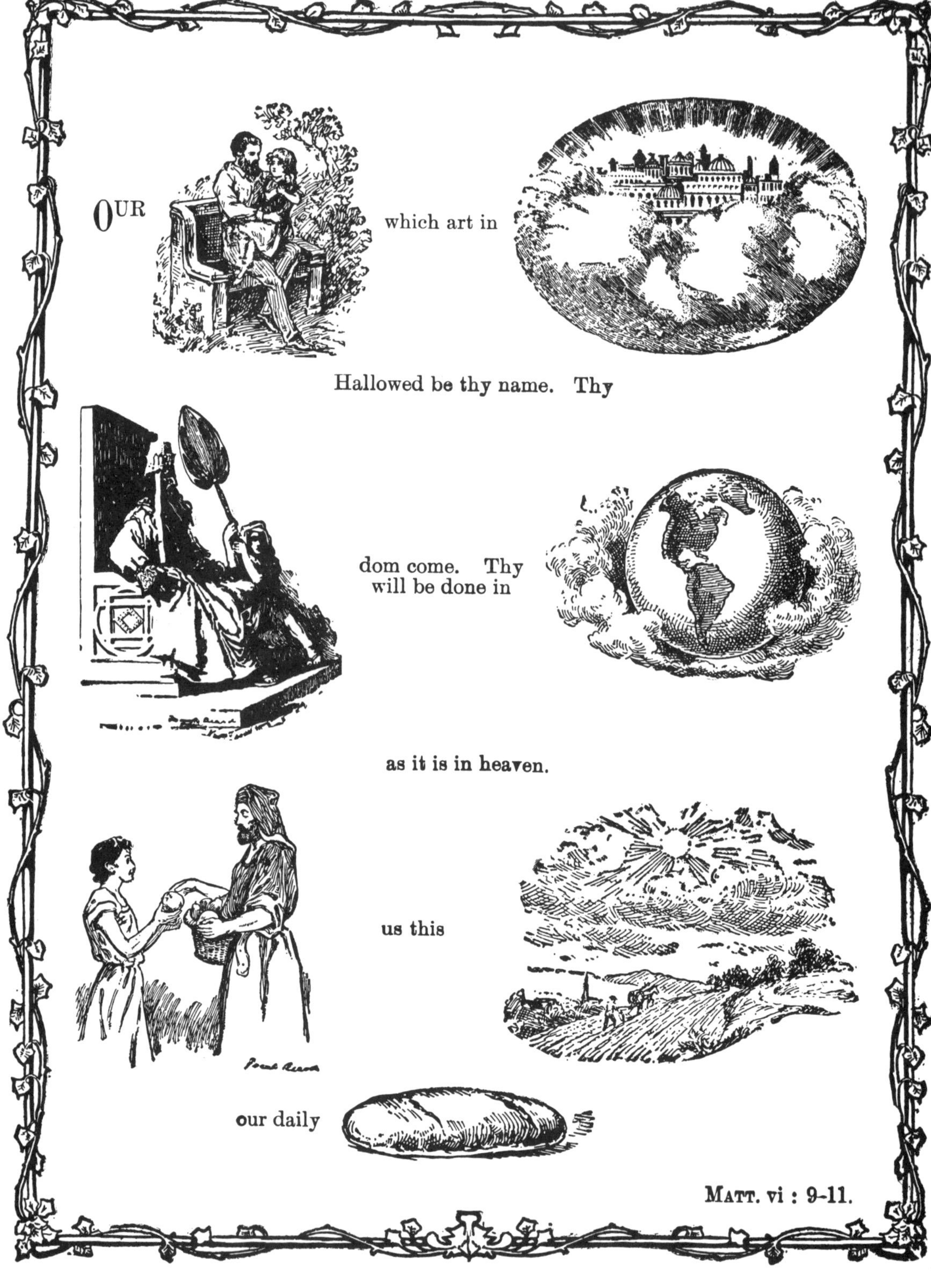
OUR
which art in
Hallowed be thy name. Thy
dom come. Thy
will be done in
as it is in heaven.
us this
our daily
Matt. vi : 9-11.

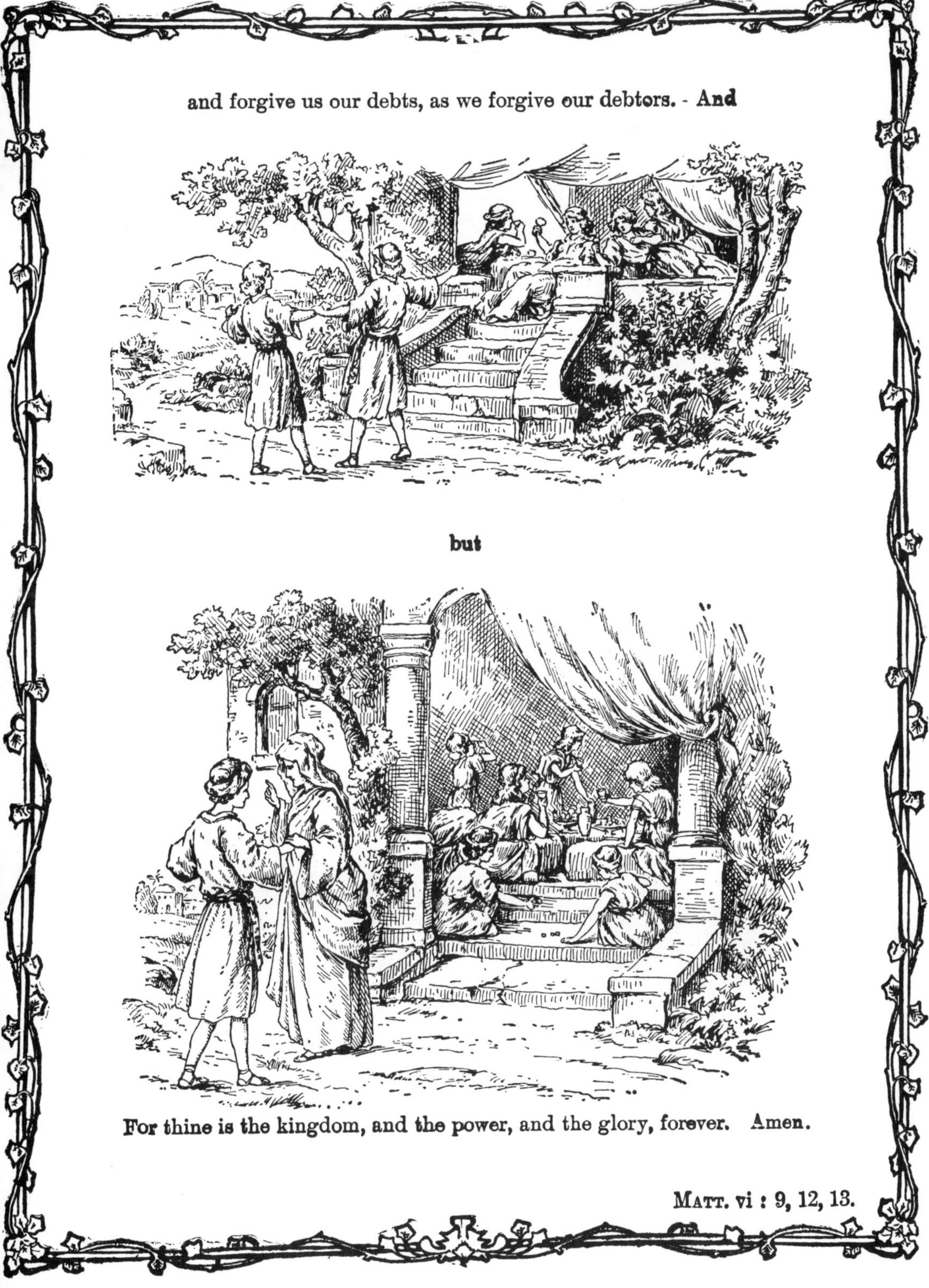

and forgive us our debts, as we forgive our debtors. - **And**

but

For thine is the kingdom, and the power, and the glory, forever. Amen.

Matt. vi : 9, 12, 13.

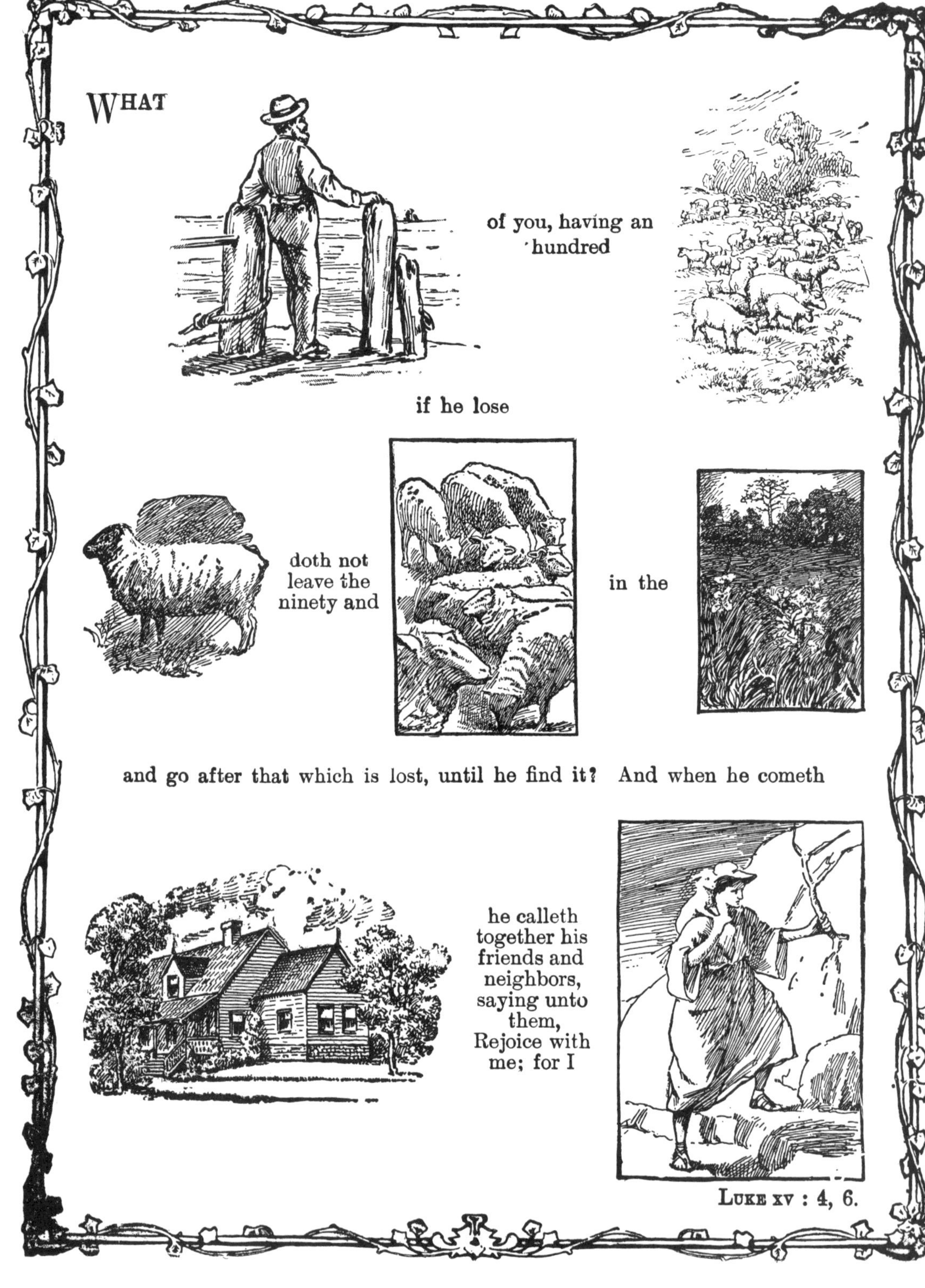

WHAT of you, having an hundred

if he lose

doth not leave the ninety and

in the

and go after that which is lost, until he find it? And when he cometh

he calleth together his friends and neighbors, saying unto them, Rejoice with me; for I

LUKE XV : 4, 6.

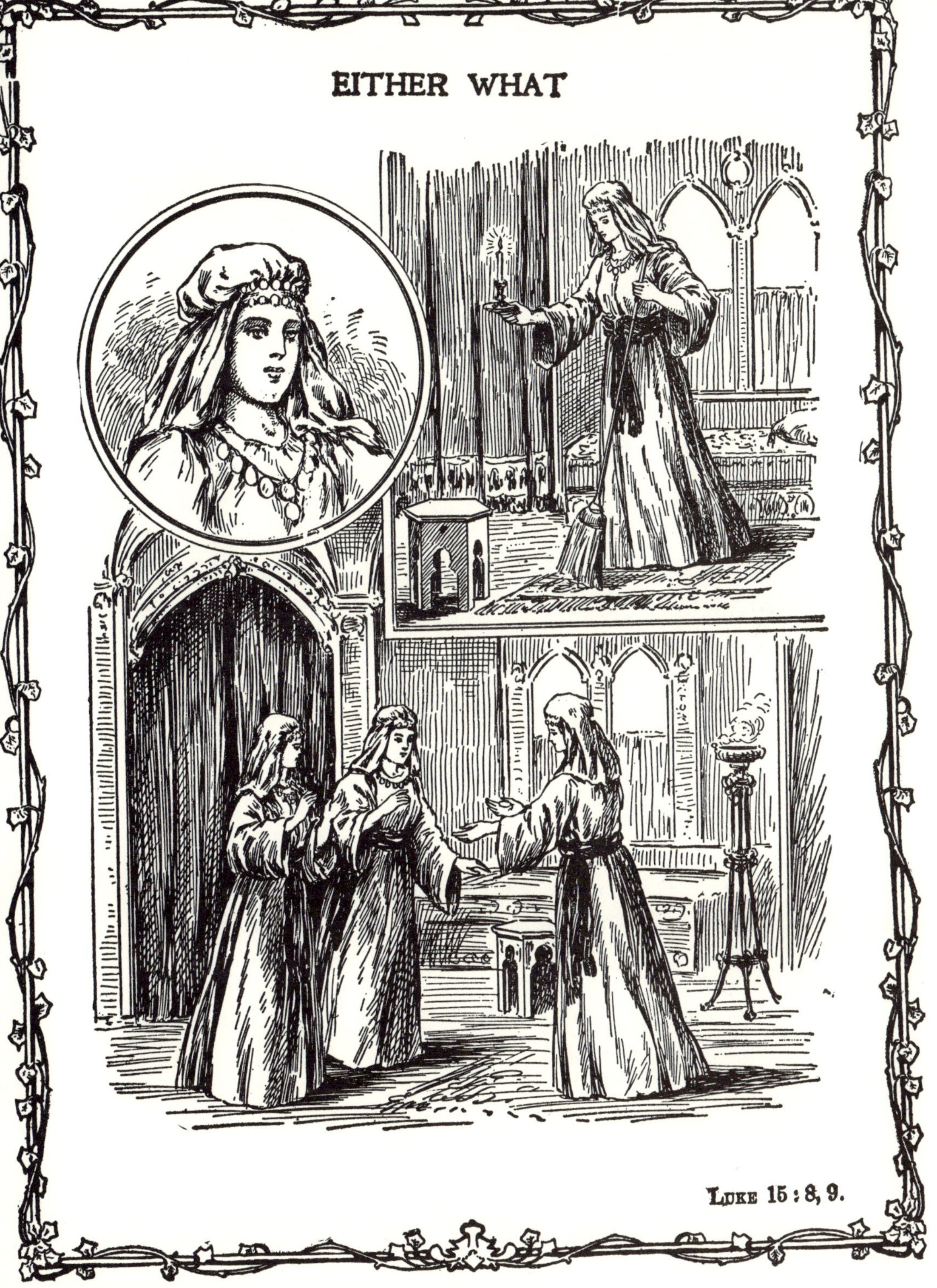
EITHER WHAT
Luke 15 : 8, 9.

I (Name)................................FILLED IN THESE ANSWERS. (Date) ....

1. What did the good Samaritan do?

....

2. What two men should have helped the wounded man?

....

3. What was the better part that Mary chose?

....

4. What was Martha troubled about?

....

5. What is the prayer on page 160 called?

....

6. What four things do we pray for specially in this prayer?

....

7. When may we expect God to forgive us?

....

8. What does the parable of the ninety and nine teach?

....

9. How many sheep in the flock and how many lost?

....

10. How many pieces of money? How many lost?

....

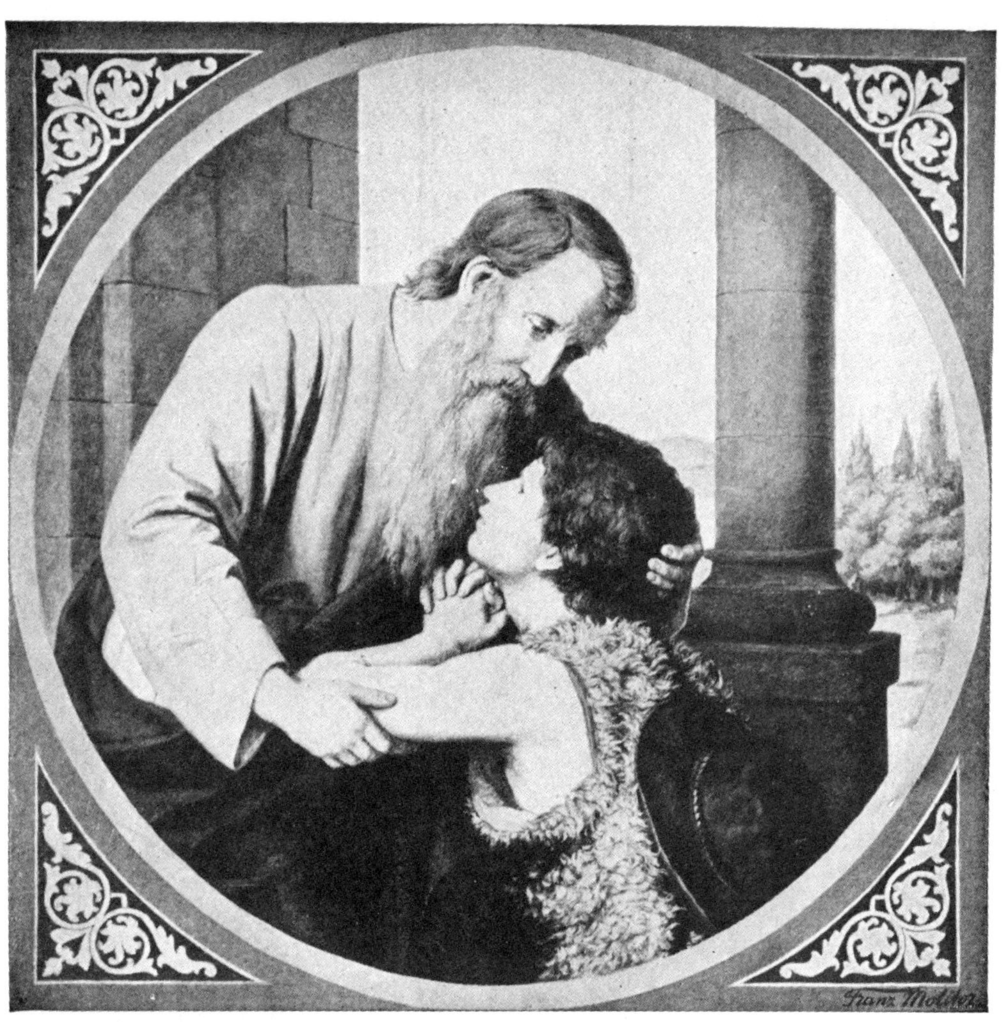

THE PRODIGAL SON.

THE SON WHO REPENTED.

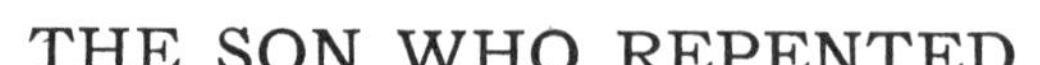

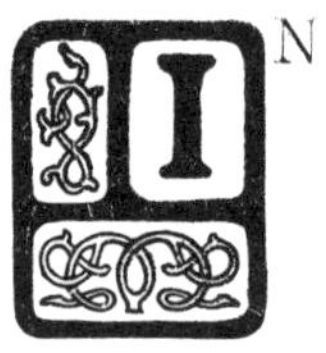

N some way or other God is always saying to us: "Though I am your Maker I am also your Heavenly Father, and I love you. Some time you will know what the Heavenly Father's love is, but now you are only just beginning to live and you can only know the beginning of love."

The Lord Jesus wanted to make a picture of his love that would forever hang in the sight of men, and so he told the story of the "Prodigal Son," and as long as the word of God stands we shall have it.

Did you ever hear it said of anyone, "That boy is restless; he will run away from home some day."

The story that Jesus told was about a restless boy who asked his father to give him his share of the property, and then when his kind father divided it between his elder brother and himself he took his share and went on a journey into the "far country." In that country, away from God and goodness, he wasted his money among wicked people and so the time came when he had nothing on which to live.

It was all the worse because there began to be a "mighty famine" in that land. It is always so when one is bound to get his happiness out of the gay things of this life. When the bright day is over a very gray day comes on, and but for God's goodness it would surely end in a black night. The foolish boy found that he had to work and the only work he could find was in a field of pigs. These he had to feed with the dry pods of the carob trees and so hungry was he that he would even have been glad to eat these dry pods himself if they had been given to him.

As he sat thinking—thinking and starving under the carob tree—"he came to himself,"—which means that he entered the room in his mind where his best self lived, and there he took a good resolve. He remembered that his father's servants were much better off than he, and he said:

"I will arise and go to my father."

He thought of the words he would say when he saw his father:

"I have sinned against Heaven and in thy sight: I am no more worthy to be called thy son."

So he went on to his father, and it must have been a long and tiresome journey for a hungry man. His father, who was always looking out for him, saw him coming when he was a long way off and came down the dusty road to meet him. When he met his boy he fell on his neck and kissed him over and over again. The son tried to confess and to beg for a servant's place, but his father would not listen. He knew that his son had come home, and that was enough. He called the servants to bring quickly the best robe, and he put it on his son, and he put a ring on his hand, and shoes on his feet, and he told them to kill the fatted calf for a feast, because, said he:

"This, my son, was dead and is alive again: he was lost and is found."

Then the whole household was full of joy and gladness.

But when the elder son came up from the field he heard the sound of music and dancing, and when he found out the reason he was angry. He would not speak to his brother, and so his father went out to urge him to come in. The elder son said that he had served his father so many years and yet never had there been a calf killed or a feast made for him. But when this prodigal boy who had spent all his living and had been wicked and disobedient came home, there was a great feast made for him. You can see that the elder son was jealous, but how sweet was the father's answer:

"Son, thou art ever with me and all that I have is thine. But it was meet to make merry and be glad, for this thy brother was dead and is alive again: he was lost and is found."

This is a true picture of Divine Love.

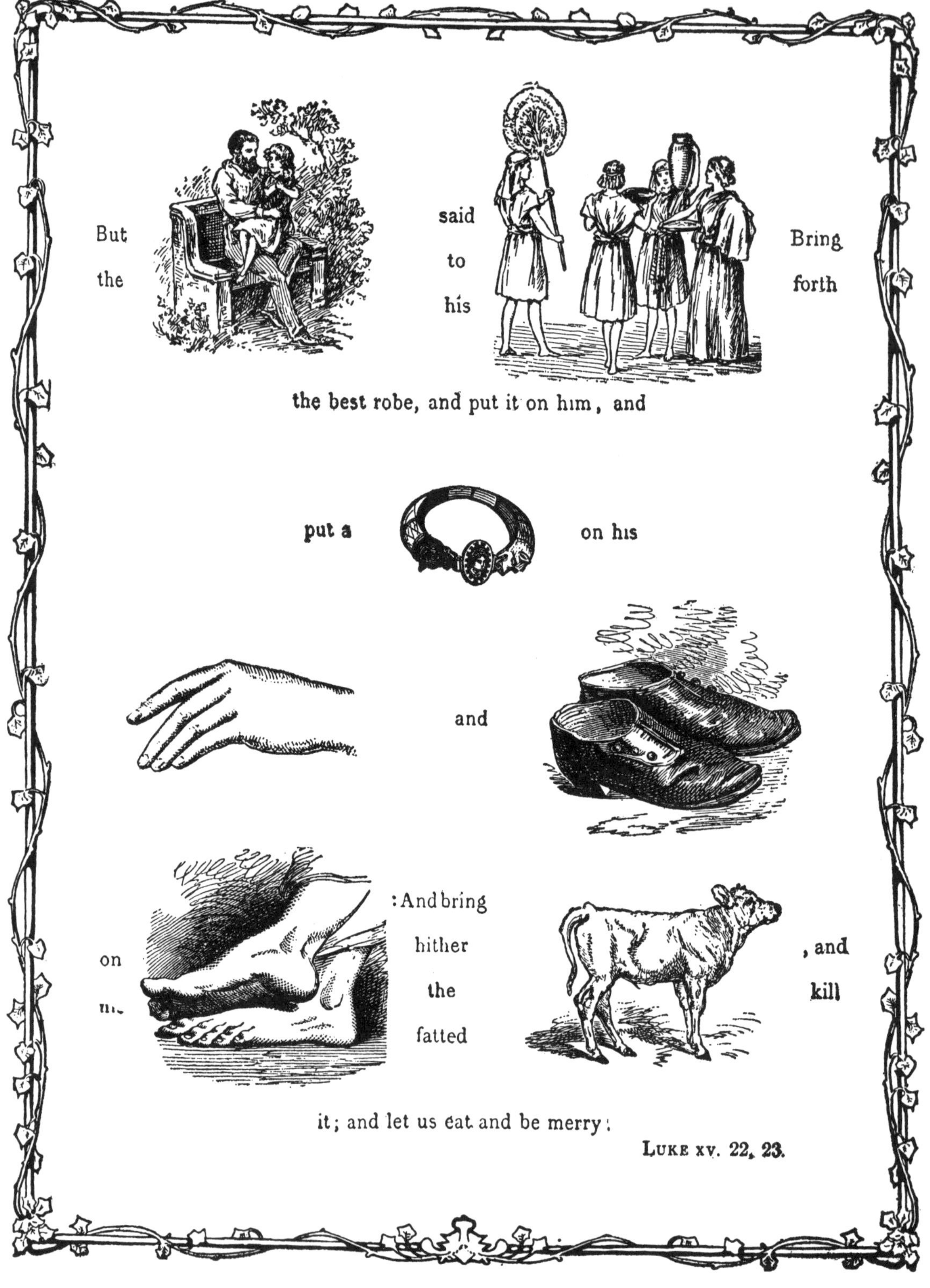

But the said to his Bring forth

the best robe, and put it on him, and

put a on his

and

on hi : And bring hither the fatted , and kill

it; and let us eat and be merry:

LUKE xv. 22, 23.

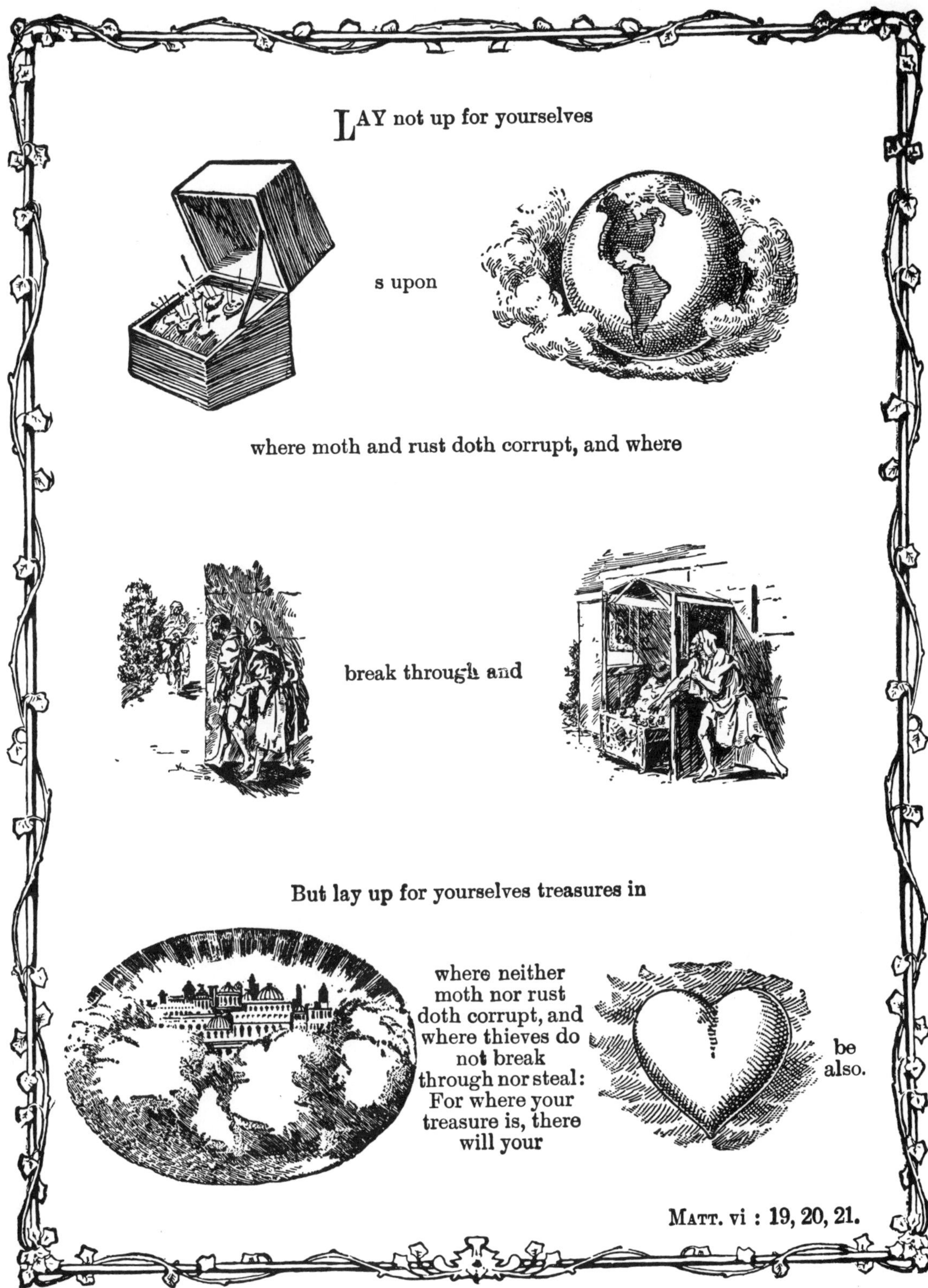
LAY not up for yourselves
s upon
where moth and rust doth corrupt, and where
break through and
But lay up for yourselves treasures in
where neither
moth nor rust
doth corrupt, and
where thieves do
not break
through nor steal:
For where your
treasure is, there
will your
be
also.
MATT. vi : 19, 20, 21.

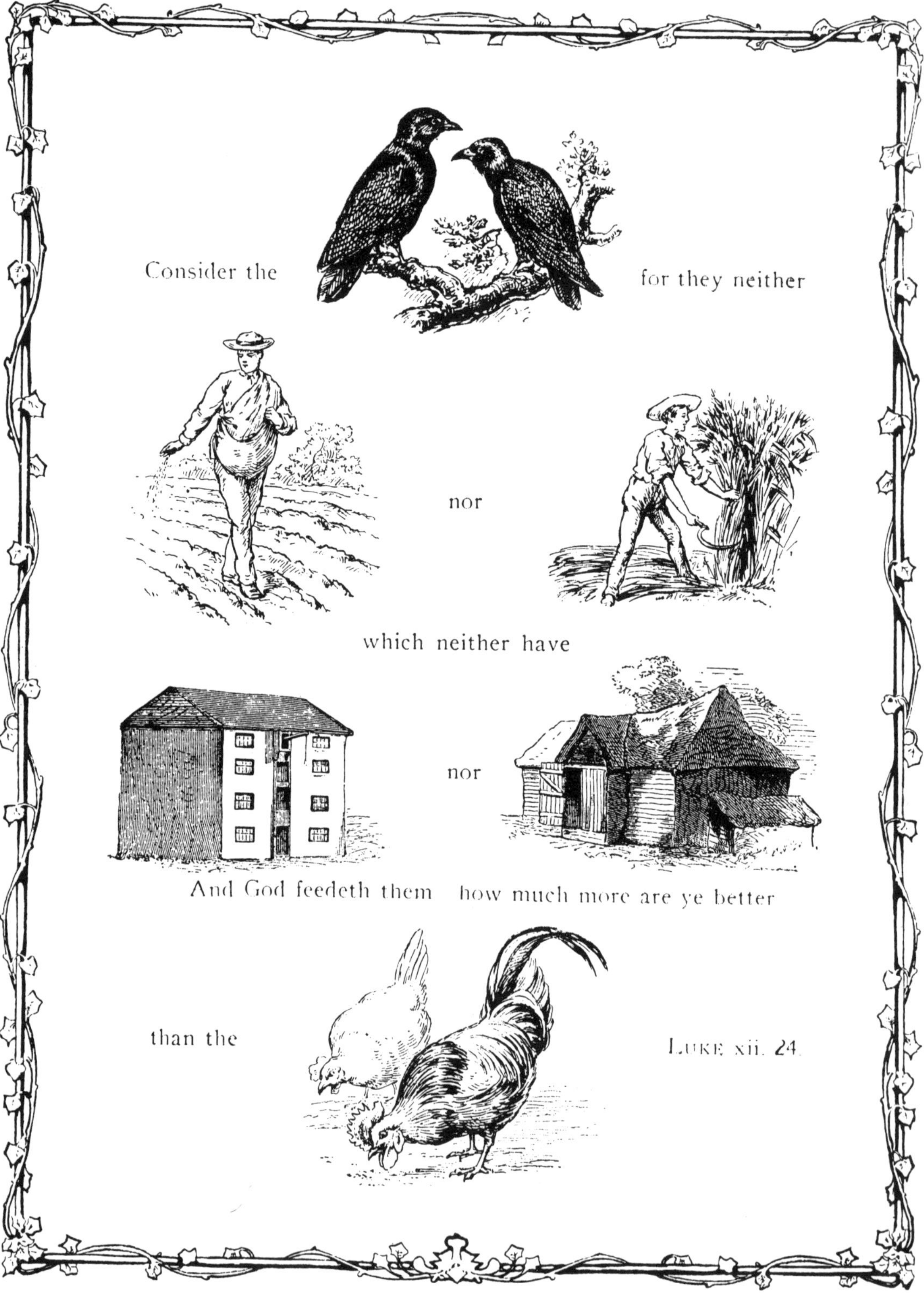
Consider the
for they neither
nor
which neither have
nor
And God feedeth them
how much more are ye better
than the
Luke xii. 24.

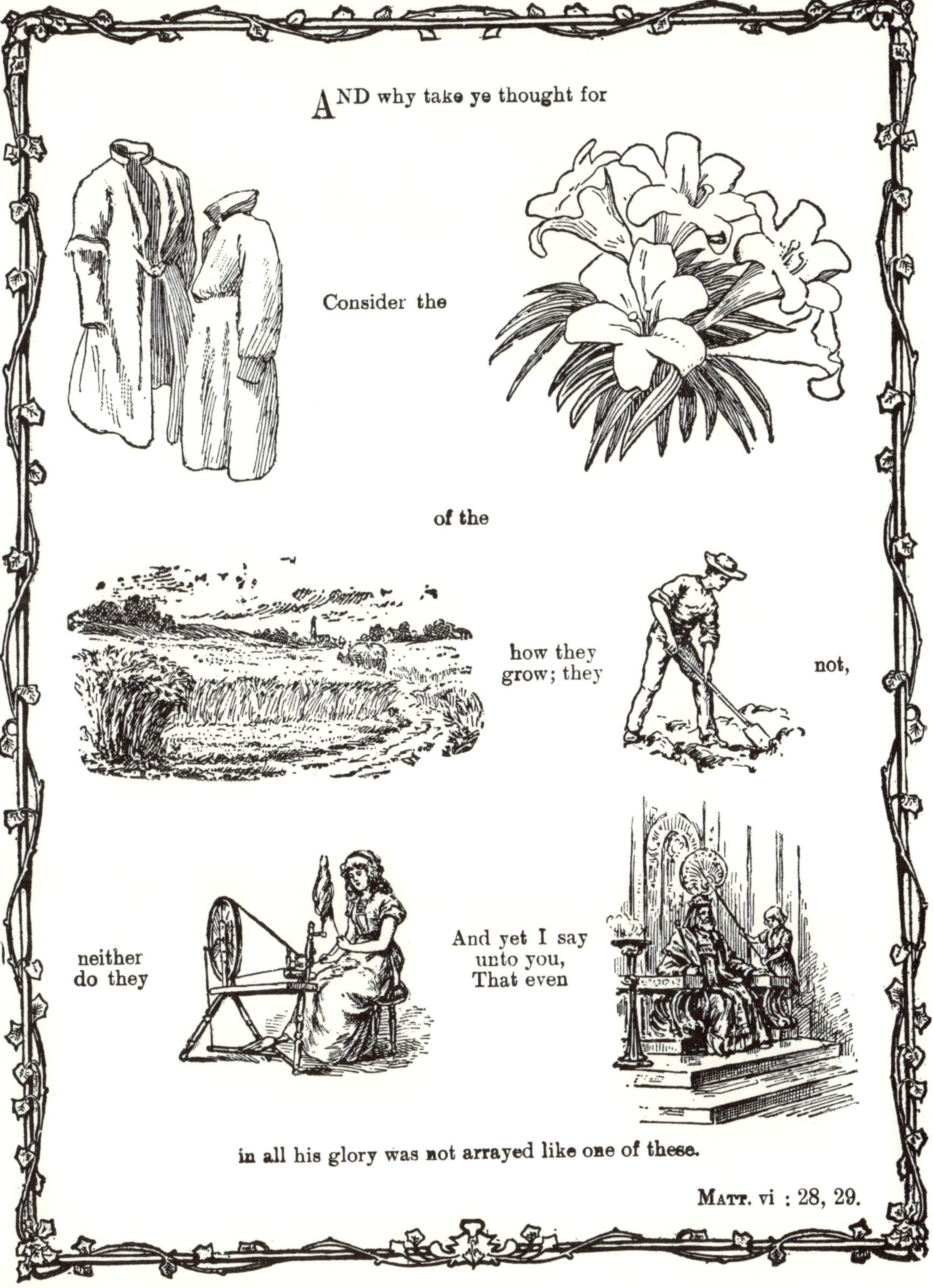
AND why take ye thought for
Consider the
of the
how they grow; they
not,
neither do they
And yet I say unto you, That even
in all his glory was not arrayed like one of these.
MATT. vi : 28, 29.

I (Name)..................................FILLED

IN THESE ANSWERS. (Date) ....

1. Why did the prodigal son come home?

....

2. What did he ask for when he returned?

....

3. Why did his father give him the best he had?

....

4. Whose great love does this parable picture?

....

5. Where should we lay up treasure and what kind?

....

6. Why should we lay up treasure in Heaven?

....

7. Who feeds the birds?

....

8. Who feeds you?

....

9. Who makes the lilies so fair?

....

10. Who was Solomon?

....

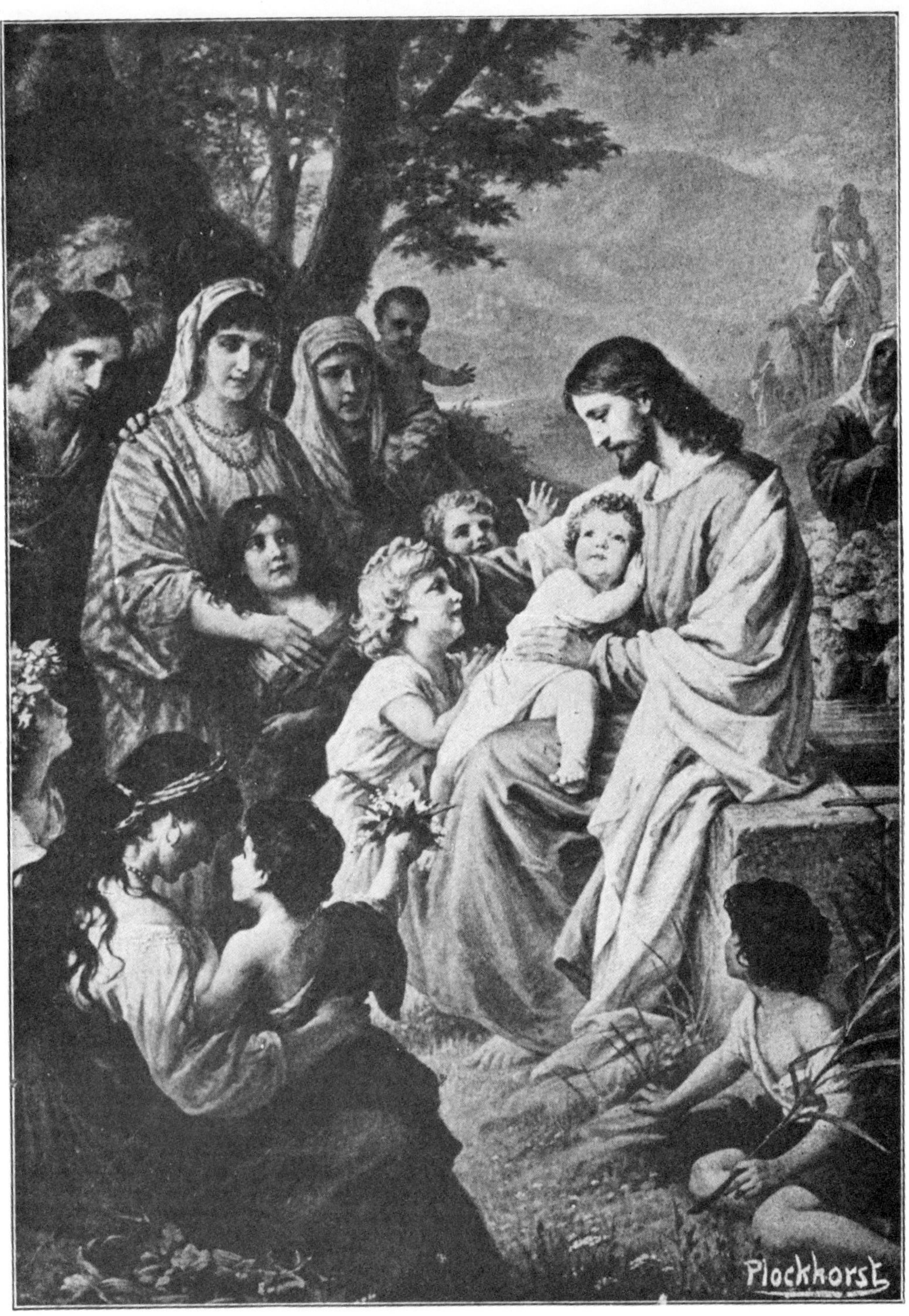

CHRIST BLESSING LITTLE CHILDREN

CHRIST BLESSING LITTLE CHILDREN.

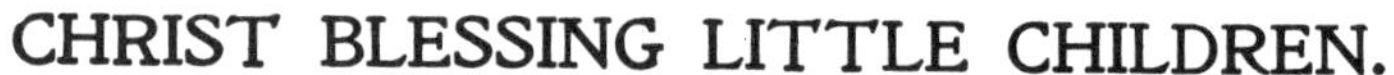

"I LOVE your Jesus because he loves little children," said a heathen child to a missionary.

It was springtime of the last year that Jesus lived on earth. He was in Peræa, beyond the River Jordan. He had gone there to hide away from the wicked priests who hated him and wanted to kill him. It was no longer safe for Jesus to preach and teach in Judea and Galilee, and the priests had even turned the hearts of the people away from him in Samaria. So the gentle Master had gone with his disciples down the Jericho road, and crossing the fords of the Jordan had come into the Peræan country, where the people were not so much under the rule of the priests as in Jerusalem. Here Jesus stayed all the winter, helping and blessing the kind people, and now the time had come for him to go back to Jerusalem and lay down his life for our sakes.

It was not a strange thing in that land for thoughtful mothers to bring little children to some wise Teacher and ask him to tell them to be always good and true. Many of the humble Peræan women had heard this young Teacher speak such wise and loving words, that they longed to have him lay his hands in blessing upon their dear children, and when they heard that he was going away, they came from their small white houses, carrying the babies—leading the little toddlers, and calling the older ones to follow, as they pressed up close to the Master's side.

It was a pretty sight to see the women wearing bright handkerchiefs on their heads—as women still do in the East—clothed in red and blue garments, hurrying forward with their dark-faced little boys, and rosy-cheeked girls and laughing

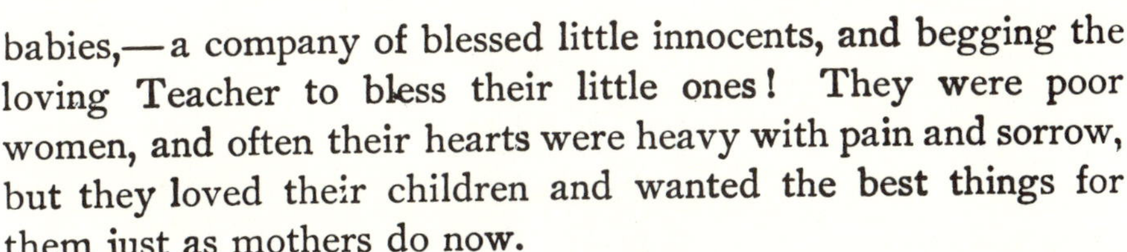

babies,—a company of blessed little innocents, and begging the loving Teacher to bless their little ones! They were poor women, and often their hearts were heavy with pain and sorrow, but they loved their children and wanted the best things for them just as mothers do now.

But so many women came, bringing so many children, that the disciples feared the Master would be wearied by their coming, and they spoke roughly to the mothers and children, telling them to go away.

Jesus heard their harsh words, and he was "much displeased." Then he spoke the beautiful words which made these mothers glad, and which will go on making hearts glad as long as the world stands:—"Suffer the little children to come unto me, and forbid them not, for of such is the Kingdom of Heaven."

Then how the little ones ran forward with eager joy to touch the kind hands and the robe of this gentle Teacher, and to nestle in his loving arms! In their young hearts they *felt* the love and tenderness with which he laid his hands upon them as he spoke sweet words of blessing, even stooping to take up the littlest ones in his arms. To be sure, they could not understand all the deep meaning of his words, but they could understand that he loved them.

What child who reads this story does not feel like saying:

"I wish that his hands had been placed on my head,—
That his arms had been thrown around me,
And that I might have heard his kind voice when he said,
'Let the little ones come unto Me!'"

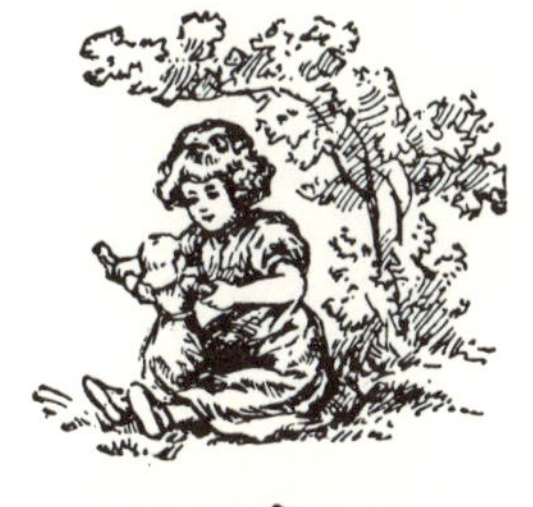

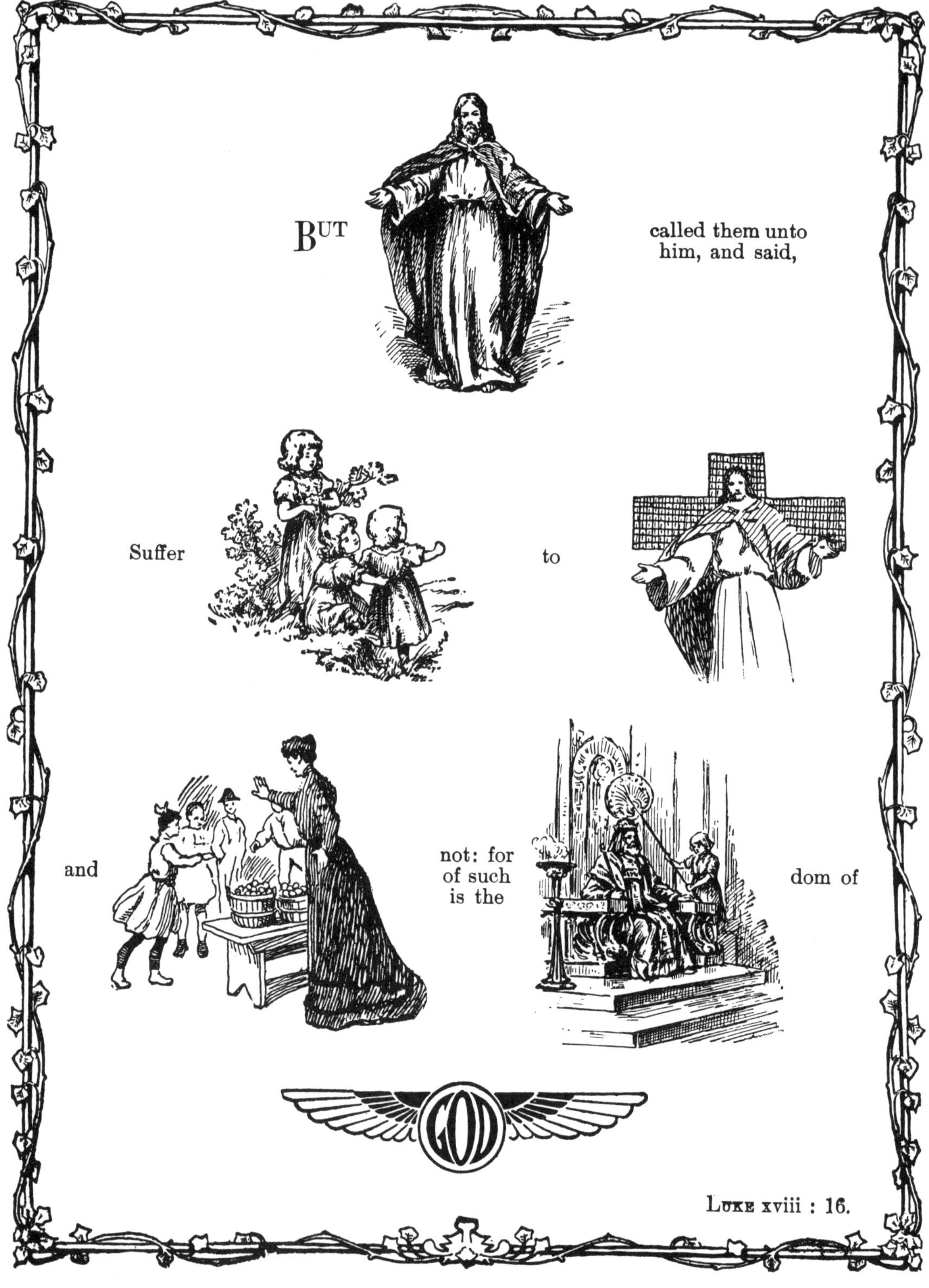
BUT
called them unto him, and said,
Suffer
to
and
not: for of such is the
dom of
GOD
LUKE xviii : 16.

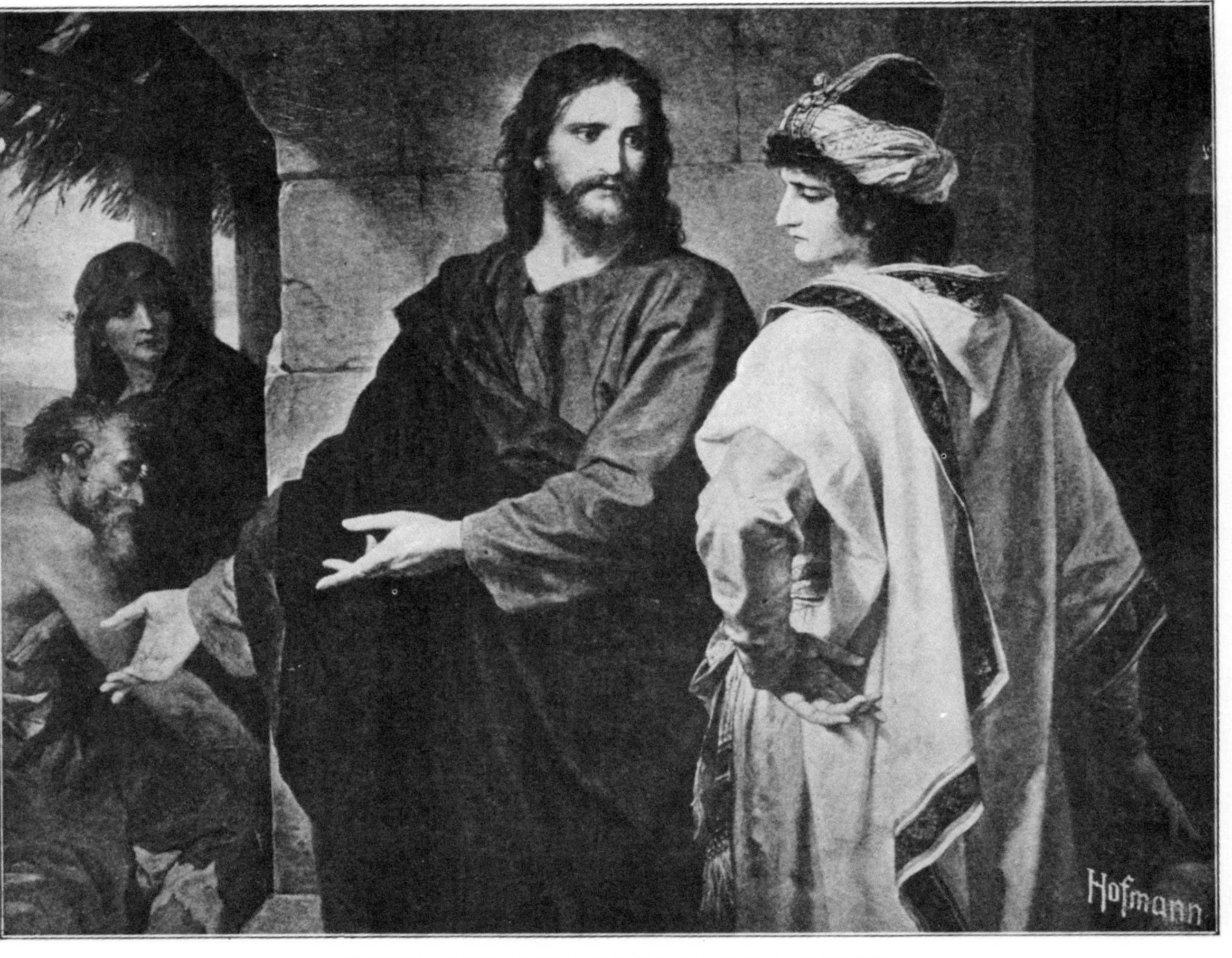

JESUS AND THE RICH YOUNG RULER.

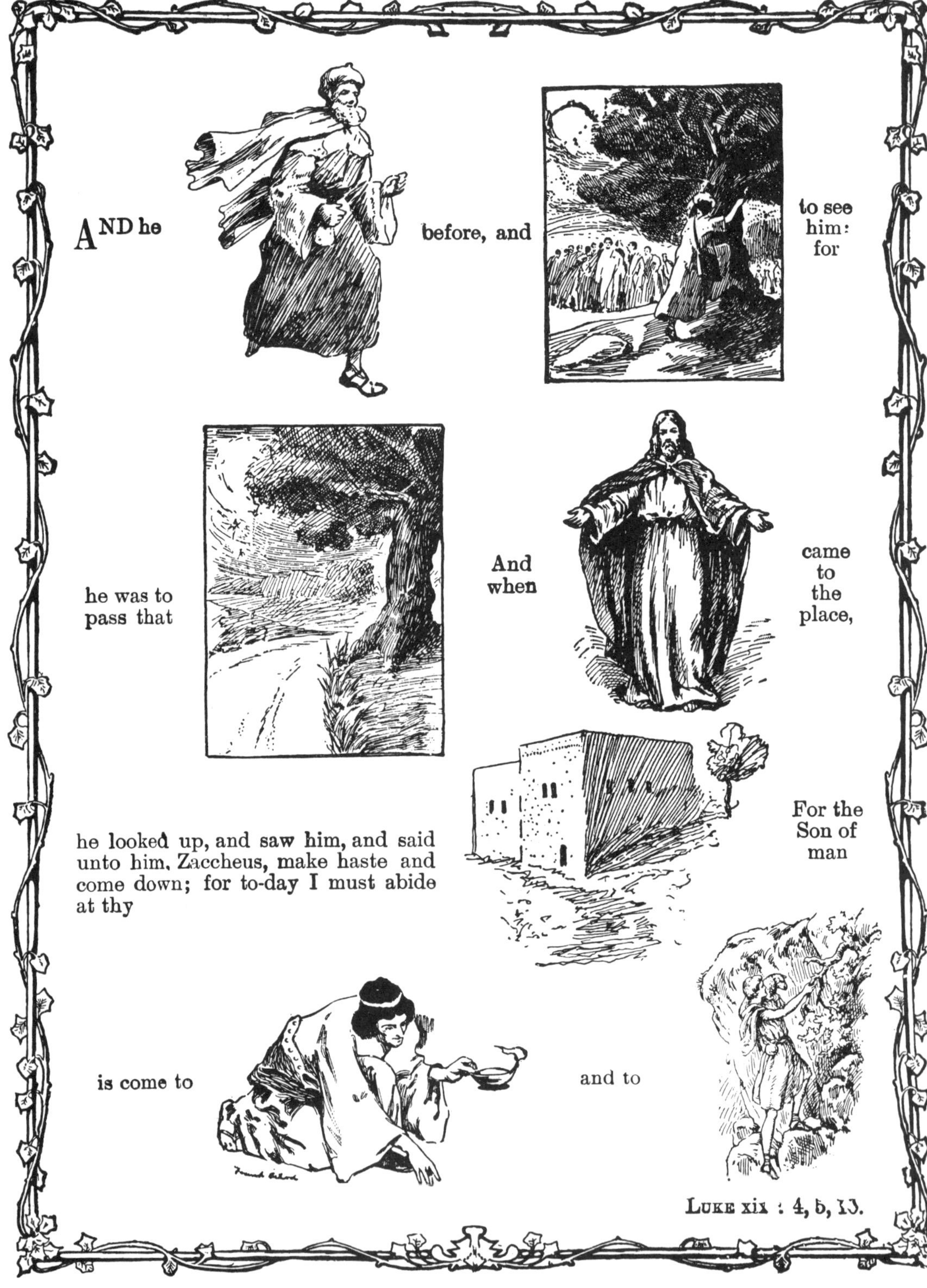

AND he before, and to see him: for

he was to pass that

And when came to the place,

he looked up, and saw him, and said unto him, Zaccheus, make haste and come down; for to-day I must abide at thy

For the Son of man

is come to and to

LUKE xix : 4, 5, 10.

HOSANNA IN THE HIGHEST.

IT was the afternoon of an April day in the land where Jesus lived. The Passover Festival in Jerusalem had called crowds of pilgrims from all parts of Palestine. Some were busy putting up little white tents and mat booths near the city walls, while others found places with friends or took lodgings in the city.

The story went from one to another that the priests and rulers would surely make Jesus a prisoner if he appeared in the temple. They had urged any who knew where he might be to tell them, and declared openly that they were going to put him to death.

Jesus understood well that the time was near when he must die, but he was not afraid of these enemies who could only kill the body, so he set out this beautiful spring day with his disciples and some dear friends from Bethany to go to Jerusalem. When they drew near to the little village of Bethphage he told two of his disciples to go into the village and ask for a young ass, which they would find there and bring to him, so that he might ride upon it into Jerusalem. When the white ass "upon which no man had yet sat" was brought, a blue garment was thrown over its back and Jesus took his seat, his friends rejoicing loudly, for they thought that now he was surely going to enter the holy city as a king. It was the custom for a prophet or a king to ride upon an animal like this, and they believed that at last their great Prophet and King was coming to his own!

Some ran ahead and threw down their outside garments of blue and yellow and brown upon the dusty road for him to ride over, while others cut green branches from the trees and cast them before him. As the crowd grew larger they shouted joyfully and waved their branches of palm, while joyous children ran ahead, gathering branches and singing praises with the rest.

It was a happy band of pilgrims indeed. When Jesus and his friends came to the top of the hill they saw another company winding up the path on the Jerusalem side of the Mount of Olives, who also welcomed Jesus with loud shouts and waving palm branches.

And what did the gentle Jesus think of all this tumult and display? He did not tell the rejoicing crowd to be silent, for he knew that the end was near, and for this once he allowed them to honor him.

Among the company who had come up from Jerusalem to meet him, were some Pharisees, who were very angry when they saw the joy of the people and heard them call Jesus a king. They shouted to Jesus to stop them, but he calmly said, that if the people had been silent the very stones would cry out! And yet, though Jesus let himself be treated as a king, it was a sad hour for him, for he well knew that he must soon lay down his life for the sins of the world, and that even his friends would fail and forsake him. None could understand his sadness as the triumphant company marched on, singing: "Hosanna! Blessed is he that cometh in the name of the Lord. Hosanna in the highest." Loudest and sweetest of all were the voices of children who loved Jesus and joyfully sang praises to him.

And still

"Sing praise, O happy children!
Sing praise to Christ the Lord,
Who calls the children to him
With gentle, loving word."

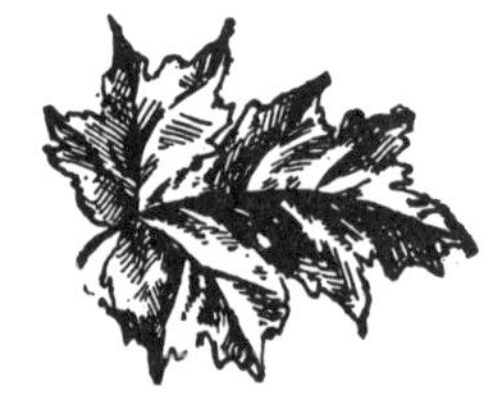

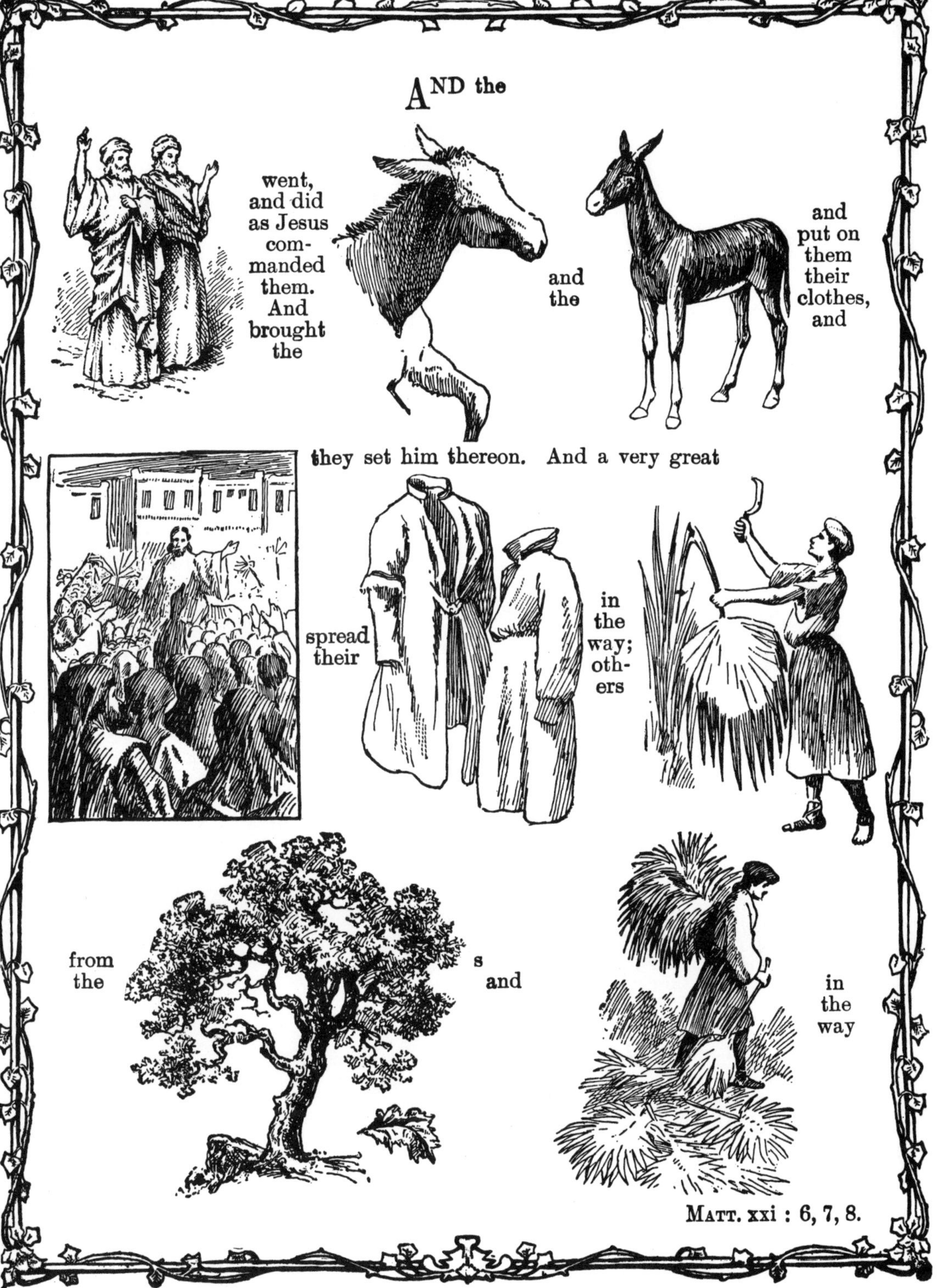
AND the
went,
and did
as Jesus
com-
manded
them.
And
brought
the
and
the
and
put on
them
their
clothes,
and
they set him thereon. And a very great
spread
their
in
the
way;
oth-
ers
from
the
s
and
in
the
way

MATT. xxi : 6, 7, 8.

THE GIFT OF LOVE.

IT was Tuesday afternoon of the last week of our Lord's life on earth. He was in the Temple, the place which he had named, "My Father's House." Soon the services for the day would end, and the Temple gates would close,—never to open again to the Lord of life!

Before going away Jesus sat down for a little while opposite the part called the "Treasury." Here were thirteen large money chests, standing against the wall. Into these the people dropped their gifts of money as they entered the Temple. Each chest had a trumpet-shaped opening made of brass into which the money was dropped. If you had been there you would have seen that each chest bore a name which showed for what purpose the money in that chest would be used, as "Wood," "Incense," "Gold Dishes," and so on.

Jesus watched the people as they came, each one dropping something into the chests. Here came a rich Pharisee, perhaps, wearing a fine robe, who dropped a handful of gold pieces into the brass mouth of the chest with a look which seemed to say, "See how rich and generous I am!" Then came a merchant, not so rich and proud perhaps, but looking pleased as he heard his silver coins tinkling among the gold pieces. Poorer people came along and cast in their money, and even though it may have been copper coins, they showed by their manner how pleased they were to be seen giving to the Lord.

But by and by came a poor woman. Jesus knew that she was a widow and so poor that she could scarcely get enough to eat. When he saw her take from her pocket two of the smallest pieces of money then in use, and drop them into the box with her head bowed as in prayer, he turned and said to his disciples, "Of a truth I say unto you that this poor widow hath cast in more than they all, for all these have of their abundance cast into the offerings of God, but she of her penury hath cast in all the living that she had."

Jesus taught his disciples this lesson so that by and by, when he was no longer with them and they had become the teachers of his Gospel, they would know and teach that true giving to the Lord's cause is not in the outward act, but in the love and sacrifice that go with the gift. The rich Pharisees and merchants who had thrown their large gifts into the Treasury, could easily spare the money, and really gave to be seen and praised of men. But the poor woman who gave only a farthing because she loved the Lord's House, Jesus said gave more than all the rest.

This story teaches that Jesus does not count as men do. He looks down below the spoken word, the outward deed, even the gift of money or service, to see what lies behind them all. If he sees there the wish to be praised, he is not pleased, but if he sees the loving desire to please him and to help some child of his, he says, "That is well, my child."

"It is not the deed we do,
Though that be never so fair,
But the love the dear Lord looketh for,
Hidden away with care
In the heart of the deed so fair."

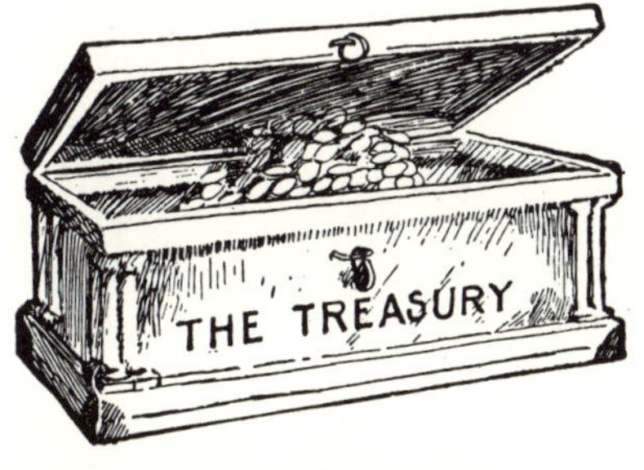

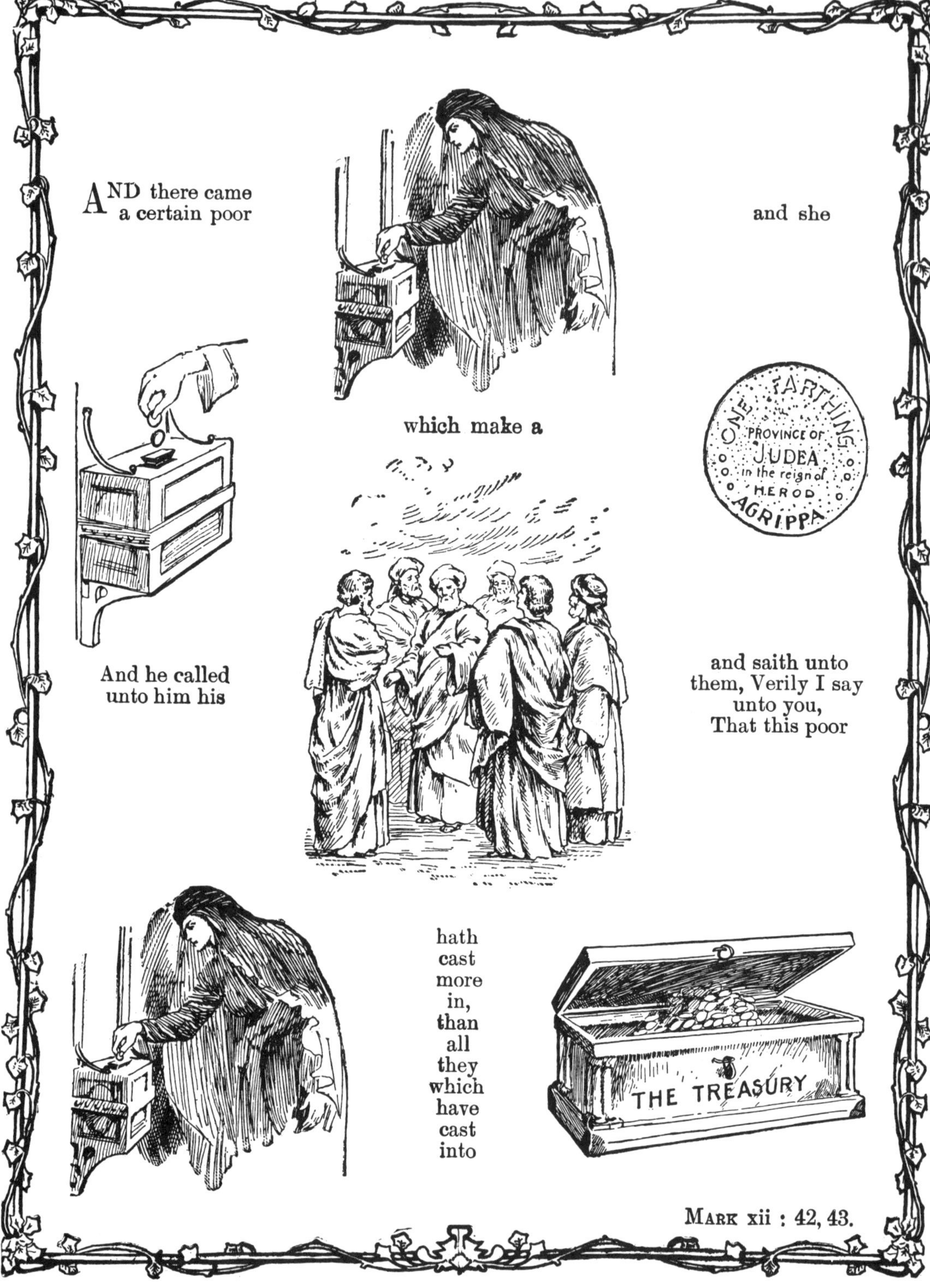

AND there came a certain poor

and she

which make a

And he called unto him his

and saith unto them, Verily I say unto you, That this poor

hath cast more in, than all they which have cast into

MARK xii : 42, 43.

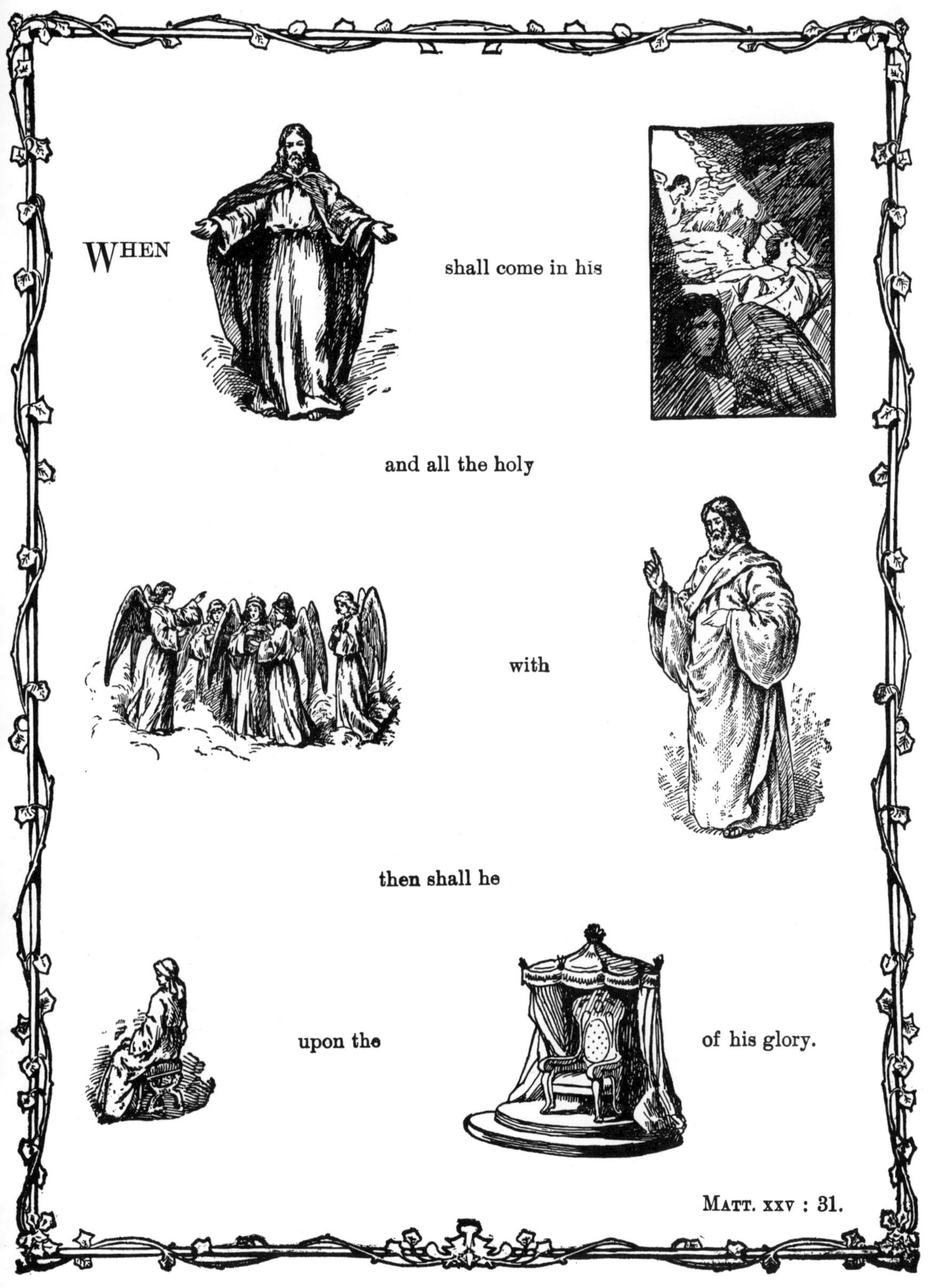

When shall come in his

and all the holy

with

then shall he

upon the of his glory.

Matt. xxv : 31.

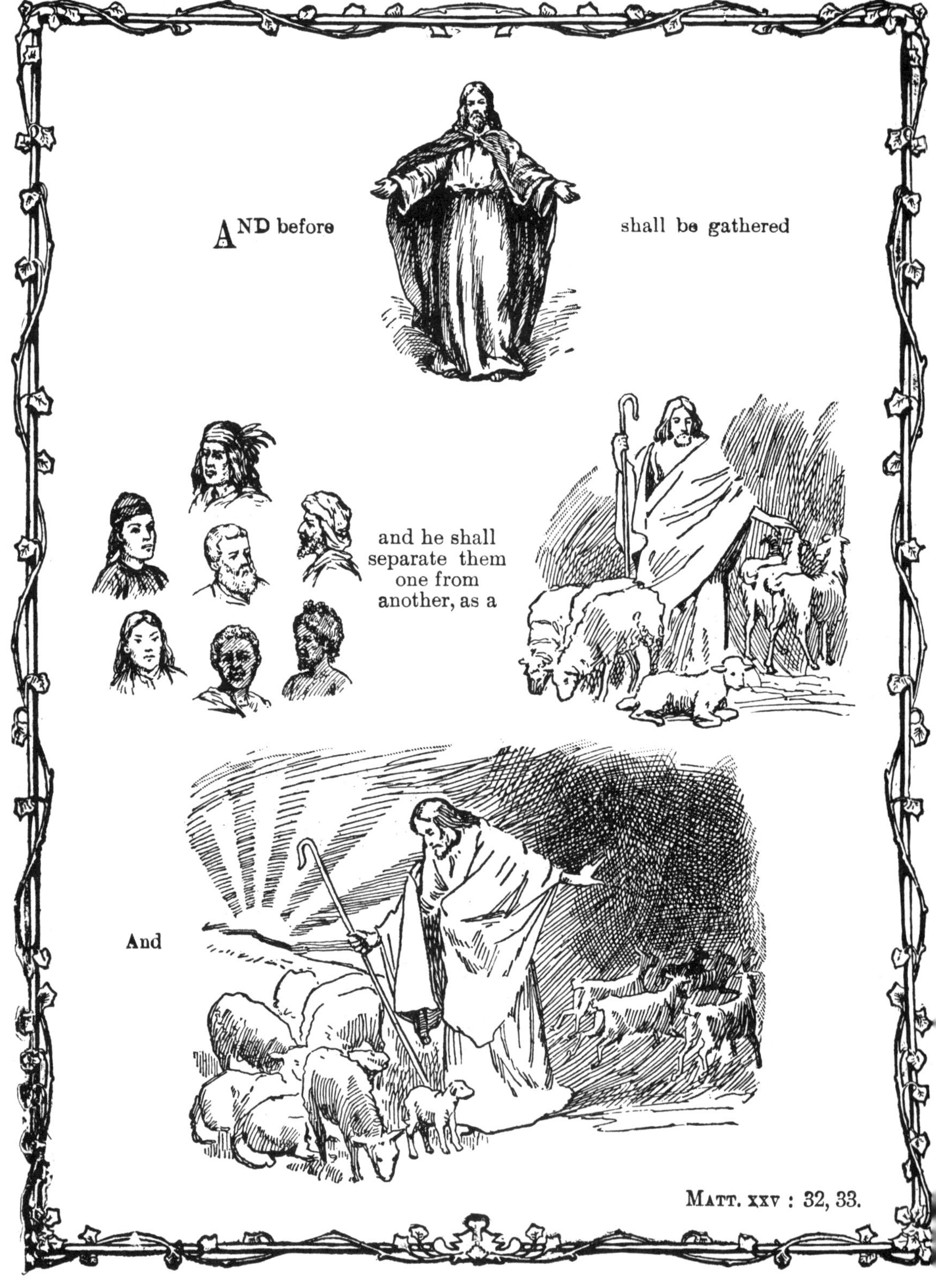
AND before
shall be gathered
and he shall
separate them
one from
another, as a
And
Matt. xxv : 32, 33.

I (Name).................................FILLED

IN THESE ANSWERS. (Date) ....

1. What did Jesus tell His disciples they were to let the children do?

....

2. Why did Zaccheus climb into a tree?

....

3. Where did Jesus eat that day?

....

4. What did Jesus say that day He had come to do?

....

5. Into what city did Jesus ride on the ass?

....

6. How did the people show their love for Him?

....

7. What part did the children have in the triumphal entry?

....

8. Why did Jesus say the poor widow gave more than the others.

....

9. When Jesus comes again will He come as a little babe or how?

....

10. Who are meant by sheep and goats and why will they be separated?

....

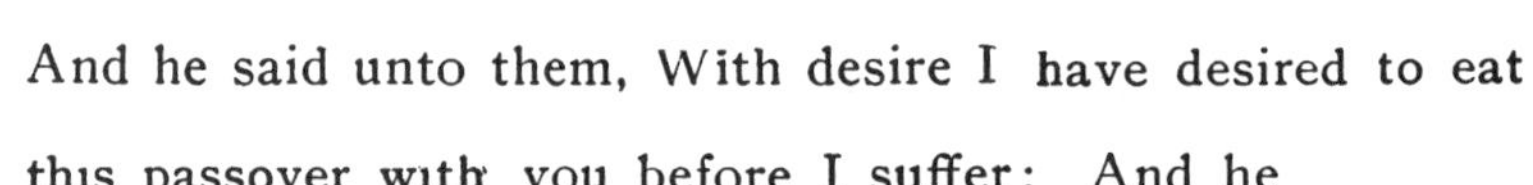

And he said unto them, With desire I have desired to eat this passover with you before I suffer: And he

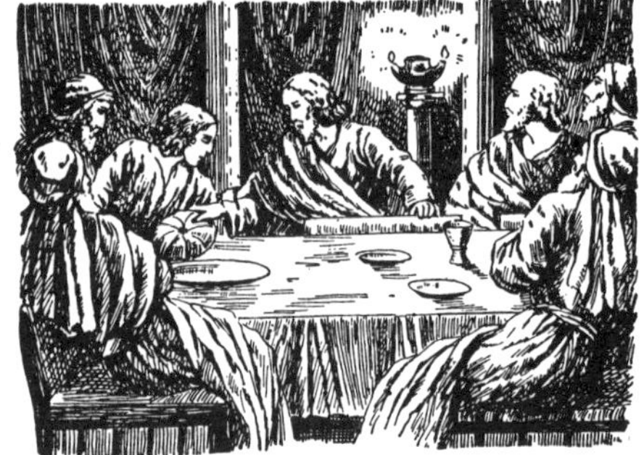

and

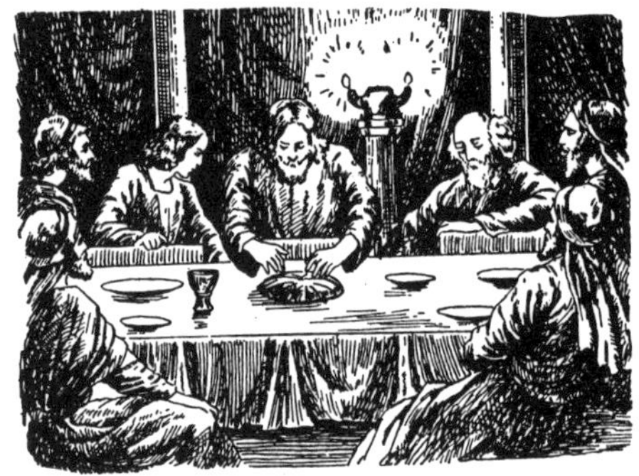

and

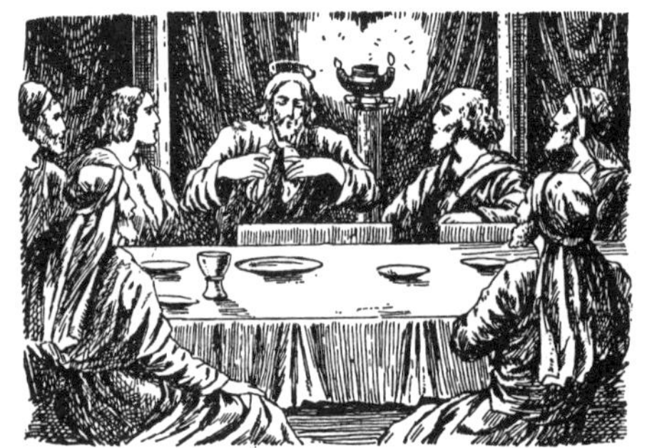

and

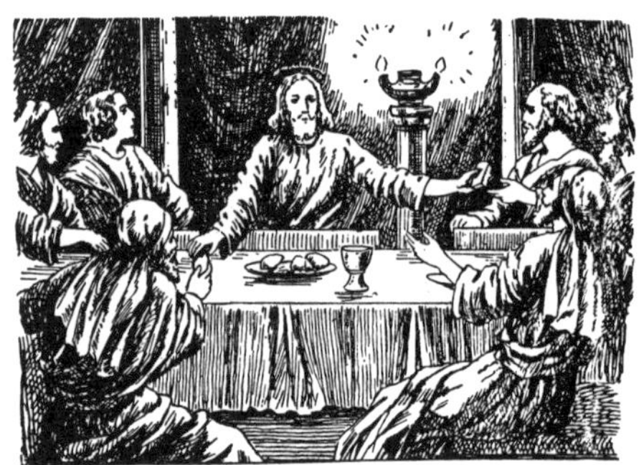

saying,

This is my body which is given for, you: this do in remembrance of me. Likewise also

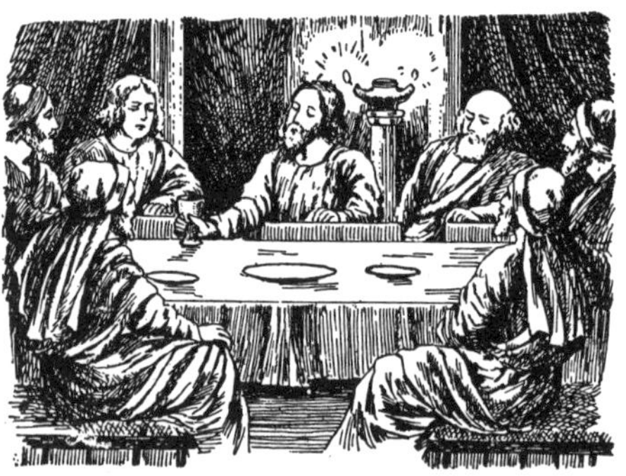

after supper, saying, This cup is the new testament in my blood, which is shed for you.

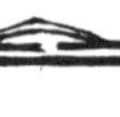

LUKE xxii. 15, 19, 20

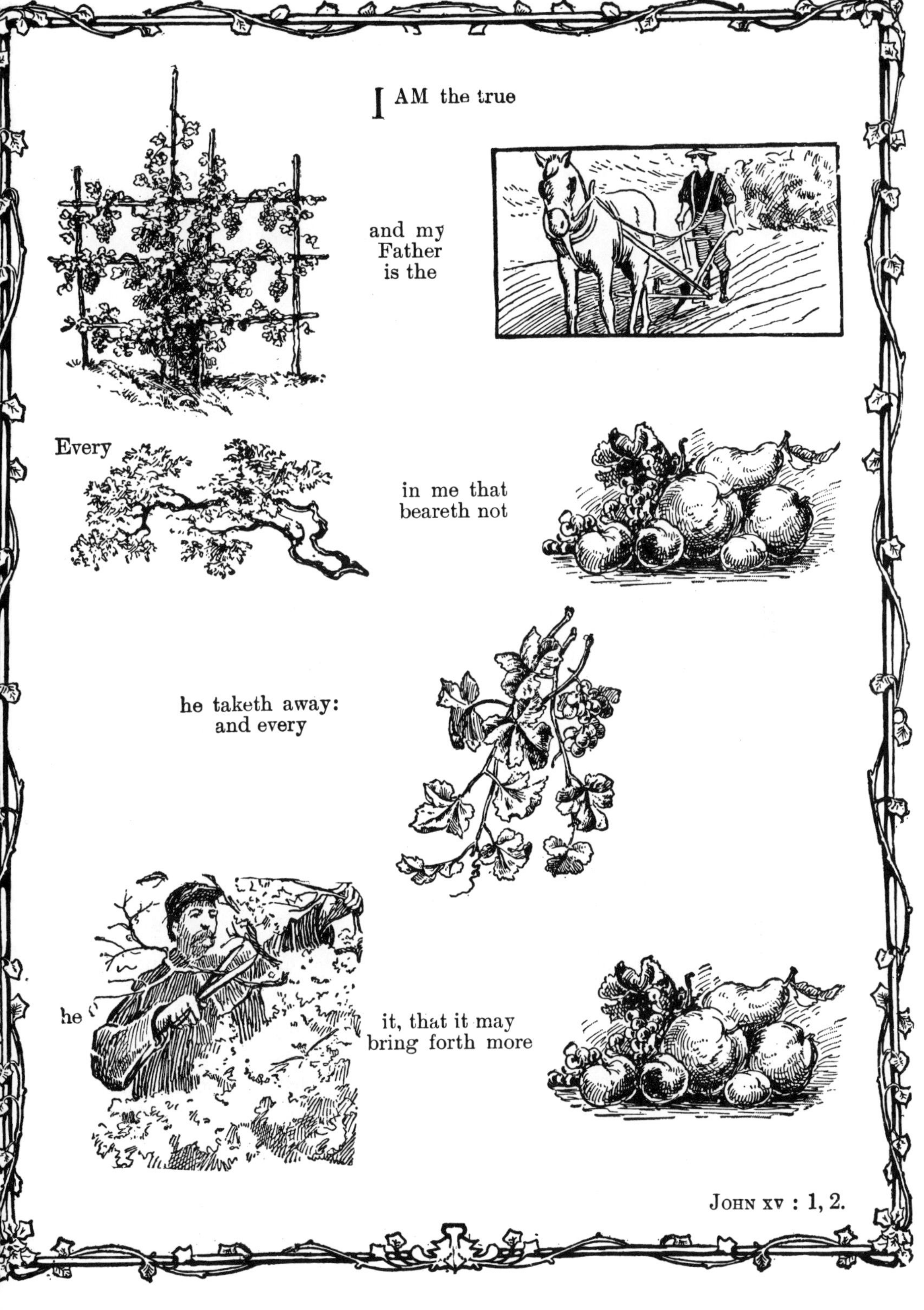

I AM the true

and my
Father
is the

Every

in me that
beareth not

he taketh away:
and every

he

it, that it may
bring forth more

JOHN XV : 1, 2.

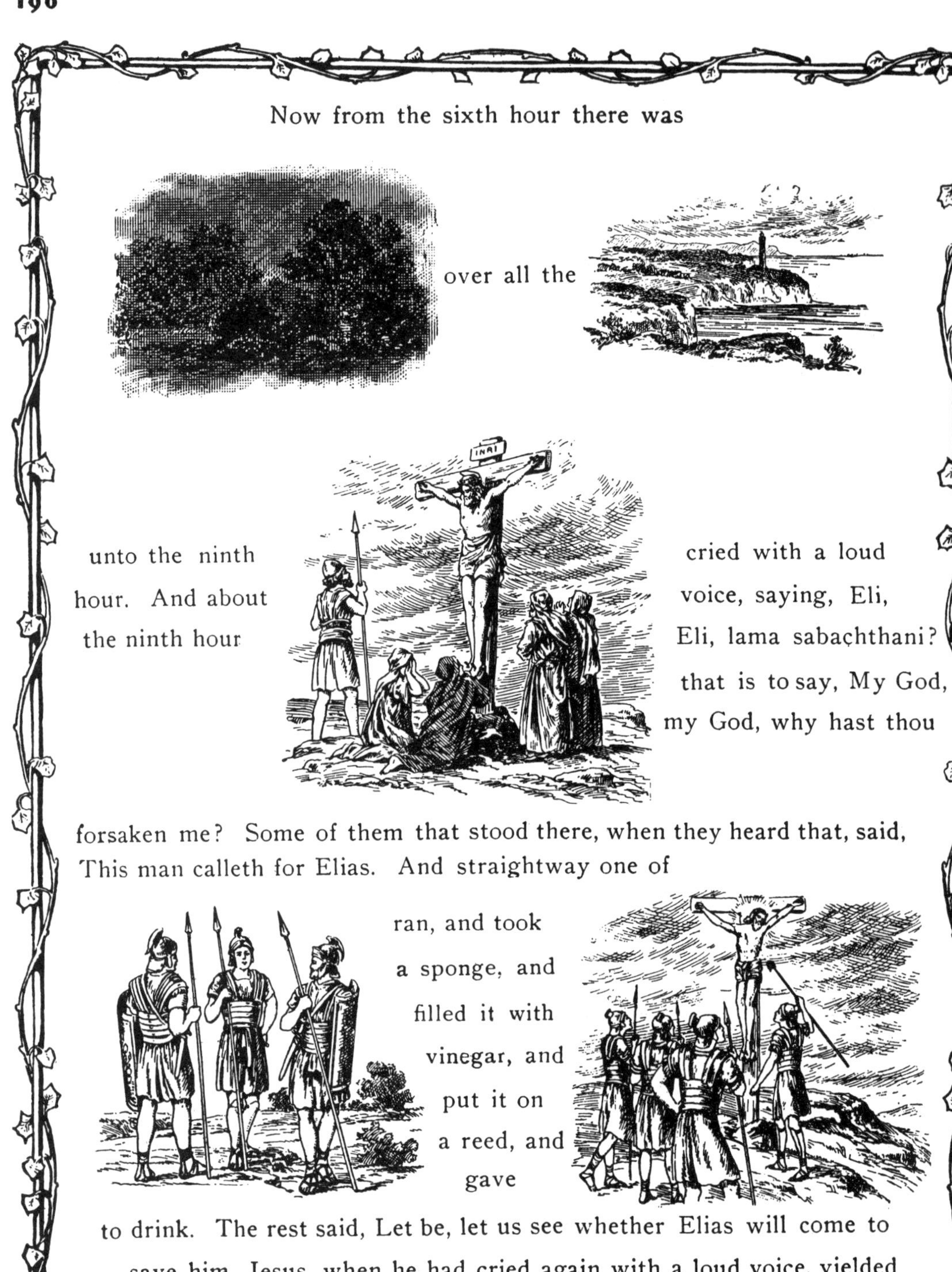

Now from the sixth hour there was

over all the

unto the ninth hour. And about the ninth hour

cried with a loud voice, saying, Eli, Eli, lama sabachthani? that is to say, My God, my God, why hast thou

forsaken me? Some of them that stood there, when they heard that, said, This man calleth for Elias. And straightway one of

ran, and took a sponge, and filled it with vinegar, and put it on a reed, and gave

to drink. The rest said, Let be, let us see whether Elias will come to save him. Jesus, when he had cried again with a loud voice, yielded up the ghost.

MATT. xxvii. 45-50.

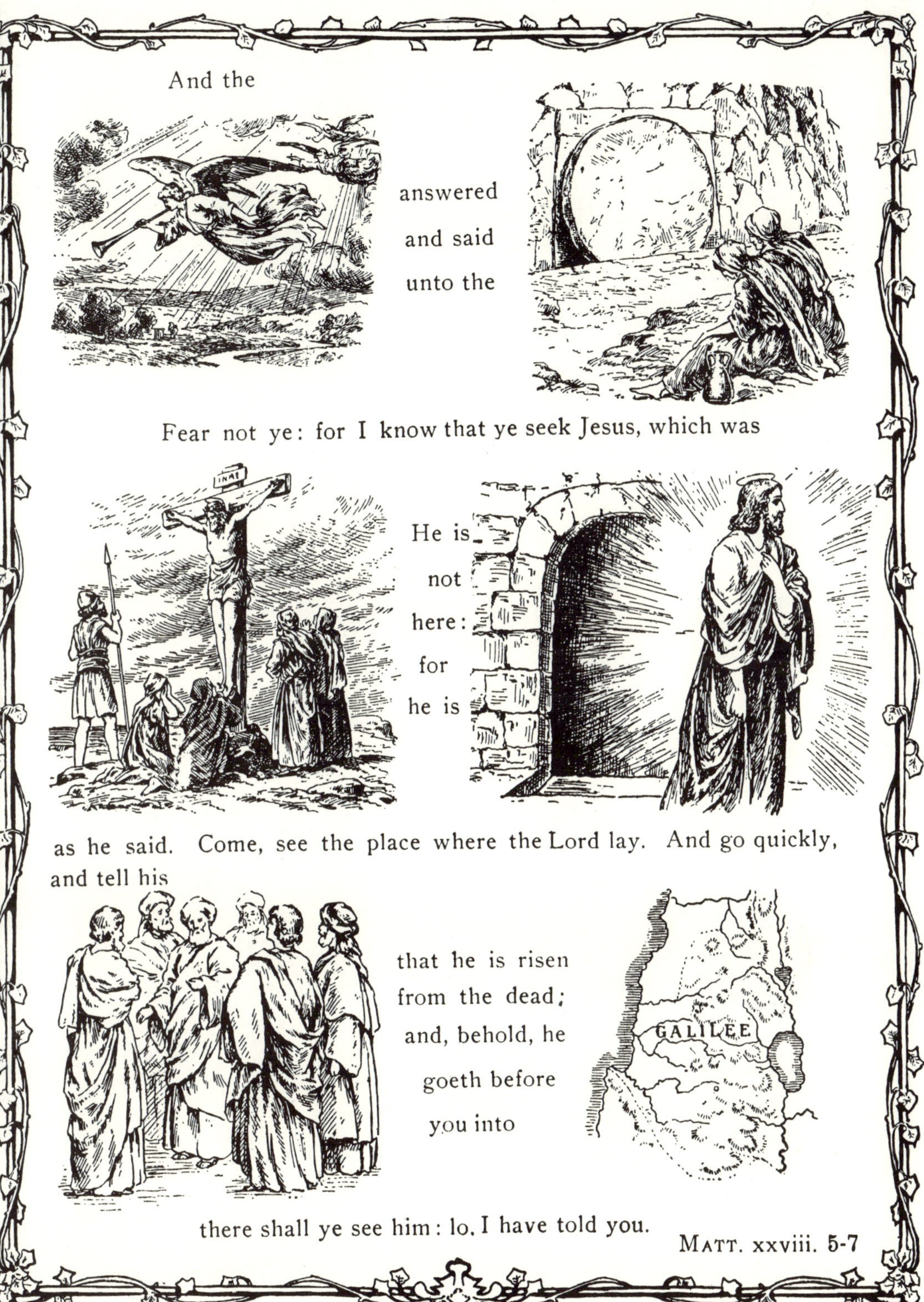

And the

answered and said unto the

Fear not ye: for I know that ye seek Jesus, which was

He is not here: for he is

as he said. Come, see the place where the Lord lay. And go quickly, and tell his

that he is risen from the dead; and, behold, he goeth before you into

there shall ye see him: lo, I have told you.

MATT. xxviii. 5-7

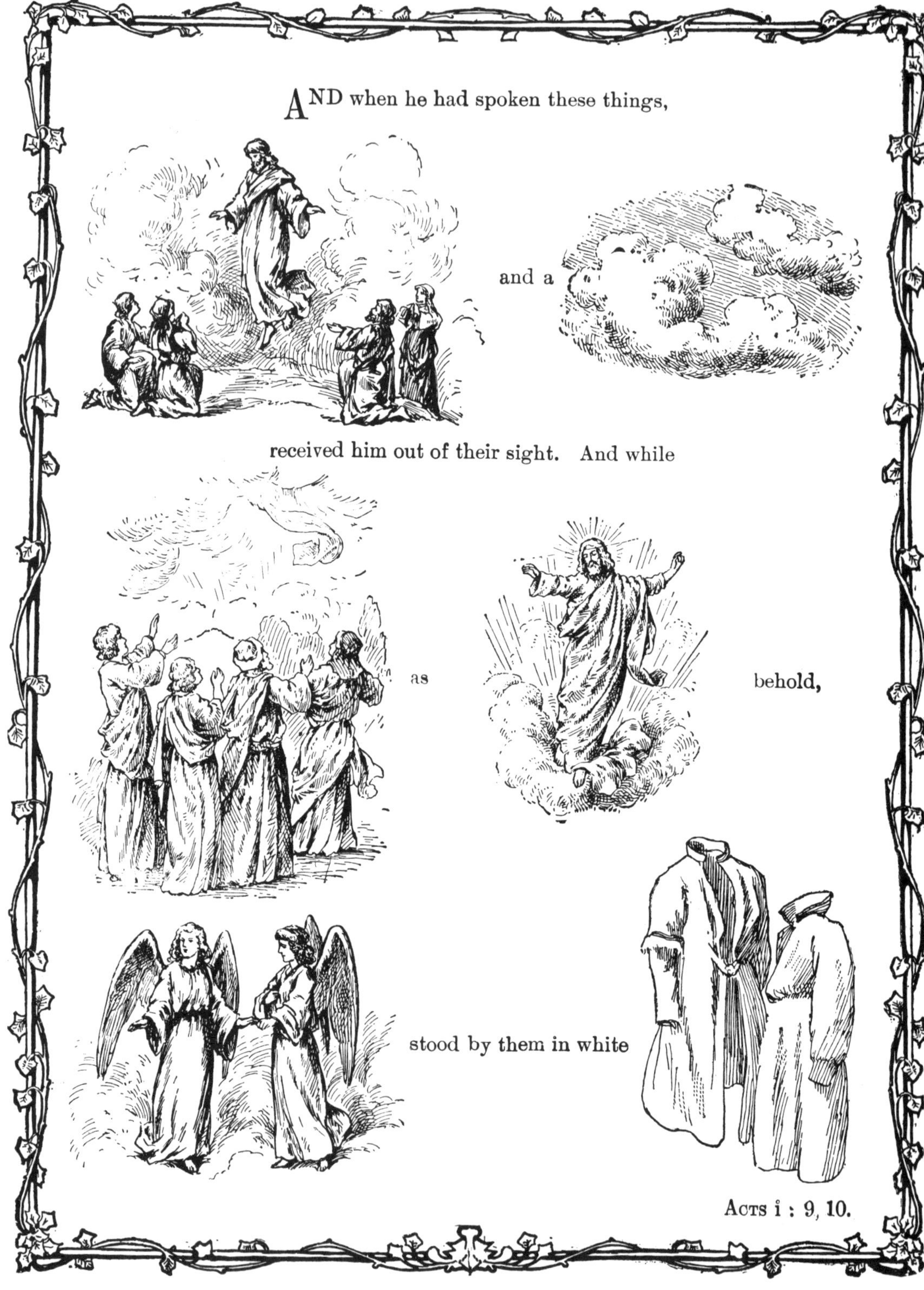
AND when he had spoken these things,
and a
received him out of their sight. And while
as
behold,
stood by them in white
Acts i : 9, 10.

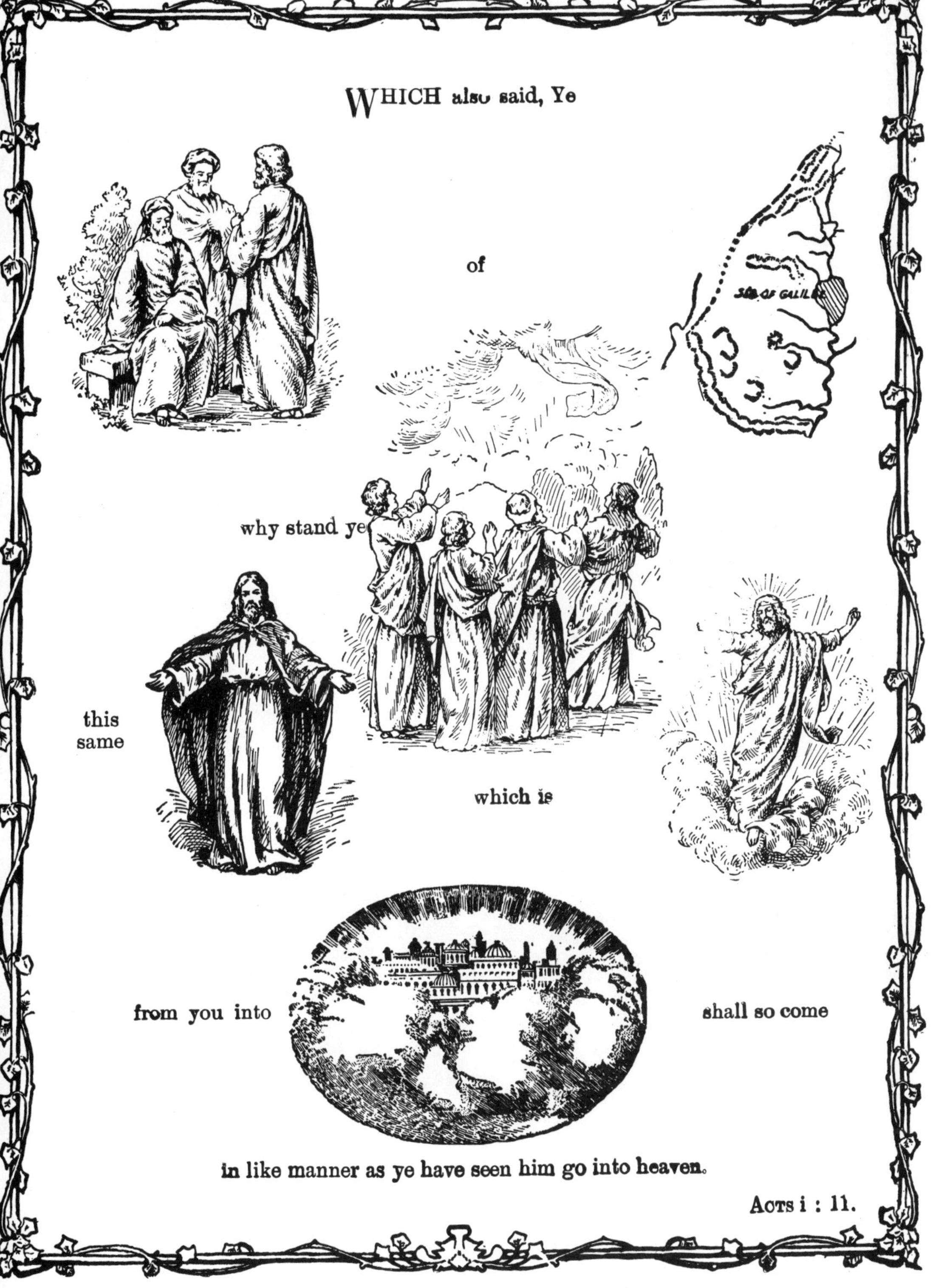
WHICH also said, Ye
of
why stand ye
this same
which is
from you into
shall so come
in like manner as ye have seen him go into heaven.
ACTS i : 11.

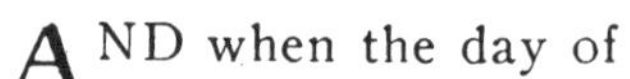

AND when the day of

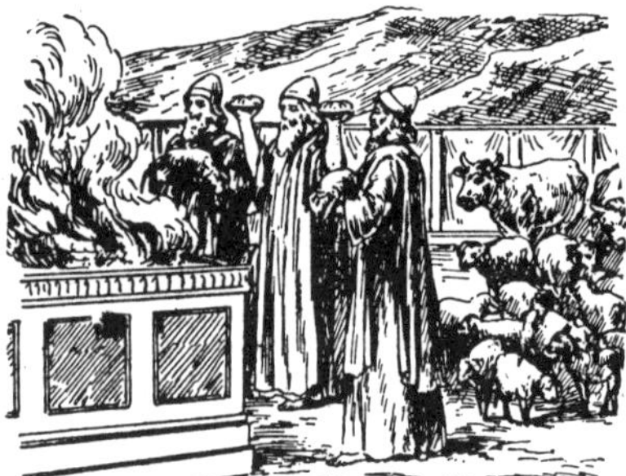

was fully come,
they were
all with one
accord in
one place.
And suddenly
there came a
sound from

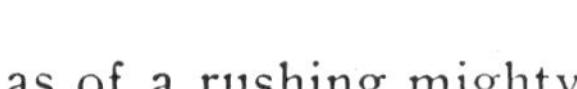

as of a rushing mighty

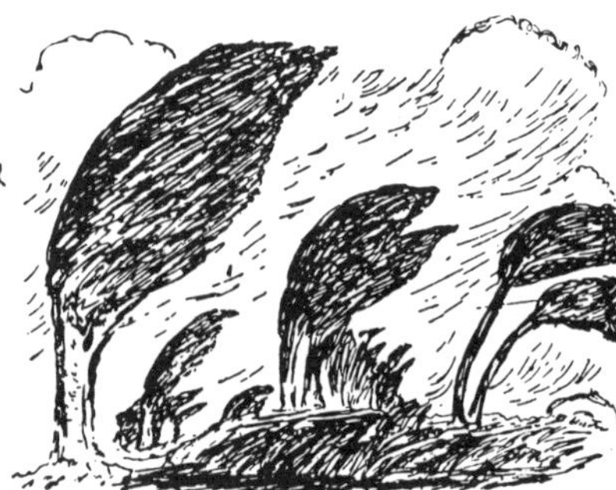

and it
filled all
the house
where

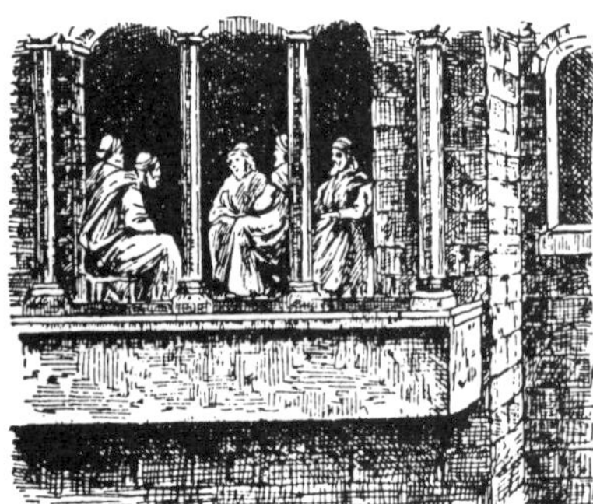

And there appeared unto them cloven tongues

like as
of fire.
and it sat

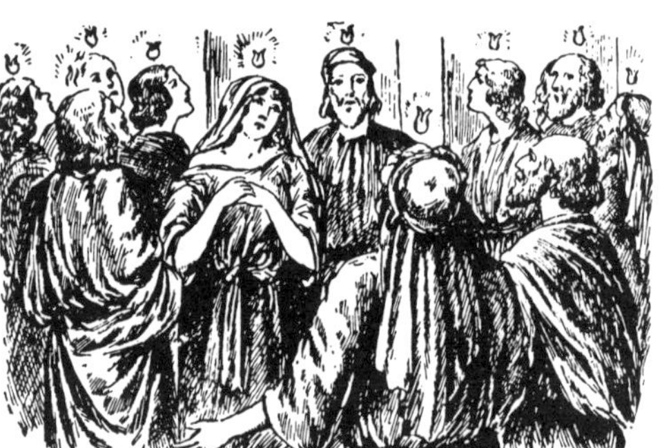

And they were
all filled with
the Holy Ghost,

and began to speak with other tongues, as the Spirit gave them utterance.

ACTS ii. 1 4.

I (Name).................................FILLED

IN THESE ANSWERS. (Date) ....

1. What did Jesus say we were to do in remembrance of Him?

....

2. What kind of vine did Jesus say He was and who are the branches?

....

3. How many times did Jesus speak from the cross?

....

4. On the day Jesus was crucified how long was it dark?

....

5. Who appeared to the women at Jesus' tomb?

....

6. What was his message to them?

....

7. How long after Jesus rose from the dead before He ascended into Heaven?

....

8. Who saw Him go, and who came from Heaven then?

....

9. What did the angels say about Jesus coming again?

....

10. Who had promised the disciples to send the Holy Spirit and when?

....

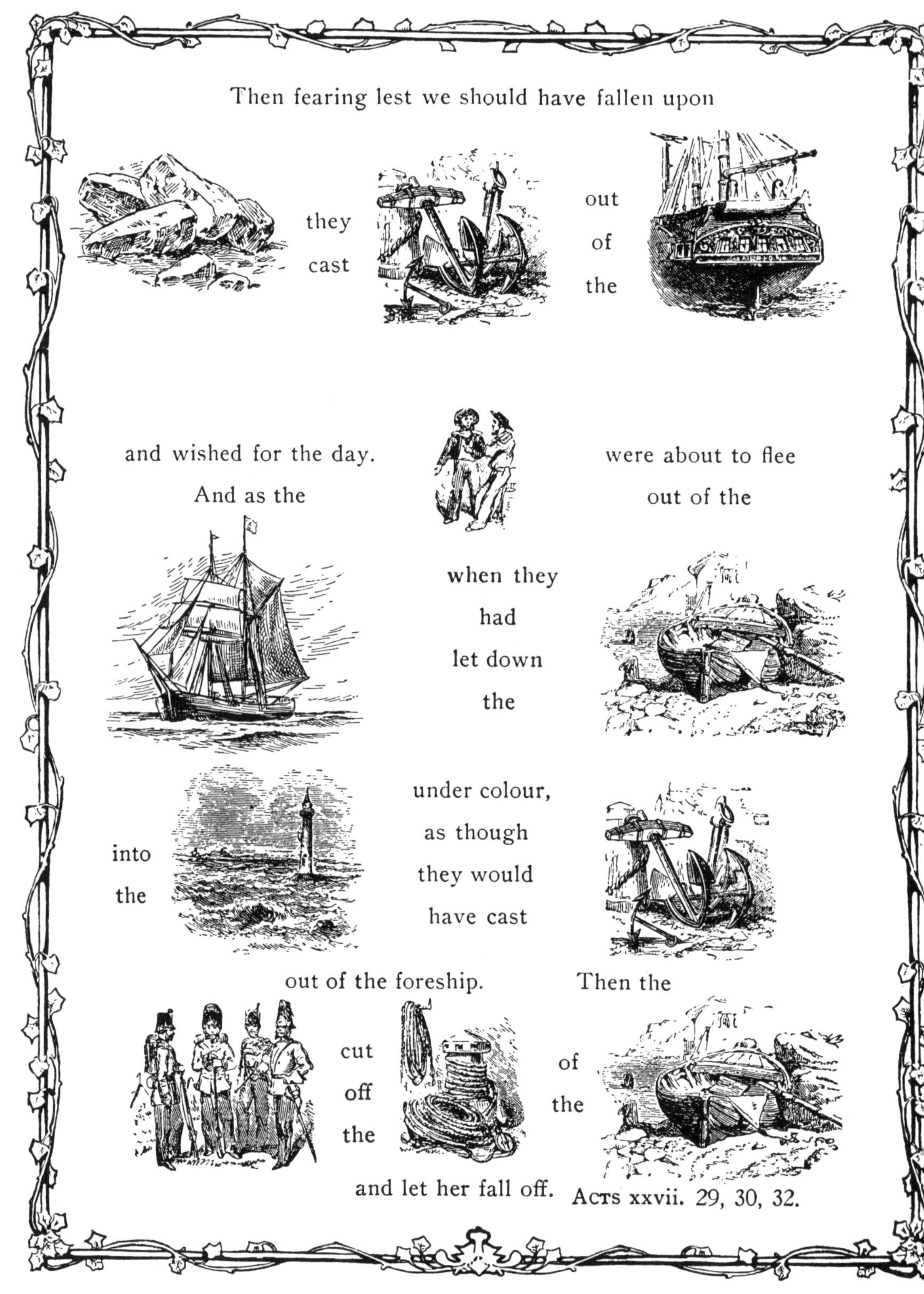

Then fearing lest we should have fallen upon

they cast

out of the

and wished for the day. And as the

were about to flee out of the

when they had let down the

into the

under colour, as though they would have cast

out of the foreship. Then the

cut off the

of the

and let her fall off. Acts xxvii. 29, 30, 32.

And when they had eaten enough, they lightened the

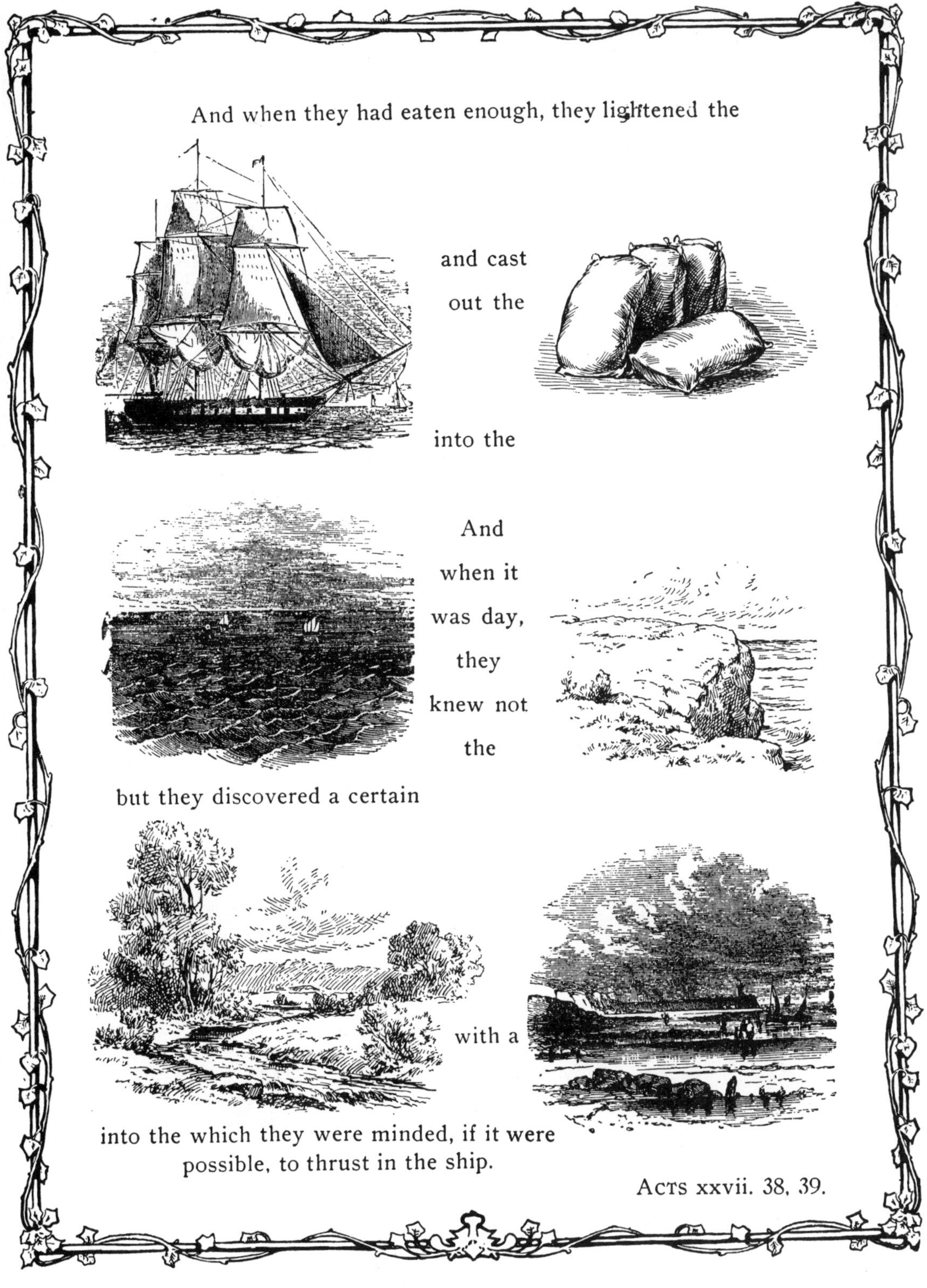

and cast out the

into the

And when it was day, they knew not the

but they discovered a certain

with a

into the which they were minded, if it were possible, to thrust in the ship.

ACTS xxvii. 38, 39.

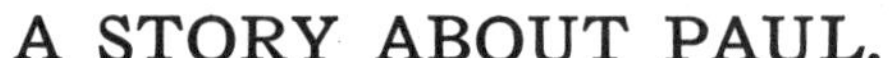

A STORY ABOUT PAUL.

PAUL was a young Pharisee who lived when Jesus was on earth. He did not believe that Jesus was the Saviour, and so he was very hard and cruel to the followers of Jesus. But there came a time after Christ was crucified when he appeared to Paul, and from that day Paul became his follower. He was never a disciple like Peter and John, but he became a great apostle, and used his great learning to help win others to believe in Jesus.

The story of this wonderful change is told in the ninth chapter of Acts.

Now that Paul had become a follower of Jesus he was persecuted by the Jews. At the time he tells this story he had been brought before the chief captain in Jerusalem, who had sent him to Felix, the governor. Felix kept Paul in prison for two years and with his Jewish wife often heard him talk about the Lord Jesus Christ.

At last another governor came who was named Festus. He, too, was kind to Paul, but could not act as Paul's judge, because Paul had said, "I appeal to Cæsar." Cæsar was still higher than the governor. By this Paul meant that he must go to Rome and be brought before the emperor himself.

Two friends went with Paul to Rome,—Aristarchus and Luke, who wrote the Acts of the Apostles. They were in the care of Julius, a centurion, on a ship that was to sail to Rome. Some wanted to wait until the winter was over but others said they must go then. There was not much to fear as the winters are very mild on the Mediterranean Sea and so the ship started. But very soon a great storm of wind arose and the people were very much frightened. Paul was not troubled for the Lord had told him that he must stand before Cæsar in Rome, and he knew that he should go there. He asked the Lord to bring them all safely through the storm and a dream was sent to him in which an angel stood by him and promised that he should stand before Cæsar, and that all on board the ship should be saved though they must first be cast upon an island.

Paul told the people on the ship this dream and it comforted them. For fourteen nights they had been tossed by the wind through the darkness and at last they were driven upon an island. The ship was broken in pieces but all the men escaped to the land.

Have you heard about the Island of Malta? This was the island and it was then called Melita. The people of the island were uncivilized but they were sorry for the shipwrecked people and were kind to them. They made a fire on the shore, and the cold, wet men were glad and thankful. Paul helped to gather sticks to make the fire and as he held them over the fire a poisonous little snake came out of them and fastened on his hand. When the people of the island saw this they expected to see Paul fall down dead, but God had a work for him to do and he did not let him die then. When the savage people saw this they said:

"He is a god!"

The head of the island was named Publius and he was very kind. He fed the men and helped them all he could and in return Paul cured his sick father of a fever, and other people, too, who came from other parts of the island. Paul was always busy helping others and he was glad to do these kind acts for the poor, sick people.

After three months a ship was ready to go to Rome and they all went away from the island. The ship was called "The Twin Brothers" and it carried Paul and all the shipwrecked men safely to Rome and not one life was lost.

This is the longest and best sea-story in the Bible.

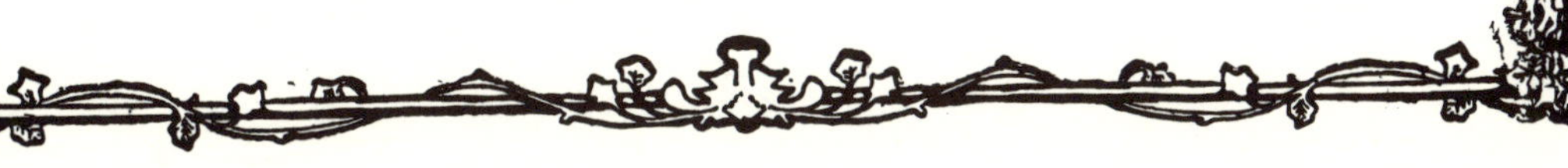

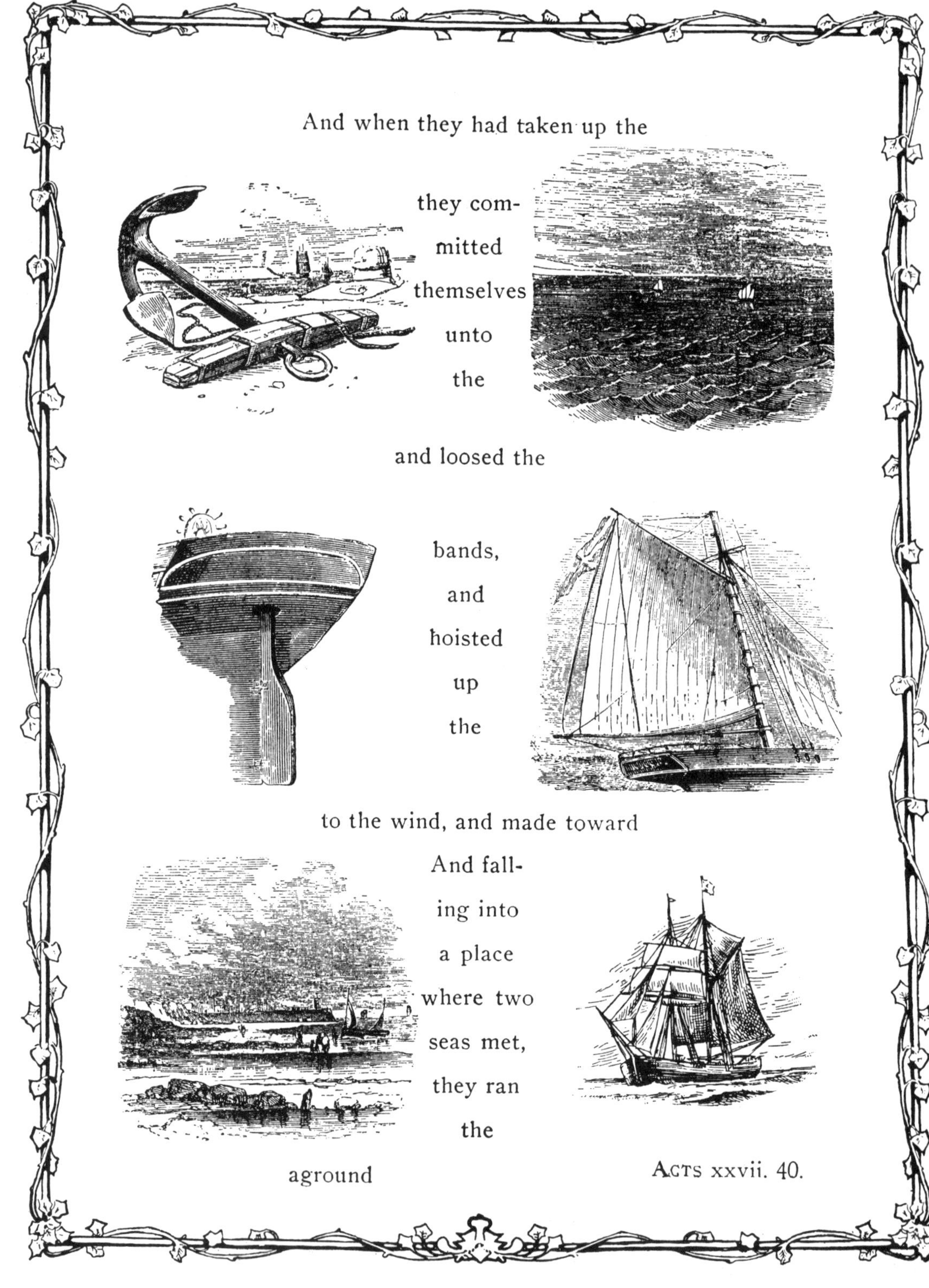

And when they had taken up the

they committed themselves unto the

and loosed the

bands, and hoisted up the

to the wind, and made toward

And falling into a place where two seas met, they ran the

aground

Acts xxvii. 40.

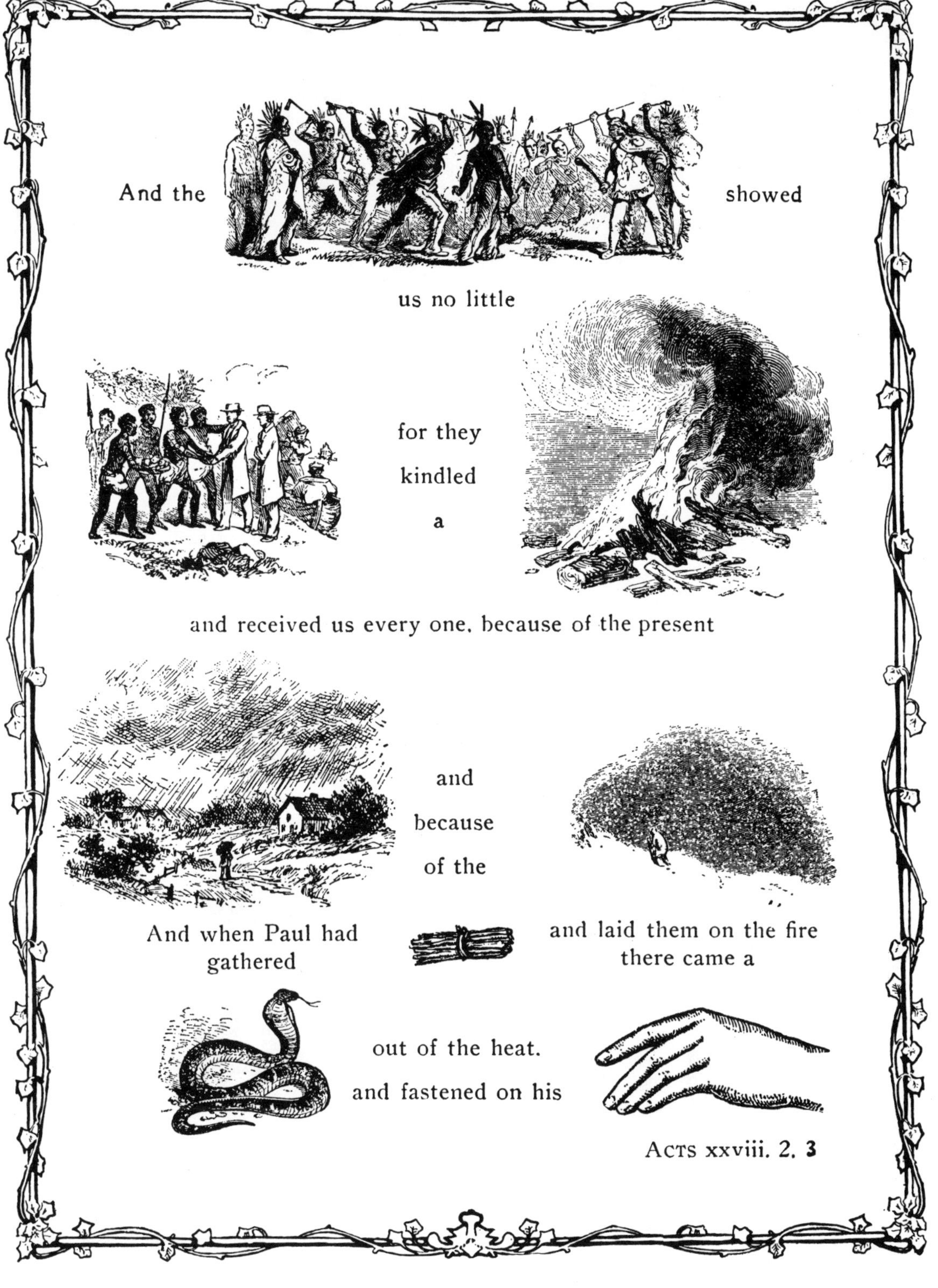

And the showed

us no little

for they kindled a

and received us every one, because of the present

and because of the

And when Paul had gathered

and laid them on the fire there came a

out of the heat, and fastened on his

Acts xxviii. 2, 3

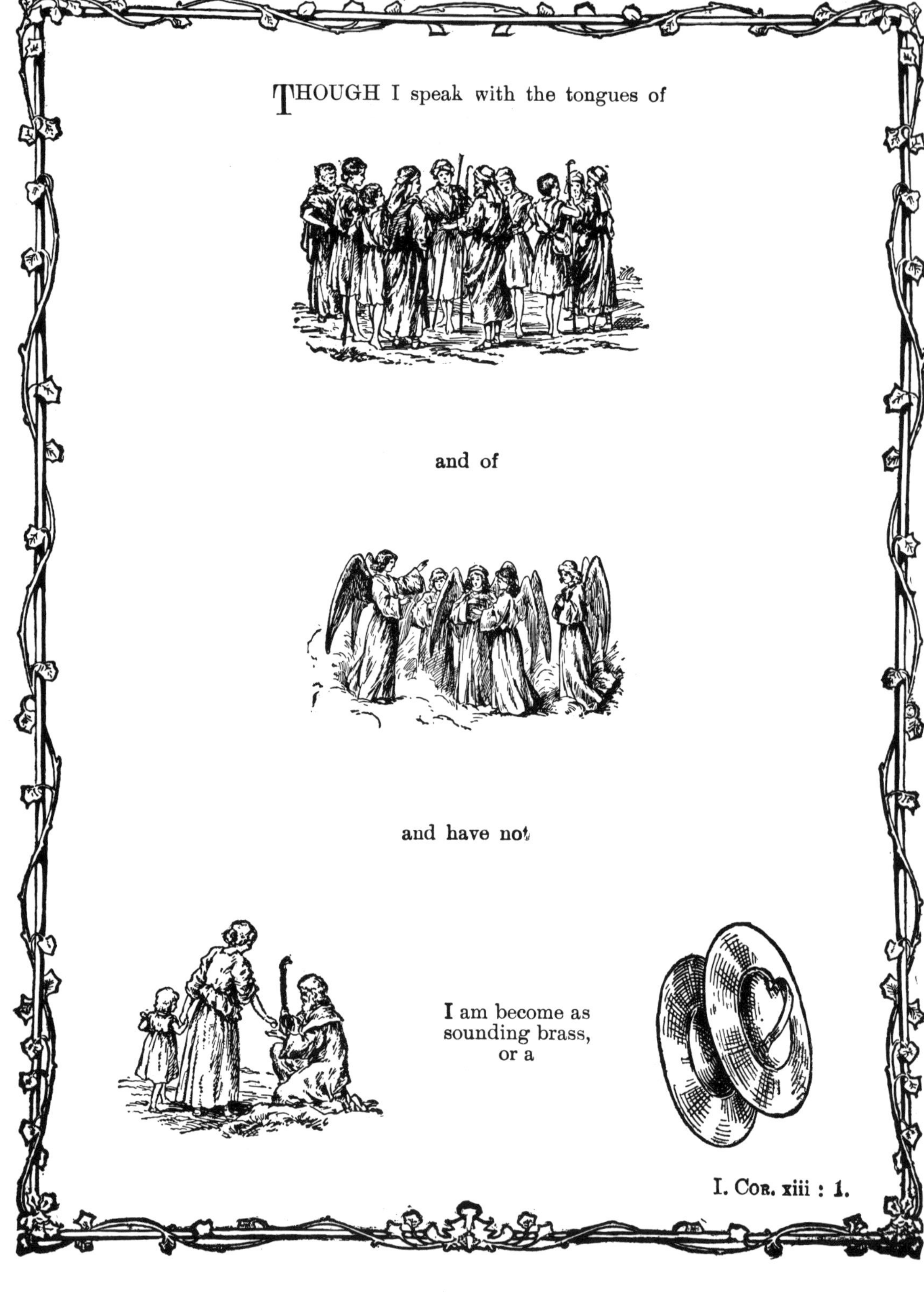

THOUGH I speak with the tongues of

and of

and have not

I am become as
sounding brass,
or a

I. Cor. xiii : 1.

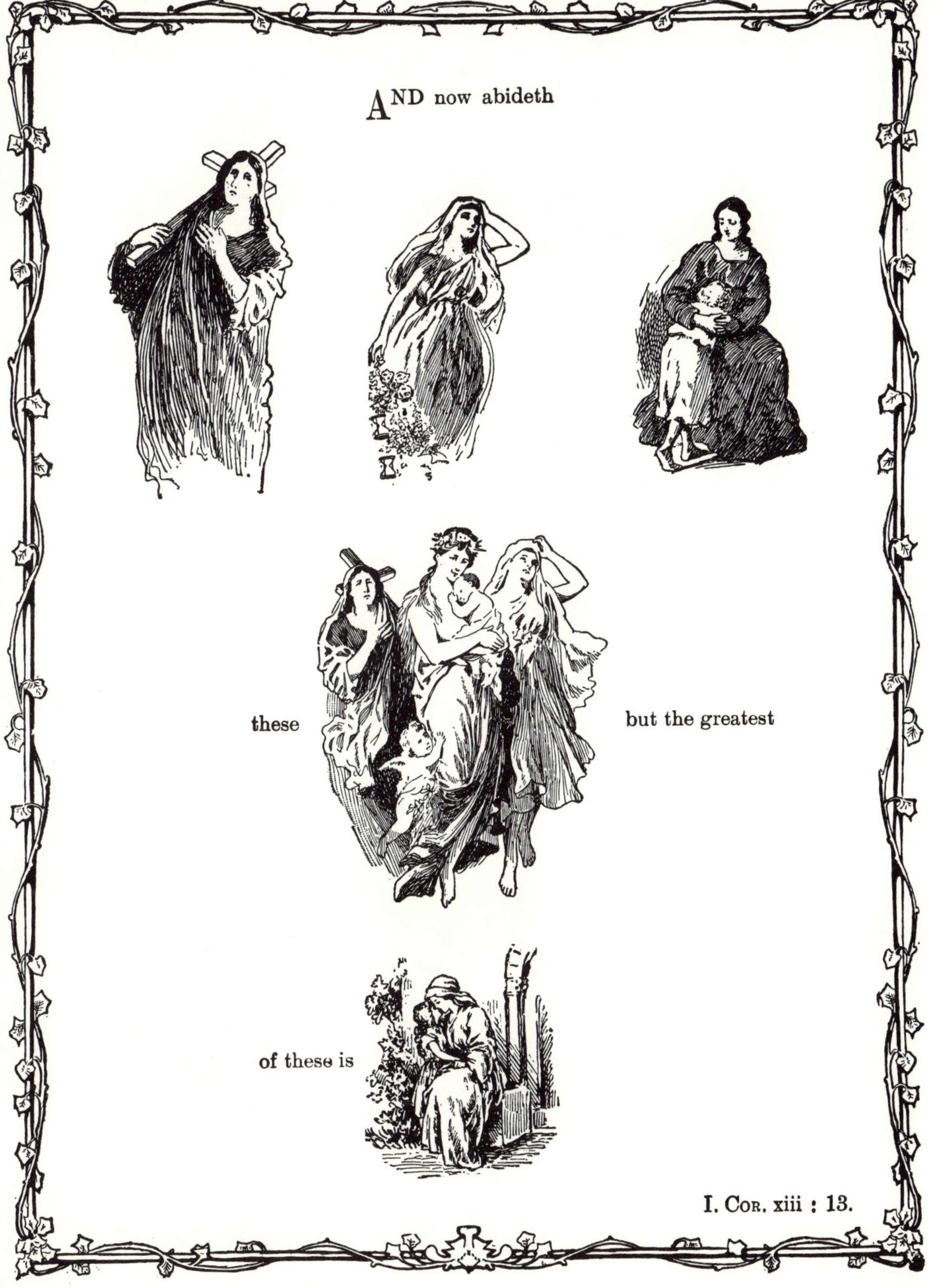
AND now abideth
these
but the greatest
of these is
I. Cor. xiii : 13.

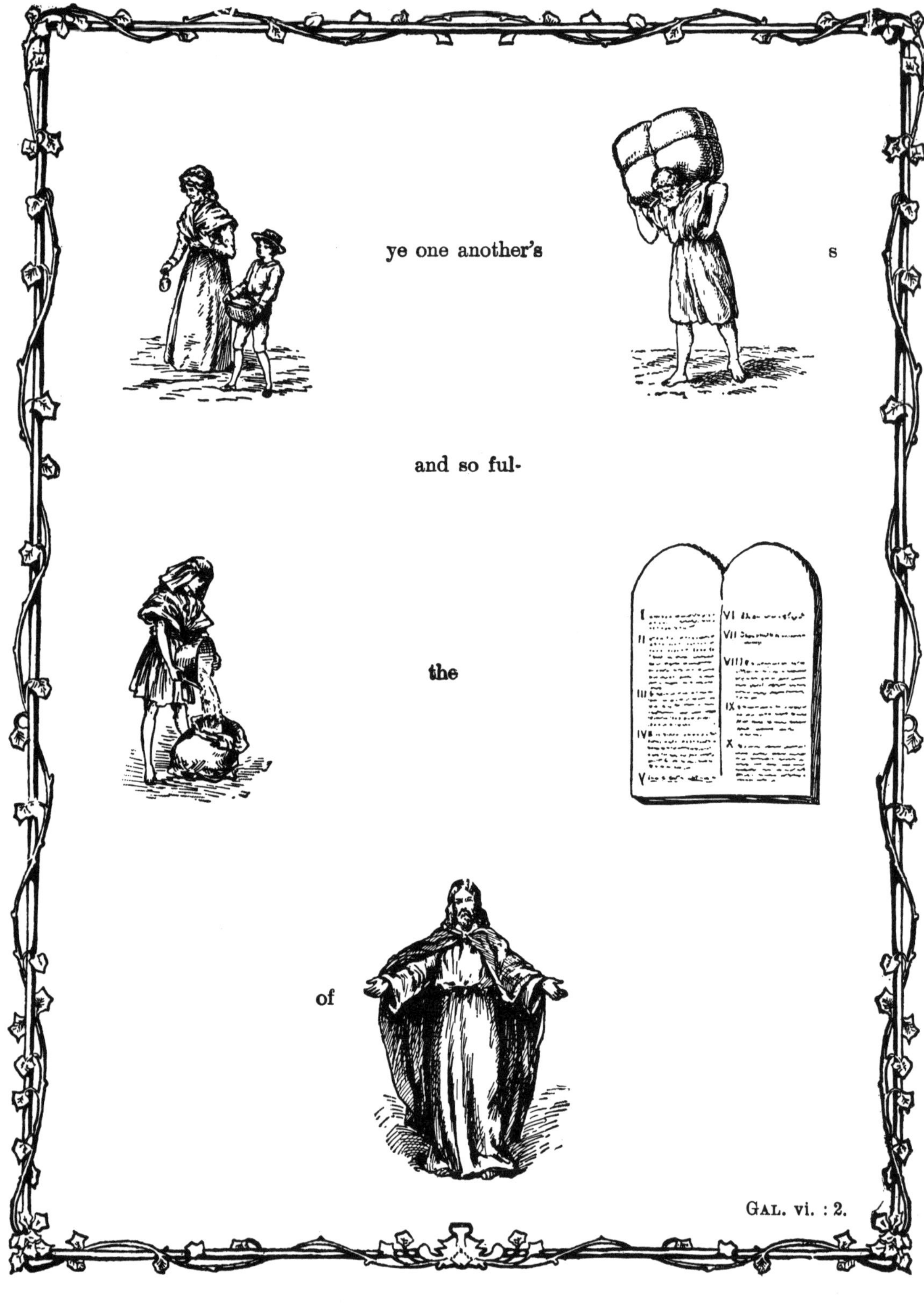
ye one another's
s
and so ful-
the
of
GAL. vi. : 2.

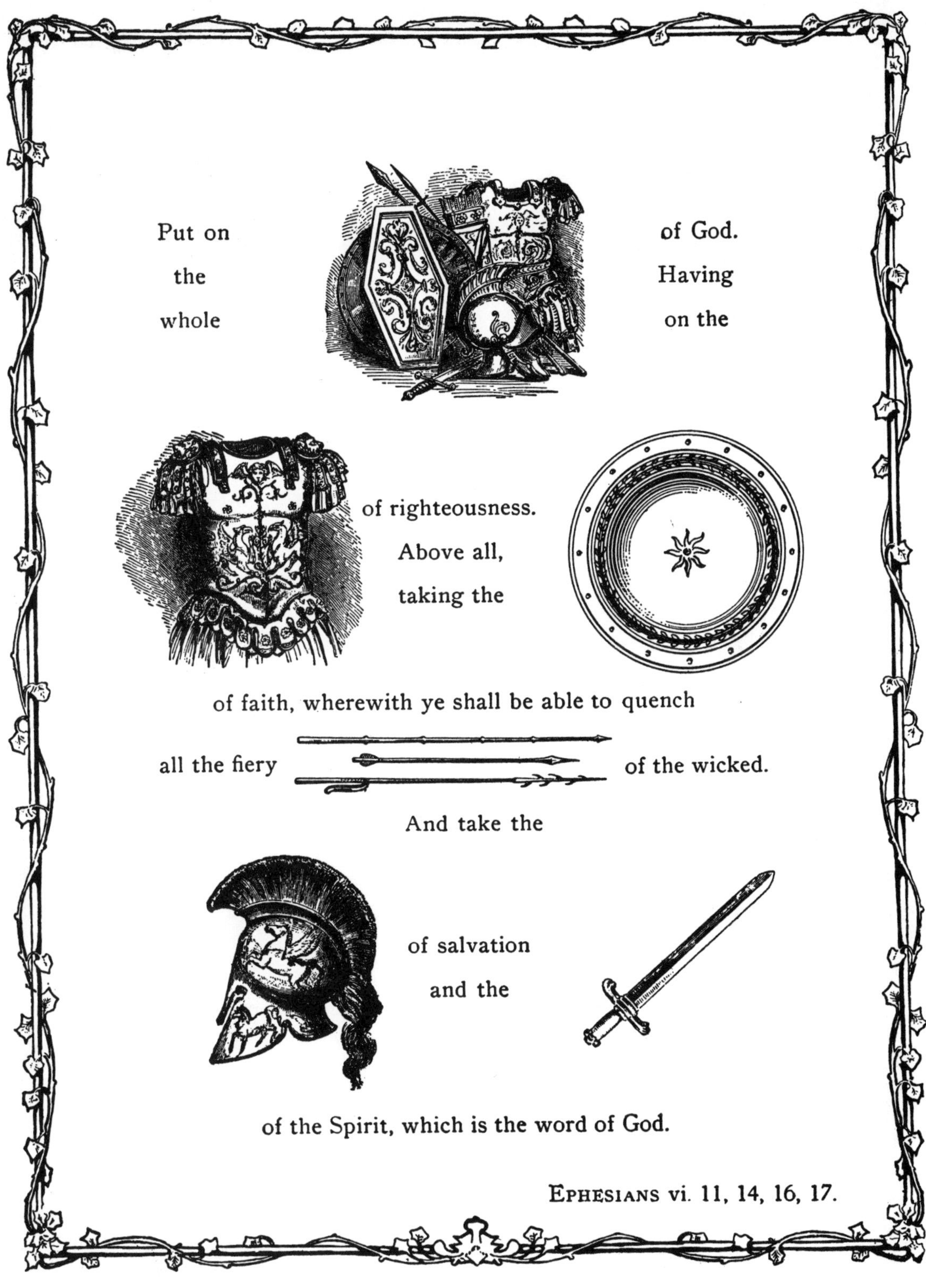
Put on
the
whole
of God.
Having
on the
of righteousness.
Above all,
taking the
of faith, wherewith ye shall be able to quench
all the fiery
of the wicked.
And take the
of salvation
and the
of the Spirit, which is the word of God.
EPHESIANS vi. 11, 14, 16, 17.

I (Name).................................FILLED

IN THESE ANSWERS. (Date) ....

1. Where was Paul going when he was shipwrecked and why?

....

2. Why were there soldiers on the ship?

....

3. What did the sailors do to make the ship light?

....

4. What was the name of the island where they landed?

....

5. How did they get ashore after the ship ran aground?

....

6. How did the natives treat the shipwrecked people?

....

7. What is meant by the word "Charity"?

....

8. What is the greatest of all Christian graces?

....

9. What must our attitude to others be in order to fulfill the law of Christ?

....

10. Why do we need the armor of God?

....

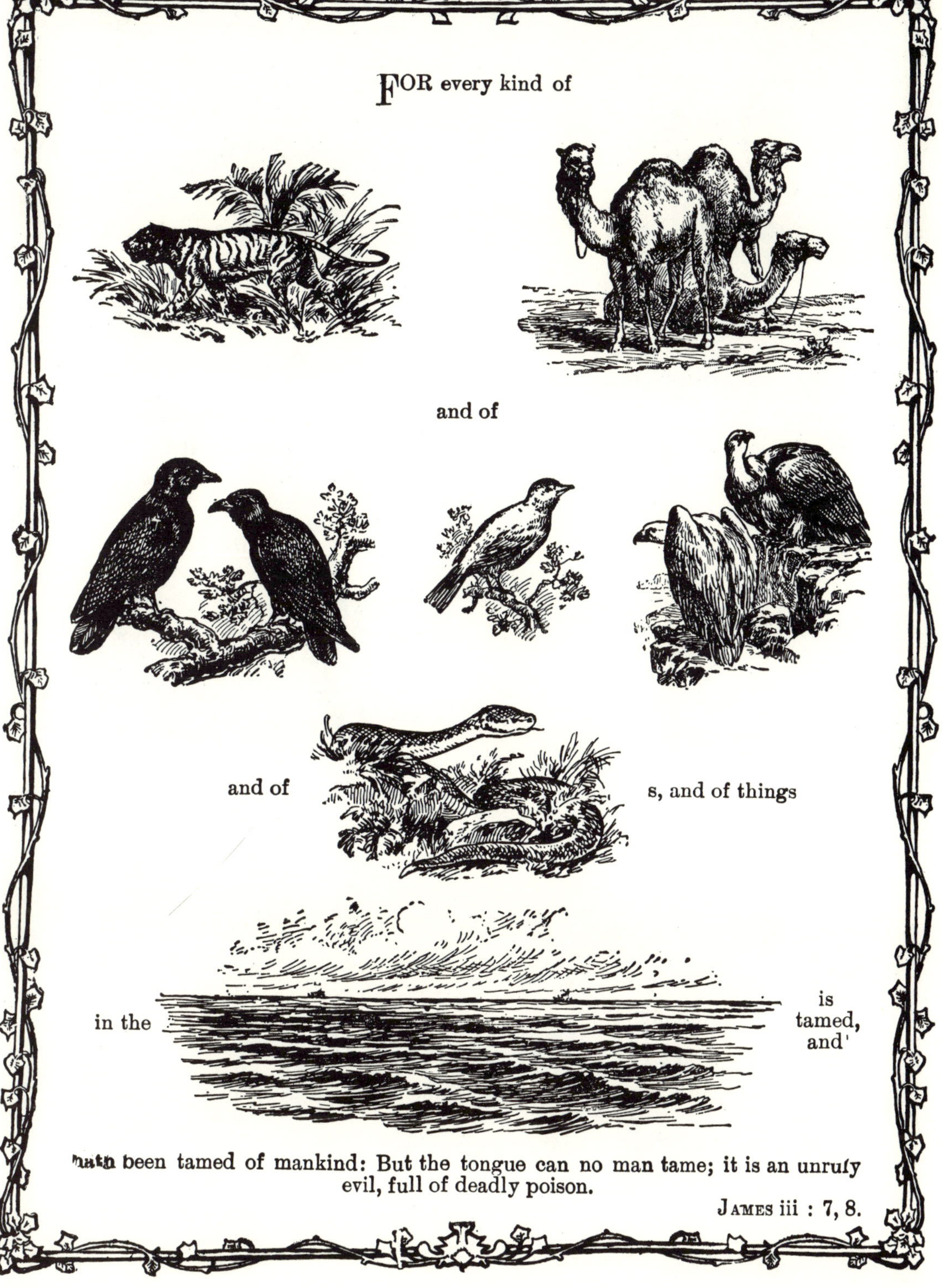
FOR every kind of
and of
and of
s, and of things
in the
is
tamed,
and
hath been tamed of mankind: But the tongue can no man tame; it is an unruly
evil, full of deadly poison.
JAMES iii : 7, 8.

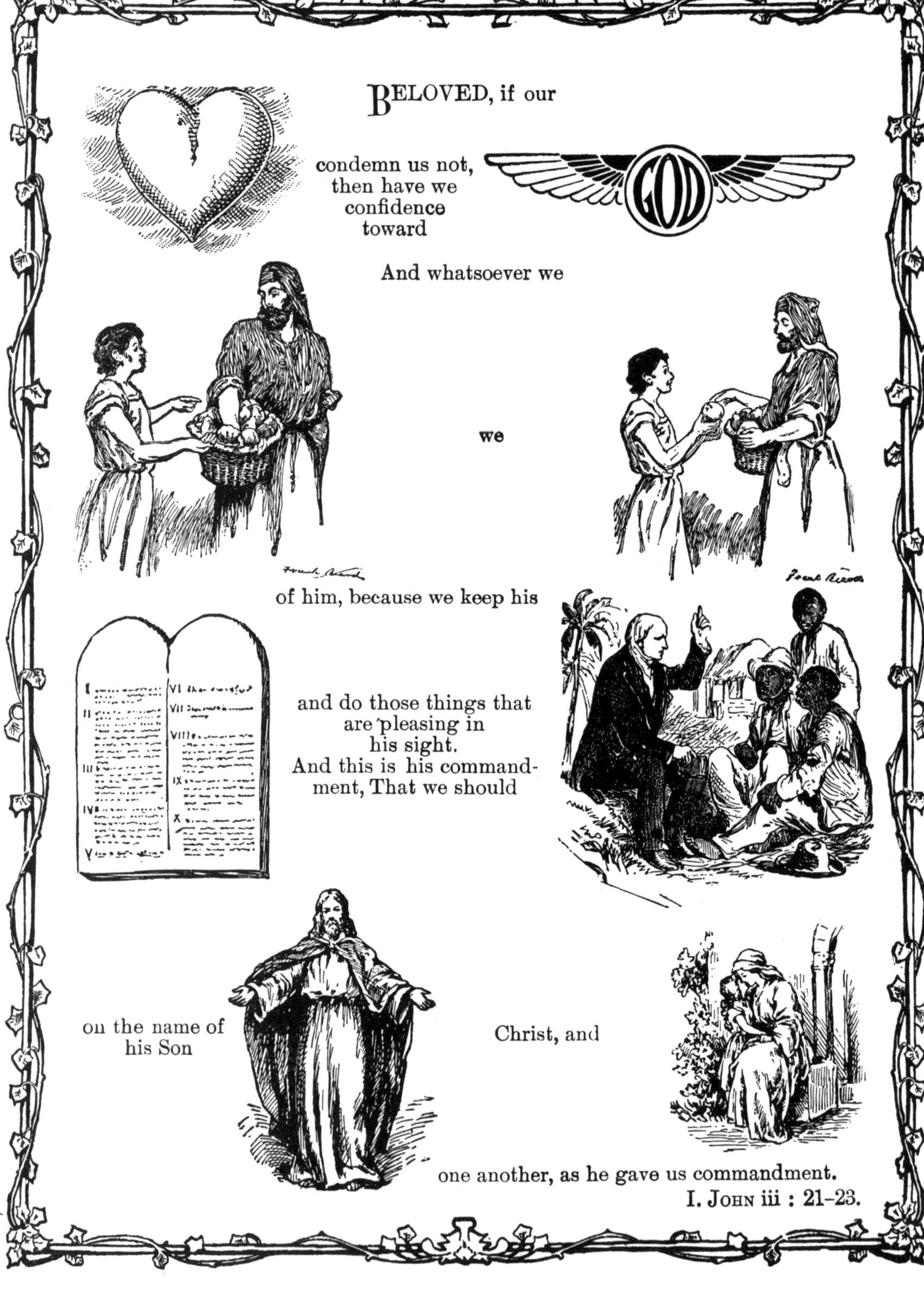
BELOVED, if our
condemn us not,
then have we
confidence
toward
GOD
And whatsoever we
we
of him, because we keep his
and do those things that
are pleasing in
his sight.
And this is his commandment, That we should
on the name of
his Son
Christ, and
one another, as he gave us commandment.
I. JOHN iii : 21–23.

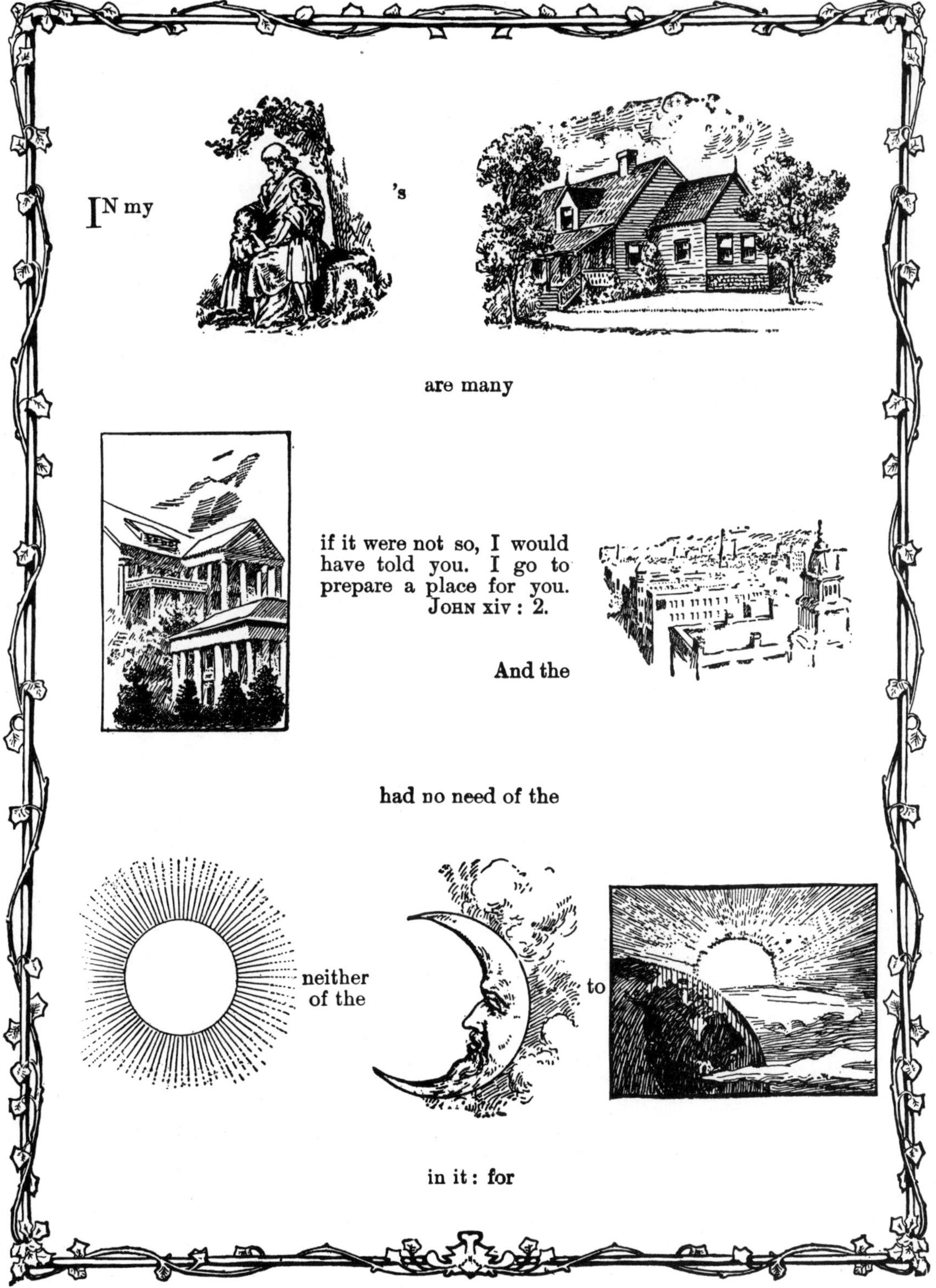

IN my 's

are many

if it were not so, I would have told you. I go to prepare a place for you.
JOHN xiv : 2.

And the

had no need of the

neither of the

to

in it : for

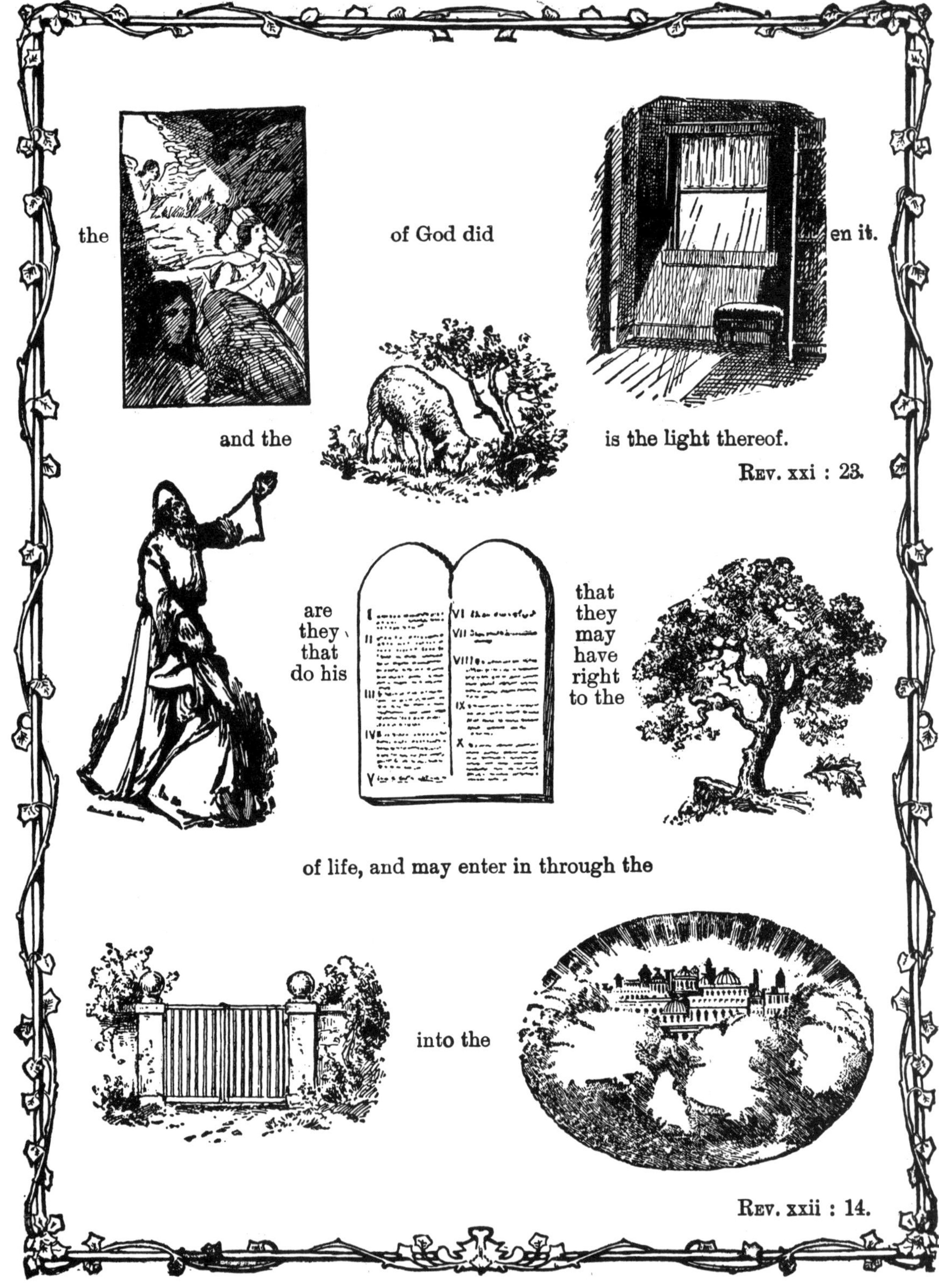
the
of God did
en it.
and the
is the light thereof.
Rev. xxi : 23.
are
they
that
do his
that
they
may
have
right
to the
of life, and may enter in through the
into the
Rev. xxii : 14.

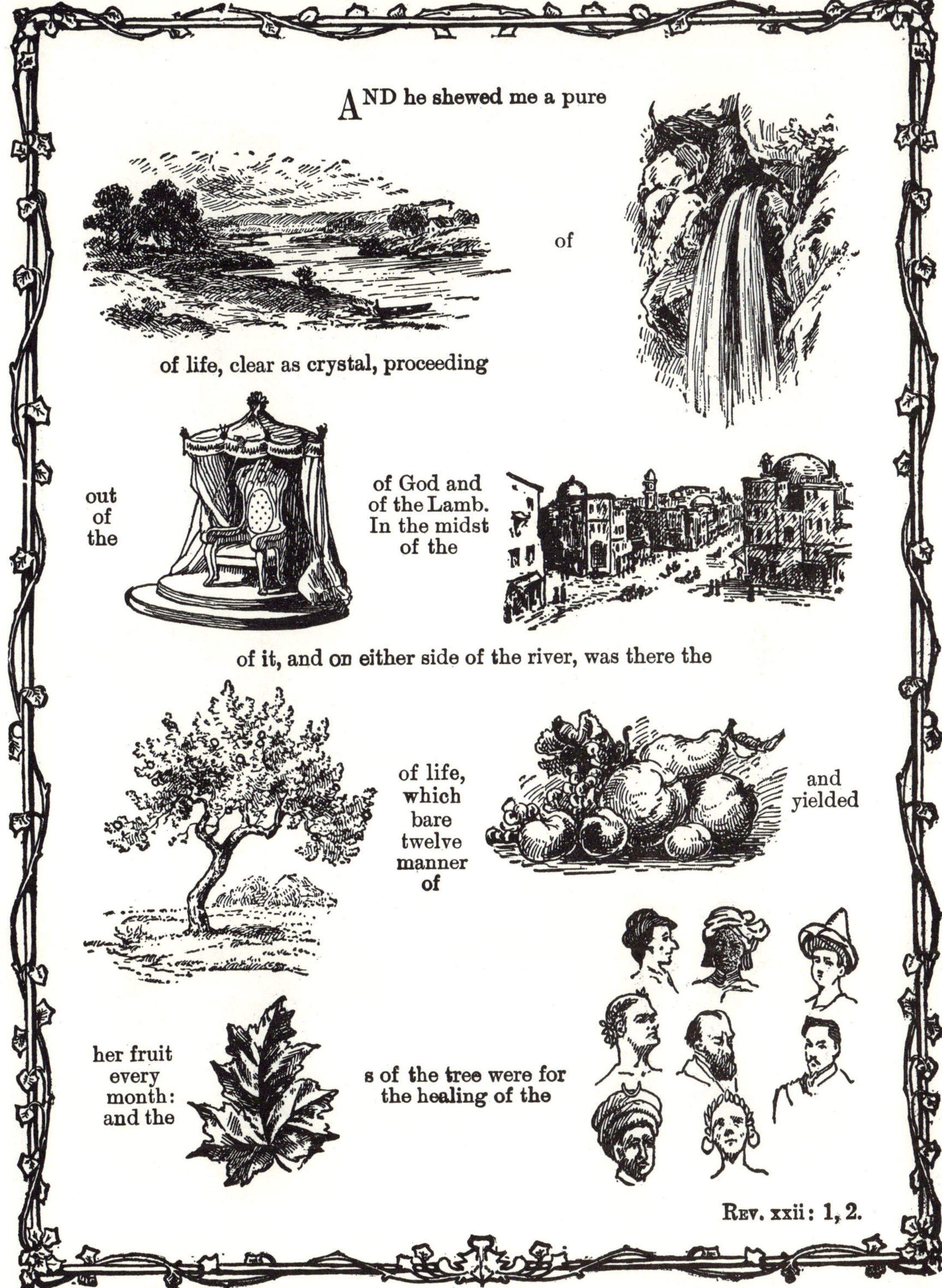
AND he shewed me a pure
of
of life, clear as crystal, proceeding
out of the
of God and of the Lamb. In the midst of the
of it, and on either side of the river, was there the
of life, which bare twelve manner of
and yielded
her fruit every month: and the
s of the tree were for the healing of the
Rev. xxii: 1, 2.

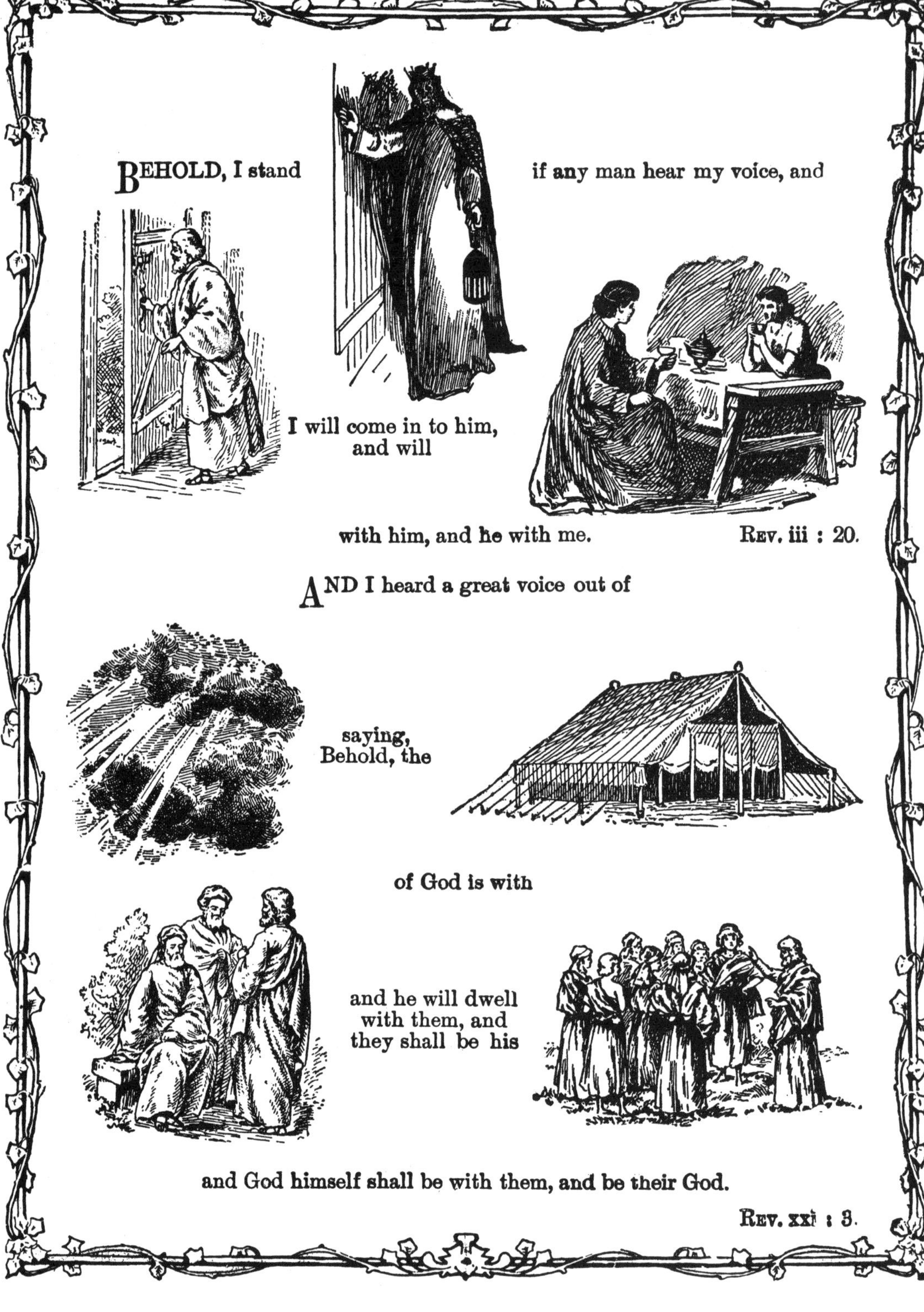

BEHOLD, I stand if any man hear my voice, and

I will come in to him, and will

with him, and he with me. REV. iii : 20.

AND I heard a great voice out of

saying, Behold, the

of God is with

and he will dwell with them, and they shall be his

and God himself shall be with them, and be their God.

REV. xxi : 3.